JANE AUSTEN AND THE NAVY

Francis Austen in his Captain's uniform about 1825. The medal is the Captain's small gold medal awarded for the Battle of St Domingo, 1806. The star is the Campanion of the Bath (Military) awarded at the Victory honours in 1815. (*Jane Austen Memorial Trust*).

JANE AUSTEN
AND THE NAVY

BRIAN SOUTHAM

Southam

Chawton 21. 7. 01.

HAMBLEDON AND LONDON

London and New York

Published by Hambledon and London Ltd

102 Gloucester Avenue
London, NW1 8HX

838 Broadway
New York
NY 10003-4812

ISBN 1 85285 251 8

Typeset by John Saunders Design & Production
Reading, Berkshire

Printed on acid-free paper and bound in
Great Britain by Cambridge University Press

Contents

Illustrations

Preface

The beginnings of this book go back four years, to the preparation I carried out in the Summer of 1995 for a Nelson Birthday Lecture, 'Jane Austen and the Navy', given at Portsmouth in the September of that year. I was happy to be invited since this was a subject I had looked at before and was keen to explore further. I was curious, for example, about William Price in *Mansfield Park* – his boyhood years at sea and the business of his promotion to Lieutenant. Another area full of interest was in *Persuasion*, how Captain Wentworth wins a princely £25,000 in prize-money, how this becomes his passport to the snobbish circles of Sir Walter Elliot and how it wins Anne Elliot's hand in marriage. What was the connection, if any, between the lives and characters of these fictional sailors and the actual lives of Jane Austen's sailor brothers Francis and Charles?

Re-reading Jane Austen's letters with this question in mind, it soon became clear to me that within the torrent of gossip and family news which fills so much of her correspondence, there is a sustained preoccupation: the fortunes of her sailor brothers – their wartime promotions and prize-money, their postings and commands, their comings and goings on leave or active service and, at home, the state of their wives in their pregnancies and the health and happiness of their infant children.

This led me to wonder more about the lives of Francis and Charles. The sole account is *Jane Austen's Sailor Brothers* (1906) by one of Francis' grandsons, John Hubback, written jointly with his daughter Edith. As a piece of family history, an affectionate tribute, it is admirable of its kind and for its time. But the facts are often sketchy and although the Hubbacks had free access to both the personal and the official papers of Francis and Charles, in other respects their source material was not extensive and a particular disadvantage was their limited knowledge of Jane Austen's letters.

Looking further into the brothers' lives, I came across material in the National Maritime Museum and elsewhere which suggested that there was another story to tell, not only more detailed but different. For example, Francis ended his days as Admiral of the Fleet, at the very top of the tree. But was this achievement and the career that led up to it such a record of success, as the Hubbacks tell us? What Francis himself had to say about his naval promotions and his opportunities at sea suggests otherwise, and that for the length of the war with France he suffered considerable frustration and disappointment. And where did Jane Austen find her model for the prize-rich Captain Wentworth? Assuredly *not* in either one of her sailor brothers.

This first biographical enquiry, limited as it was, also carried me elsewhere in the family and amongst its connections. It encouraged me to think again about Jane's father, George Austen, a mild and scholarly man of the cloth purveying advice surprisingly shrewd and worldly on Francis' first going to sea; and to look again at Henry, the family's man-of-business, with whom Francis was joined in the enterprise of an Army and Navy Agency; and further afield, at the men of influence and power such as Warren Hastings and Lord Moira (the Prince Regent's political representative in Parliament), public figures who were approached by members of the family in efforts to advance the sailor brothers; and at the naval men who became linked to the Austens through marriage, a network which included two Lords of the Admiralty, Sir Charles Middleton (later Lord Barham) and Lord Gambier, and other Flag officers who used their influence within the service, strange to say, not always to their protégés' advantage.

By this time, it was becoming clear to me that the naval dimension to the life of the Austen family was not only substantial and wide-ranging but that it was significant for Jane Austen herself. It helped to explain, for example, why the Navy first enters her writing at a relatively late stage – in 1811, on beginning *Mansfield Park*, and why she should return to naval matters in August 1815, with *Persuasion*, her last completed novel. The family background also helped to unravel the mystery of Jane Austen's little poem on the courtmartial of Captain Sir Home Riggs Popham in 1807.[1] A minor work among the *Minor Works*, it has been neglected, and understandably so. But as an excursion into 'political' verse, however brief, it stands as an extraordinary production, a total anomaly in the output of a writer famously indifferent to the world beyond the parlour. With this newly-emerging context, I was now able to return to the naval novels more alert to the service references and allusions which had previously passed me by, either unnoticed or only halfunderstood. I could sense more surely where the war-time experiences of the sailor brothers had entered into Jane Austen's own imaginative life, to reemerge in the writing of *Mansfield Park* and *Persuasion*, not only in the naval cast and subject-matter but also in other characters, most of all in the two heroines, young women left solitary at home while a brother or a loved one braved the war at sea.

It can be seen from this brief account of the book's origins that its material is varied, involving history and biography alongside literary discussion; and I have tried to present these elements so that the naval side can be followed by admirers of Jane Austen and the literary aspect by readers whose interests are primarily naval or historical.

A note on names. I have used Francis rather than Frank, although this was the name by which the elder of the sailor brothers was commonly known throughout the family. But coming to him from outside, as we do, and across so many years, Francis sounds right, especially so for an officer of such formality and punctiliousness. As to his younger brother, to the best of our knowledge, he had no nicknames and was always known simply as Charles.

Francis and Charles served their country long, life-long, and meritoriously. They were brave and enduring men in an age of endurance and bravery. Yet their names would be forgotten were it not for the eminence of their sister – the most modest and retiring of the Austens. Their interest for us today is wholly on her account. The quiet comedy of this circumstance is something she would appreciate.

For Doris
who made the space and the time for this book

Acknowledgements

I would like to thank all those who have helped me in the writing of this book, both individuals and institutions. My greatest debt is to those who read and advised me on chapters or sections in draft form: Linda Bree, A. D. Harvey, John Naylor, David Proctor, Alan Schom, David Selwyn and Robin Vick; and of these I would like to thank in particular John Naylor and Robin Vick who generously put the findings of their own naval research at my disposal.

Lt Cmdr Francis Austen RN Rtd and Alwyn Austen, great-grandsons of Francis Austen, kindly provided me with copies of documentation relating to the sailor brothers; David Willan, a descendant of Charles Austen, gave me information about the sword presented to Charles by Simon Bolivar and other gifts to him; and Helen Lefroy supplied me with documentation concerning the Rev. George Austen and other members of the family. Irene Collins advised me on clerical matters and has contributed an Appendix to Chapter 2 on Mr Austen's letter of advice to Francis.

A large number of naval, Austen and other historians were generous with their advice. These include Gwen Appleby, Mavis Batey, J. V. Beckett, Maggie Black, David Brading, Victor Bulmer-Thomas, Clive Caplan, Tom Carpenter, Jonathan Coad, Linda Colley, Tony Corley, M. P. Costelo, Patricia Crimmin, Christopher Daniel, Malcolm Deas, Frederick C. Drake, James Dunkerley, Judy Egerton, Tim Fulford, Robert Gardiner, Derek Gardner, Jim Gawler, Robert Gibson, David Gilson, Margaret Hammond, David Harries, A. D. Harvey, Karla Hayward, Rear-Admiral Richard Hill RN Rtd, Park Honan, David Hopkinson, Lt Cmdr Derek Howse, RN Rtd, Graham Hunt, Douglas Johnson, Peter Jupp, Joseph Kestner, Brian Lavery, Deirdre Le Faye, John Lynch, John McAleer, Roger Maris, Pieter van der Merwe, Edwin S. Mortimer, Susanne Notman, Wendy Osborne, Rina Prentice, Roger Quarm, Aileen Ribeiro, Nicholas Rodger, Captain A. B. Sainsbury RNR, Michael Slater, Brian Simkin, Melvyn Stokes, Patrick Stokes, Winifred Stokes, James H. Thomas, R. J. Wheeler and Margaret Wilson.

I am similarly grateful to those libraries, museums and other institutions which have granted permission for the use of documentary material and assisted me in other ways. These include Admiralty Library; Bermuda Archives; Bermuda Maritime Museum; Brasenose College Library, Oxford;

British Library; Central Library, Southampton; Centre for Kentish Studies; College of Arms; English Heritage; Guildhall Library; Hampshire County Cricket Club; Hampshire Record Office; HMS *Victory*; House of Lords Library; Huntington Library, California; Hydrographic Office of Great Britain, Taunton; India Office Library; Institute of Historical Research, University of London; Jane Austen Memorial Trust; John Murray, Publishers; London Metropolitan Archives; London Society; Museum of London; National Library of Scotland; National Maritime Museum; Nelson Collection, Lloyds of London; Pierpont Morgan Library, New York; Portsmouth Central Library; Public Record Office; Royal Archives, Windsor Castle; Royal Library, Windsor Castle; Royal Marines Museum, Southsea; Royal Naval Museum, Portsmouth; Royal Society; Survey of London; University of London Library; West Sussex Record Office.

I must apologise for any inadvertent omissions from these Acknowledgements. As to the scholarly literature, I would like to place on record my debt to the four historians of this period whose work I have found particularly useful (their works are listed in the Bibliography): Linda Colley, Tim Fulford, A. D. Harvey and Brian Lavery. On the Austen side, my greatest debt has been to the scholarly work of Deirdre Le Faye and the wide-ranging and stimulating biography of Jane Austen by Park Honan.

Notes on Officers, Guns and the Rating of Ships

The ranks of the commissioned officers, and Jane Austen is only concerned with these, rose Lieutenant, Commander, Captain – sometimes called Post-Captain (as Mary Crawford does in *Mansfield Park*, p. 60) to distinguish them from Commanders, such as James Benwick in *Persuasion* who is allowed the courtesy title of Captain but has only commanded a sloop, a small ship below twenty guns.

Admirals rose in rank Rear-Admiral, Vice-Admiral and full Admiral. At each rank, there were three grades, in ascending order Blue, White and Red, a system deriving from the seventeenth-century arrangement of the Fleet in three divisions, each with its own ensign colour. (Jane Austen gives Mary Crawford a joke about these multifarious grades in *Mansfield Park*, p. 60). At the very top came Admiral of the Fleet, the rank reached by Francis Austen in 1863, two years before his death in 1865 at the age of ninety-one.

Throughout the text I have followed the convention of the day in giving a ship's name with its standard number of guns, as in *Triton* (32). From this, an informed reader would know what kind of a ship it was (in this case a medium-sized frigate), its complement of officers and crew and its rating. The first rate included the largest vessels, three-deckers of 120 guns, with a crew of 900. These were ships-of-the-line, and their modern equivalent would be giant battleships. In the lowest ratings, 5th and 6th, came single-decker frigates with 44–20 guns and a complement between 294 and 135. These vessels were fast and manoeuvrable, 'the eyes of the Fleet' Nelson called them, equivalent to the modern destroyer. Then came sloops, with a complement of between 120 and 65. As vessels below 6th rate did not carry the post of Captain, they would normally have a Commander.

A full table of ratings, ships' complements (including details of the officers and petty officers and specialised tradesmen carried) etc is given in Lavery (1989), pp. 328–29).

Jane Austen was scrupulous in providing such precise detail. Writing to Cassandra of Francis Austen's posting to the *Triton* in April 1798, she is careful not to omit its gun-rating of '32', inserting the figure as an after-thought, ahead of the ship's name (*Letters*, p. 13). In *Persuasion*, when Mrs Croft holds forth on the 'accommodations' provided by 'a man of war', she explains that she is speaking only 'of the higher rates' (p. 70).

PART I

NAVAL LIVES AND
THE AUSTEN FAMILY

1

The Novelist and the Navy

'with ships and sailors she felt herself at home'

James Edward Austen-Leigh
Memoir of Jane Austen (1870)

Her biographer's claim was well-based. Jane Austen lived and wrote throughout the length of the Revolutionary and Napoleonic Wars and her sailor brothers Francis and Charles fought through them. With Nelson's Navy afloat, it was a high point, 'The Classic Age of Naval History' a modern scholar has called it, his book entitled *Britannia Rules*.[1] Yet there is no triumphalism in Jane Austen, no narrative of national victory, on land or sea. Austen-Leigh wrote of her brothers' 'distinguished' service 'during that glorious period of the British navy'.[2] But it could be said that this 'glorious period' passed Jane Austen by. Her attention as a novelist was not upon great events but upon private lives, not upon war but upon the character of the warriors returned from the fray, sailors home from the sea, now at home and settling to peacetime life with their families or seeking wives. Only once, in William Price of *Mansfield Park*, does Jane Austen portray a young sailor with the war to return to. And even for him, the pipe-dream is not martial success but a retirement cottage in the country, the sailor's proverbial dream. Naval heroism is kept strictly off-stage. The heroism we witness in the naval novels is the moral heroism of Fanny Price, her 'heroism of principle',[3] and the 'heroism' of 'fortitude' and self-denial that Anne Elliot witnesses in the 'sick chamber' of Mrs Smith.[4]

The closest we get to maritime adventure, or misadventure, is Louisa Musgrove's jump from the Cobb at Lyme. Like the admiring young ladies of *Persuasion*, attentive to Wentworth, or the family circle at Mansfield Park, listening to the adventures of William Price, we have to be content with sailors' tales and sailors safe on shore. The navy closest to Jane Austen's heart is that described with a sly diminuendo in the final words of *Persuasion*, a 'profession' 'more distinguished in its domestic virtues than in its national importance';[5] and it is one of the purposes of this book to determine, as well as we can, why Jane Austen should choose to confront the reader, as she does, in presenting this amusing and surprising reversal of values: the 'domestic' above the 'national' and 'virtues' above 'importance'.

The sailors in Jane Austen form a distinct group, and they stand apart from the other occupational or professional types we find in the novels. Unlike the clerical characters, including the great comic portraits, Mr Collins and Mr Elton, the naval figures are seen in a warm and romantic light, are laughed at, if at all, gently and with affection. Yet there is no emotional fuzziness; all are sharply in focus. The portraits are of individuals, each distinct and distinctively naval. Collectively, they stand as 'social portraits' of their calling, 'saturated with their professional peculiarities',[6] an observation that comes to life as soon as we think of Admiral and Mrs Croft or the occasion at Lyme when Anne Elliot visits the lodgings of Captain Harville and his family. She warms at the sight of his naval ingenuity in the 'fitting-up of the rooms', his wind-proofing of the doors and windows, and the collection of carvings, his own handiwork in 'rare species of wood . . . from all the distant countries' he has visited,

> connected, as it all was with his profession, the fruit of its labours, the effect of its influence on his habits, the picture of repose and domestic happiness it presented, made it to her a something more, or less, than gratification.[7]

It is in this very particular evocation of naval life – its manifestation in the home, its creation of 'domestic happiness' – that Jane Austen's sympathies are most abundant.

It was here, too, that her observation of the sailor brothers was at its closest and most familiar. Over the period of the war, they were not continuously at sea. Jane Austen visited them and their growing families and was welcomed as a favourite aunt. And beyond this family setting the sailor brothers introduced the Austens to a widening circle of their naval friends and Jane Austen met even more in London and in Bath, a gathering-ground for retired Admirals and for Captains and junior officers home on leave or on half-pay between ships.

The sailor brothers recognised themselves in the novels, their habits and their sayings, and allowed their sister to use the names of their ships. In this sense, Mansfield Park and, to a greater degree, Persuasion, can be seen as forming a tribute to them and to their service, a recognition that the nation's security and success in the Long or Great War (as the two French wars became known) was largely a naval achievement – in the great and dramatic victories, of which Trafalgar was only one; in the blockading of the French fleets, a stranglehold which confirmed the Navy's mastery of the seas; and in the protection of Britain's trade and its possessions overseas. Anne Elliot's first words in Persusasion (spoken, Jane Austen tells us, in 'the summer of

1814' when, with Napoleon on Elba, the war was thought to be over) put it succinctly: it is 'The Navy, I think, who have done so much for us'.[8]

It was not solely patriotism, nor family affection, which moved Jane Austen to treat her naval characters in so favourable a light, with the rogues seen or heard about only at a distance – Admiral Crawford and his 'circle of admirals' with their '*Rears, and Vices*', as Mary Crawford encountered them, 'their bickerings and jealousies';[9] and, in *Persuasion*, Admiral Brand and his brother, 'Shabby fellows, both of them' in the eyes of Admiral Croft.[10] The clue to Jane Austen's partiality is found in *Persuasion*, in Louisa Musgrove's response to the little naval colony at Lyme. Walking with Anne Elliot, she

> burst forth into raptures of admiration and delight on the character of the navy – their friendliness, their brotherliness, their openness, their uprightness; protesting that she was convinced of sailors having more worth and warmth than any other set of men in England; that they only knew how to live, and they only deserved to be respected and loved.[11]

Jane Austen invites us to smile. This is a truly ecstatic outburst, voicing the ardent sensibility of a young lady of nineteen, her eyes set on a handsome and eligible Captain, newly-returned from sea with a small fortune in prize-money. Yet Jane Austen gives us no reason to doubt Louisa's sincerity, her 'fine naval fervour'.[12] As far as 'the character of the navy' was concerned, it was a 'fervour' shared by Anne Elliot – 'She gloried in being a sailor's wife'[13] – and endorsed by Jane Austen herself.

The association suggested here between the heroine and her creator is a mild supposition with which few readers are likely to disagree. However, far closer ties have been claimed. *Persuasion* has always been regarded as a work apart, the one novel in which Jane Austen allowed herself a heroine of mature 'sensibility', a heroine who 'learned romance as she grew older',[14] whose growing older in loneliness and renunciation is coloured by nostalgia and melancholy, a faded heroine drawn with gravity and tenderness, entering upon an autumn of unmarried life. The Victorian novelist Julia Kavanagh attributed the sadness of *Persuasion*, its 'melancholy cast', to 'some secret personal disappointment';[15] while Virginia Woolf found *Persuasion* a work of 'peculiar beauty', remarkable among the six novels for its confessional quality:

> the famous talk about woman's constancy which proves not merely the biographical fact that Jane Austen had loved, but the aesthetic fact that she was no longer afraid to say so. Experience, when it was of a serious kind, had to sink very deep, and to be thoroughly disinfected by the passage of time, before she allowed herself to deal with it in fiction. But now, in 1817, she was ready.[16]

Rebecca West read *Persuasion* in the same way, glimpsing beyond it the face of Jane Austen 'graven with weeping'.[17] Many readers of *Persuasion* find themselves in agreement, detecting in the story of Anne Elliot some degree of self-revelation, some oblique image of Jane Austen's own hopes and disappointments, and seeing the 'felicity' of Anne's final reconciliation with Wentworth as wish-fulfilment, the novelist's reshaping of her own life. Was this the impulse, however veiled, behind a comment she made in the last months of her life, that Anne is a 'Heroine . . . almost too good for me'?[18]

There is an apocryphal story that mirrors this line of biographical interpretation. First made public in the *Reminiscences* (1886) of Sir Francis Doyle, it runs as follows. In 1802, taking advantage of the Peace of Amiens, Mr Austen and his two daughters travelled to Switzerland. Then aged twenty-seven – the same age as Anne Elliot – Jane Austen is said to have met 'a young naval officer, who speedily became attached' to her, but who died before they could meet again. The story is unauthenticated and was dismissed by the authors of the major family biography, *Jane Austen: Her Life and Letters* (1913). Although many families did take advantage of the Peace to travel freely on the Continent, there is no evidence whatsoever that Mr Austen or either of his daughters went abroad then or at any point in their lives, and at this time we know for sure that they were in England. Nonetheless, Doyle's report is not to be dismissed out of hand. It belongs with a group of stories handed down in the family, differing in detail, but with the common theme of a romantic encounter tragically frustrated.[19] That the young man was a 'naval officer' fits the precise moment, since during the fourteen months of the Amiens Peace there was an influx of naval officers in civilian society. This detail, at least, is not implausible.

Whatever we make of the Switzerland story, the biographical reading of *Persuasion* is supported by a contemporary witness, a Mrs Ann Barrett, a young woman who came to live in Alton, only a mile away, between 1812 and 1816. She made the acquaintance of the Austens at Chawton Cottage and struck up a friendship with Jane. The two women became sufficiently intimate for the writer to talk with her visitor about that most private of subjects, her own writing, including her current work, *Persuasion*, and its heroine. Mrs Barrett recalled Jane Austen speaking of her fear of invading the 'social proprieties' by portraying living people in her work and her endeavour 'to create not to reproduce'.* In the case of *Persuasion*, however, it was a distinction which proved to be flexible. Mrs Barrett's testimony is on record: 'Anne

---

* These particular views are well known, since they were communicated directly to Austen-Leigh and are quoted in the *Memoir* (p. 157) almost verbatim, and attributed not to Mrs Barrett by name but to an unmarried 'friend' of Jane Austen. But Austen-Leigh omits all reference to what Mrs Barrett records of Anne Elliot and *Persuasion*.

Elliot was herself; her enthusiasm for the navy, and her perfect unselfishness, reflect her completely'.[20]

Mrs Barrett's account is intriguing, pointing as it does to some degree of identification between the author and her heroine; some degree, too, of self-revelation, however guarded, however unconscious. Academics resist this kind of interpretation. But readers of *Persuasion* will speculate nonetheless, just as Virginia Woolf and Rebecca West did; and just as Roger Michell, who directed the BBC film of *Persuasion*, found it 'the most poignant of the novels':

> I was moved by the idea of the author, shortly before her death, writing a novel about lost opportunities. She died a virgin in 1817 and here she is writing an erotic love story which is full of sexual yearning. We know that there were moments in her life when she could have married, and then for one reason or another she didn't. One can't help wondering whether she was thinking, 'I missed out'.[21]

What this book sets out to explore is the less subjective and less contentious area pointed to by Mrs Barrett, Jane Austen's 'enthusiasm for the navy', something observed by her nephew, James Edward Austen-Leigh, who got to know his Aunt well in the last years of her life. In the opening chapter of the *Memoir*, Austen-Leigh refers to her 'partiality for the Navy' and 'the readiness and accuracy with which she wrote about it'.[22] He pointed to the family as being 'so much, and the rest of the world so little, to Jane Austen'; and to her sister and brothers as 'the objects which principally occupied her thoughts and filled her heart, especially as some of them, from their characters or professions in life, may be supposed to have had more or less influence on her writings . . .'.[23] In its exclusions and preoccupations, Jane Austen's naval world is no different. Like that of her own family, it is the world of the gentry, the naval gentry, the officers and the aspiring Midshipmen. Of the lower deck, the existence of ordinary seamen, we hear virtually nothing. Jane Austen's focus is tight: in *Mansfield Park*, upon the politics of 'interest' and patronage, the pulling of strings behind the scenes, the leverage needed to get Midshipman Price the commission he is unable to achieve on his own; in *Persuasion*, upon the magic touch of war and prize-money, their 'persuasive' power in transforming a nobody into a suitor now sufficiently elevated to claim the hand of a Baronet's daughter, not any Baronet's daughter, not one of 'the almost endless creations of the last century' (a standard reward for naval heroism) but the daughter of a Baronet of lineage 'ancient and respectable'.[24] For this is a world of social mobility, its naval process given caustic definition by Sir Walter Elliot 'as being the means of bringing persons of obscure birth into undue distinction, and raising men to honours which their father and grandfathers never dreamt of'.[25] How his indignation must have been fired to see common or garden Captains raised to the knighthood for their feats at sea and Flag-officers honoured with Viscountcies, some of them, like Nelson, indeed 'of obscure birth', the recipients of honours undreamt of. Doubtless, Jane Austen had overheard this complaint on the lips of many crusty old Sir Walter Elliots in Bath and in the great houses of Hampshire and East Kent, and she lays it here before us, immortalised.

Beyond what is said of Francis and Charles in the last section of this chapter, I have not set out to present the life-stories of the sailor brothers but only those aspects of their lives which bear directly upon *Mansfield Park* and *Persuasion* and which, at the same time, help to provide some of the basic information and knowledge of naval matters which Jane Austen could take for granted on the part of her contemporary readers. This was an audience found throughout the land in their rectories and country-houses, some small, like Mrs Bennet's Longbourne, some grand, like Mansfield Park or Pemberley, some middling, like Mr Woodhouse's Hartfield, or in their town houses, in London or lodged in Bath, like the John Dashwoods, Mrs Ferrars and Sir Walter Elliot exiled from Kellynch. Yet whether these were families of dignity and wealth or of small pretension, they had a common bond. They were all of them members of the gentry, bound by a traditional culture of respect for primogeniture and the ownership of land, the source of power and prestige, and all of them with someone in the Navy – a younger son, a nephew, a cousin or an uncle – someone whose career could be tracked in the *Navy List*, whose exploits at sea could be followed as the latest despatches reached England and appeared in the *Gazette*, to be copied in the London papers and the provincial press, whose postings and promotions were discussed at home and written round the family, just as they were amongst the Austens, in newsy letters meant for circulation and general reading.

Then there were the individuals and groups moving on the fringes of the gentry. We find them in such vulgarians as the Misses Steel and Mrs Elton née Augusta Hawkins of Bristol, Mr Price, the ungentlemanly Lieutenant of Marines, Wickham the steward's son, now travelling upwards with a Lieutenant's commission purchased for him in the Militia, and viewed more favourably, Sir William Lucas, successful 'in trade' and knighted, as Mayor of Meryton, for his address to the King, and the Gardiners, City Merchants of Gracechurch Street, gentlemanly in their manners and welcome at Pemberley as uncle and aunt to the young Mrs Fitzwilliam Darcy.

Yet at the heart of this mobile scene remained a stable core, families of the Austen ilk, at ease in the company of their fellow-gentry, united by their public schools, universities and clubs, their common round of receptions, balls, weddings and hunts, their cross-linkings in marriage and affinity. No more than a humble country clergyman, beyond his parish a man of no social consequence, Mr Austen was nonetheless of the gentry. Educated at Tonbridge School and Oxford, he was respected for his learning and married into the Leighs, a line boasting noble forebears, a lineage carried proudly by his wife: a grand-daughter records that Mrs Austen 'was amusingly particular about people's noses, having a very aristocratic one herself, which she had the pleasure of transmitting to a good many of her children'.[26] The daughters of the family were welcome at the great houses of Hampshire and the eldest son James (like Elizabeth Bennet) could marry into an aristocratic branch – his first wife, Anne Mathew, was a granddaughter of Peregrine Bertie, second Duke of Ancaster and the fifth Duke and Duchess were godparents to their first child. The Austens' second son Edward could enter Darcy's world, the ranks of the greater landed gentry, with estates and country houses at Godmersham in Kent and Chawton in Hampshire, inherited from his adoptive parents, the Knights of Godmersham.

This was the public Jane Austen was writing for, attentive to its tastes and interests. In the early novels, the entertainment contains a strain of literary satire directed at the current fashions for novels of 'sensibility' and Gothic fiction. By the time Jane Austen reached *Mansfield Park*, early in 1811, she was set firmly on the path of 'modern' fiction (the term Scott used in his 1816 review of *Emma*), choosing a contemporary subject and story; and her success in this style of writing was confirmed both by the reviewers and her fellow-novelists. Scott credited her with 'knowledge of the world' and with characters 'that the reader cannot fail to recognise',[27] while Maria Edgeworth found *Mansfield Park* 'like real life'[28] and, in 1818, was positively glowing about *Persuasion*. Having only read as far as Louisa Musgrove's accident, she was already singing the novel's praises. She disliked 'the tangled, useless histories of the family in the first 50 pages'. But aside from that, 'especially in all that relates to poor Anne and her lover' the novel appeared to her

> to be exceedingly interesting and natural. The love and lover admirably well-drawn: don't you see Captain Wentworth, or rather don't you in her place feel him taking the boistrous child off her back as she kneels by the sick boy on the sofa? And is not the first meeting after their long separation admirably well done? And the overheard conversation about the nut? But I must stop, we have got no further than the disaster of Miss Musgrove's jumping off the steps.[29]

These comments are useful to us, not so much as evidence of Jane Austen's impact on her fellow-novelists, but for their value in confirming both the historical accuracy and the authenticity, the reality and the realism, of her fictional account.*

Like many of the early admirers, Maria Edgeworth praised Jane Austen's handling of characters and scenes. What we would regard as an historical perspective, taking a larger, external view of the novels, has only been formed during the last thirty years or so; and to anticipate the chapters that follow I have chosen two very different, even contradictory, responses to the novels: the first from Winston Churchill, Britain's Prime Minister in the Second World War and a First Lord of the Admiralty in the First; the other from the novelist V. S. Pritchett. In December 1943 Churchill went down with 'flu and during the convalescence his daughter Sarah read him *Pride and Prejudice.* He found it soothing and comforting, and felt transported into a world free from conflict:

> What calm lives they had, those people! No worries about the French Revolution, or the crushing struggle of the Napoleonic wars. Only manners controlling natural passion so far as they could, together with cultured explanations of any mischances.[30]

Pritchett's experience of Jane Austen was totally different; in effect it contested Churchill's view:

> Our perfect novelist of comedy . . . is often presented as an example of the felicity of living in a small, cosy world, with one's mind firmly withdrawn from the horror outside. This has always seemed to me untrue. I think of her as a war-novelist, formed very much by the Napoleonic wars, knowing directly of prize money, the shortage of men, the economic crisis and change in the value of capital. I have even seen a resemblance of that second visit to Darcy's house as a naval battle; for notice there how the positions of the people in the drawing room are made certain, where Elizabeth like a frigate has to run between the lines.[31]

Although I have made no attempt to follow Pritchett into the pursuit of naval analogies or metaphors in the novels, it hardly needs saying that the Jane Austen portrayed hereafter is Pritchett's 'war-novelist' not Churchill's novelist of 'calm lives' conducted in a society untroubled by the cataclysms of the time.

---

* It is worth remarking on the trust that historians have placed upon Jane Austen as an accurate and dependable eye-witness to the naval matters of her time. Not only is this found in historians of earlier generations such as Arthur Bryant and Northcote Parkinson, for Jane Austen also features in a work as recent as *The Oxford Illustrated History of the Royal Navy* (1995) in which the Cornell Professor Daniel Baugh quotes Sir Walter Elliot of *Persuasion* in his discussion of 'naval patronage' and 'the social comprehensiveness of the officer corps' (p. 154).

The lives of the sailor brothers, both their lives at home and their careers at sea, are threaded through the chapters that follow. Nonetheless, it may be helpful at this point to give a brief sketch of their place within the Austen family and how they were seen by their sister Jane and others who knew them well.

Francis and Charles were the two youngest of the six Austen sons. The eldest was James, born in 1765, and destined to inherit his father's clerical livings and head a family of three. Next came George, born in 1766. In some way mentally defective, he was cared for away from home. Then Edward, born in 1767, adopted by distant cousins, the Knights, and through them the inheritor of considerable property at Godmersham in Kent and Chawton in Hampshire. He raised a family of eleven. Next, Henry, born in 1771, a man of many talents, soldier, navy agent, wine merchant, banker and clergyman, destined to marry his cousin, Eliza de Feuillide. Then Jane's lifelong companion, her sister Cassandra, born in 1773, a spinster, though not by choice; followed by the last three children: Francis, born in 1774; Jane, in 1775; and Charles, in 1779.

Mr Austen, an Oxford educated scholar, passed on the values of education to his children. James and Henry were taught at home before going on to St John's, his old Oxford college; unusually for girls, Cassandra and Jane were sent away for their schooling; and instead of putting Francis and Charles directly to sea at eleven or twelve, the route followed by most youngsters, he set them on an 'academic' course, entering them for the Royal Naval Academy at Portsmouth, where they received a thorough educational grounding in astronomy, mathematics and the other knowledge and skills needed to prepare them for a career at sea.

Although the Rectory was a place of learning where Mr Austen guided his children's study of the classics and encouraged their formal exercises in writing, their upbringing was far from a grind. The family reading ranged widely, including the latest novels alongside Pope, Fielding, Sterne, Johnson, Sheridan and Shakespeare. It was also lively. In the summer holidays, a small stage was set up in the Rectory barn and at Christmas plays were put on in the house, with a company made up of the younger Austens joined by friends and relations, amongst whom Eliza de Feuillide was the star. They performed popular works, including Sheridan's *The Rivals* and Garrick's *The Chances* and *High Life Above Stairs*. For a more modest evening's entertainment, the grown-ups and children would take turns in reading aloud, some of it by no means 'polite' literature, or put on their own rhyming charades or read their little poems. We can trace the influence of all this in Jane Austen's childhood writings – her extensive *juvenilia*. The effect of this strong literary background was also felt by the sailor brothers. We find this in the official letters and reports of Francis Austen, which are remarkably sustained and composed; also in the extensive private journals in which Charles recorded the events of the day, his reflections, and his reading at sea – the latest novels of Scott, the poems of Byron and so on.

Over the course of time, the sons of the family went their ways: in 1786, Edward left for two years on the Grand Tour, returning to live at Godmersham with the Knights; James took a curacy in 1790 and married two years later; Francis went off to the Naval Academy in 1786, Charles in 1791; Henry enlisted with the Oxfordshire Militia in 1793; while, outside the school terms, the two daughters remained with their parents at Steventon. In 1801, Mr Austen passed on his livings to James and left Hampshire for retirement in Bath. It was a sad parting from the old home and both Francis and Charles – Charles 'much surprised' at the news, as Jane recorded, '& means to come to Steventon once more while Steventon is ours,'[32] – returned to help with 'the final packing and farewells'.[33] Nonetheless, the family remained in close contact. The sisters would stay with Henry in London. Together, or individually, or in company with their parents, they would visit Edward at Godmersham, sometimes for months on end. Henry, too, was a frequent visitor and, in the last years of the war, Godmersham was also convenient for Charles, stationed with his wife and family at Sheerness. And Francis, newly-married in 1806, was happy to share lodgings with his widowed mother and two sisters at Southampton. There was a continual round of visits, meetings and a full flow of 'family' letters, letters for family consumption, carrying news from household to household and written to be read aloud and shared. In this way, the Austens remained together, close in feeling, understanding and knowledge, although they might be far flung, even thousands of miles apart, with Francis in the East Indies or China and Charles stationed in Bermuda, as he was for well over six years.

For the twenty years or so of war, Francis and Charles served in every theatre of operation. But it was not unbroken service. Like all naval officers, they enjoyed periods in England on half-pay when they were on leave or awaiting orders for another ship. Despite all the years of absence and the uncertainties of war-time life, in themselves they found sufficient stability to make successful marriages. It was during a home posting, in command of the Sea Fencibles on the Kentish coast, that Francis met his first wife, Mary Gibson, and between 1807 and 1821 raised a family of five daughters and six sons, three of whom entered the Navy. His wife died in July 1823, a week after the birth of their last child (who was to live for only six months). Five years later, in 1828, Francis married again. This time it was to Martha Lloyd, an intimate friend of Mrs Austen and her daughters and as their long-term companion, virtually a member of the family. Over thirty years earlier,

Martha had been Jane's and Cassandra's original choice for him. Francis recognised her abundance of 'good sense', her 'sweet temper, amiable disposition' and, what he valued most, 'what is of a far greater importance, a mind deeply impressed with the truth of Christianity'.[34]

Charles, too, was twice married. First, in 1807, in Bermuda, to Fanny Palmer, a girl of seventeen, the youngest daughter of the island's former Attorney-General. Of their four daughters, the last died in infancy, and it was following the birth of this child, in September 1814, that Fanny died too. Six years later, Charles married her elder sister, Harriet. Of Charles' second family of four, two died very young, while the two surviving boys followed their father into the Navy.

The sailor brothers passed the war unscathed. Inheriting the hardiness of the Austens – their father lived to nearly seventy-four, their mother to eighty-eight – they served on in the peacetime Navy: Charles, by then a Rear-Admiral, into his seventy-fifth year, dying on active service in Burma; Francis, to the age of ninety-one, ending as Admiral of the Fleet. Whatever similarities are to be seen in the pattern of their lives, the two men were very different in character and sensibility. In childhood, Francis carried the nickname Fly (Jane Austen uses this in one of her letters),[35] a name which brings out his boyhood character as a lively little scamp, 'Fearless of danger, braving pain', a lad with 'warmth, nay insolence of spirit'. This is Jane Austen's description of her brother in a verse-letter written in 1809, congratulating him on the birth of his first son, Francis-William junior, and recalling his own 'infant days . . . His saucy words & fiery ways'.[36] As he describes himself, in boyhood Francis was 'rather small of stature, of a vigorous constitution and possessing great activity of body'.[37] Mentally vigorous, too. When he completed his time at the Portsmouth Naval Academy, aged fourteen, his report accounted him an ideal student, hard-working and faultless in conduct, 'altho' he has a lively and active disposition'.[38] All too soon, however, Fly fades from view, to be replaced by an officer for whom the formality and stiffness of Francis sounds exactly right. In the eyes of Jane Austen he was always 'amiable' Frank. But his officers and crews found him formidable, a strict, sometimes harsh, disciplinarian – as he must have seemed, too, to his children, judging from the calvinistic severity of his letters home. He was a stickler for rules and regulations, punctilious and conscientious to a fault, a slave to 'duty'. As a devout Evangelical commanding a 'praying' ship he courted no popularity; and in himself he was a reserved and private man. Of his innermost life we can only guess. But the occasion of Mary Gibson's death in 1823 provides us with a moment's insight. The entry in his Memoir is tight-lipped and drained of emotion: 'It would be impossible and needless to describe the deep agony of the bereaved.'[39] The 'bereaved', of course, was himself.

The Hubbacks saw Francis as a man who valued 'extreme neatness, precision, and accuracy';[40]* and tales of the Admiral's oddities circulated widely in
the family. Lord Brabourne, the son of Edward's eldest daughter, recorded
two of these, one a highly characteristic story, 'one of the things most like
himself that he ever did':

> He was exceedingly precise, and spoke always with due deliberation, let the occa-
> sion be what it might, never having been known to hurry himself in his speech for
> any conceivable reason. It so fell out, then, that whilst in some foreign seas where
> sharks and similar unpleasant creatures abound, a friend, or sub-officer of his (I
> know not which), was bathing from the ship. Presently Sir Francis called out to
> him in his usual tone and manner, 'Mr Pakenham, you are in danger of a shark – a
> shark of the blue species! You had better return to the ship.' 'Oh! Sir Francis; you
> are joking, are you not?' 'Mr Pakenham, I am not given to joking. If you do not
> immediately return, soon will the shark eat you.' Whereupon Pakenham,
> becoming alive to his danger, acted upon the advice thus deliberately given, and,
> says the story, saved himself 'by the skin of his teeth' from the shark.[41]

Brabourne then proceeded to a second anecdote of 'Uncle Frank', this one:

> bearing upon the exact precision which was one of his characteristics. On one
> occasion he is said to have visited a well-known watchmaker, one of whose
> chronometers he had taken with him during an absence of five years, and which
> was still in excellent order. After looking carefully at it, the watchmaker remarked,
> with conscious pride, 'Well, Sir Francis, it seems to have varied none at all.' Very
> slowly, and very gravely, came the answer: 'Yes, it *has* varied – *eight seconds!*'[42]

Charles comes across very differently. Even as a Lieutenant of nineteen, he
remained the baby of the family, 'Our own particular little brother' Jane
called him.[43] In 1813, now a Captain and the father of a growing family, he was
'dear Charles all affectionate, placid, quiet, chearful good humour';[44] and
whenever his name enters the correspondence, Jane writes of him with
tenderness and solicitude. The *Sailor Brothers* speaks of his 'bubbling enthusiasm'[45] and 'undoubted charm'.[46] Enlarging on this, the Hubbacks enter an
intriguing note of reservation (for which, unfortunately, they provide no
illustrative stories):

---

* Although *Sailor Brothers*, written in 1904–6, comes forty years after Francis' death, more than
fifty after Charles's, it carries the full authority of an informed family account. John Hubback, its
principal author, lived at Portsdown Lodge for eight years (1850–58). Between the ages of six and
fourteen he was particularly close to his grandfather and the book carries his personal recollections
of Francis and the Admiral's tales of naval life. It also draws upon a memoir by John Hubback's
mother, Catherine, the Admiral's fourth daughter, born in 1818. She was a successful writer, with ten
novels to her name, the first of them based upon *The Watsons*, Jane Austen's unfinished story read
aloud to her by Cassandra and by her step-mother, Martha Lloyd.

His charm of manner, handsome face and affectionate disposition, combined with untiring enthusiasm, must have made him very hard to resist, and he evidently had no scruple about making his wants clear to all whom it might concern.[47]

The family biographer, James Edward Austen-Leigh, knew his Uncle as a man of 'sweet temper and affectionate disposition', qualities which 'had secured to him an unusual portion of attachment, not only from his own family, but from all the officers and common sailors who served under him'.[48] In writing this, Austen-Leigh may have been thinking of the silver salver presented to Charles by the officers and crew of the *Aurora* in 1829 and the snuff box from the ship's 'young Gentlemen' – given 'as a Testimony of their Esteem and gratitude'. One of the family voices was that of a nephew, Commander George Rice, who served under his uncle in the Second Burmese War. In his letters home, it was always 'the dear old Admiral' or the 'good old Admiral', 'without exception the kindest-hearted and most perfectly gentleman-like man I ever knew.'[49] His appearance was striking. We have a good description from Anna Austen (James' eldest daughter), who knew her Uncle as a man of 'very remarkable sweetness of temper & benevolence of character', to which

he joined great personal advantages . . . and that even to the last. When the Admiral left England in February [1850] (though in the 71st year of his age) his tall, erect figure, his bright eye & animated countenance would have given the impression of a much younger man; had it not been for the rather remarkable contrast with his hair, which, originally dark, had become of a snowy white.[50]

'To the last', too he kept a cool head and his sense of humour. Two years later, at the age of seventy-three, in the final year of his life, Charles was leading the attack on Rangoon. With a sense of occasion, he granted Spencer Ellman, Captain of the *Salamander*, the privilege of opening the bombardment. To heighten the drama of this event, Ellman trained his gun on a large pagoda and fired it himself, holding his fire until the Admiral's vessel, a steam sloop, stood in a direct line between the *Salamander* and his target. As the shot whistled over his head, Charles dryly remarked to the officers grouped around him, 'The man who fired that shot is looking for promotion'.[51]

The one thing the sailor brothers shared was a profound religious faith; and the Hubbacks went as far as to call 'their religious life . . . the mainspring of all their actions'.[52] It was a faith common to the Austens, Jane included. But for Francis it was God in the seat of judgement, religion in its severe and disciplinary aspect; and, where religion played its part, this is what came to the fore in the regulation of his ships and the upbringing of his children. Charles, too, applauded his ships' Chaplains for preaching against swearing, profanity, drunkenness and the other disorders endemic to shipboard life; he was always ready to lead Sunday worship at sea; and we know from his diaries and journals that God was never far from his thoughts. However, this was a God of love, of compassion and forgiveness, and it is these qualities that shine through his life both amongst his family and at sea.

Francis and Charles are not to be numbered among the heroes and great commanders of Nelson's Navy. Were it not for their sister, they would be forgotten. However, by 1865, the year of Francis' death, his nephew James Edward Austen-Leigh was already collecting materials for his aunt's biography, the *Memoir of Jane Austen*, published five years later. In its opening pages, alongside their sister, the sailor brothers are given pride of place. For the reception of Jane Austen, the book was momentous. Inspiring a host of essays and reviews, it opened the flood-gates of criticism and appreciation. Overnight, the novelist for a few was transformed into a popular author. Before long, the tide of interest reached Francis and Charles, and at the turn of the century Francis' grandson, John Hubback, now a prosperous Liverpool grain-merchant, helped by his daughter Edith, put his hand to the writing of *Jane Austen's Sailor Brothers*, the family tribute which set this present book in motion.

2

Naval Education and the Sailor Brothers

'for Educating Young Gentlemen to the Sea Service'

Rules and Orders (1773) of the Royal Naval
Academy, Portsmouth

Jane Austen's immediate contact with the Navy was through her brothers Francis and Charles, the youngest of the six boys in the family. Their father, George Austen, was a clergyman and there was no naval tradition on his side of the family or on the side of the Leighs, from which his wife Cassandra came. Hers, too, was a family of clerics and scholars. However, in the eighteenth century, the Navy was a traditional career for the younger sons of clergymen. While the eldest sons would follow their fathers into the Church, at some expense, since a university education was required, and ordination to the priesthood was not possible until the age of twenty-three, the younger sons could go to sea at twelve or thirteen at the cost of a uniform, a sea chest and an allowance of £30 or £40 a year. As distinct from the Army, where commissions were purchased and mess-bills could be high, the Navy was a profession in which younger sons could find honour, independence and a lift-long career.* There was a sense, too, that while the Army was a service of limited horizons, the Navy offered scope and rewarded enterprise. In Nelson's words, 'We look to the benefit of our country and risk our own fame every day to serve her. A soldier obeys his orders and no more.'[1]
Moreover, it was the Navy, rather than the Army, which embodied the heroic tradition of Britain's enterprise and success, its mastery of the seas, and its security as an island defended by its Fleet. What this meant to a youngster towards the end of the eighteenth century is wonderfully conveyed in Cobbett's recollection of his first sight of the sea and 'the grand Fleet . . . riding at anchor at Spithead':

> From the top of Portsdown, I, for the first time, beheld the sea, and no sooner did I behold it than I wished to be a sailor. I could never account for this sudden impulse, nor can I now. Almost all English boys feel the same inclination: it would seem that, like ducks, instinct leads them to rush on the bosom of the water.

---

* Between 1793 and 1815, about half the officer entry came from naval families; about 17% from clerical families, many of them rural; and about 15% from army families.

But it was not the sea alone that I saw: the grand fleet was riding at anchor at Spithead. I had heard of the wooden walls of Old England: I had formed my ideas of a ship, and of a fleet; but, what I now beheld, so far surpassed what I had ever been able to form a conception of, that I stood lost between astonishment and admiration. I had heard talk of the glorious deeds of our admirals and sailors, of the defeat of the Spanish Armada, and of all those memorable combats, that good and true Englishmen never fail to relate to their children about a hundred times a year. The brave Rodney's victories over our natural enemies, the French and Spaniards, had long been the theme of our praise, and the burden of our songs. The sight of the fleet brought all these into my mind in confused order, it is true, but with irresistible force. My heart was inflated with national pride. The sailors were my countrymen; the fleet belonged to my country, and surely I had my part in it, and in all its honours. . . .[2]

According to Francis Austen's Memoir, the decision to join the Navy was his own; and it was in April 1786, a few days before his twelfth birthday, that he entered the Royal Naval Academy at Portsmouth, to be followed five years later, in July 1791, by his brother Charles, the youngest of the eight Austen children: Francis eighteen months older than his sister Jane, Charles four years younger. That the Academy was the starting-point for their naval careers is significant, since the normal route for a prospective officer was to go straight to sea designated as a 'Captain's servant'. The regulations allowed a Captain to carry four such servants for every one hundred of the ship's company; a 74-gun ship-of-the-line, with a company of around six hundred, could carry over twenty. In effect, the boys were officer cadets, carried on the authority of the Captain, 'under his protection', as the phrase went, a private arrangement with their parents in which the Admiralty had no part. Typically, their number would be made up of relatives of the Captain, sons or nephews, and the sons of friends and fellow-officers and of men of influence, usually peers and politicians, people in a position to repay the Captain's good turn with a favour of their own. Under the Captain's surveillance, the young-sters were trained in seamanship, navigation and the other nautical skills, towards the day, not less than six years ahead, when they would face their examination for Lieutenant, having reached the age of twenty.

This was the time-honoured system of sea-apprenticeship for officers, a route jealously guarded because it placed the power of patronage securely in the hands of the serving Captains and Admirals at sea, who enjoyed the same rights. The system had a continuing importance to the Captains because over the course of time they were able to gather their 'followings' of junior officers, the well-trained, experienced and loyal protégés who looked to them for 'protection' and whom they hoped to take with them from ship to ship, subject, of course, to the agreement of the Admiralty, which would have its own views on which officers went where. Nonetheless, the Admiralty stepped carefully. During his term as First Lord, even St Vincent, a zealous reformer in other directions and no respecter of persons or institutions, steered clear of this sensitive area: 'I am very delicate about an interference with the patronage of the Captains.'[3] Flag officers, Squadron or Fleet Commanders-in-Chief in particular, were in an even stronger position to retain their following. Enjoying considerable powers of patronage and appointment, they became the acknowledged 'patrons' of their entourage. A system openly rooted in privilege and nepotism inevitably led to abuse. Yet, at the same time, it was surprisingly efficient in advancing the most able young officers, and in naval eyes at least, it proved its worth conclusively in the Navy's record of success in the Long War. Whatever other factors were involved, such as ship design, manning levels, strategy and so on, English tactics were based upon a straightforward assumption that proved to be correct, namely that in single combat an English vessel was capable of overcoming a French, Dutch or Spanish vessel of the same size. This individual superiority flowed from the morale and discipline of the English crews and the rapidity and accuracy of fire-power, factors which depended upon the quality of leadership and training provided by the ships' officers.*

The foundation of the Academy in 1729 was intended to provide an alternative route falling outside the prerogative of the Captains and wholly under Admiralty control. The Academy was to provide a two- to three-year programme of education and training for boys aged between twelve and fifteen at their time of entry. This programme completed, the youngsters were then to go to sea under Admiralty direction to complete their period of ship service before taking the examination for Lieutenant. When the Academy opened in 1733, there were places for forty 'sons of noblemen or gentlemen' (a definition which seems to have excluded, for example, the sons of merchants, doctors or lawyers, none of whom appear on the Academy lists). But it remained only half full and in an effort to increase numbers, the conditions for entry were extended in 1773 to enable a further fifteen sons of commissioned officers 'to be educated at the Public Expence'. The 'scholars' were to pay the Master £25 a year for board and lodging and provide themselves with a new uniform annually, while the officers' sons were exempted from the fees and received a clothes' allowance of £5 a year. For those who paid, as the Austen boys did, the cost was in the region of £50 a year.

---

* It was only after the Napoleonic wars that moves were made to reduce the Captain's powers of patronage. In July 1815, an Order was issued that youngsters could only be entered in a Ship's Books with Admiralty sanction. A long rearguard campaign was mounted and not until 1913 were the last elements of 'officer-nomination' removed.

Those who originally planned the Academy did so with the best of intentions. The sea-apprenticeship system, for all its success in practice, did not provide an educated officer corps and its quality of naval training was wildly uneven, depending as it did upon the conscientiousness and capabilities of individual Captains. As Captain Edward Thompson put it in 1767, formerly 'a chaw of tobacco, a ratan [a disciplinary stick], and a rope of oaths, were sufficient qualifications to constitute a lieutenant: but now, education and good manners are the study of all . . .'.[4] Moreover, the Academy paved the way for the training establishments in the nineteenth-century, *Britannia*, Osborne and the Royal Naval College, Dartmouth. In these terms, it could be counted a success, or at least a step in the right direction. But from the very beginning the Academy was short of applicants and was never more than half full. The 1773 reorganization, allowing free education for the sons of officers, improved matters but only in the short term. When Francis Austen joined the Academy in 1786, he did so in the company of eleven others, six of whom were from naval families; whereas when Charles arrived, five years later, there were only three other entrants, none of whom were officers' sons. These numbers compare badly with the high point in 1774, when there was an entry of twenty-one.

It is difficult to explain the variation in entry from year to year. But, overall, the low numbers – averaging only six a year between 1757 and 1794 – reflect the continuing and overwhelming attraction of apprenticeship at sea. The value of a Captain's immediate patronage and protection seemed far more advantageous than the Academy education, even taking account of the Admiralty guarantees attached to the progress of the College Volunteers, as they were rated at sea. The measure of this can be seen in the Long War when former students of the Academy accounted for less than 3 per cent of the Navy's officer corps.

The prime source of resistance was the body of serving Captains who saw the Academy as a threat to their vested right of patronage. They regarded College Volunteers, few as they were, as unwelcome strangers, 'academics' bringing with them a load of book-learning and virtually ignorant of practical seamanship, forced upon them under Admiralty 'orders' and enjoying Admiralty favour and protection, all which was seen as an encroachment upon the Captain's absolute command of his ship and its company. It is hardly surprising, then, that such arrangements bred hostility and resentment and that there was little affection for the Academy and its products. Its very existence was seen as an affront to the proud naval tradition that the 'ornaments' of the profession – such heroes as St Vincent, Nelson, Collingwood, Exmouth, Keats and Cockburn – went early to sea without education or training – came to the fore by their own efforts, and 'were worthy of bearing comparison with the most distinguished statesmen and diplomatists of the age'.[5]

The Academy also attracted a reputation for idleness, dissipation and worse. Disparaging views circulated at the highest levels of the Admiralty and were dispensed to prospective parents and political leaders. In 1801, the First Lord, St Vincent wrote discouragingly to one father: 'Are you so partial to that seminary as to hazard a son there?', adding darkly that he regarded the place as 'a sink of vice and abomination' which should be abolished';[6] and in 1805, Lord Barham, another First Lord, advised Pitt, the Prime Minister, that the Academy was 'a nursery of vice and immorality'.[6] Unsympathetic historians have made great play with these remarks. But are they to be taken at face value? The scholars were found guilty of many things – of idling, bullying, swearing, blasphemy, of drinking at bawdy houses – and much more that went unreported. Portsmouth was far from being the ideal training-ground for a company of boys and young men. 'The grand naval arsenal of England', 'the rendezvous and headquarters of the British Navy', it presented a squalid face, with its nightly turmoil of drunken sailors armed with pay and prize-money, its swarming prostitutes and ferocious press-gangs, altogether a scene of brutality, riot and debauchery.[8] So it comes as no surprise to hear of 'a great disciplinarian' on the Academy staff, a Mr Orchard, who 'used to flourish with direful sway an infernal horsewhip';[9] no surprise, either, to read the Academy's list of culprits, their offences and expulsion, a punishment which disbarred offenders from ever serving in the Navy again.

For the period of the 1780s and 90s, the witness most frequently cited is Thomas Byam Martin, one of the great frigate Captains of the Long War, who ended his career, like Francis, as an Admiral of the Fleet. His father, Henry Martin, formerly a naval Captain, had been appointed as the resident Commissioner of Portsmouth Dockyard. This carried with it the Governorship of the Academy, not a nominal position but an active supervisory role, with the right to visit the Academy at will. The Commissioner also held the responsibility of reporting back to the Admiralty on the progress of the scholars, the character of the staff and the overall state of the institution. On all this he was able to keep a close eye, for within the Dockyard the Academy and the Commissioner's House were adjacent. Henry Martin had been a student at the Academy himself in the 1740s and thought sufficiently well of it to enter his own son in 1785 during his time as Governor. When Byam Martin came to set down his 'Reminiscences', his criticism was directed not at any scandalous or disorderly behaviour but at the running of the place. He thought the Academy 'not well conducted, for although the masters were excellent each in his particular branch, yet a want of method tended much to waste their labors'. He recalled that there was 'an excellent second mathematical master, Mr Bradley, and a first-rate French master, M. Charrier', but concluded that 'there was a screw loose somewhere, and the machinery did not work well'.[10] How seriously are we to take Martin's criticisms? As Comptroller of the Navy (1815–31), he was a brilliant administrator, certainly qualified to assess good and bad management. But his personal experience of the Academy was very limited. He was there only eight months, as a boy of twelve, from August 1785 to April 1786. The shortness of his stay was not out of dissatisfaction, either his father's or his own, but because a plum opportunity came along, that of joining the *Pegasus* under the captaincy of Prince William, Duke of Clarence, the future William IV. Prince William, whom Martin had known since childhood, was a frequent guest at his father's home, the Commissioner's House at Portsmouth, 'an intimate visitor';[11] 'and to my great joy', writes Martin, 'I was sent from the academy to join the ship at Plymouth'.[12]

Perhaps the Academy's management was faulty. Nonetheless, at this time, there was certainly continuity to its leadership. The Master, William Bayly, held office for over twenty years, from 1785 to 1806; John Bradley, the Second Master, for almost thirty years, from 1767 until his death in 1794; and Henry Martin was Governor from 1780 to 1790.

Whatever the state of the 'machinery', conditions at the Academy must have been good enough to satisfy Mr Austen. Although we have no record of the exact circumstances under which Francis was entered, we learn from the Memoir that this was arranged 'through the kindness and Interest' of the Commissioner. As Steventon was only forty miles from Portsmouth, we cannot suppose that Mr Austen would have consigned his sons there for eleven months of the year without first visiting the Academy and speaking with the Master. A scholar and teacher himself – four or five private pupils lodged with the Austens at the Rectory – he would want to satisfy himself as to the Academy's level of education as well as its living conditions, together with the conduct of the scholars and the standard of moral and religious welfare. Clearly, in 1786 he was satisfied on all these counts; and following Francis' time at the Academy, five years later, he was happy to enter Charles. And Francis kept in contact with the Master until the time of Bayly's death in 1810.

In this light, the remarks of Barham and St Vincent smack of rank prejudice. St Vincent is notorious for the violence and extremity of his dislikes. In a bad mood he could be viciously abusive,[13] whereas in 1801, the same year in which he described the Academy as a 'sink' which 'should be abolished', he was writing equally to another father about the chances of admission for his son without the least note of warning.[14] Whatever the state of the Academy – and the circumstantial evidence suggests that it was no worse than any other boarding establishment of the time – induction on board ship might be no better. There, vice and brutality, 'the scenes of horror and infamy', as one Captain described them,[15] were out of the public eye; and Mr Austen would be right to judge that the Academy provided a more humane, and better educated, point of entry than baptism at sea.*

It was easy for experienced officers to mock the products of the Academy. When it came to navigation, there was still a 'by guess and by god' school relying on accumulated experience, 'sea sense' and rule-of-thumb. For these old sea-dogs, calculations and chronometers, together with the rest of the scholars' education, smelt of book-learning and refinement quite at odds with the bruising realities of life in a ship at sea; and, in their support, they could point to the heads of instruction set out in the Academy's articles of 1773 which spoke of subjects both academic and gentlemanly: 'that the Scholars be instructed in Writing, Arithmetick, Drawing, Navigation, Gunnery, Fortification, and other useful Parts of the Mathematicks; and also in the French Language, Dancing, Fencing, and the Exercise of the Firelock [i.e. the musket] . . .'.

The Mathematics included logarithms, geometry, plane and spherical trigonometry, navigational calculations, surveying, mechanics, chronology (the science of time measurement) and astronomical observation. The two last, together with the mathematical elements, were of particular importance, since they provided the key to the calculation of longitude, the knottiest of all navigational problems, solved only around 1760, with the discovery that longitude could be worked out, after exhaustive calculations, from the measurement of lunar distances and by the use of chronometers of sufficient accuracy. The Admiralty put considerable emphasis on this part of the curriculum and picked the staff accordingly. It was traditional for the Master to be an astronomer with nautical experience and the Academy had its own Observatory. William Bayly, the Master during the Austens' time, was a respected astronomer and had carried out chronometer trials on behalf of the Board of Longitude on Cook's great voyages of 1772 and 1776. The Second Master, John Bradley, a nephew of James Bradley, the third Astronomer Royal, was another accomplished astronomer experienced in the testing of chronometers. Serving Captains interested in their use could come to the Academy for advice and it assisted in checking chronometers employed in sea trials for the Board of Longitude. But why the 'gentlemanly' arts? French – in Nelson's eyes 'absolutely necessary'[16] – because it was fitting that those committed to a life of travel should command at least one

---

* Francis was himself to take this view in 1823 when he entered Francis-William, his eldest son, for the College, and again in 1830 with the entry of his fourth son, Herbert-Grey.

foreign language and French was a *lingua franca* as much at sea as in the courts of Europe and beyond, where a ship's captain and his officers might find themselves filling a political or diplomatic role as Britain's representatives or envoys – in remote parts, virtually ambassadorial. Twenty years later, this was to be Francis' experience in China. It was on such occasions that the Portsmouth lessons in Dancing could also prove their worth in courtly diplomacy. As Nelson explained to the Earl of Cork, 'You will see almost the the necessity of it, when employed in Foreign Countries; indeed, the honour of the Nation is so often entrusted to the Sea Officers, that there is no accomplishment which will not shine with peculiar lustre in them.'[17] Nor were Drawing and Writing purely academic or recreational pursuits. The punctilious keeping of records was a strict Admiralty requirement and the maintenance of log books, letter books, remark books, journals and countless other memoranda and reports fell heavily upon junior officers, a labour of recording which often included drawing maps, making plans of naval dispositions, port facilities and fortifications, charts of shoals and headlands with their off-shore depths and currents. There was also the need to record such mundane yet vital data as dispositions for the stowage of ballast, cargo, supplies and water casks, all of which could affect the ship's centre of gravity, its depth in the water fore and aft, and hence its 'trim', its navigability and speed.

The Exercise of the Firelock, what we would call musketry, was essential training, for firearms were frequently employed at sea when ships engaged at close quarters. Seamen not manning the guns would join the marines on the upper decks, or in the rigging, to provide small-arms fire with muskets and pistols, and it usually fell to the youngest Lieutenant to serve as Lieutenant at Arms, commanding the seamen and training them in the use of small-arms, which were also used by boarding parties, or in repelling boarders, and by prize-crews guarding the crews of captured vessels when sailing them to a friendly port. Unfortunately, none of Francis' Academy reports seem to have survived, but from those of Charles we learn in some detail what was covered in the practical and theoretical aspects of seamanship. The Attendant writes that in 1793–94 'Austin'* and the other scholars were

> frequently with me in the Rigging House, seeing the several Ships Rigging fitted etc. – and also at the Academy running over the Rigging and Blocks of the model of the *Victory*, and rigging and unrigging the Academy Yacht, sailing her out to Spithead and St Helens, telling them the names, Bearings, distances and marks of

* This misspelling stems from the original misspelling of both Mr Austen's and Charles's names in The Commissioner's Report for the year 1 March 1791 to 29 February 1792. For this, and all the details from the Academy reports which follow, I am grateful to Robin Vick, working on PRO MS ADM 1/3504 & 1/3505; and see Vick (1996a).

the Out Buoys on the Sand heads. I observed they took notice, and have made Improvements (for the time they were under my care) both in the Practic and Theorical parts of seamanship.

Understanding the construction of the ship was an important area. In foul weather, or following action at sea, damage could call for running repairs which had to be made without the resources of a dockyard and the expertise of a shipwright. In desperate situations, the Captain would have to rely on the ship's carpenter and the carpenter's crew, with their limited knowledge; and his own training might make the difference between security and disaster. Again, we can turn to Charles Austen's report. According to the shipwright, in 1793–94 'Austin' attended twenty-six lessons (more than any other scholar):

and having shewn them the manner of bringing to and fastening the Main Wales, Lower, Upper, Quarter Deck & Forecastle Clamps, scarphing the beams etc. of the Swift Sloop – also the use of the Draught, laying off and taking the Bevellings of the Square and Cant Timbers, Crossing and levelling the Floors, getting up and securing the Frame bends and the use of the Bollard Timbers and Nause Pieces on the Tiger, building at this Port – they have made good Improvement therein.

In 1794–95 'Austin' attended thirteen lessons with the Shipwright:

and having shewn them the manner of laying off the Square & Cant Timbers, taking the Bevellings & applying the same – also the disposing & securing the Frames, placing the Ring & Eye bolts with their several uses etc. of the Prince of Wales – also the disposing the Stantions, placing the Bases & Perpendiculars for taking off the body & sheer etc of the several French Ships dock'd at this Port – they have made good progress therein.

The 1793–94 report of the Gunner records that 'The Young Gentlemen have been very attentive to, and have made good Progress in learning the nature and use of the Cannon'. If 'good progress' were the standard words of approval, appearing with some frequency, they were not without weight since twice-yearly examinations were conducted by the staff in front of a formidable Board comprising the Academy Governor, the Port Admiral and the six Senior Captains then in Portsmouth Harbour or at Spithead. The members of the Board put their names to an account of each pupil's performance, which was then forwarded to the Admiralty. Such a congregation of naval talent and experience would be eagle-eyed when it came to assessing the performance of these aspirant officers, especially as very few, if any, of the Board members would themselves have attended the Academy in their own early days. Almost to a man, these would be officers whose academy had been a ship at sea.

Whether this picture of the Academy training would have softened naval attitudes is a moot point. What is clear, however, is its practical nature and the value, too, of the other seemingly academic or recreational parts of the course. The intention of its founders had been to introduce a leavening to the naval dough, to create a new style of officer, both educated and accomplished in the social graces, less the sea dog and more the gentleman, appropriately so for a profession which attracted the sons of peers and where, amongst the serving officers, there were Members of Parliament. Judged purely on its numbers, the Academy could not be counted a success. But as a method of naval education, while by no means faultless, it was undoubtedly thorough and certainly served the Austen brothers well.

According to his Memoir, Francis' time at the Academy was a story of success from beginning to end:

> Very soon after his admission into this seminary, he was distinguished by all the Masters as a youth of superior abilities, which joined a possessing appearance and a degree of regularity in his conduct but rarely seen in so young a boy, gained him the esteem and regard of them all, and especially of Mr Bayly who to the day of his death always treated him with the most flattering marks of attention . . .

By the end of 1788, after a stay of two and three-quarter years, his 'Plan of Learning' completed,* Francis was ready to begin his life at sea. Henry Martin, the Governor, duly addressed their Lordships at the Admiralty requesting his discharge into the frigate *Perseverance* (thirty-six guns and a complement of 164) then fitting out at Portsmouth, 'as Captain Smith will be glad to receive him', and recommending him for promotion to Midshipman when he had served his time as Volunteer. A copy of the Commissioner's letter was read out to Francis' fellow-scholars as an encouragement to follow in his ways of 'diligence, exertion and orderly behaviour'.[18] The Commissioner's report was couched in glowing terms:

> I beg leave to observe to their Lordships that this Young Gentleman had completed his plan of Mathematical learning in a considerably shorter time than usual, his assiduity indeed has been uncommon, and his conduct during the whole

---

* The 'Plan of Learning' refers both to the student's course of study and to its record. The latter was the student's pride and glory, the centre-piece of his course, an enormous volume, its pages 14 inches high and 10 inches wide, with a printed title page: 'A Plan of Mathematical Learning Taught in the Royal Academy Portsmouth Performed by [space for the student's name] A student there 17[years to be entered]'. Francis' own 'Plan' (MS. NMM.AUS/14), running to 400 pages and dated 1788, is a work of art with its immaculate calligraphic penmanship, decorative sectional headings, maps and diagrams (including some fold-outs). The sections are: Arithmetic, Geometry, Trigonometry, Globes, Geography, Chronology, Navigation (98 pages); Spheres, Astronomy, Latitude, Longitude (30 pages); Day's Works (includes Ship's Reckoning, Journal of a Voyage etc), Marine Surveying, Fortification (28 pages); Gunnery (20 pages); Mechanics. In Francis' case, the completion of the 'Plan' seems to have signified his fitness to go to sea.

time he has been at the Academy has been in all respects so properly correct, that I have never had a complaint or one unfavourable report of him from any Master or Usher altho' he had a lively and active disposition.[19]

With this exemplary record, it is hardly surprising that Francis was the outstanding scholar of his year and (in his own words) had 'attracted the particular notice of the Lords of the Admiralty by the closeness of his application, and been in consequence marked out for early promotion'.[20]

On 23 December, Francis was taken off the Academy roll and in early February 1789, under Captain Isaac Smith, the *Perseverance* set sail from Portsmouth, one of a small Squadron – the *Crown* (64), two frigates and two sloops – ordered to the East Indies under Commodore* the Hon. William Cornwallis, designated Commander-in-Chief in the East Indies station, (later, one of the great Admirals of the Long War).[21]

In the *Perseverance*, Francis carried with him a long letter from his father. Dated December 1788, it was a document of 'Memorandums' he would treasure until the end of his life.

The letter throws a revealing light on Mr Austen. As the family biographers have observed, the document is 'wise and kind' and written with 'courtesy and delicacy'.[22] Also a homily, it offers advice which is shrewd and astute, which tacitly recognises the drawbacks to his son's situation as someone from a non-naval family seeking to advance in a service where patronage and connections count for so much. Immediately, on board the *Perseverance*, an Academy cuckoo in the nest, the young Volunteer must set himself to making a good impression on his shipmates and superiors, the Captain in particular, and must begin to build up his precious network of alliances. Alongside the youngsters already established on board, the Captain's protégés, most of them ranked above him as Midshipmen or Master's mates, Francis was at a disadvantage – and it was this disadvantage that Mr Austen now sought to overcome.

The Hubbacks rightly call it 'a very charming letter'.[23] Yet Mr Austen set it off with a striking preamble, a statement which has the effect of turning this 'charming' letter into something more formal, a document of 'Memorandums', of guidance *in absentia*, to be taken to heart and acted upon. It is suffused with the spirit and style of Chesterfield's *Letters to His Son*, a volume published fourteen years previously, in 1774; and it looks very much as if Mr Austen chose to address his own son in exactly the same tradition.**

* Commodore was a temporary rank granted to a Captain when in command of a Squadron. It ranked alongside an Army Brigadier-General.

** Chesterfield's *Letters* was taken up as a model of its kind. Three years later, the book was in its eighth edition, with other pirated editions from Dublin. Many different versions appeared, including a versification, *The Fine Gentleman's Etiquette* (1776) and by 1775 a selection entitled *The Principles of Politeness and of Knowing the World* was in its fourth edition.

Chesterfield's *Letters* display the concerns and rhetorical skills of an experienced diplomat-politician. No one would charge Mr Austen with teaching 'the morals of a whore, and the manners of a dancing master' (as Dr Johnson said of Chesterfield). Nonetheless, following his second paragraph, reminding Francis of his religious 'Duty', in the remainder of his letter Mr Austen is no less calculated and no less adept than Chesterfield in taking up material issues. The wisdom purveyed is, in the best sense, worldly wisdom, directed to setting Francis' feet on an upward path. This emphasis is caught in Mr Austen's use of two words in particular, 'friend' and 'prudence'. For someone at the beginning of their career a 'friend' is a precious possession. Not a friend in our modern sense of a companion with whom we have a bond of common feeling and interests, but a 'friend' in the sense, now outmoded, of someone in a higher position, a 'friend' at court, a patron, able to do you a good turn, open doors, and advance you on your way. It was a meaning long-established in English political life. Bacon's essay 'Of Followers and Friends' defines the relationship succinctly: 'There is little friendship in the world, and least of all between equals . . . that that is, is between superior and inferior, whose fortunes may comprehend the one the other.' Accordingly, Mr Austen refers to 'your good Freind the Commissr.', someone to whom Francis is so 'much . . . obliged'; and advises him of the ways to make 'friends' of the ship's captain and officers. 'Prudence', too, has an enviable pedigree. It stands alongside justice, temperance and fortitude, as one of the four cardinal virtues of scholastic philosophy. And it belongs to the same political sphere as 'friend'. To act with 'prudence' is to act with self-interest. 'Prudence will oblige a man to do that which may do most for his safety' is the illustrative quotation in Johnson's *Dictionary*. So we can understand the force of Mr Austen's closing injunction: to write both to the Master of the Academy and the Commissioner is not a matter of mere courtesy but a first step in naval statecraft, the prudential and due deference to powerful 'friends'. As to the Commissioner, the letter was timely and effective. Just over a year later, in 1790, Henry Martin became Comptroller of the Navy, the head of the Navy Board,* a high official Francis came to regard as his first patron.

Memorandums for the use [of] Mr F. W. Austen on his going to the East Indies Midshipman on board his Majesty's Ship Perseverance Cap: Smith Decr: 1788.

---

* Broadly speaking, the Admiralty was concerned with the officers and direction of the Fleet, while the Navy Board, a subordinate body, was responsible for the non-commissioned officers, the ships, the dockyards, naval supplies and the administration of everything comprised under the term *matériel*.

My Dear Francis,

While you were at the Royal Academy the opportunities of writing to you were so frequent that I gave you my opinion & advice as occasions arose, & it was sufficient to do so; but now you are going from us for so long a time & to such a distance that neither you can consult me nor I reply but at long intervals, I think it necessary therefore before you [sic] departure to give you my sentiments on such general subjectes as I conceive of the greatest importance to you, & must leave your conduct in particular cases to be directed by your own good sense & natural Judgment of what is right.

The first & most important of all considerations to a human Being is Religion, or the belief of a God & our consequent duty to *him*, our *Neighbour*, & *ourselves* – In each of these your Catechism instructs you, & for what is further necessary to be known on this subject in general, & on Christianity in particular I must refer you to that part of the *Elegant Extracts* where you have Passages from approved Authors sufficient to inform you in every requisite for your belief & practice. To these I refer you & recommend them to your frequent & attentive perusal; observing only on this head, that as you must be well convinced how wholly you depend on God for success in all your undertakings, you will easily see that you are bound in interest as well as duty regularly to address yourself to him in Prayer, Night & Morning; thankfully acknowledging the Blessings you have received already & humbly beseeching his future favour & protection. Now this is a Duty which nothing can excuse the omission of times of the greatest hurry will not hinder a well disposed mind from fulfilling it – for a short Ejaculation to the Almighty, when it comes from the heart will be as acceptable to him as the most elegant & studied form of Words.

Your behaviour, as a member of society to the Individuals around you *may* be also of great importance to your future well-doing & certainly *will* to your present happiness & comfort – You may either by a contemptuous unkind & selfish manner create disgust & dislike; or by affability Good humour & Compliance become the object of Esteem & Affection – which of these very opposite paths 'tis your interest to pursue I need not say. – The little world, of which you are going to become an Inhabitant, will consist of three Orders of Men – All of whom will occasionally have it in their power to contribute no little share to your pleasure or pain; to conciliate therefore their good will, by every honourable method will be the part of a prudent Man. – Your Commander and Officers will be most likely to become your Friends by a respectful behaviour to themselves, & by an active & ready Obedience to Orders. – Good humour, an inclination to oblige, & the carefully avoiding every appearance of Selfishness will infallibly secure you the regards of your own Mess & of all your Equals. – With your Inferiours perhaps you will have but little intercourse, but when it does occur, there is a sort of kindness they have a claim on you for, & which, you may believe me, will not be thrown away on them. – Your conduct, as it respects yourself, chiefly comprehends Sobriety & Prudence – the former you know the importance of to your Health your Morals & your Fortune, I shall therefore say nothing more to enforce the observance of it. I thank God you have not at present the least disposition to deviate from it.

Prudence extends to a variety of Objects. [Ag?] ree any Action of your Life in which it will not be your interest to consider what she directs. She will teach you the proper disposal of your time & the careful management of your Money – two very important trusts & for which you are accountable. – She will teach you that the best chance of rising in life is to make yourself as useful as possible, by carefully studying everything that relates to your Profession, & distinguishing yourself from those of your own rank by a superior Proficiency in nautical Acquirements.

As you have hitherto, my Dear Francis, been extreamly fortunate in making Friends, I trust your future conduct will confirm their good opinion of you; & have the more confidence in this expectation because the high Character you acquired at the Academy for propriety of Behaviour & diligence in your studies, when you were so much younger & had so much less experience, seems to promise that riper Years & more knowledge of the world will strengthen your naturally good disposition – that this may be the case I sincerely pray, as you will readily believe when you are assured that your good Mother, Brothers, Sisters & myself will all exult in your reputation & rejoice in your happiness.

Thus far by way of general hints for your conduct. – I shall now mention only a few particulars I wish your Attention to. – As you must be convinced it will be the highest satisfaction to us to hear as frequently as possible from you, you will of course neglect no opportunity of giving us that pleasure & being very minute in what relates to yourself & your situation: On this Account, & because unexpected occasions of writing to us may offer, 'twill be a good way always to have a letter in forwardness. You may depend on hearing from some of us at every opportunity.

Whenever you draw on me for money, Captain Smith will endorse your Bills, & I dare say will readily do it as often & for what sums he shall think necessary. At the same time you must not forget to send me the earliest possible notice of the amount of the Draft & the name of the person in whose favour it is drawn. – On the subject of Letter writing I cannot help mentioning how incumbent it is on you to write to Mr Bayly, both because he desired it & because you have no other way of expressing the sense I know you entertain of his very great kindness and Attention to you. – Perhaps it would not be amiss if you were also to address one letter to your good Freind the Commissr: to acknowledge how much you shall always think yourself obliged to him.

Personal Cleanliness, in the hot Country you are going to, will be so necessary to your Comfort & Health that I need not recommend it – I shall only therefore beg of you to be particularly carefull of your Teeth.

Keep an exact account of all the Money you recieve & spend, lend none but where you are sure of an early repayment, & no account whatever be perswaded to risk it by Gaming.

I have nothing to add but my Blessing & best Prayers for your health & prosperity, & to beg you would never forget you have not upon Earth a more disinterested & warm Friend than
Your truly Affect:ᵉ Father
Geo Austen

[Double foolscap, showing signs of fire damage down the folds, hence a few words missing.]

"A note on the religious aspect of the 'Memorandums'" is given in Appendix 1.

The very specific aim of this letter, its calculated purpose in turning the boy's mind to the task of advancing in his career as smoothly and rapidly as possible, is brought out very sharply when we compare it with other Chesterfieldian letters of advice from an older to a younger man. One notable example written during the Long War is from Vice-Admiral Peter Rainier to a nephew of twenty just appointed to his first command.[24] A comparison with Mr Austen's letter is by no means to the clergyman's disadvantage. Civilian though he might be, Mr Austen was remarkably successful in framing his advice to fit a service career and we can understand why the letter remained so singularly important to Francis throughout his life. Seventy-six years later, at the time of his death in 1865, now senior Admiral of the Fleet, it was found among his private papers, as Deirdre Le Faye describes the document, 'water-stained, singed at the edges and frayed by constant reading'.[25]

Henry Martin's successor as Governor in 1790 was the new Dockyard Commissioner, Captain Charles Saxton, a well-connected naval officer; and when it was the turn of Charles Austen to enter the Academy, in July 1791, at the age of twelve, the numbers were rising. There were twenty-six scholars in all, nine of whom were the sons of naval officers. On the 12th of that month, the Commissioner formally reported to Philip Stephens, the Secretary of the Admiralty, that Charles had been tested by the Master and 'found to have made such progress in his education as qualified him to enter on the plan of Learning', having satisfied Bayly, in an oral examination, that he possessed a sufficient competence in 'Latin, Writing & Arithmetick to the Rule of Three'.

During that summer, the Austens may have paid a visit to Portsmouth to see Charles at the Academy. A report of this seems to have travelled round the family and we find an elder cousin, Eliza de Feuillide (the future Mrs Henry Austen) writing flippantly to her confidante, her cousin Philadelphia Walter: 'as to Cassandra it is very probable as you observe that some son of Neptune may have obtained her approbation as she probably experienced much homage from those very gallant gentlemen during her aquatic excursions. I hear her sister and herself are two of the prettiest girls in England.'[26]

Charles made a good start. In February 1792, the Governor rendered his annual report to Admiralty, with Charles's record:

Mathematical	Is learning of Euclid – having gone through Arithmetic and Logarithms.
French	Very diligent.
Fencing	————————
Drawing & Writing	Writes & draws but midling. Is very industrious.
Dancing	Dances tolerably.
Head Master	Has a very good Capacity, is very attentive to his studies and of a good disposition.
Governor	Good capacity & behaviour with very considerable industry.

As to the staffing and general state of the Academy, the Governor had this to say:

I pray leave to observe that at this juncture there is a good harmony and mutual agreement not only among the Scholars, but the several Masters, except the Dancing Master, of whose neglect frequent complaints have been made to me, and I have been as frequently obliged to reprove him, but hope my admonitions will effect a better observance in future. And I am to remark that the duty of the Fencing Master, from his infirmities, has been performed by a substitute for many months past. . . .

In the following year, 1792–93, the numbers had risen to twenty-eight, including ten in the naval entry, with another sound report for Charles:

Mathematical	Has proceeded in his Plan as far as Current Sailing.
French	Very diligent & behaves very well.
Drawing & Writing	Writes & draws pretty well.
Dancing	Dances indifferently.
Head Master	Is of good disposition and capacity; diligent and makes good progress
Governor	Of good capacity, well disposed & industrious.

In 1793–94, the numbers were steady at twenty-eight, with a fall to six in the naval entry. A sound report again for Charles

Mathematical	Has proceeded in his Plan as far as Lunar Observations.
French	Pretty diligent.
Drawing & Writing	Writes & draws pretty well – Behaves well.
Dancing	Dances very well.
Fencing	No Fencing Master has attended during this time.
Gunner in Ordinary	The Young Gentlemen have been very attentive to, and have made good Progress in learning the nature and use of the Cannon.
Head Master	Has a pretty good Capacity and is very attentive to his studies.
Governor	Of a tolerable Capacity [other boys are of 'good Capacity'] & very attentive and well behaved.

The Governor, who seems to have been attentive to the affairs of the Academy, reported his satisfaction:

> I pray leave to observe that at this Juncture there is a pretty good Harmony and Agreement among the Scholars and the several Masters; and that upon my frequent visiting the Academy, I find the latter are very diligent in, and give due attention to their Business, and the methods used by them in educating the Young Gentlemen are very regular, familiar and instructive, and agreeable to the Plan approved of by
> C. Saxton

In 1794–95, Charles' final year, the Academy numbers were down to twenty-three, with six in the naval entry. He was discharged on 14 September 1794 'To go to sea in the *Daedalus*'. Possibly, for this reason, no reports were made on Mathematical, French, Drawing and Writing, Dancing or Fencing; those for Firelock, Gunner and Attendant repeated the previous year word-for-word.

The Academy records for Francis and Charles are piecemeal and incomplete. But nothing in them gives any hint of the unnamed depravities suggested by St Vincent and Barham. Nor does George Austen's 'Memorandums' suggest anything amiss. Quite the contrary. Our impression is of an institution with teachers of high ability in astronomy and mathematics, achieving its objectives and turning out trainees with a sufficient grounding in the essentials of nautical knowledge and at no disadvantage in this respect to the Young Gentlemen who went directly to sea. It is a pity that we have no personal recollections of Academy life at this period, nothing to guide us to its real character. Our sole picture of the sailor brothers, no more than a glimpse, comes in a letter written years later to Charles, in which Captain Philip Broke recalled him as 'such a good temperd sociable little fellow in our *evening tea party* at the Academy – that I always recollect you with pleasure'.[27] At least, we can judge from this that, whatever the shadows, there were good times to be remembered and the lasting glow of friendship.

No doubt both Francis and Charles encountered the drawbacks to the Academy route. Doubtless, too, Mr Austen wrote a second comprehensive and inspiring letter, this time to Charles, encouraging him in similar terms to take the necessary steps to form a network of naval connections and 'friends', to exercise the 'Prudence' (Mr Austen's embracing term) of self-interest and exploit his 'superior' nautical learning.

As it turned out, Francis and Charles were not left to make their own way in forging naval contacts. There were naval men on their mother's side: Captain Henry Stanhope (Rear-Admiral in 1801) and Captain Charles Chamberlayne

(Rear-Admiral in 1795).[28] However, as third cousins, they were probably too remote to be of help. But in 1792 there occurred two family events which promised to secure the brothers' future, equipping them with an embryonic network of patronage and interest, contacts which were to reach to the very heart of naval command, the Board of Admiralty itself.*

The fortuitous events of 1792 were two marriages, which brought to the Austens a formidable phalanx of naval connection. The first, in March, was the marriage of James, their eldest brother. His bride was Anne Mathew, the daughter of Edward Mathew, a former Governor of Granada and Commander-in-Chief of the Windward and Leeward Isles, and soon to be General Mathew. Anne's mother, Lady Jane Bertie, was a daughter of the second Duke of Ancaster. She brought with her, on her mother's side, Captain Albemarle Bertie, to become Rear-Admiral in 1804, Vice-Admiral in 1808 and Admiral in 1812; and Captain Sir Thomas Bertie, Rear-Admiral in 1808, Vice-Admiral in 1813 and Admiral in 1825. On the Mathew side, it was the General's nieces Louisa and Jane, the daughters of his brother Daniel, who brought the two most important naval husbands into the Austen circle: Captain James Gambier, a future Lord of the Admiralty, with three spells in office, nine years in all, between 1795 and 1808, and his brother Captain Samuel Gambier, Secretary of the Navy Board 1795–96 and a Commissioner of the Navy from 1796 to 1813. Moreover, the Gambiers' Aunt Margaret (née Gambier) was married to one of the leading officials of the period, Sir Charles Middleton, a vigorous reforming Comptroller of the Navy from 1778 to 1790, First Naval Lord in 1795 and, as Lord Barham, First Lord of the Admiralty in 1805–06. James Gambier was brought up by the Middletons and succeeded Sir Charles as First Naval Lord in 1795.

The second stroke of fortune was the marriage of an Austen cousin, Jane Cooper (daughter of Mrs Austen's sister, Jane Leigh) to Captain Thomas Williams. Although, as another cousin observed, 'his present fortune is but small . . . he has expectation of future preferment'.[29] It was a family affair, celebrated at Steventon in December 1792, with Jane and Cassandra as witnesses, and officiated by Tom Fowle, Cassandra's future fiancé. The happy outcome for Charles was the Captain's patronage. On leaving the Academy in September 1794, he transferred directly to his cousin's ship, the *Daedalus* (32).

---

* The Navy was directed by the Lords Commissioners of the Board of Admiralty, usually seven in number. The First Lord, who could be either a civilian or an Admiral, had a seat in the Cabinet, where the central issues of war policy were decided. These included naval strategy, the disposition of the Navy worldwide and the levels of manning and finance put before Parliament. The First Lord relayed these decisions to the Board. Following the First Lord was the Senior professional member, the First Naval (later Sea) Lord, who gained in importance when the First Lord was a civilian. There were usually two other naval members and three civilians, these usually government supporters in Parliament. See Rodger, 1979.

It was a classic instance of long-term naval good fortune based on family connection. Charles came to be enrolled in Captain Williams' 'following' and the Captain's name – later Admiral Sir Thomas Williams – occurs again and again in the record of Charles' advancement over the next two decades – just as in Francis' naval record, the recurrent name is Admiral James Gambier. After the death in 1794 of Francis' first patron, the former Portsmouth Commissioner and Governor of the Academy, Sir Henry Martin, who had succeeded Middleton as Comptroller of the Navy in 1790, Gambier was to take his place.

What influence these senior officers and high officials could exert on behalf of the sailor brothers, how this influence was exerted and the part played by Mr Austen in setting these forces in motion, is something we come to in Chapters 5 and 6. To these processes, Jane Austen was a more than interested spectator; they were material for the novelist's imagination; and in *Mansfield Park*, they enter the story of William Price's commission, Henry Crawford's efforts on his behalf, and the shadowy manoeuvrings, involving Admiral Crawford, which bring it about.

3

Young Francis at Sea

'the ornament of his Country & his profession'

Jane Austen, *The History of England*

Francis had the good fortune to join a ship where his Academy education was valued and where he rapidly found his feet. As he describes himself, at the age of fourteen, he was a boy of great self-confidence, 'rather small of stature' yet 'of a vigorous constitution and possessing great activity of body'; and in time, he became 'a decided favourite' with Captain Smith and the other officers.

He set himself to make good the shortcomings in his training at the Academy and 'was not long in acquiring a competent knowledge of the practical parts of seamanship to which he was urged by the natural energies of his mind and a general thirst for knowledge'. He acted on his father's injunction to distinguish himself 'from those of' his 'own rank by a superior proficiency in nautical acquirements'. Above all, this 'proficiency' lay in his sound grasp of the methods, still relatively new, of determining longitude, an area which called for the specialised knowledge in which his two mathematics teachers, Bayly and Bradley, had long experience. It was soon noticed that Francis possessed 'a more than usual degree of theoretical knowledge', an aspect of his Academy education which was not scorned but put to good use. Francis records the outcome with characteristic self-esteem and directness: 'he became in a very short time a very good practical observer which in those days was rather an uncommon thing. In this he was encouraged by his captain, himself an excellent nautical astronomer, having been two voyages round the world with the celebrated circumnavigator, Cook.' For Captain Smith had, in Cook's words, 'been bred to the Sea under my Care'.[1] A first cousin of Mrs Cook, Smith went to sea with Cook in the 1760s, serving his apprenticeship under Cook's instruction as a nautical surveyor and draftsman on the Newfoundland Survey, and subsequently joining the great voyages of the *Endeavour* and *Resolution* in company with William Bayly, later to be appointed the Academy Master. Cook was enthusiastic about the new method of determining longitude by lunar distances and, when this became possible, on his second Pacific voyage, by chronometer – and its was from Cook himself that Smith learned his nautical astronomy, an association recorded in the log-books of the *Endeavour* and *Resolution,* where the names of Cook and Smith sit side-by-side in the daily record of observations. For naval men of this period, Cook was the peace-time hero of the seas, 'The ablest and most renowned Navigator this or any country hath produced'.*

What this great tradition – begun in the exploits of Cook and handed on in the teaching of Bayly, Bradley and Captain Smith – meant to Francis we can only imagine. On this matter his Memoir is silent. But more than once he must have been treated to his Captain's favourite story, his claim to fame: that on the landfall at Botany Bay on 28 April 1770, Cook had picked him out, calling to him, 'Isaac, you shall go first'.[2]

During the boy's first year, Captain Smith would have seen to it that Francis caught up on what the Academy training failed to provide, 'the practical parts of seamanship': the training that could only take place, day in, day out, as a working member of the ship's crew, literally learning the ropes, handling the sails aloft with the topmen, knotting, splicing and reefing the sails in all weathers, foul and fair, something for which sail drill at Portsmouth gave little preparation. Gun drill, too, was wholly different. Here, theory was replaced by exhausting and dangerous practice. Even on a frigate, the relatively small guns were upwards of a ton in weight, to be manhandled on rolling decks in the sequence of loading, running out, aiming and firing.** Not that Francis was expected to be master of these skills. But even as a Midshipman he could find himself in charge of a section of guns, and, as a future officer, in these or any other duties, he needed to know what he would be ordering his men to do, what could be asked of them and when exhaustion would set in. Above all, he had to learn the secret of disciplined teamwork – how it was achieved and maintained, how vital it was to the crew's morale, and how a well-trained ship's company, working together, could mean the difference between survival and death, between victory and defeat, between winning prizes and losing them.

There was also learning to cope with shipboard life, acclimatisation to what in sailors' talk was called 'the wooden world', an isolated and contained community, described in his father's letter as 'The little world of which you are going to become an inhabitant': the finding of his place in its structure of command, in its routines and tempo, in its confines of space, its constraints on freedom, its range of punishments, with the proximity, night and day, of his shipmates, some of them friendly boys of his own age, others envious and

---

* The tribute of Admiral Sir Hugh Palliser, Cook's patron, colleague and friend, heading the memorial inscription on the monument to Cook erected by Palliser on his estate at Vache Park, Buckinghamshire. The words echo Cook's declared ambition 'not only to go further than anyone had done before, but as far as it was possible for man to go' quoted in MacLean (1972), p. 184.

** The standard armament of the *Perseverance* were 12 pounders, this being the weight of the ball they fired: 8 feet long, these guns weighed over a ton.

resentful of his status as a young gentleman and jealous of he favour the found with the Captain for his skills in navigation. And not for these alone. For Francis was also talented in nautical drawing, in hydrography and the making of charts and in sketching the coasts, headlands and other features that came in view. These exercises formed a part of the youngster's training that Captain Smith was able to supervise knowledgeably out of his own experience as a naval surveyor and draftsman with Cook, and they were gifts that Francis was to employ throughout his life as a sailor. In the biography which he supplied to Marshall's *Royal Naval Biography* of 1824 he draws attention to this, remarking that since boyhood he had been 'very fond of practical astronomy and hydrography',[3] skills which he later deployed in making charts of the China Seas, the Canton River, and sketches of the Nanka Islands he was able to deliver to the East India Company following his return from China in July 1810;[4] and a further record of Francis' skilful charting is to be found today in the archives of the United Kingdom Hydrographic Office at Taunton.

The first milestone in Francis' career at sea was reached in December 1789, ten months after his joining the *Perseverance*, when his rating was raised from Volunteer to Midshipman, an advance which normally took place after three years at sea, his time at the Academy counting as two. He now moved from the Gunroom, where he messed with the other youngsters, to the Cockpit, joining the other Midshipmen and Master's Mates; and, as a Midshipman, henceforth he was formally regarded as a Superior Petty Officer with the right to walk the quarter-deck with the commissioned officers. This alteration in status and rating did not mean that his duties changed overnight, since his progress and responsibilities were dictated by ability and experience, not by the rating he carried on the ship's books. With his Academy training and the Captain's encouragement, we can be sure that Francis was already playing a responsible role in the noonday calculation of the vessel's course, its speed and position, using astronomy, dead-reckoning* and the chronometer; and in the course of time he would help to maintain these entries in the ship's log-book. Over the course of the next three years Midshipman Austen would also take his place in the ship's watch system, under the orders of the division's Lieutenant, having responsibility for a subdivision. He would take on specific duties, such as charge of the signals or command of a ship's boat; and, in the event of action, he might stand by as an *aide* to the Captain or as deputy to one of the Lieutenants in charge of a division of guns.

---

* This was the traditional method of estimating a ship's position by calculating the distance travelled over the previous twelve hours and charting the courses steered by the compass, then correcting these measurements for current, drifting and the ship's trim. Without astronomical checking and correction, dead-reckoning was a rough-and-ready method.

Throughout this time, Francis' eyes were set on the great ordeal for every Midshipman, his passing for Lieutenant. According to the letter of the regulations, at the age of twenty (nineteen, after 1806) or above and with not less than six years' service at sea, three of these to have been served as a Midshipman, he would come before a Board of three serving or former Captains (Commissioners for the occasion) convened to judge whether or not he was fit to hold the King's commission. The procedures were well known. He would be expected to produce a number of certificates from his Captain: of age and rated service, and testifying to his 'Sobriety, Obedience, Diligence, and Skill in the Profession of a Seaman'.[5] He would also be asked to show his personal log books for the ships in which he had sailed. He could be examined in navigation, seamanship and gunnery, including the different methods of fixing longitude; the calculation of azimuth altitude and double altitude; holding a course in the face of shifting winds, changing waves, currents and tides; the action to be taken in facing hazards such as the loss of masts and rigging; the calculation of high-water times for specific ports; the orders for clearing the ship and preparing for engagement – in effect, he could be questioned on everything he should have learned over the last six years.

In practice, some candidates got through on the nod; some were asked only token questions; others were grilled. It could depend on the mood of the Board and the severity of individual Commissioners. Admiralty influence or political pressure or family interest could be at work behind the scenes. And there was stretching and evasion of the regulations. Sometimes under-age candidates came armed with false certificates. Extra years of sea-time could be added by entering a boy's name on the ship's books before he actually arrived, or having him entered on the books of several ships, or by the purchase of another youngster's certificates and changing the name. In Francis' time, these malpractices were known and tolerated.* For as long as the Board was satisfied with the candidate, it could choose to turn a blind eye. Influence and interest to one side, at the end of the day the Board's prime concern was that the candidates coming before them were fit to carry out the duties of a Lieutenant in the conduct of a ship at sea. This practical test was the decisive issue.

But passing the examination for Lieutenant was not enough. Promotion itself was a further step, since a Lieutenant's commission was a document appointing him to a specific vacancy on a named ship.** 'Elderly'

---

* As First Lord, St Vincent led the Board in tightening up on these 'inroads and abuses', seeking 'to restore the Navy to its pristine vigour' Letter to Rear-Admiral Duckworth, 29 March. 1801 (Smith, 1922, i. 339).

** This is a 'Ship's Commission'. 'General Commissions', appointing the recipient to a rank and not to a post on a named ship, were generally introduced only in 1860.

midshipmen, 'oldsters' (as they were described), without patrons or interest could be found on every ship, stranded for years waiting for a commission to arrive, if ever. This is the very predicament which Jane Austen creates for Midshipman Price in *Mansfield Park*. For all his experience in action and his 'professional knowledge'[6] from seven years at sea, having passed for Lieutenant, he is consumed with anger and frustration at the long wait and bitter at seeing others junior to him get their commissions first. His desperate situation answers the test of history, for this part of *Mansfield Park* is set in the winter of 1812–13, and in 1813 the actual queue of passed Midshipmen awaiting commissions was almost two thousand long.

But for Francis Austen, it was plain sailing. Unlike William Price, he enjoyed immediate patronage of the highest order. After his time in the *Perseverance* under Captain Smith (in the opinion of Cornwallis, 'a most excellent man'),[7] he removed to the *Crown*, the Flagship of Commodore Cornwallis, returning with him to the *Perseverance* when the *Crown* was ordered back to England and following him yet again when, in November 1791, Cornwallis moved his pennant to the *Minerva* (38), recently arrived on the station. As Commander-in-Chief in the Eastern Seas, Cornwallis was authorised to make promotions on the spot. Moreover, Lord Chatham, First Lord of the Admiralty, had personally encouraged him to fill vacancies in his Squadron as he wished, with the assurance that 'young men' from outside would not be forced upon him by the Admiralty, 'knowing how few occasions you have in peace of providing for your followers'.[8] Chatham's favour was not extended only on account of Cornwallis's long and distinguished service. Chatham had an eye upon the the mainland as well. For at Fort William, the seat of Government at Calcutta, was someone else worth obliging, the Commodore's elder brother, General Lord Cornwallis, the Governor-General and Commander-in-Chief of India.

Swept along by such a confluence of power, patronage and political interest, Cornwallis's following could hardly fail. On 28 December 1792, four months short of his nineteenth birthday, Midshipman Austen duly passed for Lieutenant and at Old Harbour, Andaman Islands, Cornwallis appointed him Lieutenant of an armed brig, the *Dispatch* (12), loaned from the East India Company. As Francis proudly recorded, this was an event which confirmed the Commodore's recognition of the 'particular merits of the young man, especially as there were on the Ship a number of very deserving Midshipmen, most of them greatly his senior in the service, of good connections and strongly recommended for promotion'. If this success sounds all too easy, it is worth remembering that Cornwallis would suffer neither fools nor incompetents. He gave his support to Francis because he wanted to have him as an officer, and in this matter there was no higher accolade, nor one more difficult to obtain. As Alan Schom points out, Cornwallis 'always demanded the finest officers in his squadrons and expected nothing less than the best from them'.[9] So Francis may be forgiven the complacency with which he remembered the reaction of his former messmates, some of them those familiar 'elderly' Midshipmen, 'oldsters' soured with waiting and envious of his success:

> It was not in the nature of things that even a marked preference for one so much their junior in age as well as in the service should not strike some sensations of an unpleasant description amongst the Gentlemen of the Cockpit, but to their honour and the credit of the young Lieutenant be it mentioned there was not one of them who did not with every appearance of cordiality congratulate him on his promotion.

The voyage out to India had taken seven months. The Squadron left Spithead on 9 February 1789, with calls on the way at Madeira, on the 28th, Tenerife and Rio de Janeiro, where it rested for three weeks, arriving at Madras on 3 September. Cornwallis reported to the Admiralty 'the great progress of Scurvey among most of the Seamen' and blamed this partly on the failure to get a delivery of sauerkraut – rich in vitamin C and the Navy's anti-dote before lemons and limes were adopted; the vessel bringing it was caught in severe weather and crashed into Ramsgate pier. He also blamed the supplies of pork and beef, ancient meat left over from the war with America and kept in store for no less than five or six years. Yet close to hand there was a ready source of fresh meat in the nest of shipboard rats. A Midshipman on the *Crown*, Edward Pelham Brenton (later famous for his five volume *History* of the Navy) remembered these vermin 'as tame as rabbits. We used to catch them with fish hooks, stab them with forks or cutlasses, and dress and eat them'.[10]

Fort George, Madras, was the official residence of the naval Commander-in-Chief. After the formalities of his arrival in India were completed there, Cornwallis sailed northwards up the Coromandel Coast, arriving at Diamond Harbour, Calcutta, two weeks later. The most recent conflict with France had ended in 1783. Preoccupied with its own internal affairs, for the time being France had given up any territorial ambitions and confined itself to a limited trading role. It was, as Francis comments, 'a period of profound peace'.

There was, however, a minor interruption, which kept the ships of the Squadron occupied, on and off, over the next two and a half years. In December 1789, Tippoo Sultan of Mysore, a native ruler supported by the French, attacked Travancore, the capital of one of the East India Company's native allies. Cornwallis immediately took part of the Squadron southward and round to the Malabar Coast, urged by the Governor-General to search any French merchantmen found in the area and prevent the possible landing of troops, arms and military supplies. This blockade was maintained for over two years, with several skirmishes. French vessels objected to being stopped and searched; a French Squadron arrived in July 1791; and in November 1792 these clashes led to a minor engagement when the *Phoenix* (36), in company with the *Perseverance*, was fired upon by a French frigate, with some loss of life. However, blockade duty was sporadic, and not all the Squadron – now enlarged with the arrival of four more frigates in 1791 – was involved. For much of the time the movements of the *Perseverance* were determined less by military considerations than by the monsoons. From November to March, naval forces were usually stationed at Madras and from May to December went round to Bombay, before the North East monsoon set in, the aim being to keep to the leeward of the peninsula. These voyages were varied with visits, as Francis records, 'to numerous settlements in the vast extent of territory occupied by the English in the East. This afforded him an opportunity of seeing a great variety of places and through his captain's kindness . . . he was on several occasions introduced to the notice of persons of the first consequence and distinction in India.' With Mr Austen's 'Memorandums' in mind, Francis would have seized these opportunities. Moreover, his father would have primed him on the family connection with Warren Hastings (discussed in Chapter 5), a connection which led to the highest levels of the East India Company, with all that this could do to open doors and effect introductions during Francis' time in the Company's domain. Although its political role had been reduced by the Acts of 1773 and 1784, its trading monopoly and control of the administration remained, and its realm of patronage was undiminished.

Just as the Company continued to hold a dominant role in the life of British India, so it formed the nucleus of Anglo-Indian society in the outposts where Francis and his gentlemanly shipmates were made welcome. Here, the Academy's dancing lessons could be put to good use, a detail that, twenty years later, Jane Austen wove into the story of Midshipman Price. Following his years away at sea, to the West Indies and beyond, William entertains Sir Thomas Bertram with what he 'could relate of the different modes of dancing which had fallen within his observation'.[11]

Our knowledge of Anglo-Indian society at this time owes a good deal to the observations of the diarist William Hickey. His trading interests brought him to Fort William and Calcutta, where he met Captain Smith (a 'very fine fellow') and, in January 1790, he came across Commodore Cornwallis paying a call on his 'noble' brother, the Governor-General: 'very unlike him both in person and manner . . . The commodore was a living Trunnion, but more of a brute than Smollett made his hero' – Commodore Hawser Trunnion, an old sea-dog, outwardly ferocious but kind at heart, was a leading character in *Peregrine Pickle*, published in 1751. After three weeks in Calcutta, during which time he 'abused or found fault with everybody and everything', the Commodore took his departure. As Hickey records, he was a man of 'rough temper and disposition'. He felt out of place and out of humour in the drawing-rooms and 'polished' society of the English settlements, and was prepared to show it. On the other hand, he was highly regarded by the ordinary sailors and ready to address them in 'tar-like' language. He carried several affectionate nicknames, including 'Coachee', 'Mr Whip', 'Billy Blue' and, the name by which he was most widely known, 'Billy Go-Tight' – because, although ruddy-cheeked and a convivial drinker on land, at sea he was notably abstemious. Famed throughout the Navy as a character, he was an aristocratic seaman of the old school, someone, according to Hickey, who could make himself quite at home amongst the 'savage people', said to be 'a race of anthropophagi or cannibals', of the Andaman Islands.[12]*

There was, in fact, some truth to Hickey's joke. A reserved man, reputed a woman-hater, Cornwallis much preferred visiting 'our new settlements', such as Fort Cornwallis on Prince of Wales' Island (the island of Penang) set up by the East India Company in 1786, and exploring the Andamans and the coasts of Siam and Malaya, 'to being stuck up in a pompous style at one of the old ones'.[13] Moreover, he was under secret orders from the Admiralty to carry out a general survey, to include the East Coast of India, the Andamans and the Malay Peninsula, as part of the Government strategy to combat the strong Dutch trading presence in the region.

As a member of Cornwallis's following, Francis was able to enjoy these voyages across the Bay of Bengal and eastwards to the Andaman Sea. For all his quirks and eccentricities, Cornwallis was an ideal mentor. He loved nothing more than travelling in remote places and understood how valuable this experience could be for young sailors. He addressed the Admiralty on this very point, stressing the 'great variety of this station' and how 'useful' service here would be 'to our young folks in future'.[14] A stern moralist, he added a warning to the Admiralty Board: that India was 'in general distructive to officers, and to the Younger part in particular, where nothing is heard of but *making of money*'.[15] This was not making money through prizes, for few were to be had. Cornwallis's indignation was at the level of corruption amongst the contractors of ships' supplies and he waged an unending war against these established abuses, the 'little dirty tricks' which he reported back

---

* It is worth balancing this picture with the impression of Zachary Macaulay, a leading figure in the Slave Trade Abolition movement and a fervent Evangelical. He found Cornwallis a man of 'Intelligence, courtesy, frankness' who 'unites firmness of mind and strictness of discipline' (letter of 4 February 1797, in Knutsford, 1900, p. 258).

in letter after letter to the Admiralty. He also addressed himself to a fellow-spirit, Sir Charles Middleton, Comptroller of the Navy Board from 1778 to 1790, who resigned in disgust, having been frustrated in his own attempts to put through a similar programme of reforms at home.[16]

Effective support from London was not forthcoming, but praise from the very top was unstinting. Chatham, the First Lord of the Admiralty, applauded Cornwallis for his 'zeal and attention'; and Admiral Hood, the First Naval Lord, assured Cornwallis that 'not only the Board of Admiralty but every other Board you have had to correspond with, are most perfectly satisfied with every part of your conduct, and convinced that you have been unremitting in your pains for bringing the expenses of his Majesty's squadron under your command as low as possible'.[17] However, the cleansing of such ancient stables was beyond the strength of one man, even someone with the vigour and reforming zeal of a Cornwallis. It was his old friend Admiral Howe who put the proper gloss on the matter, advising him that to eradicate such corruption was 'an Herculean labour, unless you can find purity in the natives!' – and such 'purity' was not to be found. 'But be not discouraged in your most commendable pursuit', Howe added, understanding very well that Cornwallis was not a man to be deterred.[18]

Francis would have known nothing of Cornwallis's stream of complaint to London. Yet he was well aware of the Commodore's immediate campaign, since, as long as Cornwallis was in Indian waters, the ships of the Squadron were bombarded with orders and memoranda laying down the law on dealings with contractors and the purchase of supplies, and drawing attention to such incidents as the discovery of a recent and needless purchase of sail canvas – the bolts having been stowed away between decks. In all this, Francis would have observed the fierce rectitude of his commander, a lone crusader against one of the Navy's chronic ills. If Commodore Cornwallis led his young officers on the path of exploration and adventure and taught them a disdain of formality and pomp, he also set them an example of moral courage and leadership, a lesson Francis was not to forget.

In February 1792, peace was made with the Tippoo. After returning to Madras, Cornwallis set off for the Andamans to investigate the possibility of using the islands as a naval base to the windward of the Bay of Bengal. By December, he was again in Madras. By this time, rumours were heard of an impending war in Europe. Two months later, in February 1793, Cornwallis was promoted to Flag rank as Rear-Admiral of the White. One by one, in varying states of unseaworthiness, the ships of the Squadron returned to England – the *Perseverance* in March 1793 – until only the *Minerva* remained. It was joined by an improvised Squadron of three Indiamen drafted into the

Bombay Marine, the East India Company's private navy. By this time England was at war with both France and Holland – news of its outbreak reached Madras on 1 June and Calcutta on 11 June – and it was reported that four or five French frigates and a corvette (the equivalent of an English sloop of twenty guns) were off Pondicherry, the capital of the French settlement located southwards along the coast from Madras. With the help of the Company's Squadron, Cornwallis successfully blockaded Pondicherry, which surrendered in August.

Unfortunately, Francis' Memoir tells us nothing of these events, nor of Cornwallis's strange yet admirable ways. What we learn, summarily, is that Francis remained only five weeks as Lieutenant in an armed brig, the *Dispatch*, before it was laid up for repair. He then rejoined the *Minerva* in February 1793 as a supernumerary Lieutenant, remaining there until June, when Cornwallis, seeing no further use for the *Dispatch*, returned it to the East India Company, leaving the ship's officers free to return to England. Francis signed off from the vessel on 3 June and, at the beginning of July, took his passage home in a Company ship, landing at Southampton, after a voyage of four-and-a-half months, on the evening of 13 November, and arrived at Steventon the next day.

We can imagine the warmth of the young Lieutenant's homecoming, and his entertaining the Steventon household, after an absence of five years, with his anecdotes of Cornwallis, his tales of India, the 'anthropophagi' of the Andamans, the kingdoms of Siam and Malaya, their sights, manners and 'modes of dancing'; and illustrating his account with the sketches and water-colours of the landmarks and exotic scenes taken on his travels; and producing from his sailor's chest the gifts for his mother and sisters, among them the finest of all muslins, genuine Indian muslins – the spotted, checked and sprigged muslins that Jane Austen mentions so frequently in her letters to Cassandra – the 'true Indian muslin' (as against the coarser home-produced fabric) that Henry Tilney purchases for his sister's gown, boasting at his own expertise and at the bargain price of 'but five shillings a yard'.[19] Francis may also have been the source for a short Indian sequence in *Sense and Sensibility* in which Marianne Dashwood and Willoughby make fun of Colonel Brandon's experiences there:

'That is to say', cried Marianne contemptuously, 'he had told you that in the East Indies the climate is hot, and the mosquitoes are troublesome' . . . 'Perhaps', said Willoughby, 'his observations may have extended to the existence of nabobs, gold mohrs, and palanquins'.[20]

In return, Jane was able to welcome Francis with presents of her own, the amusing little pieces written during the years of his absence. There was 'Jack & Alice', a parody 'Novel' 'respectfully inscribed to Francis William Austen Esq Midshipman on board his Majesty's Ship the Perseverance by his obedient humble Servant The Author'.[21] As Claire Tomalin suggests, this is a fantastical tale which Francis and Jane may have started on together before he left for India. It contains a hero 'amiable, accomplished & bewitching', a family 'a little addicted to the Bottle and the Dice', a young lady caught in a man-trap, her legs 'entirely broken', a cook who marries a titled Lady, and a village scene of drunkenness, brawling and murder.[22] A tale of violence for a brother whose calling inevitably led to violence. In *Volume the First* we find other pertinent little jokes: 'a man of War of 55 Guns' (an uneven gun-number was an impossibility)[23] and 'The Adventures of Mr Harley', 'a short, but interesting Tale' thirteen lines long. This, too, is dedicated to Francis on board the *Perseverance*, 'inscribed' 'with all imaginable Respect'. The hero, Mr Harley, 'one of many children' was 'Destined by his father for the Church & his mother for the Sea, desirous of pleasing both, he prevailed on Sir John to obtain for him a Chaplaincy on board a Man of War. He, accordingly, cut his Hair and Sailed.'[24] The conflicting ambitions of Mr Harley's parents raises an intriguing speculation, since Francis himself was highly devout and became known in the Navy for his piety. According to the *Memoir*, 'he was spoken of as "*the* officer who kneeled at church"' (this would be during the prayers, when the usual practice was to remain seated); and his nephew, James Edward Austen-Leigh (himself a clergyman) wrote of Francis, with studied emphasis, as being 'a very religious man'.[25] Could it be that 'Mr Harley' catches some hint of a debate that arose at Steventon in the 1780s when the boy's career was under discussion? Whether daring or indiscreet, Jane Austen was not averse to planting events of family history into her writing under a veneer of literary humour.

'Jack & Alice' and 'Mr Harley' are undated. But a flattering reference to Francis appears in 'The History of England', dated 26 November 1791, in *Volume the Second*. The section on Queen Elizabeth holds a stirring prediction for brother Francis, a future which promises to be as glittering as that of his namesake, Sir Francis Drake:

> It was about this time that Sir Francis Drake the first English Navigator who sailed round the World, lived, to be the ornament of his Country & his profession. Yet great as he was, & justly celebrated as a Sailor, I cannot help foreseeing that he will be equalled in this or the next Century by one who tho' now but young, already promises to answer all the ardent & sanguine expectations of his Relations & Freinds, amongst whom I may class the amiable Lady to whom this work is dedicated, & my no less amiable Self.[26]

(The 'amiable Lady' of the last lines is Cassandra.) What supports the connection of this passage with Francis rather than Charles is not simply the coincidence of names, which Jane Austen plays upon, but the fact that Drake, like Francis, was a notably religious sea-captain. He would always sail with a chaplain on board and it was said that the sound of prayers and psalms on his ships was unceasing.*

Jane could be playfully flattering, and respectful too, of her brother's piety. It was an Evangelical faith which was to shape his career. Yet alongside success, over the years it was to bring him more than his share of disappointment.

---

* Mr Austen's library may well have contained a copy of Camden's *Annales* which recounts these details, as well as Drake's heroic exploits, and which would have been familiar to the Austens in their family reading. The *Annales* was first published in Latin, part one in 1615, part two in 1627; and in English in 1625 and 1628, as *Annales of Britain, The History of Elizabeth*. Camden recounts that in 1580, Drake's father acted as a naval chaplain (3rd edn, 1635, i. 219–25).

Captain

4

Lives in the Service

'the true Sailor way'

Jane Austen to Cassandra, 30 June 1808

During the Long War, the sailor brothers served in all the theatres of action and saw duty of every kind: patrolling the North Sea; blockading the French fleet in the Channel ports, the Mediterranean and off the coast of Spain; carrying troops; escorting convoys in the Baltic, to the West Indies, to India and onwards to China; and patrolling on the North American station, from Halifax to Bermuda. There was the excitement of long pursuits and Fleet engagements, of interception, boarding and the capture of prizes; and for Francis, the glory of having served under Nelson and winning his approval as 'an excellent young man';[1] and, his lifelong disappointment, missing Trafalgar. There was also the frustration of dull routine patrolling in home waters and periods when one or other of the brothers was kicking his heels in England, on half-pay, impatient to be at sea, waiting for a ship or orders to sail.

Much of this comes in *Jane Austen's Sailor Brothers* and to fill in the fine detail we have the benefit of their official records, including log books, letter books and order books, navigation notes, remark books and so on, together with their private journals and diaries. We read of 'Old England' and France 'the Great Nation', 'strange sails' sighted, 'contrary winds', the state of the watch, the 'readiness' of their vessels, ships 'lost' and ships 'distressed', 'flags of truce', and engagements with French men-of-war, frigates and brigs and American privateers. Among the historic papers preserved by Francis is the 'Order of Battle and of Sailing' addressed to him as Captain of the *Canopus* 'Dated on board the *Victory* in Carlisle Bay Barbadoes 5th June 1805' and signed 'Nelson & Bronte', an order issued during the pursuit of the combined French and Spanish Fleet to the West Indies and back, ahead of Trafalgar.[2]

There are visits to harbours and remote landing places and anchorages for wooding and watering, inspections of batteries and fortifications. For Francis, there was an unwelcome spell of duty ashore, from July 1803 to April 1804, during the first year of 'The Great Terror', the invasion scare when it was feared that Napoleon would despatch *La Grande Armée* across the Channel, 'a ditch', according to Napoleon in November 1803, 'that shall be

leaped when one is daring enough to try'.[3] At the forefront of the Channel
Fleet, commanded by Cornwallis, were the forward blockading Squadrons;
and behind them the heavier protecting Squadrons at the rear; and behind
them waited Britain's third line of defence, the Sea Fencibles. These were
volunteers manning so-called gunboats (often no more than armed fishing
vessels), in readiness to meet Boney and his barges. Poets might sing of their
bravery and readiness. Wordsworth's sonnet 'To the Men of Kent, October
1803' hailed them as the 'Vanguard of Liberty' and cheered them on:

> In Britain is one breath;
> We are all with you now from shore to shore: –
> Ye men of Kent, 'tis victory or death![4]

Francis, however, was not enthused. Indeed, he doubted their effectiveness.
As far as he was concerned, and he was ready to put this on record in his official report, the force was 'a non-descript half-sailor half-soldier as efficient as
neither'.[5] Nonetheless, he took his duty seriously. His district covered a
twenty-mile stretch of the East Kent coast from the North Foreland to
Sandown Castle, just north of Deal. Within a few weeks of his appointment
he had rendered the Admiralty a description of the coastline, setting out in
detail the possible landing-places for an invading force, with predictions of
likely success or failure according to the tides and weather.[6] It was a task in
which Francis had a personal interest, for only twenty miles inland was
Godmersham Park, his brother Edward's family seat. The Corps
Commander, Admiral Lord Keith, received good accounts of the Fencibles
serving under Captain Austen. In January 1804 Keith's report to the
Admiralty showed that, with a force of 250 men and seventeen boats, 'Every
boat in the district is in perfect readiness'.[7] In the event, Francis was doubly
fortunate. Although Napoleon spoke of the Channel as 'a mere ditch' and
ordered a song to be written 'to go to the tune of *Chant du départ*, for the
invasion of England',[8] the Fencibles were never put to the test, and it was in
Ramsgate, his headquarters, that Francis met his future wife, Mary Gibson, in
February 1804.

There were moments of glory. For Francis, one of these came in March
1800 – serving in Nelson's Mediterranean Fleet – an encounter off Marseilles
with three French vessels, two of which he drove onto the rocks and the third,
La Ligurienne, he captured after a sharp engagement under the guns of two
shore batteries, with no loss of life to the crew of his sloop, the *Peterel* (16),
thirty of whom (out of 110) including the First Lieutenant and the Gunner,
were away manning prizes. For this act of skill and bravery Francis was
promoted from Commander to Captain. There were also historic engagements such as the Battle of San Domingo in 1806, in which he served as Flag

Captain of the *Canopus* (80) (see Illustration 13), winning a gold medal and the thanks of both Houses of Parliament. Charles, too, was distinguished in the heart of battle, promoted Lieutenant for his part in driving a Dutch ship-of-the-line, the *Brutus* (74), into Helvoetsluys following Admiral Duncan's historic victory at the Battle of Camperdown in December 1797. And once again he won promotion at sea, from Lieutenant to Commander, in 1804, for his part in a series of engagements, including the capture of three men-of-war and two privateers.

It was this promotion that took Charles away from European waters, to spend six-and-a-half years patrolling the Eastern seaboard of North America. His duty, in the main a policing role, was somewhat unwelcome and certainly unheroic: enforcing the right of search for English deserters on American vessels, preventing American trade with Napoleon's Europe, and intercepting the traffic in slaves between the British West Indies and the Southern States of America. There was, however, one consolation. For it was on his home station of Bermuda that he met his wife, Frances Palmer, a bride of just seventeen, with whom he returned to England in August 1811 with his two infant children. Only three months later, his old patron, now Rear-Admiral Sir Thomas Williams, newly-appointed Commander-in-Chief of the Nore, found a place for Charles as his Flag Captain in the *Namur* (90), a guard-ship* anchored off Sheerness.

In the belief that Napoleon was securely out of the way on Elba, the close of the Long War was celebrated in the Spring of 1814. For Francis it ended quietly. In May, he returned from escort duties in the Baltic and signed off the *Elephant* (74) at Spithead. He wrote at once to the Admiralty of his 'readiness to serve whenever and wherever their Lordships may think it fit to employ me'.[9] Withdrawing his request almost immediately, he came to settle with his wife and five children at Chawton House, the Hampshire property of his brother Edward. Charles, on the other hand, saw out the war, active to its very end. Soon after his wife's death in September 1814, he resigned his post in the *Namur*, took command of the *Phoenix* (36) and set sail for the Mediterranean. After Napoleon's escape from Elba in March 1815, he was sent in pursuit of a Neapolitan Squadron said to be in the Adriatic. He was involved in the blockade of Brindisi and was then ordered to the Greek Archipelago in the suppression of piracy, a mission which ended in disaster in February 1816. Under a pilot, the *Phoenix* was driven ashore by a hurricane near Symrna on the coast of Asia Minor. Charles' Diary entry for Wednesday 21st records the consequence: 'Thus in two short hours was the Phoenix from a well appointed Frigate in good order reduced to a wreck. How uncertain are all human

* A guard-ship functioned as a collecting station for seamen (some of them press-ganged in London and towns along the Thames) to make up crews for outgoing vessels.

events'. Although all the ship's boats were stove in, the crew managed to swim to shore and safety – and Charles was able to close on a note of heartfelt gratitude: 'Thank God I found no life had been lost'.[10] The Court Martial in April cleared Charles of any error or negligence. Nonetheless, it was, as Marshall records, 'the most unfortunate event in his professional career'.[11]

Back in England by the end of June, he stayed in London with the Palmers to be within calling distance of the Admiralty for another command, but with little hope. His misfortune dismayed the family and James's daughter Caroline dolefully noted that 'No blame fell on the Captain, yet such a misfortune is always a disparagement; and the war being over, he knew he was likely to wait long for another ship'.[12] So it proved. A blot on his record, it was ten years before he went to sea again.

With Jane Austen's death in 1817, strictly speaking, our interest in the sailor brothers comes to an end. However, their story is quickly completed. In 1820, still under a cloud, Charles was offered a post in the Coast Guard service commanding a district, first for two years at Padstow, in North Cornwall, then at Plymstock near Plymouth. It was a job usually kept for superannuated naval officers and seemed a sad end to his career. However, following his second marriage in August 1820, and a further four children in the next six years, he had little choice but to carry on. Much of his time, his mother reported, was spent 'on horseback' on tours of inspection around the Custom Houses and Revenue Stations in his area. When smugglers were sighted, in vessels from France and the Channel Islands carrying gin, brandy, rum, silk and tea, 'he sends out his Boats & Men, but does not go himself'.[13] It is not surprising that Charles kept his silence, saying nothing of these years in the wilderness, from 1817 to 1825, in the service record he provided for the naval biographers: Marshall, in the 1820s, and, twenty years later, O'Byrne. The *Sailor Brothers* also holds its silence over the Coast Guard years.

Charles' return to sea is a fine example of naval alertness, a combination of his impulsive determination and the turn of fate. On leaving the Coast Guard service, he took a house at Gosport, a favourite settlement for Navy men, with its proximity to Portsmouth and its views of the Fleet at Spithead. One day in May 1826 he happened to be watching a frigate, the *Aurora* (44), which was about to sail

> when he saw the anchor let go and the Captain's flag half-masted. He immediately took a small boat and went alongside, when he heard of Captain Maxwell's death. Thereupon, he posted up to the Admiralty, with this intelligence and asked for the appointment. To the question how soon could he be ready he replied 'Tomorrow'. As any delay in despatching the *Aurora* was objectionable he got the appointment. He returned at once, joined the frigate and sailed within four days of the death.[14]

The *Aurora* was ordered to the Jamaica station, where he was, as he recorded, 'most successful' 'in crushing the slave trade'.[15] In addition, the *Aurora* formed part of the naval presence in the Caribbean, showing the flag in support of British interests in the emergent states of South America. Charles was appointed the Squadron second-in-command. After three years, he joined the *Winchester* (52) (see Illustration 14) as Flag Captain to Admiral Sir Edward Colpoys, the Station Commander-in-Chief. Unluckily, he fell from a mast during a gale and was invalided home at the end of 1830. In 1838–41 he saw active service again, in command of the *Bellerophon* (80) in the campaign against Mehemet Ali, Viceroy of Egypt, and took part in the bombardment of Acre, service which won him the Companion of the Bath. In 1846, Charles was promoted Rear-Admiral and in January 1850, at the age of seventy-one, became Commander-in-Chief of the East Indies and China Station. It was to be his final posting. He directed the British naval forces with success in the Second Burmese War and in April 1852 led the capture of Rangoon. Later in the year, however, heading a combined naval and military expedition up the Irrawaddy, he suffered a recurrence of cholera and died in the line of duty on 7 October, at the age of seventy-three. It was, at least, a death he was prepared for: 'He is said to have written up his reports, penned a line to his wife, said his prayers, took to his bed and died, peacefully and alone'.[16] One of his officers wrote home to the family: 'Our good Admiral won the hearts of all by his gentleness and kindness while he was struggling with disease, and endeavouring to do his duty as Commander-in-Chief of the British naval forces in these waters. His death was a great grief to the whole fleet. I know that I cried bitterly when I found he was dead.'[17]

Following the Long War, Francis' career was less remarkable but even more impressive for its sheer duration. Although he was regularly honoured and promoted – CB in 1815, Rear-Admiral in 1830, KCB in 1837 (at the last investiture by William IV), Vice-Admiral in June 1838 (to mark the Coronation of Queen Victoria) – it was no less than thirty years before he was to go to sea again, a period of being 'laid up upon the Shelf' (as the saying went)* that ended only in December 1844 when, at the age of seventy-one, he was appointed Commander-in-Chief, North American and West India Station, returning to Caribbean waters after an absence of forty years.

Apart from ceremonial duties, tours of inspection, and moving between his official residences at Bermuda and Halifax, Nova Scotia, there were operations to direct against slave-traders of all nationalities sailing under Brazilian and Portuguese flags. Gun-boat diplomacy was called for along the coasts of Venezuela and Nicaragua, in his own words, 'to protect property

---

* A vessel laid-up is dismantled and moored in a harbour, as unfit or unwanted for further service.

from apprehended outrage in consequence of revolutionary insurrection'.[18] Francis remained in post until May 1848, when Cochrane, now Vice-Admiral the Earl of Dundonald, arrived to take over the command, a reunion of old comrades who had sailed together in the Mediterranean half-a-century before.

Francis' remaining years were passed at Portsdown Lodge, his home since 1828. It was the very spot for a sailor, Portsdown Hill overlooking Portsmouth and the harbour and with a view beyond, out to the Isle of Wight and the Fleet anchored at Spithead. Further honours and promotions were to come: Admiral in 1848, GCB in 1860, in 1862 both Rear-Admiral and Vice-Admiral of the United Kingdom,* appointments which lost him a £300 pension but which together brought an income of almost £800. In the following year, Francis reached the pinnacle of his career, the Navy's highest rank, Admiral-of-the-Fleet. In the words of Queen Victoria, it was 'a well-deserved reward for your brilliant services'[19] – a gracious and flattering remark, and regally bestowed, but empty, nonetheless. The truth of the matter was less momentous. Promotion above the rank of Captain was not on the basis of bravery or 'brilliant services' but strictly according to seniority as determined by the date of entry onto the Captain's List. So, although promotion was slow in the years following the Long War, given the log-jam created by the number of Captains on the List, nonetheless, for those blessed with good health and staying power, Flag rank was an assured prize. Byam Martin, himself an Admiral of the Fleet from 1849 until his death in 1854, put this 'well-deserved reward' in perspective. It was, he wrote, achieved by a 'casual progressive rise in rank', 'no compliment whatever; it is a *professional inheritance*, the *gift* of *old age*, and *survivorship*: it follows as a matter of *right*, as one of the gradations of rank in the service, and no thanks to any one'.[20]

Francis lived on a further two years. His entry in the *Dictionary of National Biography* comes immediately before that of his sister Jane. It concludes, 'full of years and honours, he died on 10 August 1865.'[21] Aged ninety-one, he had been in the Navy seventy-nine years. The memorial in the local church at Wymering is modest, a simple stone tablet, recording only his name, his rank, his GCB, the year of his birth at Steventon Rectory and his death at Portsdown, and that he was 'One of Nelson's Captains'.** Beneath this inscription is a quotation from verse 30 of Psalm 107: 'So he bringeth them unto the haven where they would be', words every sailor would recognise.

---

* These were honorific titles bestowed on distinguished officers of Flag rank, usually on their retirement.

** This was an honoured title which was not restricted to Nelson's Captains at Trafalgar. In 1815 Frances Lady Shelley so described Admiral Benjamin Hallowell, who commanded the *Swiftsure* at the Battle of the Nile but missed Trafalgar (Edgcumbe, 1912, p. 77).

They close that great passage of the Bible, beginning at verse 23, 'They that go down to the sea in ships', a passage Francis would have read week after week and month after month in leading the Sunday service for his crews at sea.

The simplicity of his memorial tablet was matched by the modesty of his funeral. This was conducted at the little church at Wymering nearby. It was held without any naval ceremony. The Admiralty had offered to stage an elaborate, full-scale Service Funeral, befitting his rank, with a detachment of sailors to provide the last Salute, according to custom. But his three surviving sons – George, a former Navy Chaplain, Herbert, a serving Navy Captain, and Edward, like George, a clergyman – declined, just as their father wished.

Jane Austen was an intensely private person. She kept no diary, left no autobiography, no memoir or recollections. This gives her letters a singular importance, since, alongside what we gather from *Mansfield Park* and *Persuasion*, they provide the only direct evidence we have of her perception of the sailor brothers and their world. Yet, invaluable as the letters are, the quantity is small. Time, dispersal and sheer carelessness have all played their part. But there was also deliberate destruction. In the 1860s, when her nephew, James Edward Austen-Leigh, was gathering material for the *Memoir*, he found to his disappointment that 'Her nearest relatives, far from making provision for such a purpose [a biography], had actually destroyed many of the letters and papers by which it might have been facilitated. They were influenced, I believe, partly by an extreme dislike to publishing private details'.[22] The principal culprit in this was Cassandra. According to the family, one bout of incineration took place at the time of Jane's death in 1817 and a second in the early 1840s, two or three years before Cassandra's own death in 1845. At the time, she told her niece Caroline that she 'looked them over and burnt the greater part'.[23] From other letters, she cut sections out. Francis' youngest daughter Fanny was another culprit. Immediately after her father's death in 1865, without consulting anyone in the family, she destroyed the letters he had preserved carefully over many years.

As a consequence, we have only 162 letters out of a possible total of three thousand or more. Of these, there remain only six letters to Francis and one to Charles, although we know that during the brothers' time at sea or abroad, they were in regular correspondence with Jane. In the case of Francis, there was an exchange of letters every three or four weeks, and with Charles somewhat less frequently.* Not only that. Caroline Austen recalled that her Aunt 'wrote very fully to her Brothers when they were at sea',[24] 'very fully' borne

---

* Charles' diary for 1815 includes lists of 'Letters Written' and 'Letters Received'. In the period 8 February to 1 April, amongst his other correspondence he records three letters written to Jane and one to Cassandra, and one received from Jane (NMM, MS AUS/101).

out in her letters to Francis which run to fifteen hundred words and longer, occupying three or four printed pages.

The paucity of surviving material is tantalising. It leaves us with periods of Jane Austen's life for which we have no information whatsoever, neither letters nor family records. The precise nature of the difficulty becomes clear when we look at dates. The earliest letter we have is 9 January 1796 with Jane Austen already twenty-one. There are seven letters in 1796, none in 1797, nine in 1798, six in 1799, with a gap of sixteen months before the first of five letters in 1800. The ten letters of 1801 are followed by a gap of three-and-a-half years before the only letter of 1804 – and so on up to her last letter, dated 27 May 1817, six weeks before her death. The coverage is spotty and rarely continuous. The closest we get to a sequence is a group of six letters to Cassandra, written between 1 December 1798 and 23 January 1799. But even within this group, at least as many letters again are missing. The other problem is that we have virtually no letters written *to* Jane Austen, none at all from either of the sailor brothers, and we can only guess at their side of the correspondence from Jane's replies. Yet the picture is not entirely bleak. Ninety-six of the letters (amounting to 90 per cent by volume) are written to Cassandra. Addressing her sister, Jane Austen writes with a freedom and a degree of self-revelation that she allows to no one else – these are not letters to be read aloud or passed round the family – and they give a vivid sense of the writer's personality, the range of her interests, her observation of society and her picture of the wartime world. Some parts of the letters read like diary jottings, particularly in letters taken up and put down again across a period of several days, sometimes as long as a week.

These are not literary letters. They contain few references to her writing and virtually no discussion of it. Nor are there any memorable 'anthology' passages such as we find in the great letters of her contemporaries – Keats, Byron, Shelley or Wordsworth. What they do reveal is Jane Austen's private self, the flow of her feelings and the play of her ironic, sometimes ferocious wit. This can be a far from 'gentle Jane', a discovery that can be disconcerting. The writer who displays herself, in private, to be as mocking and merciless as the caricaturists of the age, anatomising her victims in waves of mockery, disgust and outrageous laughter. These are the unladylike letters which miraculously escaped family censorship, the scissors and the fire.

The occasion for the sisters to write to one-another with such frequency, as often as every three or four days, was the understanding within the family that as the six boys went their different ways the sisters were not to be left cooped up with their parents. While one sister remained at home, the other would often be away staying in London with brother Henry or at Godmersham with Edward, with a changeover at the end of three or four months. During these times apart, Jane and Cassandra kept in regular contact, exchanging family gossip and local news. Writing from Steventon, Jane had much to say about her clothes, about the births, marriages and deaths of the neighbourhood, and such events as a grand ball at Hurstbourne Park, a great country house near Andover, the seat of John-Charles Wallop, 3rd Earl of Portsmouth. The Austens were *persona grata* in these circles. As a boy of six, Lord Portsmouth had boarded at Steventon Rectory for a few months as one of Mr Austen's pupils. Jane was far from awed by the company and on the following day she penned her description of the evening's entertainment for Cassandra, then at Godmersham, sketching her fellow-guests with malicious glee: 'There were very few Beauties, & such as there were, were not very handsome': among them, poor Mrs Blount 'much admired', appearing 'exactly as she did in September, with the same broad face, diamond bandeau, white shoes, pink husband & fat neck'; Miss Cox, in whom could be 'traced . . . the remains of the vulgar, broad featured girl who danced at Enham eight years ago'; and Sir Thomas Champneys' daughter, 'a queer animal with a white neck'. Mrs Warren 'has got rid of some part of her child, & danced away with great activity, looking by no means very large' while Mr Warren 'is ugly enough; uglier even than his cousin John', but 'does not look so *very* old'. The Miss Maitlands, 'both prettyish' but with 'a good deal of nose'; General Mathew has 'the Gout, & Mrs Maitland the Jaundice'; and towards 'Miss Debary, Susan & Sally', 'I was as civil . . . as their bad breath would allow me'.[25]

In such a setting and with such a foreground, the war seemed far away. Yet great victories, especially those with an exotic touch, such as Nelson's at the Battle of the Nile in August 1798, were quickly embraced by the world of high frivolity and fashion. Only a month later, society ladies were patriotically dressing themselves *à la Nile* in Mamolouc robes and cloaks.* Amused at the fashion, for a grand ball at Kempshott Park, Lord Dorchester's Hampshire residence, Jane Austen followed suit, abandoning her familiar 'white sattin cap' (as she wrote to Cassandra) for a borrowed 'Mamalouc cap', a toupée modelled on the Egyptian fez and adorned with Nelson's rose feather emblem, 'all the fashion now, worn at the Opera, & by Lady Mildmays at Hackwood Balls'.[26]

Jane Austen's own perception of the war, as we find it in the letters, places the sailor brothers as the principal players in a world of uncertainties – about their safety, the readiness of their ships, their voyages and destinations, their arrivals at Portsmouth, Southampton, Deal or Sheerness, and their comings and goings around the family homes. News of their whereabouts arrived

* The Mamelukes were the ruling class of Egypt from the thirteenth into the early nineteenth century.

circuitously, sometimes through family letters, sometimes found in the news-papers, sometimes carried by fellow-officers. It could make for tragi-comedy, almost farcical were it not so sad. Writing to Francis with the news of their father's death, Jane's letter is addressed to the *Leopard* at Dungeness. But learning that he may now have sailed round to Portsmouth, she picks up her pen to convey the 'melancholy news' once again.[27] Like their letters, the sailor brothers could be long-delayed, becalmed on a homeward voyage, or for days fighting their passage up the Channel in the teeth of a gale. For these uncer-tainties Jane Austen coined a phrase of her own, 'the true Sailor way', as she described Francis' unexpected return at the end of June 1808, his having been away since February, convoying to St Helena:

> My dear Cassandra
> I give you all Joy of Frank's return, which happens in the true Sailor way, just after our being told not to expect him for some weeks. – The Wind has been very much against him, but I suppose he must be in our Neighbourhood by this time. Fanny is in hourly expectation of him here. – Mary's visit in the Island is probably short-ened by this Event. Make our kind Love & Congratulations to her.[28]

The letter forms a link in the chain of family affection, joining Jane and Fanny Knight (Edward's eldest daughter) at Godmersham, twenty miles or so inland from Deal or Dover, at whichever port Francis might arrive, to Cassandra at Southampton; she, in turn, will pass on the news to Mrs Francis Austen, relaxing on the Isle of Wight as a distraction from the anxiety of waiting.

Letters could take as long as four months, with news long outdated. Here, at the beginning of December 1798, Jane dashes off a quick letter to Cassandra, updating her sister on the complications and frustrations which loomed large in their sense of what the sailor brothers were doing and how they might be contacted:

> I am so good as to write to you again thus speedily, to let you know that I have just heard from Frank. He was at Cadiz, alive and well, on October 19, and had then very lately received a letter from you, written as long ago as when the 'London' was at St Helen's. But his *raly* latest intelligence of us was in one from me of September 1, which I sent soon after we got to Godmersham. He had written a packet full for his dearest friends in England, early in October, to go by the 'Excellent'; but the 'Excellent' was not sailed, nor likely to sail, when he despatched this to me.[29]

(St Helen's was the Fleet anchorage off the eastern end of the Isle of Wight adjacent to Spithead; '*raly*' is a piece of mockery, imitating the fashionable pronunciation of 'really').

At this time Francis, a First Lieutenant in the *London* (98), was serving in the Fleet under St Vincent blockading the Spanish Navy at Cadiz. Communication with their brother might be getting more difficult but 'alarm' was to be joked away:

> Frank writes in good spirits, but says that our correspondence cannot be so easily carried on in future as it has been, as the communication between Cadiz and Lisbon is less frequent than formerly. You and my mother, therefore, must not alarm yourselves at the long intervals that may divide his letters. I address this advice to you two as being the most tender-hearted of the family.[30]

(Letters were collected from the blockading vessels and taken to Lisbon in neutral Portugal for transmission onward to Britain.)

In November 1800, Jane directs Cassandra's attention to the newspapers for an account of a success at sea that Francis had enjoyed four months earlier:

> Mr Holder's paper tells us that sometime in last August, Capt: Austen & the Petterell were very active in securing a Turkish Ship (driven into a Port in Cyprus by bad weather) from the French. – He was forced to burn her however. – You will see the account in the Sun I dare say. –[31]

(The Holders were neighbours at Ashe Park House, two miles from Steventon.)

Jane gives the barest detail, knowing that Cassandra would see in the newspapers that Francis was with Sir Sidney Smith's Squadron off Alexandria, that the 'Turkish Ship' was a wreck, a line-of-battle ship from which Francis drove off a force of French who were salvaging the guns and other usable parts when he outsmarted them by setting fire to the vessel.

Long into the war, the uncertainties of communication remained. After his years of service on the North American station, it seemed that Charles might be on his way back to England, soon to arrive. But, as Jane tells Cassandra, the news comes by a roundabout and questionable route: 'Capt. Simpson told us, on the authority of some other Captn just arrived from Halifax, that Charles was bringing the Cleopatra home, & that she was probably by this time in the Channel –'. But it was late in the evening, at one of Henry Austen's Sloane Street parties, and 'as Capt. S. was certainly in liquor, we must not quite depend on it. – It must give one a sort of expectation however, & will prevent my writing to him any more'.[32] The lightly ironic ending is characteristic. Anxieties and uncertainties about the sailor brothers can be dissolved in humour, or, at least, be reduced to 'a sort of expectation'.

How closely the sisters followed the course of the war is evident in Jane's letter of 1 November 1800 telling of Francis' readiness (four months previously) to sail in Sir Sydney Smith's Squadron from Jaffa to join the Turkish Fleet in the blockade of Alexandria, the town held by Napoleon's troops since 1798 in the French occupation of Egypt:

> We have at last heard from Frank; a letter from him to You came yesterday, & I mean to send it on as soon as I can get a ditto, (*that* means a frank,) which I hope to do in a day or two. – En attendant, You must rest satisfied with knowing that on the 8th of July the Petterell with the rest of the Egyptian Squadron was off the Isle of Cyprus, whither they went from Jaffa for Provisions &c., & whence they were to sail in a day or two for Alexandria, there to wait the result of the English proposals for the Evacuation of Egypt.[33]

The 'Frank/frank' pun is a typical piece of word-play, an irreverent device that runs through Jane Austen's writing, even to the final page of *Persuasion*, where we read that 'Anne was tenderness itself, and she had the full *worth* of it in Captain Went*worth*'s affection'.[34]

These extracts are little snippets from letters of considerable length. *In situ*, the references to the sailor brothers are given no special prominence. Jane Austen moves rapidly on, jumping from topic to topic, providing Cassandra with a quick bulletin-like round-up of recent events in the family and the neighbourhood, wherever she happened to be. The one exception to this is a group of six 'interrupted' letters written to Cassandra across the Christmas and New Year of 1798–99, in which news of the sailor brothers is the single topic continuing from letter to letter. The group begins with the letter of 1 December 1798 (quoted above pages 58 and 59), reporting Francis 'alive and well' off Cadiz. On 18 December, Jane mentions Charles' frustration at being stuck in the *Scorpion* (16), a brig stationed in home waters and engaged in routine duties far from any scene of action. As Jane puts it, 'our dear Charles begins to feel the Dignity of Ill-usage' and the family sets in motion its resources of 'interest'. 'My father will write to Admiral Gambier', Francis' patron, and she thinks 'it would be very right in Charles' to address his own patron, Sir Thomas Williams.[35] This was on Tuesday. By Wednesday, Jane reports, the Gambier letter is sent. Gambier deals with the matter promptly and five days later, on Christmas Eve, Jane is able to quote his reply: the young officer must be patient and learn his 'Duty' in a 'small vessel'. Nonetheless, 'his wish to be in a Frigate' is noted.[36] Gambier goes on to say that promotion is in prospect for Francis, still a Lieutenant. Their father immediately writes to his regular Admiralty informant, George Daysh, Clerk in the Ticket Office, asking Daysh to contact him as soon as Francis' commission comes through. Jane Austen continues in playful mood:

Your cheif wish is now ready to be accomplished; & could Lord Spencer [First Lord of the Admiralty] give happiness to Martha [Martha Lloyd, whom the Austens hoped would be Francis's wife] at the same time, what a joyful heart he would make of Yours [i.e. if he were to get married on the strength of this promotion] – I have sent the same extract of the sweets of Gambier* to Charles, who poor fellow! tho' he sinks into nothing but an humble attendant on the Hero of the peice, will I hope be contented with the prospect held out to him. – By what the Admiral says it appears as if he had been designedly kept in the Scorpion –. But I will not torment myself with Conjectures and suppositions; Facts shall satisfy me.[37]

Jane then turns her attention to Francis again and the speed of communication:

Frank had not heard from any of us for ten weeks, when he wrote to me on the 12th of November, in consequence of Lord St Vincents being removed to Gibraltar. – When his Commission is sent however, it will not be so long on its' road as our letters, because all the Government dispatches are forwarded by Land to his Lordship from Lisbon, with great regularity.[38]

This letter was begun on a Monday, continued on a Tuesday, with the very latest news squeezed into a postscript the following day, Wednesday 26th, and it is late on the Tuesday that Jane adds news just received from Charles. Again, she speaks playfully: 'he has written to Lord Spencer himself to be removed. I am afraid his serene Highness will be in a passion, & order some of our heads to be cut off'.[39] Two days later, on 28 December, Jane Austen is able to announce the 'Good News'. The mechanism of 'interest' has turned:

My dear Cassandra
Frank is made. – He was yesterday raised to the Rank of Commander, & appointed to the Petterel Sloop, now at Gibraltar. – A Letter from Daysh has just announced this, & as it is confirmed by a very friendly one from Mr Mathew to the same effect transcribing one from Admiral Gambier to the General, We have no reason to suspect the truth of it. – As soon as you have cried a little for Joy, you may go on, & learn farther that the India House have taken *Captn Austen's* Petition into Consideration – this comes from Daysh – & likewise that Lieut. Charles John Austen is removed to the *Tamer* Frigate – this comes from the Admiral. – We cannot find out where the Tamer is, but I hope we shall now see Charles here at all

---

* Possibly there was some bitter-sweet extract from the gambier/gambir plant or a confection of this name, unrecorded by food historians. Nelson uses a similar phrase, 'the sweets of Jamaica' in referring to the benefits Admiral Sir Peter Parker and his son Vice Admiral Christopher Parker gained from their service in the West Indies (letter of 12 September 1801, (Nicolas (1845), iv. 488); and for Admiral Pellew 'sweets from America' were the prizes he felt deprived of in the War of 1812 (letter to Sir Richard Keats, 5 March 1814, quoted in Parkinson, 1934, p. 406).

Events. This Letter is to be dedicated entirely to Good News. – If you will send my father an account of your Washing & Letter expences &c, he will send You a draft for the amount of it, as well as for your next quarter, & for Edward's Rent. – If you don't buy a muslin Gown now on the strength of this Money, & Frank's promotion, I shall never forgive You. –

Mrs Lefroy has just sent me word that Lady Dortchester means to invite me to her Ball on the 8th of January, which tho' an humble Blessing compared with what the last page records, I do not consider as any Calamity. I cannot write any more now, but I have written enough to make you very happy, & therefore may safely conclude. –

Yours affect:^ly
Jane.

Steventon
Friday Decr 28th
Miss Austen
Godmersham Park
Faversham
Kent^40

(Mr Mathew is Daniel Mathew, whose daughter Louisa married Admiral Gambier. '*Captn Austen's* Petition' was for a refund of his passage money home from India made in a Company ship and paid for by Francis in June 1793. After further referrals, his application was finally disallowed by the Court of Directors in March 1801).

On Tuesday, 8 January, Jane writes of a ball at Lord Dorchester's that very evening, at Kempshott Park: 'Charles is not come yet, but he must come this morning, or he shall never know what I will do to him . . . I have got him an invitation, though I have not been so considerate as to get him a *Partner*.'[41] This was the ball at which she wore her 'Mamalouc cap'. But, as she writes the next day, she went unaccompanied. 'Charles never came! – Naughty Charles. I suppose he could not get superseded in time' (i.e. relieved of his duties aboard ship).[42]

At this point two or more letters are missing, and the last of the group, begun on Monday 21 January and ended two days later, brings the sequence to a close. Towards the opening, we hear of Charles' preference for joining his new ship, the *Tamar* (38) at Portsmouth, which would be more convenient for Steventon, rather than at Deal, where the ship is presently waiting to set sail:

Charles leaves us to-night. The 'Tamar' is in the Downs, and Mr Daysh advises him to join her there directly, as there is no chance of her going to the westward. Charles does not approve of this at all, and will not be much grieved if he should be too late for her before she sails, as he may then hope to get into a better station. He attempted to go to town last night, and got as far on his road thither as Dean Gate; but both the coaches were full, and we had the pleasure of seeing him back again. He will call on Daysh to-morrow to know whether the 'Tamar' has sailed or not, and if she is still at the Downs he will proceed in one of the night coaches to Deal.[43]

As we hear at the close of the letter, written two days later, although Charles ends up in Deal, his good fortune continues. It turns out after all that the *Tamar* is not ready to sail and needs a refit. So, instead, he is to rejoin his patron, Sir Thomas Williams, as Second Lieutenant on the *Endymion* (24) – a vessel in which his appetite for action was to be satisfied.

Towards Charles, the youngest of the family, Jane Austen displays an especial tenderness. 'Our own particular little brother' she calls him, writing to Cassandra in January 1799,[44] her affection carried in an allusive turn of phrase, adapted from Fanny Burney's *Camilla*, a novel published only three years earlier, in which Sir Hugh Tyrold refers to the heroine as 'my own particular little niece'.[45] We can see why he was such a favourite. Winning £30 as his share in the capture of a privateer, with the expectation of a further £10, he bought gold chains and topaz crosses for his sisters. (See illus. 2). This was the gift Jane Austen was to return years later in *Mansfield Park* where William Price brings his sister 'a very pretty amber cross . . . from Sicily'.[46] These gold chains and crosses, Jane wrote to her sister, would make them 'unbearably fine',[47] a thought that Charles, no doubt, would be delighted by, since he paid attention to his sisters' gowns and expressed his admiration for them. In turn, Jane Austen would comment on his radiant health. Charles arrives at Steventon 'in very good looks indeed',[48] is raring to dance (a touch of William Price here). On the night of his arrival at Gosport (next to Portsmouth), where would brother James look first for Charles but in 'the assembly room in the Inn, where there happened to be a Ball', 'a likely spot enough for the discovery of a Charles', writes Jane. All to the good that he was not to be found there, 'for it was in general a very ungenteel one, & there was hardly a pretty girl in the room'.[49] This was on 8 November 1800. Two weeks later, Charles occupies her mind once again, and once again it is her brother the dancer:

> Naughty Charles did not come on tuesday; but good Charles came yesterday morning. About two o'clock he walked in on a Gosport Hack. – His feeling equal to such a fatigue is a good sign, & his finding no fatigue in it a still better. – We walked down to Deane to dinner, he danced the whole Evening, & to day is no more tired than a gentlemen ought to be.[50]

(Deane House, two miles from Steventon, was the home of the Harwoods.)
The most revealing view of Charles comes a few years later, when he was

appointed to the *Namur* anchored in the Thames estuary at the mouth of the River Medway, just off Sheerness. As a measure of economy, instead of taking lodgings in the town of Sheerness, he had quarters on the *Namur* itself with his young wife and their two infant children. (The ill-odour of the town may have influenced his decision, as well; according to Commander James Gardner, it was known in the Navy as 'Sheernasty', 'the – hole of the world'.)[51] At first, Fanny was enthusiastic about living on board ship, finding it comfortable and inexpensive and thinking of it only as a temporary home. But when the novelty wore off, drawbacks began to appear. The quarters were damp and confined and in Winter and periods of bad weather the children had to be put on shore to be looked after by others – at Godmersham, Chawton, or by Fanny's sister in London. Moreover, Charles was very short of money and needed to get a posting away from the *Namur* with command of a frigate. This would give him the chance of prize-money to support his growing family. During 1812, a frigate was on the cards. But somehow the opportunity passed and Jane Austen notes his predicament with sympathy and humour, laughing gently at the folly of presumption: 'Poor Charles & his frigate. But there could be no chance of his having one, while it was thought such a certainty.'[52] This must have been a possibility, again, during 1813. But by October Fanny was writing to her brother-in-law in Bermuda that for the time being Charles had given up any hope of getting a Frigate, nor would his patron, Sir Thomas Williams, be in line for a better command.[53]

Their nearest Austen home was Godmersham, at a distance of forty miles, a journey of about five hours, depending on the weather and the crossing from ship to land. Fortunately, brother Edward enjoyed company. A full house 'suits him exactly, he is all alive & chearful',[54] Jane observed. Edward made Charles and Fanny welcome and it was at Godmersham that Jane Austen saw them most regularly. During one such stay, in October 1813, she reported back to Cassandra, 'I shall be most happy to see dear Charles, & he will be happy as he can with a cross Child or some such care pressing on him at the time'. The 'cross child' in question – the eldest of his children (there were now three) – is 'little Cassy' aged four and three-quarters, capable, Jane Austen fears, of 'some immediate disagreableness'.[55] The letter is put down and continued again the following day, the family having arrived the evening before. Jane Austen's affection and concern for him are evident and there is a warm picture of 'dear Charles' in the final lines:

> They came last night at about 7. We had given them up, but I still expected them to come. Dessert was nearly over; – a better time for arriving then an hour & 1/2 earlier. They were late because they did not set out earlier & did not allow time enough. – Charles did not *aim* at more than reaching Sittingbourn by 3, which c^d

not have brought them here by dinner time. – They had a very rough passage, he w^d not have ventured if he had known how bad it w^d be. – However here they are safe & well, just like their own nice selves, Fanny looking as neat & white this morn^g as possible, & dear Charles all affectionate, placid, quiet, chearful good humour.[56]

But 'poor little Cassy is grown extremely thin & looks poorly'.[57] There was talk of her coming ashore for another visit, to recuperate under Cassandra's care at Chawton. However, the girl was unwilling to leave her parents and

Papa & Mama have not yet made up their mind as to parting with her or not – the cheif, indeed the only difficulty with Mama is a very reasonable one, the Child's being very unwilling to leave them. When it was mentioned to her, she did not like the idea of it at all. – At the same time, she has been suffering so much lately from Sea sickness, that her Mama cannot bear to have her much on board this winter. – Charles is less inclined to part with her. – I do not know how it will end, or what is to determine it.[58]

That the decision is left hanging, its conclusion uncertain, points to some unsatisfactoriness in Charles' situation.

The last glimpse of Charles comes in November 1815. Jane addresses Cassandra from Henry Austen's London home. It is a letter full of writing news. Mr Haden, the surgeon attending Henry, 'is reading Mansfield Park for the first time & prefers it to P&P'.[59] The proof-correction and printing of *Emma* is well advanced, and she is in correspondence with John Murray about its dedication to the Prince Regent. Charles, away at sea in the *Phoenix* (36), is pursuing pirates around the Greek Archipelago. Constantly on the move, he received not a single present to celebrate his birthday in June – as he wrote in a letter to Cassandra, a letter in which Jane finds so much of her brother's 'Disposition & feelings':

Thank you very much for the sight of dearest Charles's Letter to yourself. – How pleasantly & how naturally he writes! and how perfect a picture of his Disposition & feelings, his style conveys! – Poor dear Fellow! – not a Present! – I have a great mind to send him all the twelve Copies which were to have been dispersed among my near Connections – beginning with the P. R. & ending with Countess Morley. – Adeiu. – Y^rs affec^ly.[60]

Jane's fanciful gift, the copies of *Emma*, were tokens of affection in which Charles stood in need. For in September 1814, just before he left the *Namur*, Fanny had died in childbirth and the baby daughter two weeks later. We know from his diaries at sea how these losses pursued him, how his sleep was haunted with recollections of his children and their dead mother, phantasies of reunion, dreams 'of Dearest Fanny that I was again blessed with her society'.[61]

What Jane Austen recognised, above all, in Francis was his seriousness. It was a quality she respected and responded to, without failing to lighten it with a balance of humour on her own side. Her letters might be long, yet his were longer still, and packed even tighter with facts and information about the places he travelled to – features which she acknowledges and, in her own style, chides him for, in a letter which runs to three full printed pages: 'Behold me going to write you as handsome a Letter as I can. Wish me good luck . . .'[62] She concludes on an equally playful note: 'I hope you continue beautiful & brush your hair, but not all off. – We join you in an infinity of Love'.[63] A further letter, written nearly three months later, with Francis still serving in the Baltic, is even longer, as if in competition with his weighty missives:

> My dearest Frank
> The 11th of this month brought me your letter & I assure you I thought it very well worth its 2s/3d. – I am very much obliged to you for filling me so long a sheet a [sic] paper, you are a good one to traffic with in that way, You pay most liberally; – my Letter was a scratch of a note compared with yours – & then you write so even, so clear both in style & Penmanship, so much to the point & give so much real intelligence that it is enough to kill one.[64]

In the following year, Edward Austen showed Jane the letter of a lawyer, 'Excellent Letters' from an 'excellent Man' she remarked to Cassandra. 'They are such thinking, clear, considerate Letters as Frank might have written.'[65]

For Jane Austen, Frank's excellence and all it conveyed was a personal quality – not his professional excellence, his achievements at sea, everything that is embraced in the idea of his 'national importance' as a sailor, but the excellence of those 'domestic virtues' celebrated at the end of *Persuasion*.[66] This was a part of his life which she knew very well. For just as Francis was away for long periods – one voyage, to the East Indies and China, lasted seventeen months – he also spent long periods at home. One of these was from June 1806 until the following April. In July 1806 he married Mary Gibson and, in the Autumn, joined with his mother and sisters in setting up home at Southampton, first in lodgings and then in a rented house in Castle Square. Then, again, eight years later, following his return from the Baltic in May 1814, with his mother and sisters nearby at Chawton Cottage, Francis moved into the Great House and remained there and in the neighbourhood of Alton for the rest of Jane's life.

'Snug' is Jane Austen's word, very much a naval word, for what she felt as comfortable closeness and intimacy; 'snug' was the sailor's word for sails tightly reefed before an oncoming storm; and 'snug' is how she found the Francis Austens settled in at Chawton House. She writes about one such occasion to her niece Fanny Knight. The family gathering included Fanny's father, Edward, the owner of the Chawton estate; his eldest son Edward, now twenty; Cassandra and Jane; and Francis and his wife: 'We had a pleasant party yesterday, at least *we* found it so. – It is delightful to see him [Edward] so chearful & confident. – Aunt Cass: & I dine at the Gt House to day. We shall be a snug half dozen'[67] (Francis' five children were too young to be counted.)

What connects Francis with Captain Harville, himself the epitome of *Persuasion*'s 'domestic virtues', is his skill as a handyman. In September 1796, when Francis was between ships and staying with Edward, Jane tells Cassandra of his using a lathe for the first time: 'He enjoys himself here very much, for he has just learnt to turn, and is so delighted with the employment, that he is at it all day long' and soon produces 'a very nice little butter-churn' for three-year-old Fanny.[68] A decade later, during the Southampton period, he is helping with dress patterns, 'of course . . . cut out to admiration'.[69] His skills were a by-word in the family: at Godmersham, when Edward's boys are fired with 'sporting Mania' they occupy themselves in the evenings with making rabbit nets, '& sit as deedily to it, side by side, as any two Uncle Franks could do'.[70] Three-and-a-half months later, in January 1814, Jane Austen began *Emma* in which we find another Frank, Frank Churchill, 'most deedily occupied'[71] in repairing Mrs Bates' spectacles, fastening those little rivets which were beyond her daughter's eyesight and dexterity.

There are other sly touches which the family readers would connect with Francis. Knowing his precise and well-formed hand they would recognise an allusion in the exchange between Emma and Mr Knightley, the little scene in which she praises Frank Churchill's as 'one of the best gentleman's hands I ever saw', while Knightley, touched with dislike and jealousy, declares he cannot 'admire it . . . It is too small – wants strength. It is like a woman's writing', a criticism resisted by Emma and Mrs Weston in vindicating Churchill 'against the base aspersion'.[72] Again, remembering Churchill, any recipient of Francis Austen's substantial missives would have smiled to read of the 'Short letters from Frank'.[73]

Behind the exploits of the sailor brothers lurked the ever-present shadow of death. When a cousin writes to Mrs Austen following the Battle of St Domingo, it is 'to congratulate us on Frank's Victory and Safety'.[74] Yet, strange as it may seem, the greatest threat was not death in action – this accounted for only about 7 per cent of the 100,000 seamen estimated to have been killed during the years 1793–1815 – but death from disease and accidents which ran at the astonishingly high rate of 80 per cent. The remaining 13 per cent were put down to natural disasters, those 'dangers of the sea'. For sailors, these were familiar words. In the *Book of Common Prayer*, one of the prayers to be 'used in his Majesty's Navy every day' was an appeal to God to 'Preserve us from the dangers of the sea' and from 'the violence of the enemy'. Those dangers included fire, a particular hazard for vessels carrying large quantities of gunpowder.[75] 'Yellow jack', as yellow fever was known, was a scourge which killed many times the numbers who died fighting the French in the West Indies. Hence the Ward-room toast, 'A bloody war or a sickly season', meaning promotion, one way or the other, for the lucky ones who survived. It was a harsh logic, which Nelson applied to himself and his father's position as a clergyman:

> I wish I could congratulate you upon a rectory instead of a vicarage; it is rather awkward wishing the poor man dead, but we all rise by deaths. I got my rank by a shot killing a post-captain, and I most sincerely hope I shall, when I go, go out of the world the same way; then we all go in the line of our profession – a parson praying and a captain fighting.[76]

Early on in the war, the reality of death on service entered the Austen home when news came of Tom Fowle, Cassandra's fiancé. This was not the expected news of his safe arrival in the West Indies, but news of his death from yellow fever off St Domingo in February 1797 and of his burial at sea. According to Jane, in the face of this tragedy her sister behaved 'with a degree of resolution & Propriety which no common mind could evince in so trying a situation'.[77] We are to understand by this that Cassandra kept her grief to herself and maintained a Christian acceptance of her loss, acknowledging that 'the Goodness which made him valuable on Earth will make him blessed in Heaven' – the words of consolation Jane sent to her cousin Philadelphia Walter on the death of her father in 1798.[78] The correct behaviour was to bear up 'with great fortitude', just as Mrs Austen succeeded in doing at the time of her husband's death in 1805;[79] 'to be tranquil & resigned', as Jane hoped that Fanny Knight would be at the death of her mother in 1808.[80] At the time, Fanny's brothers Edward and George were taken from school at Winchester to be cared for at Southampton and Jane was able to report to Cassandra at Godmersham that 'They behave extremely well in every respect, showing quite as much feeling as one wishes to see ...',[81] an observation that no doubt Cassandra was to convey to their father Edward.

In the surviving letters, we find no reference to the dangers faced by Francis and Charles or to the possibility of their death. The closest we get to these matters is in the remarks Jane Austen made on the death of troops in battle:

those who lost their lives with Sir John Moore at Corunna in 1809; and two years later, in 1811, a comment she made after reading a newspaper report of the massacre of British infantry at the Battle of Albuera.

Early in January 1809, Francis was at Spithead on the *St Albans* (64), ready to take charge of the disembarkation of the British forces returning from Spain. On the 11th, Jane wrote to Cassandra from Southampton reporting that 'The St Albans perhaps may soon be off to help bring home what may remain by this time of our poor Army, whose state seems dreadfully critical'.[82] On the 16th, Moore was killed during the retreat and on the 30th Jane wrote to Cassandra again:

> I am sorry to find that Sir J. Moore has a Mother living, but tho' a very Heroick son, he might not be a very necessary one to her happiness. – Deacon Morrell may be more to Mrs Morrell. – I wish Sir John had united something of the Christian with the Hero in his death. – Thank Heaven! we have had no one to care for particularly among the Troops – no one in fact nearer to us than Sir John himself.[83]*

Moore was reported to have said nothing religious on his death-bed – quite the opposite. What he did say, according to the newspapers, was a good deal about public opinion in England and his hope that his military failure would not be held against him. His last messages were not to his mother or members of his family but to Lady Hester Stanhope and other society friends.

There is a surprising change of tone between the letters of the 11th and the 16th: from the sympathetic note of the first – 'our poor Army, whose state seems dreadfully critical' – to the relief, seemingly flippant, certainly brisk and pragmatic, at having 'no one to care for particularly among the Troops'. And readers have also paused at Jane Austen's reaction to a newspaper report of the Battle of Albuera, an engagement which took place on 18 May 1811 with appalling bloodshed. Of the British infantry alone, 4400 of the 6500 were killed. Once again, Jane Austen expresses her relief that these are deaths of people unknown, in itself a tough-minded and strictly rational attitude. But the comment seems deliberately, and emphatically, throwaway, a remark slipped in between trivialities: between news of a jilted young lady and of

---

* In linking the 'Christian' and the 'Hero' Jane Austen may have been thinking of Dr Johnson's words in *Rambler* 44: 'The Christian and the hero are inseparable'. Deirdre Le Faye comments that ' "no one nearer than Sir John himself" implies *some* family connexion' but 'None has been traced' (*Letters*, p. 400). There was, however, a connection through the Rev. Samuel Cooke, Vicar of Great Bookham, Surrey, 1769–1820, married to Mrs Austen's first cousin and namesake, Cassandra Leigh. Mr Cooke was Jane Austen's godfather. The Cookes' medical practitioner was Dr John Moore, Sir John's father. Nothing known about the connection of the Morrell family with the Austens. (Philip Morrell of a later generation was the husband of Lady Ottoline).

returning from a visit to a Miss Webb. The formulation is stylish, euphonious and offhand:

> I am very sorry for Mary; – but I have some comfort in there being two Curates now lodging in Bookham, besides their own Mr Warneford from Dorking, so that I think she must fall in love with one or the other. –
>
> How horrible it is to have so many people killed! – And what a blessing that one cares for none of them! – I return to my Letter writing from calling on Miss Harriot Webb, who is short & not quite straight, & cannot pronounce an R any better than her Sisters. . . .[84]

From the evidence of these extracts alone we cannot pretend to know where Jane Austen's sympathies really lay. What we do see is a writer enjoying her skills and serving up an item, artfully casual, artfully inconsequential, for her sister's entertainment. We could well suppose this to be a literary device, the writer's strategy for holding death at a distance, a habit of heart and mind that in war-time the sister of the sailor brothers could cultivate in private as a device of self-protection. Then, when the danger of war was past, the thick skin could be put on display, as it is in *Persuasion* – for all the world, including her family and the sailor brothers themselves, to enjoy. The occasion for this is the author's barbed reflection on the sight of Mrs Musgrove overwhelmed with grief at the memory of her son, a Midshipman who died at sea, whether or not in action Jane Austen does not say:

> her large fat sighings over the destiny of a son, whom alive nobody had cared for. Personal size and mental sorrow have certainly no necessary proportions. A large bulky figure has as good a right to be in deep affliction, as the most graceful set of limbs in the world. But, fair or not fair, there are unbecoming conjunctions, which reason will patronize in vain, – which taste cannot tolerate, – which ridicule will seize.[85]

'which ridicule will seize' – the writer defines her own artistic act, in this instance her mode of humour. We are treated to Mrs Musgrove's 'large fat sighings', her 'large bulky figure', an observation reminiscent of that catalogue of physical defects and blemishes she conducted for Cassandra's private entertainment in describing the guests at Lord Portsmouth's ball, the 'very few Beauties' with their broad faces, white necks, large noses and bad breath.'[86] Just as she treats the slaughter at Albuera, it is all of it a display of verbal skill; to what degree self-protective or simply heartless, we, the outsiders, are left to guess.

5

Patronage and Interest

'I trust in heaven that these changes in the Administration may bring in some of our friends, there is no getting on without friends in power.'

Captain Thomas Fremantle to his wife,
from the *Ganges* at sea, 23 May 1804

As there is no biography of Mr Austen, our impression of him largely rests on the scattered details given in the *Memoir*, where he comes across solidly, if conventionally, as a man of learning, for forty years a devout parish priest, and a loving husband and father of a happy and successful family. His letter to Francis adds depth and unexpected detail to this picture. It reveals a man of practicality and resourcefulness fully alive to the need to cultivate influential 'friends'; a man of foresight in supplying his son with a palatable dose of worldly wisdom, an effective philosophy of achievement for an ambitious young sailor, this mundane calculation decently balanced with a leavening of spiritual advice.

Mr Austen's readiness to act on his son's behalf was put to the test in 1794. At the time, Francis was serving as a Lieutenant in the *Lark* (16), a sloop patrolling the Downs and the North Sea on the routine duties of reconnaissance and message-bearing that a small and lightly-armed vessel could handle. For a ship of this size, there was little likelihood of action. The French had not yet established a presence in home waters. What engagements there were involved ships-of-the-line and frigates, and it was to a frigate that Francis was keen to get a posting.

In the Spring of 1794 Francis had seen the frigates in home waters organized into Squadrons and patrolling the Channel systematically. This provided young officers like himself with the opportunity to distinguish themselves in action with the hope of promotion. Promotion he was impatient for, having been a Lieutenant for nearly two years, a period in which some of his contemporaries had risen – some by merit, some by the fortunes of war and some by the exercise of 'interest' – to the rank of Commander or even Captain. For a junior officer seeking a transfer, the accepted procedure was to hand a formal letter of application to his ship's Captain, who would decide whether or not to forward it to the Flag-officer of the Squadron or the Commander-in-Chief of the Fleet. It lay in their hands to make a transfer within their own command, subject to Admiralty confirmation. Otherwise, the Commander-in-Chief could merely forward the application to the Admiralty, accompanied by his own observations, leaving the decision wholly to the Board.

As a commissioned officer Francis could by-pass this route and address the First Lord himself directly by way of a formal Memorial, setting out his request with a statement of service, reciting his past achievements and Captains served under. These applications from junior officers came thick and fast (some wrote in monthly!) and the Admiralty had a standard response. For that reason, an officer with 'friends' would solicit their support, asking them to write to the First Lord, or better still, for those who were *persona grata* at this level, to see him. In the language of these matters, this is how 'just claims' might be advanced, how a 'Patron and Friend' might 'serve' or 'promote' another's 'interest', and how, given 'the instability of Ministerial promises', it was necessary for the 'friend' to 'follow up the application' in person to receive the First Lord's due 'Consideration', which the First Lord would grant to 'oblige' this powerful 'friend', providing that 'the nature of the Service and his duty to his Country will permit it'.[1]

Such directness and informality of approach was possible within a Navy of this size. In 1794, the entire Fleet numbered 420 ships of war, from sloops to 1st rates, with an officer corps of just over 1400. According to Lady Spencer, during the 1790s, when her husband was First Lord, 'no sea captain ever returned without being asked to dinner by us'; and, at the time of Trafalgar she could claim that 'All the captains in the fleet were our particular friends'.[2] Even in 1809–12, with the officer figure at its highest, the total number was not above 4700. The degree of contact between junior and senior ranks meant that commissions and appointments could be made on the basis of personal knowledge or recommendation in a way which would not be possible in a larger organization. It was for this reason that Collingwood welcomed St Vincent's appointment as First Lord in 1801. Collingwood was confident that St Vincent would 'keep the Admiralty as active as his predecessor', the politician Spencer, 'with more knowledge of the character and ability of all the officers'.[3] What this meant for the Fleet at sea comes across strongly in a letter Nelson wrote to St Vincent in January 1804, reiterating their shared belief 'that it was absolutely necessary merit should be rewarded on the moment; and that the Officers of the Fleet should look up to the Commander-in-Chief for their reward'.[4] It was through this system that Flag-officers were able to build up their loyal 'followings' of younger officers whose professional skill and personal qualities they knew, trusted and rewarded.*

* The connection between the officers and ship's companies was very different. Into the period of

In the applicant's support, parents, relatives and acquaintances of the family, however far distant, might be called in if they were people of standing and influence, best of all if they were officers of Flag-rank, since naval 'interest' provided the surest long-term guarantee. Occasionally, it could be dispensed with. When James Gardner took his examination, in 1795, he found one of the commissioners was Captain Harry Harmood, 'an intimate friend of my father's,' another 'Sir Samuel Marshall, the deputy controller of the navy...a particular friend of Admiral Parry, my mother's uncle'. Interest was to hand. But after passing him, 'they said the certificates I produced ought to get me a commission without interest.'[5]

Between old comrades there was a triple bond: professional loyalty, naval honour and mutual interest. Thus Rear-Admiral Pellew wrote in 1806 to his old friend Rear-Admiral Markham, an experienced member of the Admiralty Board now enjoying his second term of office: 'Do me all the kindness for my son you can; I may live to return it to one of yours, for you see the wheel goes round and round.'[6] It was a wheel that revolved down the generations. Nelson owed his rapid promotion – from Lieutenant to Commander 'and onwards' to Captain in exactly two years and two months – to the patronage of Rear-Admiral Sir Peter Parker, his Commander-in-Chief in the West Indies. And when Sir Peter's grandson came into the *Victory* in 1803, Nelson reminded himself that the young Lieutenant was 'to get both steps as fast as possible – his grandfather made me what I am'.[7] Young Parker's 'steps' followed in rapid succession: Commander in May 1804, Captain in October 1805.

Pellew speaks of one day returning 'the kindness' that Admiral Markham will do for his son. Something more than gratitude, this is 'obligation', the grease in the turning of the wheel. It was a responsibility taken seriously, the duty of repaying a favour, a credit in store, whose redemption, in the *quid pro quo* and the scratching of backs, might come far in the future, as it did when Nelson was able to meet his 'obligation' towards Admiral Parker twenty-five years later in extending his own patronage to his patron's grandson. Throughout the political and public life of the nation, the Navy included, patronage or protection was a recognised principle, spoken of as an honourable tradition. Protégés recorded their patrons' names with pride; and, within this, obligation was seen as an equally honourable connection, signifying gratitude to the benefactor. This human side to the relationship

the American War, Captains and Admirals recruited crews from their own home areas, a system which encouraged personal loyalties and bonds of mutual obligation. However, these private and informal arrangements could not survive the growing complexity of the state, its processes of bureaucracy and centralisation accelerated by the exigencies of the Long War. Naval recruitment passed into the hands of the Impress Service and it was only favouritism that permitted Captains such as Pellew to take their own locally-raised crews from ship to ship.

comes across clearly in Nelson's letter to Admiral Parker announcing his intentions for Sir Peter's grandson: 'It is the only opportunity ever offered me, of showing that my feelings of gratitude to you are as warm and alive as when you first took me by the hand: I owe all my Honours to you, and I am proud to acknowledge it to all the world.'[8]

Criticism, when it arose, was usually not at the system as such but at its malpractice in creating officers unfit to command. It was a criticism as old as the Navy itself. Two centuries earlier, Raleigh, a naval man, had complained of the 'preferment' which brought on 'people very raw and ignorant' and 'very unworthily and unfittingly nominated' while 'men of desert and ability' were 'held back' (Raleigh, *Selections*, p. 151). Early in the period of Francis and Charles, Mary Wollstonecraft was writing of sailors 'compelled to pull a strange rope at the surly command of a tyrannic boy, who probably obtained his rank on account of his family connections, or the prostituted vote of his father, whose interest in a borough, or voice as a senator, was acceptable to the minister' (*A Vindication of the Rights of Men*, 1790 quoted in *A Wollstonecraft Anthology*, 1977, ed. Janet Todd, p. 68).

War-time called for higher standards. Nonetheless, the abuses of 'interest' persisted. In his *Essays on Professional Education* (1808, 1812), Richard Lovell Edgeworth charged 'modern corruption' with undermining the 'system of impartiality, on which the glory and existence of the British navy depends', with 'political connexion, and the parliamentary interest of . . . family and friends' at work (p. 222).

A more expert witness was Captain Lord Thomas Cochrane. During a Commons debate on the Flogging of Soldiers (13 March 1812) he made a powerful contribution:

> Great parliamentary interest had enabled the first families in the kingdom to force their children into the service, who were too young to understand the authority entrusted to them. Many of them insisted on their decks being as clean and as shining as the floor of a drawing room in the summer season, and that their kitchen utensils should be scoured as bright as silver, with a variety of other useless and fantastic commands; and if such commands were not obeyed, they flogged severely those who had those articles in charge. The discipline of the navy depended on the commanding officer of each ship; and if they continued to flog for such offences the navy must soon go to ruin. It was going, he said, as fast as possible. Gentlemen might think otherwise, but he knew it to be true, and he was afraid they would all be convinced of it too soon. The family interest he had alluded to prevailed also to such a degree, that even the Lords of the Admiralty had lists made out; and when an officer went to offer his service, or to solicit promotion for services performed, he was asked – are you recommended by my lady this, or miss that, or madam t'other; and if he was not, he might as well have staid at home.
>
> (*Parliamentary Debates*, xxi. col. 1290).

As was customary, the sailor brothers supplied the wording for their entries in John Marshall's *Royal Naval Biography*, and these are cast in the spirit of gratitude made public. Charles names Sir Thomas Williams as 'his early friend and patron';[9] and Francis writes of 'Lord Gambier and the late Sir H. Martin, Comptroller of the Navy' as his 'first naval patrons', and 'Vice-Admiral Gambier' as his 'friend'.[10] In his Memoir, Francis records that he was fortunate enough to enjoy his friendship with Martin, which went back to his days at Portsmouth, up 'to the latest hour of that excellent man's earthly existence'; and he came to regard Martin's death, in August 1794, as a handicap to his progress: 'and though the subsequent occurrences of his professional career afford no reason to suppose he did not obtain Promotion quite as early as he ought yet at the same time is there strong ground for believing the decease of his Patron delayed it very considerably'.

Political, as distinct from naval, interest was more diverse and transitory. In the hands of Ministers, Peers, and great landowners with the patronage of pocket boroughs, it could be immediate and dramatically effective. But as the motto at the head of this chapter reminds us, it could also be fickle and short-term, depending on the succession of Ministries, which politicians were 'in' and which were 'out'; and claims from outside the profession, unless they carried the 'King's pleasure' or the hand of the Prime Minister, were never assured of success. In this vein, the Duke of Northumberland, with several parliamentary seats in his gift, explained to Edward Pellew, 'it will in some measure authorize me to interfere in your affairs at the Admiralty, because we have a Vote or two on certain occasions to use as an Allure'.[11] Run of the mill MPs, unless they were dedicated party-men, carried little weight, a circumstance that Jane Austen exploits in the plotting of *Mansfield Park*. Sir Thomas Bertram, a country member, is a dutiful Parliamentarian; but knowing that his interest is strictly limited, he is happy to leave it to Admiral Crawford to help his nephew, a Midshipman, on his way to a commission.

Bombarded with political applications, especially around election times, First Lords were also wary of favouring applicants unlikely to bring them credit or whose advancement would raise the hackles of the profession. In such cases, their replies would be prompt, polite and unobliging. And professional First Lords had stronger reasons for standing their ground. Although, by virtue of their office, they were temporary politicians, members of the Cabinet and appointees of the Ministry, unlike the true political First Lords, the career politicians, they had to answer the scrutiny and expectations of their fellow-Admirals, indeed of the Navy as a whole, to which they would return when their term at Whitehall was over. They were more resistant to outside interference, more protective of naval matters, and, in war-time, more concerned to maintain an officer corps of proven merit, with favour and favouritism from the outside kept to a minimum.

Of these naval values St Vincent was a jealous guardian. A commander, as Nelson testified, of outstanding 'professional zeal and fire',[12] in 1801 he was serving as Commander-in-Chief of the Channel Fleet when Addington invited him to join the new Ministry. Amongst senior ranks the verdict of Admiral Collingwood was widely held: 'The navy, I doubt not, will be ably directed by Lord St Vincent. His ambition, which has ever been his ruling passion, has kept him all his life in the continual exercise of his powers, and established in him habits of business which will enable him to keep the Admiralty as active as his predecessor, with more knowledge of the character and ability of all the officers'.[13] In these respects, St Vincent was in a far better position than the two previous First Lords, Spencer and Chatham, both of them civilians who had to rely for advice on their First Naval Lords and any other Admirals they trusted. His eye firmly on priorities, soon after taking office St Vincent made his policy on promotion widely known. A brief statement appeared both in the *Times* and the *Naval Chronicle*,[14] announcing that he intended to give preference to those officers who had been longest on the half-pay list. With a dig at Chatham and Spencer, the *Times* commented that if St Vincent succeeded in keeping to 'such a rigorous and impartial line of conduct . . . it will be more than any of his Predecessors have been able to accomplish'.[15] In making this a public announcement, St Vincent was warning off the Parliamentarians: he had no intention of being a cipher, a tool of his political masters. Nonetheless, pressure from Whitehall was inevitable. When he was instructed by Ministers that he must promote Commander Lord Thomas Cochrane, he retorted that 'The First Lord of the Admiralty knows *no must*',[16] and when he did promote Cochrane, in August 1801, it was for gallantry in action. He was equally resistant to the claims of the 'Aristocracy' and denounced the misuse of 'interest' by which 'the influential secure the plums of the Service for the inefficient and lazy'.[17] He answered the Dowager Countess of Macclesfield with the advice that the 'best road' to promotion for her candidate was 'the undeviating pursuit of his Profession'.[18] St Vincent's criteria were 'service' and 'merit', his preference for seamen who were 'hardy' and 'practical';[19] and he advised one correspondent that 'Having refused the Prince of Wales, Duke of Clarence, Duke of Kent and Duke of Cumberland, you will not be surprized that I repeat the impossibility of departing from any principle which would let in such inundation upon me which would tend to complete the ruin of the Navy'.[20] 'The Service has been most shamefully and scandalously prostituted,' he wrote to Captain Lord Garlies at the end of March 1801, 'and I am moving heaven and earth to stop the torrent.'[21] He reported himself 'surrounded with applications, independent of the commands of His Majesty's Ministers'.[22]

Where he was keen to help was in cases of 'friendless merit',[23] especially 'the children of the service' ('legacies to the Service' was Nelson's phrase),[24] the applicants from naval families. He declared himself readier to 'promote the son of an old deserving officer than any noble in the land.'[25] When he did feel under pressure, he would find an alternative inoffensive to the Navy, as in the case of a protégé of the Duke of Sussex, appointed to the sinecure Agency of Antigua Hospital, an expedient which answered the Duke's request 'without wounding the feelings of a great number of meritorious young Men, who have stuck by His Majesty's Service during the whole of the late arduous war, and disgusting the whole Navy'.[26] Notwithstanding his strict principles and objectives, St Vincent was forced to confess, as he did to Nelson, that he found 'a just disposition of the Patronage is the most difficult thing I have to perform'.[27]

Lord Barham (the former Sir Charles Middleton) followed in the St Vincent tradition. During his time in office, from 1805 to 1806 (a veteran of seventy-nine), like St Vincent he feared inundation, reporting to Cornwallis the endless representations pouring in from 'Admirals and Captains for their children, from the King's Ministers, members of Parliament, peers, eminent divines . . . if I steer clear of injustice I shall think myself fortunate . . . The applications are so numerous, and opportunities of complying with them so few that my whole time is spent in answering unreasonable demands'.[28] We might well ask what was the essential difference between 'demands' reasonable and 'unreasonable'. A communication to Barham from Downing Street in May 1805 makes the point nicely:

> Mr Pitt will speak to your lordship in favour of Captain Codrington. The object is an appointment to the Orion. The captain is brother of the member for Tewkesbury and has not recently attended [the House of Commons] although an uniform supporter; the cause, I have been privately told, is that he conceives he has been treated with inattention in respect to his brother. Mr Codrington is a respectable country gentleman, with a large fortune, and it seems desirable that he should be gratified. I have not the least acquaintance with Mr Codrington or the captain, though I have understood the latter to be a fair officer in point of service.[29]

By the standards of the day, as an undisguised political request this was eminently reasonable. Not a personal favour on behalf of Pitt, it was for the safeguarding of the Ministry, of which Barham was a member. What the note does not say is that Christopher Bethell Codrington, an MP for fifteen years, was not in truth 'an uniform supporter', but a former Whig whose support for Pitt could not be depended on, and whose vote had to be bought. Of course, silence on these matters was part of the convention. And another protocol was observed. This was the assurance that the officer in question (a

Captain since 1795) was one whose performance would not reflect badly on his 'friends'. The letter was dated 23 May. Captain Codrington's appointment to the *Orion* (74) came the following day. It proved to be 'meritorious'. At Trafalgar, the *Orion*, sailing No. 11 in the Weather Column in the Order of Battle, fought with honour and success under the command of Edward Codrington, a gallant officer, to whom the *Intrepide* (74) lowered her colours after a fierce engagement.

Certain areas of naval high command and policy lay indisputably with the Cabinet, including strategy, the disposition and command of Fleets world-wide and the levels of manning and the financing of the Navy overall, these last two matters laid before Parliament annually and voted upon. Barham's success was to defend the areas of command, appointment and promotion which were the Admiralty's rightful preserve, and for this he was respected by the politicians and throughout the Navy itself. An exchange which throws a particularly revealing light on this situation took place between Barham and Nelson in the month before Trafalgar. Barham called Nelson to the Admiralty, handed him the Navy List and asked him to make his own choice of officers for the new Mediterranean Fleet. 'Choose yourself, my Lord', Nelson replied, 'the same spirit activates the whole profession. You cannot choose wrong.' But Barham would not have it and handed the list back to Nelson. 'This is my secretary,' Barham said, 'Give your orders to him.'[30] Such an expression of mutual trust was only possible as long as the 'spirit' of leadership at Whitehall visibly represented the best interests of the Navy and was not at the call of the politicians; when, in other words, the First Lord had succeeded, in vital matters, in insulating the Admiralty from political pressure and preserving the autonomy of its most vital decision-making.

This was not the situation during the time of Barham's predecessor, Henry Dundas, Lord Melville, Treasurer of the Navy from 1783 to 1800, and First Lord for twelve months from May 1804. His appointment had nothing to do with the needs of the Navy or Melville's knowledge of it, and everything to do with the fact that he could deliver the votes of forty-three out of the forty-five Scottish Members of Parliament. Had he not been impeached for financial irregularities going back to his time as Treasurer, bringing his term as First Lord to an end, Melville 'would soon have given us a Scotch navy', as the Whig politician William Windham remarked.[31] Samuel Whitbread, a prominent back-bencher interested in naval affairs, led the attack on Melville. Whitbread's reward came in February 1806 when his brother-in-law Charles Grey, took over from Barham (then over eighty) as First Lord. Whitbread promptly sent in an early batch of applications, a passing out of favours to servants of yesteryear which makes extraordinary reading:

There was 'the brother to our apothecary at Biggleswade', Mr Okes, who 'wants to be made a lieutenant. He is son to old Okes of Cambridge to whom we are indebted for early cures'; 'your sister is particularly anxious to recommend someone for an Admiralty messenger's place; Lee Antonie recommends a naval officer and my sister Lady St John another . . . pray order two letters to be written that I may send an answer to each.' And finally 'Can you do anything for the son of our old roll and butter manufacturer at Eton?'[32]

Politicians were also at the helm in the 1790s. In 1788, finding Admiral Lord Howe obstructive and difficult to work with, Pitt replaced him with his own elder brother, John, Earl of Chatham, knowing that he would them have free access to the Admiralty Board. Chatham was followed in December 1794 by Earl Spencer. With a line of politicians in office, political patronage held sway, leading to St Vincent's forceful complaint, when he arrived in February 1801, at the overstock of Admirals promoted by Spencer and 'the list of post-captains and commanders' swollen 'to an enormous size' by the 'numerous connexions of the Spencer Family'.[33] He expressed his determination 'to restore the Navy to its pristine vigour'.[34] As a life-long sailor, St Vincent had no time for politician First Lords. Yet his years in the Navy had taught him the need for political backing and he lost no time in buttressing his own position in Parliament, bringing in supporters on whom he could rely. In the General Election of July 1802, eleven out of his twelve candidates, constituting the 'Admiralty' interest, were successful, including Troubridge, his principal follower, whom he brought into the Admiralty as First Naval Lord. St Vincent also cultivated alliances, where he could, with the other eighteen naval MPs. Naval officers were said to make awkward politicians and wretched speakers, and naval lore was that on nautical topics they should 'observe a passive and dignified silence' and leave the debate 'solely to landsmen'.[35] But this was a wisdom difficult to follow during St Vincent's term. His shake up of the naval administration between 1801 and 1804 was seen as a direct attack upon the Navy Board and the Board's Parliamentary dependents and supporters (largely those with a financial interest in ship-building and ships' supplies) turned a heavy fire-power on the First Lord. However, for a crucial debate in March 1804, St Vincent was able to summon Edward Pellew, the MP for Barnstaple, possibly the most dashing, successful and popular of frigate Captains. Coming directly from his Squadron at Ferrol, off the coast of Spain, Pellew addressed the Commons with authority and skill, more than once reminding the House that he spoke out of his 'professional experience' and came hot from his Squadron. He assured the House that 'our Navy was never better found, that it was never better supplied, and that our men were never better fed or better clothed'.[36] It was what one MP described as 'the best sea speech that ever was heard'.[37] It was an undoubted victory for St Vincent. Pitt's critical motion was defeated by 130 votes to 71. But rewarding Pellew was not so easy. To promote Pellew meant promoting those Captains who stood above him on the Captains' List; and there was a similar problem with St Vincent's other supporters. In order to reach them, he was forced to extraordinary lengths. So when the promotions were gazetted on 23 April, no less than eight Captains, including Pellew, jumped the Blue to become Rear-Admirals of the White and twenty-two Captains became Rear-Admirals of the Blue. The Navy was rendered top-heavy with a burden of Flag officers far in excess of the available Flag commands. It was a classic example of political pressure distorting the professional interest of the service, the very thing that St Vincent had protested against on entering office three years before.

We are not certain what steps were taken by Francis to move from the *Lark*. But we do know that he told his father of his wish to transfer to a frigate. Mr Austen's options were limited. Lacking political, territorial or commercial 'interest', the name of Austen carried no weight whatsoever and a letter from himself, merely as parent, would cut no ice at the Admiralty. Seemingly, the obvious step would be to invoke naval interest, in particular, Sir Charles Middleton, a member of the Admiralty Board since May 1794, and since 1792 joined to the family by the marriage of James Austen. However, there is no evidence that Mr Austen made any move in that direction. Instead, in October 1794, he chose to approach Warren Hastings. Hastings was an old friend of both the Austen and Leigh families (from which Mrs Austen came) and was on particularly good terms with Mr Austen himself. Although Hastings had occupied no public office since his Governor-Generalship of Bengal (in effect, of all British India) ended in 1785 and although he had been on trial since 1787 on charges of corruption, nonetheless he continued to wield considerable influence. Throughout the years of his impeachment and trial, he enjoyed the favour of the King; and, in Parliament, he had the support of the 'King's friends', a group known in this regard as the 'Hastorians'. In social circles, only by the Whig aristocracy was he ostracised and as far as the public was concerned, he was a successful and popular figure.

Hastings' power-base was the East India Company, with its immense field of patronage – from the granting of vastly profitable shipping and trading contracts to the appointment of 'writers' or civil servants in the administration of the Company's territories and of cadetships in the Company's armed forces. These posts offered a rewarding career for the younger sons of the gentry, the most successful of whom returned as nabobs of vast wealth. Within the Company's patronage the naval aspect was significant since it maintained its own Marine, many of whose officers had served in the Navy, and in Indian waters it often worked alongside the Navy, a relationship which was of growing importance during the Long War. We have already seen an example of this in Chapter 3 with the support provided to Cornwallis when the weather-beaten ships of his Squadron were forced to return home for refitting and Company ships were called in to strengthen his force. Conversely, it was the Navy which provided the escorts for the great convoys of East Indiamen which set out for India and China.

A Company patronage much sought after was Freight or Treasure Money. This was paid to Captains for the secure carriage of gold or silver bullion or specie (minted coins) in naval vessels, an important service even in peacetime in Eastern and Far Eastern seas plagued by pirates. By the end of the eighteenth century London had become the centre of the world bullion market. So there were plentiful opportunities for earning a 1 or 2 per cent commission on cargoes of Treasure to the value of hundreds of thousands of pounds.* Company Treasure was one of the items of patronage in Hastings' gift during his Governorship and many of the young Captains favoured during his years of office (1773–85) were by now flag officers of the highest rank. They knew the truth of Admiral Vernon's adage that naval laurels were 'handsomely tipped with gold';** they remembered whom to thank for those favours; and were ready to repay their debt when Hastings came to seek their 'interest' in return.

The beginning of the Long War put the Company in particularly good standing since the building and fitting-out of its larger ships ensured a supply of trained shipwrights for the Navy's accelerated building programme. The largest of the East Indiamen, already heavily armed against pirates and privateers, were easily converted into fighting vessels and trained sailors from the Company service were provided to man them.+ In addition, the Company raised a further three thousand sailors at its own expense. This level of co-operation and support was continued for the duration of the war, and from its one hundred strong fleet the Company was able to offer transports for troops and military supplies. Understandably, these measures found favour

* The Freight arrangement lasted until 1864. The sole beneficiaries were the ships' Captains and their Squadron or Fleet Commanders who took a one-third share of the commission. There were statutory 'war-rates' and 'peace-rates' and a distinction was made between Private Treasure and state-owned or Public Treasure, on which the Government tried to stop paying any allowance after 1801. But vested interests were at stake in so valuable a perk and the story of the epic battle between the Navy, to preserve it, and the Government, to remove it, can be followed in Dillon (1956), ii. 270–73 and Lewis (1965), pp. 242–45.

** Quoted in Rodger (1988), p. 258. Admiral Keith, reported to be the richest naval officer of his time, earned £67,000 in his Flag share of freight money in the two years between December 1799 and November 1801 while Commander-in-Chief in the Mediterranean.

+ Ships of up to 1200 tons employed on the China trade could carry 36 or 38 guns, and the smaller vessels from 32 down to 12 guns. They also carried a small arsenal of muskets, grenades, pistols, bayonets, cutlasses and boarding-pikes.

in Parliament as well as with the Admiralty and added further to the Company's already substantial influence. At any time during this period, from sixty to one hundred MPs were Proprietors of India Stock, with a direct investment in the Company's trading activities and success; and within this Parliamentary group was a growing number of Company Directors and plutocratic nabobs.* Of these, the Hastings supporters were not less than thirty or forty strong, long indebted to him for the profitable years of his Governorship. There was also an identifiable naval lobby with Company or Indian connections. These were officers who had either served in the Company's navy or, like Cornwallis, MP for Portsmouth, had close contact with it during tours of duty on the East Indies station. So Mr Austen was not mistaken in approaching Hastings for help.

Although only one letter of their correspondence survives, this, together with an entry in Warren Hastings' Diary, tells us all we need to know of the understanding between the two men and it throws into sharp relief the difference between Hastings, a man who knew his way around the Admiralty and the personalities involved, and Mr Austen, careful and competent in his own way, but an innocent in these circles of power.

Hastings' Diary entry, made in London, is dated 4 November 1794:

> wrote to Adm.¹ Affleck, & sent him Mr Austen's letter, in behalf of his Son. – rec'd his answer – that all patronage centered in the 1st Lord of the Adm ỿ but whenever I can hook in a word for him I will – promising his best endeavours.[38]

Brief as it is, Hastings' Diary entry here is unusually detailed for although he was scrupulous in making a daily record, the entries are normally very sparse, often limited to the state of the weather, his wife's health and medicines, and visitors and social calls. So this service for Mr Austen Hastings felt worthy of record.

Around this date Hastings must have written a second time to Mr Austen, who replied

Steventon 8th Novʳ 1794.

Dear Sir

I have had the favour of both your letters, & must ever acknowledge myself much your debtor, for the friendly manner in which you have undertaken our cause, & the application you have made in behalf of my Son. – As to the event of it I am not very sanguine, convinced as I am that all Patronage in the Navy rests with Lᵈ

---

* Philips (1940), p. 299, puts the total at sixty MPs in 1784, ninety-five in 1802, rising to 103 in 1806, following which the numbers fall. Namier and Brooke (1964) give these figures (p. 152):

	Directors	Nabobs
1774–80	9	17
1780–84	9	22
1784–90	12	33

Chatham; however as it may be of material service to us to have a warm Friend at the Board, I am very thankful you have procured us one in Adl: Affleck. If I mistake not he had formerly some acquaintance with my family, & perhaps his recollection of that may be an additional motive with his regard for you to endeavour to assist us. Should we not succeed in our first object of getting him promoted, it might forward his views to have him removed to a Flag Ship on a more probable Station; & this is a circumstance you might, if you had no objection, suggest to the Admiral when you meet him [in] Town. And here I must not omit to inform you that we have by the Application of a Friend gained, as we hope, another L^d of the Admiralty, Mr Pybus, in our interest, a circumstance you will mention or not as you think proper.

I shall not trouble you with anything farther on this subject than to assure I should not have introduced my son to your notice, had I not been convinced that his merits as a Man & a Sailor will justify any recommendations.

    I am, Dear Sir,
        Your much obliged
        & faithful Servt
        Geo. Austen.[39]

In expressing his doubt as to the outcome of Hastings' application to Vice-Admiral Philip Affleck, Mr Austen betrays an outsider's ignorance of the way in which the day-to-day business of the Admiralty Board was actually conducted. While Chatham, as First Lord, was nominally the dispenser of all promotions and appointments, he was notoriously lazy and famous as a late riser, so famous that it became his nickname, 'the late Lord Chatham'; and of one particular piece of Admiralty bad management Nelson remarked that 'Lord Chatham did better sleeping'.[40] 'Ministerial concerns' was his familiar excuse for missing the Board's daily meeting and on his departure from office in December 1794 there was indignation (but no surprise) that hundreds of Admiralty letters were found unopened at his home. Much of his business he delegated to Affleck, the First Naval Lord, an arrangement which the other members of the Board were happy to accept. Affleck had a distinguished naval record. He achieved Flag rank in 1787, was appointed Commander-in-Chief of the West Indies station in 1790 and joined the Admiralty Board in April 1794. So in winning over Affleck as the Austens' 'warm Friend at the Board', Hastings showed his understanding of the Admiralty's workings, knowledge which he may well have gathered from Affleck himself, since they were friends of long standing, going back to the time when they both held junior positions in the East India Company.

As an alternative to promotion, which would be to the rank of Commander, in charge of a sloop, Mr Austen proposed that Francis be transferred 'to a Flag

Ship on a more probable Station', a vessel more likely to contend with the French in a Fleet engagement. As Francis was then serving in the Downs and the North Sea, a favourable move would be to the Channel, the Western Approaches or the Mediterranean, where the enemy was more likely to be encountered. In making this suggestion, Mr Austen was well-informed (quite probably by Francis himself). For it was by gallantry in action that junior officers performed 'meritoriously' and found their reward in promotion. Following a successful Fleet engagement, First Lieutenants on ships-of-the-line could hope for promotion directly to Post Captaincy, jumping the intervening rank of Commander. As Francis had now served as a Lieutenant for two years, he could feel qualified by time and experience to be given such an opportunity.

In the second paragraph, Mr Austen goes on to mention 'the Application' of a second, unnamed 'Friend' which he hopes will have 'gained' the 'interest' of another 'Ld of the Admiralty, Mr Pybus'. Charles Small Pybus, an ambitious but unsuccessful career politician, MP for the Admiralty seat of Dover, had been a member of the Board since 1791. He was there as a junior civil Lord, known as a 'signing member', of no particular influence or power, but available for the daily duty of signing orders and other routine papers. Like Affleck, Pybus had Company connections. His father had been an Indian civil servant and a member of the Council of Madras and the son would have been acquainted with Hastings as well.

Finally, it is worth noting the formal courtesy of Mr Austen's letter at its opening and close and the necessary reassurance that Francis, with 'his merits as a Man & A Sailor', will live up to any 'recommendations' that Hastings, Affleck, Pybus or anyone else might offer on his behalf. In other words, in backing the young Lieutenant, they would not be putting their own reputations nor the value of their interest and patronage at risk. This was a serious matter since accidents at sea were all too often the work of officers advanced beyond their experience and ability. When the *Bellerophon* (74) 'lost her foremast and bowsprit', sailing into Portsmouth 'a cripple', Cuthbert Collingwood (then a senior Captain of 13 years standing) cited this single accident as signifying a general malaise:

> This was not the fault of the ship nor the weather, but must ever be the case when young men are made officers who have neither skill nor attention, and there is scarce a ship in the Navy that has not an instance that political interest is a better argument for promotion than any skill.[41]

Sadly for Francis, this arrangement was overtaken by events, the impressive line-up of Admiralty interest recruited to no immediate purpose. Whatever Hastings and Mr Austen had achieved in October and November was frustrated the following month. Chatham, having lost the confidence of the Navy and the public, went out, and Spencer came in. Affleck's power was curtailed and Francis was forgotten. The key figure in these changes was Sir Charles Middleton. Although he had resigned as Comptroller of the Navy in 1790, disgusted by the waste and corruption he found in naval supplies, Pitt continued to treat him as his confidential adviser on naval affairs and in May 1794 appointed him to the Admiralty Board. On 19 December, the very day Spencer took office, Middleton presented two memoranda: one, 'Information', outlining the unsatisfactory conduct of Board business under Chatham, until it 'fell into my hands' and his remedies, either taken or proposed. Middleton was highly critical of the handling of 'offices and appointments . . . It has been managed in a most irregular and incorrect way and the service and the office has felt the consequence of it'.[42] However, given Affleck's seniority on the Board, Middleton had not so far ventured to interfere with his running of things. The second memorandum, 'Project of Business', outlined Middleton's proposals for the timetabling of the Board's working day and the organisation of its office and procedures. Spencer accepted both sets of recommendations. In this new climate Affleck lasted only five months and in May 1795, when Middleton took over as First Naval Lord, his place was filled by Middleton's nephew, Captain James Gambier (promoted to Flag rank two months later).

At this point, Francis, still languishing in the *Lark*, was first introduced 'to the notice of' Gambier. It was a fateful meeting. Besides the family connection established by the marriage of James Austen, both Francis and Gambier were men of strong religious conviction. As Francis wrote glowingly (too glowingly, as it proved) Gambier 'soon became his warm friend, and never lost sight of his Interest, nor neglected any opportunity of forwarding it to the utmost of his power, until he had obtained the rank of Post Captain' (this was five years ahead, in 1800). The immediate benefit of Gambier's patronage was Francis' removal from the *Lark* to the *Andromeda* (32) and, having seen Gambier again, onwards to the *Prince George* (98) and then on to the *Glory* (98). These three moves, made in the space of six months between May and November 1795, were in pursuit of a senior Lieutenant's position on a Flagship, for with the Admiral's support, a young officer had the opportunity to take the next vacancy to command a sloop. But Francis was dogged with bad luck. In the *Prince George*, where he was supposedly 'on the road to promotion', to his disappointment he found himself ranked by the Admiral commanding as eighth of the nine Lieutenants, although by seniority he should have been third. Then the move to the *Glory* proved to be a dead end. She was one of a Squadron escorting troops out to the West Indies, a very cockpit of action. But the convoy, a large fleet of transports, which sailed in December, was driven back by foul weather and was kept at Spithead until mid-March 1796. His 'sanguine hope of Promotion . . . thus fallen to the ground', Francis applied once more to 'his firm friend at the Admiralty for a removal to a Frigate, and through his kindness was early in March appointed Third of the Shannon a new Fir built Ship of 32 guns . . . fitting at Deptford'.* However, misfortune once more. The Captain, Alexander Frazer, was a brute. In desperation, the crew petitioned the Admiralty, charging him as 'one of the most barbarous and one of the most unhuman officers that ever a sect of unfortunate men eaver had the disagreeable misfortune of being with . . .'.[43] But their plea went unanswered,** and to escape Frazer's tyranny, Francis 'again made Interest with his friend at the Admiralty'. He left the *Shannon* at the end of June and remained in England on half-pay until September, when he joined a former shipmate, John Gore, who had been a Lieutenant in the *Perseverance* and was now Captain of the *Triton* (32), another new fir-built frigate. She was a friendly ship and Francis stayed for just over a year as First Lieutenant. The *Triton* was attached to the Channel Fleet, 'cruizing to the westward'. Their small success was to capture five French privateers and some other vessels 'of inconsiderable value'. But this was not a path to promotion and, by what Francis calls an 'unwished for' act, Gambier, 'finding no prospect of it on the home station', removed him to the *Seahorse* (38), which was ordered to a more likely command, the Mediterranean. On Francis' behalf, Gambier sent recommendations to St Vincent, the Commander-in-Chief, hoping 'to obtain his advancement'.

We can suppose that Jane Austen followed every twist and turn of these events, just as she did four years later, in 1798, in a similar situation when her father conducted a rapid and highly effective correspondence with Gambier. For our detailed knowledge of this episode we are lucky enough to have a sequence of three letters from Jane to Cassandra reporting Mr Austen's approach and its speedy and successful result: firstly, in the advancement of Francis, appointed by St Vincent as First Lieutenant in the *London* (98), and, secondly, in the removal of Charles from an unpromising post in a sixteen-gun brig to something worthwhile in a thirty-two gun frigate.

Jane writes to Cassandra of these matters with economy and amusement. It is familiar ground to both of them, a routine they have watched many

---

* Oak was the traditional wood for ship construction. But war-time shortages brought the introduction of pine for sloops and frigates. 'Fir built' ships, as they were called, although marginally faster, were regarded as inferior and less durable.

** Neither was this a setback to Frazer's career. A Captain since 1 July 1793, he held a succession of commands, and became a Rear-Admiral of the Blue in 1811.

times before; and, armed with his own experience, Mr Austen knows exactly what to do. Charles is unhappy on his brig, the *Scorpion*, and 'begins to feel the Dignity of Ill-usage', as Jane puts it. 'My father will write to Admiral Gambier.' Since Middleton's resignation from the Board in November 1795, Gambier had taken the position of First Naval Lord. 'He must already have received so much satisfaction from his acquaintance with & Patronage of Frank, that he will be delighted I dare say to have another of the family introduced to him.' And Jane has her own serious suggestion to add: that 'it would be very right in Charles to address Sir Tho^S on the occasion' – this being Charles' own patron, Captain Sir Thomas Williams.[44]

This was Jane's news of 18 December. The next day the letter to Gambier was sent. Five days later, on 24 December, Jane was able to send her sister a copy of Gambier's reply to their father's 'application', adding her own amused commentary:

Steventon Monday Night Dec:^{r} 24th

My dear Cassandra,

I have got some pleasant news for you, which I am eager to communicate, & therefore begin my letter sooner, tho' I shall not *send* it sooner than usual. – Admiral Gambier in reply to my father's application writes as follows. – 'As it is usual to keep young officers in small vessels, it being most proper on account of their inexperience, & it being also a situation where they are more in the way of learning their Duty, Your Son has been continued in the Scorpion; but I have mentioned to the Board of Admiralty his wish to be in a Frigate, and when a proper opportunity offers & it is judged that he has taken his Turn in a small Ship, I hope he will be removed. – With regard to your Son now in the London, I am glad I can give you the assurance that his promotion is likely to take place very soon, as Lord Spencer has been so good as to say he would include him in an arrangement that he proposes making in a short time relative to some promotions in that quarter.' – There! – I may now finish my letter, & go & hang myself, for I am sure I can neither write nor do anything which will not appear insipid to you after this. – *Now* I really think he will soon be made, & only wish we could communicate our fore-knowledge of the Event, to him whom it principally concerns. – [45]

On pages 60 to 61 readers can follow the continuation of this letter. Towards its close, Jane Austen wonders if the bombardment has not gone too far, a well-grounded anxiety, for a package of letters received from Francis at the beginning of the month had included one 'for Lord Spencer';[46] now came the news that Charles had written too:

The Lords of the Admiralty will have enough of our applications at present, for I hear from Charles that he has written to Lord Spencer himself to be removed. I am afraid his serene Highness will be in a passion, & order some of our heads to be cut off. – [47]

Cassandra would readily pick up the *Arabian Nights' Entertainment* joke casting Spencer as the Sultan.[48] The absoluteness of the First Lord's command over the fortunes of her brothers, matched with the Austens' attempts to put their case, had its comic side. No joking matter in the family circle at large. But in writing to Cassandra, Jane was free to indulge her sense of the ridiculous. Nonetheless, whatever action Gambier took was prompt and effective. Only four days later, on 28 December, Jane could open her letter triumphantly: 'Frank is made . . . yesterday raised to the Rank of Commander'. There was further good news. Mimicking the style of the *Gazette*, she announced 'that Lieut. Charles John Austen is removed to the *Tamer* Frigate'.[49]

What these letters bring out is the informal courtesy with which such requests were answered; the speed with which favoured applications, weighted with interest, could be met; and, more than that, the openness (today we would call it the transparency) with which the operation was conducted. It was these circumstances and the sharing of news and letters at Steventon that provided Jane Austen with an insight on the workings of interest and the machinery of naval administration. Armed with this knowledge, years later she had the confidence to recreate this area in *Mansfield Park*.

A much more important episode in Francis' career took place in 1805. It illustrates the vagaries of 'interest' and the possibilities of conflict that could arise between the needs of the service, an officer's ambitions for himself and the intervention of 'friends'. The sequence of events opened in May 1804 when Francis was appointed Flag-Captain to Rear-Admiral Thomas Louis in the *Leopard* (50). Louis was then in command of the Squadron blockading Boulogne and Francis remained there with him until February 1805, when Louis was transferred to Nelson's Mediterranean Fleet, arriving there to be welcomed by Nelson on 26 March as an 'old Crocodile', a beloved veteran of the Nile campaign, Louis raised his flag in the *Canopus* (80), with Francis continuing as his Flag-Captain. It was now approaching five years since Francis had last held an independent command. This was the *Peterel* (16), the sloop in which he enjoyed success in the Mediterranean, with the capture or destruction of over forty enemy vessels, small as they might be. But since October 1800 his career had been less rewarding. Following his promotion to the rank of Captain, his first appointment was as Flag-Captain to his patron, Admiral Gambier in the *Neptune* (98). Then came the Peace of Amiens, followed by his service with the Sea Fencibles, before joining the *Leopard*. None of these posts gave him the same freedom of command he had enjoyed in the *Peterel*, nor did they provide the opportunities for distinction. His position as Flag-Captain might seem to carry prestige. But it was a customary appointment for Captains recently promoted. Directly under the Admiral's eye, it was the least independent of commands in the Navy and in a blockading force, carried little chance of prize-money. It was not surprising then that Francis was impatient to have command of a frigate, an ambition which he confided to Admiral Louis during his few weeks on shore between his appointment to the *Canopus* and their sailing in March 1805. Louis felt Francis' wish was 'perfectly reasonable' and said he would make no objection to his 'quitting his Flag'.[50] To strengthen his hand, Francis called not on Gambier but on the help of a prominent public figure and military man, Lord Moira, who gave him a letter to hand to Nelson personally when the *Canopus* joined his Fleet in the Mediterranean.

On the face of it, a commendation from Moira could be expected to carry weight. As the Prince of Wales' political representative in parliament, Moira was an important figure in public life. As Lord Rawdon, he had a distinguished military career going back over thirty years to the American war and, more recently, had led British forces in Belgium and Holland. As Moira's circle included both Gambier and Warren Hastings, it could have been that Francis gained an introduction through their good offices. A more likely route, however, led through Henry Austen, by now established as an Army and Navy Agent* and on his way to becoming an established banker. One of his partners in the Army Agency, Captain Charles James, a protégé of Moira's, may have introduced his patron as a client seeking loans. However, Moira was a very bad risk. A spendthrift, living far beyond his means, he was also unwisely generous in helping out the Prince of Wales, whose boast it was that 'Moira and I are like two brothers, when one wants money he puts his hand in the other's pocket'.[51] As the Prince's pocket was notoriously empty, it was a saying that did little to strengthen Moira's credit. Nonetheless, despite Moira's reputation for high-living and chronic indebtedness, Henry made him a number of personal loans, and we can suppose that it was Moira's sense

---

* Army Agents served as middlemen between the Army's Paymaster-general and the Regimental Paymasters, handling the financial business of regiments and acting as private bankers for the officers. Between 1793 and 1801, Henry had served in the Oxfordshire Regiment of Militia, for part of this time as Adjutant and Paymaster, and in setting up the Agency he was able to exploit his Regimental and wider military connections. Francis was a sleeping partner in the Navy Agency, which acted in a more limited role for Naval officers, looking after their financial affairs, providing advances on pay, and so on.

of obligation which led him to provide the letter to Nelson in 1804.

As it turned out, the only beneficiary of this business was Moira himself. The letter made no headway with Nelson and Moira's indebtedness to Henry Austen, running at £6000 when he left England to take up the Governorship of Bengal in 1813, was never paid. By Henry's account, it was this that brought him down: by April 1814, 'my credit as a banker was impaired . . . confidence withdrawn and business destroyed . . . insolvency ensued in March 1816'[52] and his financial career ended by this act of 'unexampled treachery'.[53]*

Whatever led to Moira's involvement, he wrote to Nelson on 11 February 1805. Francis, who was then on leave prior to joining the *Canopus*, was able to carry the letter from him and hand it to Nelson on boarding the *Victory* off Sardinia six weeks later.

Although the letter is now lost, Nelson's reply tells us all we need to know.

> VISCOUNT NELSON TO EARL MOIRA, in St James's Place, London 1805, March 30. Victory. – Capt. Austin delivered me your Lordship's letter of Febry. 11th. A frigate would have been better calculated to have given Capt. Austin a fortune out of the Medn. than coming under my command, where nothing is to be got except the French fleet should put to sea, of which I have yet some faint hopes; if they do not in the April I shall think they will remain in port all the summer and then I shall return to England for a few months to try and recruit for another campaign.

Nelson then turned to other matters, arguing that if Napoleon is to be defeated, the 'blow' should be struck in Europe and that 'our Troops and Ships' should not be frittered away in 'buccaneering expeditions' to Mexico or Peru 'when they are so much wanted for more important occasions and are no use beyond enriching a few individuals'. This would be in response to news from Moira that such 'expeditions' to South America were being urged at this time by the Venezuelan patriot Francisco de Miranda supported by a naval man, Captain Home Riggs Popham (an episode that comes into Chapter 7). Following an expression of concern about Lady Moira's health and a polite signing off, Nelson returned to Francis' affairs, the real purpose of Moira's letter, in a '*Postscript*':

> You may rely upon all attention in my power to Capt. Austin. I hope to see him alongside a French 80 gun ship and he cannot be better placed than in the *Canopus*, who was *once* a French adl.'s ship and struck to me. Capt. A. I knew a little of before; he is an excellent young man.
>
> I am, &c
>
> Nelson and Bronte[54]

Nelson's letter is that of a practised naval diplomat – polite, correct and unobliging. 'Excellent young man' as he is, Captain Austen is not to look for

---

* See Appendix 8: Henry Austen's Banking Style.

any favours. Entering the Mediterranean, he joins a Fleet and cannot expect the freedom to go cruizing for prizes. His duty is in the *Canopus* and his success will be 'in action', with the recognition and reward that will follow. To understand why Nelson treated Moira's letter so coolly we need to look at the relationship between them. After taking his seat in the House of Lords in October 1801, Nelson heard Moira expressing remarkably liberal views on the future of Ireland and the treatment of debtors. Politically naïve, Nelson came away so convinced that Moira was a man of 'ability, honour and strict integrity' that he decided to break his resolution never to allow anyone to make use of his proxy in a House of Lords vote.[55] But he soon discovered Moira was no paragon and that, manoeuvring and plotting on behalf of the Prince of Wales, he was deeply involved in Whig party politics. As Nelson explained to Pitt, his own idealistic 'sailor politics' was 'England's welfare'; and he was not prepared 'to range' himself 'under the political banners of any man in or out of place'.[56] 'I will stand upon my own bottom and be none of their tools', he wrote to Lady Hamilton. 'When I come home' (it was August 1804 and he was in the Mediterranean) 'I shall make myself understood. I like both Pitt and Lord Melville, and why should I oppose them' (as he would, associated with the Foxite Moira). 'I am free and independent.'[57] So, distancing himself from Moira, he withdrew his proxy.

A request turned down in this style – in fact it was Nelson's standard letter-of-reply to such applications - could raise no objection, for national interest stands first.* Nor could Moira (or Francis, should he see the letter) take offence since it was Nelson's practised style to hint at his previous dealings with the 'excellent young man'. Francis would remember these occasions well: in May 1799 when he carried vital despatches across the Mediterranean from St Vincent at Gibralter to Nelson at Palermo, warning him of the French fleet running fast into the Mediterranean before a westerly gale.[58] Nelson immediately sent Francis on with further despatches warning the blockading Squadron at Malta. And there was another occasion, on 1 January 1800, when Francis reported back to Nelson the safe delivery of his letters to Corfu, further letters brought back from Corfu and the positions of a third-rate and a frigate of the Mediterranean Fleet.[59] For a Commander-in-Chief, in the midst of war, these services were trivial. But they were not unremembered by Nelson, a fact he brings to Moirs's attention.

On this occasion, in 1805, Nelson kept to his word and Francis remained in the *Canopus*, soon to accompany the *Victory* on the longest pursuit of the war, little short of seven thousand miles, across the Atlantic and back – lasting

---

* Another example of this formula-response, written in 1799, can be found in Friendly (1977), p. 93. Nelson assures his correspondent of his 'inclination to be useful' to Lieutenant Francis Beaufort who 'cannot be better off than 1st Lieut. of so fine a frigate' etc etc.

from mid May to late July – in search of Villeneuve and the combined French and Spanish Fleets.

After that fruitless journey, the British force renewed the blockade of Cadiz. After two years at sea, Nelson returned to England on leave and to receive fresh orders as Commander-in-Chief of the Mediterranean Fleet, which he rejoined on 27 September off Cape St Vincent. It was an event for which Francis, in the *Canopus*, was waiting. His formal letter of welcome, written the very next day, carried his request for a frigate.

Canopus off Cadiz Sept 28th 1805

My Lord,
Rejoicing as I do from the bottom of my heart, at your Lordship's return to this station, I should be unjust to my feelings, were I to neglect the occasion of requesting you to accept my sincere congratulations on the event, which will not, I am confident be less conducive to the comfort and satisfaction of Individuals than advantageous to the public service; I could say much more on the subject, but that I wish not to risque incurring the suspicion of useing Flattery, more especially as I am about to ask a favor.

In the extensive fleet which will now be under your Lordship's orders, it is not improbable but some vacancy may happen in the command of a Frigate; should such be the case and your Lordship free from any previous promise, I venture to solicit the refusal of it; and I do this with the greater confidence when I reflect on the uniform kindness and attention with which your Lordship has honored me, from whence I am induced to hope my endeavours to secure your favorable opinion, have been not altogether unsuccessful.

It may not be superfluous to mention, that previous to my quitting England to join the Canopus, Admiral Louis was apprized of my wish to get into a Frigate, which he was good enough to say he thought perfectly reasonable, and that he should not have any objection to my quitting his Flag, whenever I could gain the situation I wanted.

I have the honor to be
My Lord,
your Lordship's obedient
humble servant
Francis W. Austen

The Rt. Honble.
Lord Vist: Nelson K. B.
Etc etc etc[60]

At the time, Frances received 'no positive promise' from Nelson but believed that he would attend 'to my wishes', as he afterwards wrote to his fiancée, Mary Gibson. Nelson's immediate tasks were to instruct his Captains on the

Plan of Battle and assess the condition of the Fleet. Although, as he reported to the Admiralty on 2 October, he found it 'in very fair condition and good humour', the ships were 'getting short in their water and provisions' and 'in order that the Fleet may be all prepared for service before the winter sets in',[61] arranged for detachments to go to Gibralter and Tetuan. The first to leave, on 3 October, were six ships-of-the-line led by the *Canopus*. On the afternoon of their departure, Louis and Francis dined with Nelson on the *Victory*. Louis, heavy with foreboding, remonstrated: 'You are sending us away, my Lord, - the Enemy will come out, and we shall have no share in the Battle'. Nelson replied reassuringly with characteristic vigour and confidence:

> The Enemy *will* come out, and we shall fight them; but there will be time for you to get back first. I look upon *Canopus* as my right hand (she was his second astern in the Line of Battle); and I send you first to insure your being here to help to beat them.

These words remained etched in Francis' memory and forty years later he sent a verbatim account of the exchange to Sir Harris Nicolas for his edition of Nelson's *Despatches and Letters* published in 1844-46.[62] For Louis, not Nelson, was proved right. As Francis feared, the enemy did 'come out' and the *Canopus* missed the battle, losing 'all share in the glory of a day, which surpasses all which ever went before'.[63]

The careful record that Francis kept of these events is contained in a long serial letter to Mary Gibson. It was begun on 15 October, with the *Canopus* at sea off Gibralter and completed in Cadiz Bay three weeks later, amidst the wreckage of the French and Spanish Fleets. For the historical record, it is a document of the first importance, establishing precisely what it meant to a naval officer to miss a great victory at sea and at what cost to his fortune and career. And, at a personal level, it reveals Francis' emotional vulnerability, a human frailty shown nowhere else in his letters and personal papers.*

The letter opens evenly, reporting in a 'methodical' way (Francis' word) the events of the twelve days since leaving Nelson on 3 October – the contrary winds delaying the journey,** the loading of supplies, the watering,+ dining with the Governor of Gibralter and a performance of *Othello* by officers of the garrison, which he and Admiral Louis quit at the end of the first act. Soon, however, anxiety breaks through at the prospect of missing the battle, with the consequent loss of honour and reward: 'having borne our share in a

---

* For the text of this letter, in preference to the version printed in *Sailor Brothers*, I have used a more accurate transcript in the possession of Mr Alwyn Austen.

** According to Francis' letter, 2 October. But the *Victory's* log gives 6 p.m., 3rd October.

+ The Log Book of the *Canopus* records that at Tetuan and Gibralter they took on board provisions for four months, including cattle, fodder, water and onions (NMM, MS AUS/2B).

tedious chase and anxious blockade, it would be mortifying indeed to find ourselves at last thrown out of any share of credit or emolument which would result from an action'.

Three days later, on 18 October, Francis writes in low spirits, now escorting a Malta-bound convoy from Cadiz, putting 'us compleatly out of the way, in case the Enemy should make an attempt to get to sea, which is by no means improbable, if he knows Lord Nelson's force is weakened by the detachment of so many ships'

These fears proved all too real. From Spanish intelligence, Villeneuve learned of the six ships-of-the-line missing from Nelson's fleet and decided to break the blockade.* On 19 October, the enemy's preparations for sailing were spotted and Nelson sent after Louis a sloop with orders for his immediate return. But by this time the *Canopus* was some way eastwards into the Mediterranean, and the orders reached Louis only on 21 October. Francis takes up his letter again at this point:

> We have just bid adieu to the Convoy without attending them quite so far as was originally intended, having this day received intelligence by a vessel dispatched in pursuit of us that on Saturday, the 19th. The enemy's Fleet was actually under way and coming out of Cadiz; Our situation is a peculiarly unpleasant and disastrous one for if they escape Lord Nelson's vigilance and get into the Mediterranean, which is not very likely, we shall be obliged with our small force to keep out of their way, and on the other hand should an action take place it must be decided before we could possibly get down even were the wind fair, which at present it is not. As I have no doubt but the event would be highly honorable to our arms, and be at the same time productive of some good Prizes, I shall have to lament our absence on such an occasion on a double account, the loss of pecuniary advantage as well as professional credit. And after having been so many months in peril of constant and unremitting fag, to be at last out by a parcel of folk just come from their homes, where some of them were sitting at their ease the greater part of *last* war, and the whole of *this*, till just now, is particularly hard and annoying.**

On 26 October came the first news of Trafalgar. It was brought to the *Canopus* – trapped by Westerly gales and still off Tetuan – by Commander Peter Parker in the *Weazle* (18), a schooner attached to the inshore reconnaissance Squadron at Cadiz. The Log Book of the *Canopus* notes his time of arrival at 12.15 a.m., the news of victory 'alas! dearly purchased'- and ends, public-spiritedly, with rousing words for the ship's company, 'May those he has left behind him in the service strive to imitate so bright an example!!!'[64]

* A second factor, wholly outside Francis' knowledge, was that Villeneuve was to be replaced as Fleet commander and, learning of this, was intent on setting to sea before the order got to him.

** This refers to the news received a few days earlier that Nelson's Fleet had been reinforced by the arrival of five men-of-war from England.

A day later, with the *Canopus* anchored off Tetuan, Francis returns to his letter. Towards Nelson, the simple expression of his feelings rings true; and his judgement of Nelson's gifts as a leader is sound, if stilted. About his own sense of personal misfortune he writes unashamedly:

> You perhaps may not feel this quite so forcibly as I do, and in your satisfaction at my having avoided the danger of battle, may not much regret my losing the credit of having contributed to gain a Victory; not so, myself; I do not profess to like fighting for its own sake, but if there have been an action with the combined Fleets, I shall ever consider the day on which I sailed from the Squadron as the most inauspicious one of my life.
>
> Alas! my dearest Mary, all my fears are but too fully justified. The Fleets have met and after a very severe contest, a most decisive Victory has been gained by the English 27 over the Enemy's 33* – Seventeen of their Ships are taken and one is burnt, but I am truly sorry to add that this splendid affair has cost us many lives, and amongst them a most invaluable one to the Nation, that of our gallant and ever to be regretted Commander-in-Chief, Lord Nelson, who was mortally wounded by a Musket shot, and only lived long enough to know his Fleet was successful. In a public point of view, I consider his loss as the greatest which could have occurred, nor do I hesitate to say there is not an Admiral on the list so eminently calculated for the command of a Fleet as he was; I never heard of his equal, nor do I expect again to see such a man – to the soundest judgement he united prompt decision, and speedy execution of his plans and he possessed in a superior degree the happy talent of making every class of persons pleased with their situation and eager to exert themselves in forwarding the public service. As a national benefit, I cannot but rejoice that our arms have been once again successful, but at the same time I cannot help feeling how very unfortunate we have been to be away at such a moment, and by a fatal combination of unfortunate though unavoidable events to lose all share in the glory of a day, which surpasses all which ever went before, is what I cannot think of with any degree of patience, but as I cannot write on that subject without complaining, I will drop it for the present till time and reflection have reconciled me a little more to what I know is now inevitable.

Four days later, on 31 October, having passed the Straits of Gibralter, the *Canopus* is keeping watch off Cadiz. Francis reports all he knows of the battle and its aftermath, with the losses on both sides, and Vice-Admiral Collingwood now in command of the remains of Nelson's Fleet. Then nagging bitterness breaks in and Francis returns to his own predicament:

---

* For Francis, this figure was more than a mere statistic. During September, when Louis' Squadron had been placed in the forward line of the close blockade, the log of the *Canopus* records Francis' eye-witness account of the Combined Fleet in Cadiz harbour: 'Their whole force consisted of thirty-three sail of the line and five frigates', all but two 'apparently quite ready for sea'; and 'Of the ships of the line seventeen were French and sixteen Spanish, of which last two were three-deckers' (with upwards of 100 guns) (*Sailor Brothers*, p. 147–48).

By the death of Lord Nelson I have again lost all chance of a Frigate, I had asked his Lordship to appoint me to one when he had an opportunity, and though I had no positive promise from him, I have reason to believe he would have attended to my wishes. Of Admiral Collingwood I do not know enough to allow of my making a similar request and not having been in the Action I have no claims of service to urge in support of my wishes. I must therefore remain in the Canopus, though on many accounts I am more than anxious to get into a Frigate.*

Just as Francis says, having missed the 'Action', he has no 'claims of service' on which to argue his case; and with Admiral Collingwood, the new Fleet commander – a reserved and somewhat unapproachable man – he has no standing. So it was that Francis remained stuck on the *Canopus,* a well-designed vessel (captured from the French at the Battle of the Nile in 1798) but now slow and lumbering and badly in need of a refit. In the coming months, she carried him out to the West Indies in pursuit of the French Squadron from Rochefort, leading to the Battle of St Domingo in February 1806, a victory which answered his hopes in returning him to 'Old England. Oh, how my heart throbs at the idea!" he wrote to Mary Gibson.[65] For his part in the action Francis was awarded a Captain's small gold medal** and a memorial vase by the Patriotic Society of Lloyd's.[66] Along with his brother officers, he also received the thanks of both Houses of Parliament. When he had first taken command of the *Canopus,* a year before, his brother James had sent him good wishes: 'May Health, Success & Honour attend you'.[67] St Domingo brought him a measure of 'Success & Honour', together with a modest share of prize-money. But the great prize, the longed-for command of a frigate, remained as elusive as ever.

To this train of events, there is a strange postscript. Unknown to Francis, Nelson had acted on the application he sent in on 28 September and had made a positive recommendation to the First Lord,[68] who had duly instructed Collingwood that Francis should be given a 40-gun frigate, the *Acasta:*

Admiralty 7th November 1805

Sir, - In any arrangement which the late events may give rise to, I shall be glad if Captain Austen, now in the Canopus, could be put into the Acasta which will be vacant by the removal of Captain Dunn into Sir John Duckworth's flag-ship. I

---

* Francis Austen was not alone in viewing Nelson's death as a personal setback. See this extract from a letter of Captain Thomas Fremantle, of the *Neptune* (98), who took part in the Trafalgar action. Writing to his wife on 28 October 1805 'off Cadiz', he believes he has 'gained considerable credit'. Nonetheless, 'The loss of Nelson is a death blow to my future prospects here, he knew well how to appreciate Abilities and Zeal, and I am aware that I shall never cease to lament his loss whilst I live' (Fremantle, 1940, iii. 221).

** See Appendix 3: Commemorative Gold and Lesser Medals.

shall send you a list of such other officers as I am desirous of having brought forward into particular ships as soon as the same can be prepared.

I am . . .
Barham[69]

Evidently Barham felt that Nelson's wishes in this matter should be respected and that ahead of any other promotions and appointments arising from Trafalgar Captain Austen's command of the *Acasta* should be singled out and made a first priority for Collingwood's attention. But circumstances – in this case, the vagaries of communication and the pressure of events – worked against Francis yet again. Duckworth was totally unaware of Barham's order, having left Plymouth for Cadiz on 2 November, not in the *Acasta*, as was planned, but in the *Superb* (74) with Richard Keats as his Flag-Captain. Reaching Cadiz on 15 November, he had little time with Collingwood who set sail for Carthagena as soon as Duckworth, his new second-in-command, arrived. Duckworth was then joined by Dunn in the *Acasta* just before he left in pursuit of a French Squadron. In this hurried sequence, no opportunity arose to remove Dunn into the *Superb* as there was no vessel suitable for Keats. Hence Nelson's intentions were frustrated and Barham's order negated. Dunn remained in the *Acasta* and Francis in the *Canopus* with Louis, now Duckworth's Second-in-Command, and so they remained until after the Battle of St Domingo.

What we see in the Trafalgar episode and its aftermath are the accidents and uncertainties of patronage and circumstances. Had Nelson survived, or the *Canopus* returned in time, or Barham's orders been followed, Francis' career would have taken a different direction. As it was, on his return from St Domingo at the end of April 1806, he was to remain in England without an appointment for another twelve months. During this time, Moira's help was called upon again, early in 1807. In February, Jane wrote to Cassandra that 'as the 1st Lord [Thomas Grenville] after promising Ld Moira that Capt. A. should have the first good Frigate that was vacant, has since given away two or three fine ones, he has no particular reason to expect an appointment now.'[70]

In fact, an appointment came only a month later; not, however, to a 'good frigate' but to the *St Albans* (64) in which Francis was to serve for three and a half years, mainly in long-distance convoying to St Helena, the Cape and China. The most tedious of duties and low in prestige, it was rewarding financially as the trading companies, the East India Company in particular, found it politic to be generous in acknowledging naval protection. Francis was conscientious and well thought of by the ships under his care, as he noted in his Memoir:

The captains of the eight ships he convoyed, in a letter expressive of their sense of his gentleman-like conduct to themselves as well as his attention to the safety of the convoy requested his acceptance of a piece of plate as a testimony of their satisfaction and best wishes.[71]

On his side, Francis was appreciative of their generosity in helping the laggards and he wrote to the Company directors, commending 'the cheerfulness and alacrity with which they repeatedly towed for many successive days some heavy sailing ships of the convoy, a service always disagreeable, and often dangerous'.[72] The slowest of the Indiamen was the *Retreat* and he picked out her Captain for particular praise:

> I cannot conclude without observing that the indefatigable attention of Captain Hay of the *Retreat*, in availing himself of every opportunity to get ahead, and his uncommon exertions in carrying a great press of sail both night and day, which the wretched sailing of his ship, when not in tow, rendered necessary, was highly meritorious, and I think it my duty to recommend him to the notice of the Court of Directors as an officer deserving a better command.[73]

The East India Company signified its appreciation of Francis' concern for their vessels, in January 1808 voting him two hundred guineas 'for care and attention' in escorting a convoy of thirteen vessels from St Helena to England, 400 guineas for further escorting, and 500 guineas 'in anticipation' of his convoying out to China in April 1809.[74] If Francis was conscientious in his convoying, he also had a sense of what was due to him and was prepared to argue for it. An instance of this came in 1810, when he delivered to the Company's Agent at Deal '93 Chests of Treasure said to contain 470,000 Dollars or Bullion to that amount', a cargo he brought from China to Madras and onwards to England via St Helena, escorting a convoy of thirteen Company ships. For these services, the Company proposed to pay £525 for the convoying and freight money of £1177. Francis was happy with the first payment but asked £2 per cent 'upon the Treasure brought home . . . instead of the sum mentioned', a claim which the Company met, the figure increased to £1500, a sum that Francis finally accepted.[75]

After the *St Albans*, Francis had two further commands, as Flag-Captain to Gambier, in the *Caledonia* (120), the Flagship of the Home Fleet, and his last command of the war, the *Elephant* (74) from July 1811 until May 1814.

No doubt it was Gambier's continuing patronage that kept Francis at sea over these years. Command of the *St Albans* he resigned in September 1810, wishing to have some time at home with his growing family before joining the *Caledonia* in December. But this appointment was short-lived. The *Caledonia* was an enviable vessel, the Navy's first and most successful three-decker of 120 guns. Built in 1808, she was the pride of the Navy, said to be 'weatherly' and 'faultless'.[76] It was no secret that other senior officers had their eyes on her; and, in the Spring of 1811, she was taken from Gambier, commanding the Home Fleet and assigned to Admiral Pellew, who arrived to raise his flag as Commander-in-Chief of the Mediterranean Fleet, the Navy's key command. At once, he turned it into a 'family ship'*– the Navy's term. It was a cosy arrangement. The Admiral brought with him his son-in-law as Flag-Captain and his brother as Captain of the Fleet (a kind of Chief-of-Staff or Adjutant-General. With the rank and pay of a Rear-Admiral, he was responsible for the issue of public orders, the distribution of stores and the handling of all returns and official papers).

This unwelcome news reached the Austens rapidly, via their trusty Admiralty source, Mr Daysh. At the time, Jane was staying in London with Henry, who was finding out more, and she quickly wrote to Cassandra at Godmersham:

> Saturday. – Frank is superseded in the Caledonia. Henry brought us this news yesterday from Mr Daysh – & he heard at the same time that Charles may be in England in the course of a month.– Sir Edwd Pellew succeeds Lord Gambier in his command, & some Captain of his succeeds Frank; & I beleive the order is already gone out. Henry means to enquire farther to day; – he wrote to Mary on the occasion. – This is something to think of. – Henry is convinced that he will have the offer of something else, but does not think it will be at all incumbent on him to accept it; & then follows, what will he do? & where will he live?[77]

This episode illustrates the drawbacks of Flag-Captaincy. Not only was it an appointment without independence, it was also without security, since it was an appointment within the Admiral's 'following', linked to his command and when that changed (as in Gambier's case it did), the Flag-Captaincy went with it – leaving Francis, after only five months, high and dry, with the unexpected problem of what to 'do' and where to 'live'. This upset was a sufficient signal that Pellew's interest was in the ascendant – he was valued as the finest Admiral in the Fleet – and Gambier's on the wane, now that his own two

---

* To appoint members of one's own family was a perk of office which ran on unchecked for a further thirty years. Tolerance for this near-abuse wore thin. An internal memorandum of 1 January 1845 by John Barrow, Second Secretary to the Admiralty, observed that 'much jealousy and inconvenience to the Service has almost invariably arisen from . . . "family ships"' (Hattendorf, 1993, p. 707) and the Admiralty directive issued to the Service prescribed strict limits to this custom:

In the future it is decided that a flag officer elected for a command shall only be permitted to nominate one commissioned officer to his flagship in addition to his flag lieutenant, from his immediate family (viz. sons, grandsons and brothers) and that officer not to be captain or commander. (PRO. ADM 12/447, 1 January 1845)

When they reached Flag rank, both Francis and Charles made good use of their patronage rights on behalf of their own families (see Appendix 5).

patrons were gone – Pitt, dead in 1806 and his uncle, Lord Barham, in retirement – and his recent spells as First Naval Lord on the Admiralty Board
(1804-06 and 1807-08) were at an end.[78] Gambier's departure was a blow, for
in his second spell, the First Lord, Lord Mulgrave, a soldier-politician, had
left him with the effective power and authority, in Collingwood's words, 'the
direction and all the patronage of the navy.'[79]

It was a change of fortune which the Austens must have watched with
dismay. Moreover, as the war with Napoleon was increasingly fought out on
the mainland of Europe, while the Navy's diplomatic and economic activities
increased, its combative role was in decline and the opportunities for 'pecuniary advantage' and 'professional credit' that Francis had missed at Trafalgar
were now few and far between.

By the end of the war, several former students from Francis' time at
Portsmouth had reached Flag rank. It was a galling reminder that despite a
strong start – he was appointed First Lieutenant* on no fewer than six out of
the first ten ships in which he served as an officer – his own promotion was
dishearteningly slow. Thomas Byam Martin, who arrived at the Academy only
eight months before him, had become a Rear-Admiral of the Blue in August
1811 and was now a Rear-Admiral of the Red. Francis Gardner, who arrived
two months after Francis, had become a Rear-Admiral of the Blue in August
1812 and was now a Rear-Admiral of the White. Henry Hotham, who arrived a
few months after Francis had left, was already a Rear-Admiral of the White.
And George Byng, who came even later, eighteen months after Francis, was
now a Rear-Admiral of the Blue – the rank Francis was to reach only in 1830.
Their achievement was a consequence of seniority on the Captain's list. While
it took Francis over seven years to rise from Lieutenant to Captain, by May
1800, Martin got there in three years, by November 1793; Gardner in two and
three quarter years, by May 1794; Hotham, moving at unparalleled speed, in
five and a half months, by January 1795; and Byng in just under five years, by
June 1795. And this same pattern – a rise from Lieutenant to Captain in a
period of one, two or three years – is also found on a much larger scale for that
majority of officers who took the standard route, not the Academy, but
straight to sea as young gentlemen, the element common to both groups being
strong and effective patronage. A particularly wounding example was that of
John Whitby. Exactly the same age as Francis, he sailed as a fellow-
Midshipman in Cornwallis's Squadron in 1789. In four years, aged nineteen,
Whitby had risen to become Captain of the *Minerva*, the Squadron Flagship, a

---

*The First Lieutenant ran the administration of a ship, acted as the Captain's eyes and ears, visiting
the quarters of the crew, the warrant officers, the midshipmen and the various ship's offices and
areas, and was expected to know how everything was running; and he acted as the Captain's deputy
or replacement in his absence, injury or death in action.

promotion Francis witnessed as he was then serving in the vessel as a Lieutenant. There was no merit in the case. One of the crew noted that Whitby 'was too young', 'could work the ship well, but that was all'.[80] However, these modest abilities were no handicap. His patrons were Vice-Admiral Sir John Jervis (to whom he was related) and Cornwallis himself, both of whom had to step in to protect Whitby when the harshness of his discipline drove his crews to the point of mutiny. According to a member of the *Minerva*'s crew, when there was a spate of punishment for the sailors' swearing, Cornwallis instructed him never to 'flog a man again without his permission'.[81]*

Those Portsmouth students who were successful enjoyed equally potent interest, whether naval or political. Thomas Martin's father was the Academy Governor and Dockyard Commissioner and in 1790, months before the youngster was commissioned, became Comptroller of the Navy and MP for Southampton; and the boy's patron was his first Captain, the Duke of Clarence, the future William IV. Gardner's progress was the work of his father, Admiral Sir Alan Gardner. Hotham's uncle was Admiral Sir William Hotham, Commander-in-Chief in the Mediterranean, where the youngster's meteoric rise was engineered. And Byng, the eldest son of Viscount Torrington, the scion of a famous naval line, enjoyed the active and powerful support of William Henry Cavendish Bentinck, 3rd Duke of Portland, a political grandee who formed the Tory Ministry of 1807-09.

Yet, on the face of it, Francis too was well supported. After the death of Sir Henry Martin in August 1794, Gambier, soon to be a member of the Admiralty Board, took over as his 'patron' and 'friend' at the very time when the young Lieutenant was ready for promotion. What, then, went wrong? Why was Francis unable to keep up with his peers? One drawback may have been his earlier service in the East Indies under Cornwallis. Vacancies in a small Squadron in peacetime were rare. As a consequence, his commission as a Lieutenant, in December 1792, came relatively late – that is in comparision with Martin, Gardner and Byng, all of whom enjoyed more than eighteen months' seniority over Francis.

A more likely weakness seems to have been Gambier himself, judging from his fruitless activity in moving Francis from ship to ship in 1795-96. These attempts to get his protégé a post for speedy promotion led nowhere and Francis' arrival on the *Prince George* found him placed lower in the order of Lieutenants than his entitlement by seniority, a real slap in the face for the young officer and disparaging of his patron. By this time, Francis must have

---

* Whitby's small claim to a place in history is as the messenger who brought the news of Nelson's death to Emma Hamilton. He was sent by Sir Andrew Hamond, Comptroller of the Navy. He also brought the news to members of Nelson's family. Whitby's obituary notice in the *Naval Chronicle* (January-June 1806), xv. 352) brings out the closeness of his friendship with Cornwallis.

realized the consequence of having a patron who was widely disliked, the root of the problem lying in Gambier's religiosity and its impact on the ships he commanded. It was not that there was any objection to religion as such. The sailors admired Cornwallis as 'a religious and good man' as much as for his seamanship and humanity.[82] Hymns and prayers were a natural comfort in facing the perils of war and the dangers of the sea, and a solace for the injured and dying. Sunday church services, 'a marked eccentricity in the Navy of the 1750's',[83] became a regular feature of shipboard life and when there was no Chaplain on board, the ship's Captain would conduct them. Sermons provided an occasion for urging obedience and promoting the virtues of sobriety, clean-living and clean speech as duties to God as well as obligations of the ship's discipline. Nelson, respected and loved by his officers and men, was famous throughout the Fleet as a God-fearing Christian. He was ready to lead his ships in prayer and (one seaman recalls) assembled his crews 'in Nelsonian style . . . to return thanks to Almighty God, the giver of all victory'.[84] On the practical front, Nelson was rare among naval commanders in requesting the Society for the Propagation of Christian Knowledge to deliver consignments of Bibles and Prayer Books to his ships. For this he was known as 'the bible Admiral', a nickname inherited by Gambier[85]– but with a sting, for unlike Nelson, Gambier was known as a 'blue-light', the sailors' derisive term for the sanctimonious. He was given other names, equally descriptive: 'Preaching Jemmy' and 'Dismal Jimmie'; and the vessels he commanded were known as 'praying' ships.

All this reflected Gambier's Evangelical upbringing with his uncle and aunt, Sir Charles and Lady Middleton, both of whom were leading figures in the group around Hannah More and Wilberforce actively campaigning on issues of slavery, poverty, drink, female education and other religious and humanitarian causes of the day. The letters of Hannah More show the importance she attached to having, in Middleton/Barham, a First Lord who 'Prays for the success of his measures'.[86]

Gambier's offence, as it was seen, was not Evangelicalism as such but his pious determination to impose a narrow code upon unwilling crews. It was not only that the seamen were hectored in sermons and at Gambier-led psalm-singing and prayer meetings, and that they had tracts and hymn-books forced upon them. With the preaching of temperance there was intrusion into their customary rights and further resentment when he tried to interfere with their other pleasures, such as they were. For example, at the beginning of the war, Gambier ordered all the women on board the *Defence* (74) – these were the 'doxies' (as the sailors called the prostitutes who flocked daily to the ship while it lay in port) – to show their marriage lines, a requirement which sent the women packing and 'created a very unpleasant feeling among the tars'.[87] As for the officers, it was said that with Gambier in command, the road to promotion was not by way of professional merit but along the narrow path of Evangelicalism and all that followed in terms of sobriety, decency of language and religious observance.

If it was Gambier's unpopularity which held Francis back during the 1790s, this may also have reduced his chances of getting a 'good' frigate in the later stages of the war. On the religious front, there were whisperings of an Evangelical cell at the Admiralty around the Gambier-Middleton (Barham) axis. Upon Barham's entering the Admiralty as First Lord in April 1805, the MP Thomas Creevey announced to a friend that Pitt had made the appointment of 'a superannuated Methodist* at the head of the Admiralty, in order to catch the votes of Wilberforce and Co. now and then.'[88] Three years later, the *Monthly Repository*, a keen-eyed Unitarian journal surveyed the great institutions and   found Evangelicals everywhere: thriving 'at the Bank', bearing sway at 'India-house', counting votes 'in parliament', with 'a footing in the Royal Palace', having successfully 'invaded the Navy'.[89]

The anti-Gambier camp was further strengthened in 1809 by what was known as the Basque and Aix Roads affair. There were two strands to this. The first involved Gambier's clash with Rear-Admiral Eliab Harvey, his second-in-command. Harvey volunteered to direct the assault on a powerful French Squadron sheltering in Aix Roads, off Rochefort in the Bay of Biscay. However, the Admiralty had already selected Lord Cochrane, a relatively junior Post Captain, of less than eight years standing, to carry out the fireship attack, and it was left to Gambier to explain to Harvey on the spot that the operation had already been placed in Cochrane's hands. Deeply offended, Harvey threatened to strike his flag and resign his commission, and went on the criticise Gambier's conduct as commander, threatening to impeach him for bad management of the Channel Fleet. According to Gambier's evidence at the subsequent Court Martial, Harvey made these threats 'in the most violent and disrespectful manner . . . with insulting gestures and language' and continued his noisy complaints publicly, on the Quarter Deck, according to

---

* Not a member of the true Methodist society of the Wesleys but a loaded term thrown insultingly at any pious, active and reforming Christian, in particular the Anglican Evangelicals. This latter group were seen as fanatics alongside the orthodox Anglicans distinguished for their sober conservatism and rational orthodoxy of religion. This usage is perfectly illustrated in *Mansfield Park*: Edmund Bertram, with his conscientious resolutions on carrying out his duty as a resident parish priest, is moving in an Evangelical direction, at a time when around 60 per cent of incumbents were non-resident. After hearing him hold forth disapprovingly on her brother's elopement with Maria Bertram (now Mrs Rushworth), Mary Crawford congratulates him, ironically, on his 'sermon . . . At this rate, you will soon reform everybody at Mansfield and Thornton Lacey; and when I hear of you next, it may be as a celebrated preacher in some great society of Methodists, or as a missionary into foreign parts' (p. 458). Part of the insult here is in Methodism's character as a working-class movement. Around 80 per cent of its membership were artisans, labourers, colliers, miners, etc.

Captain Bedford, in the presence of not less than thirty of the officers and crew. Bedford also reported that Harvey spoke of Gambier's 'Methodistical, Jesuitical conduct'; and, according to Cochrane, Harvey remarked sarcastically that 'He was no canting Methodist, no hypocrite, nor a psalm-singer. I do not cheat old women out of their estates by hypocrisy and canting'.[90] Charged with 'imputing disrespect to his superior officer',[91] Harvey did not dispute the evidence against him and apologised. He was sentenced 'To be dismissed his Majesty's Service'. However, despite the gravity of his offence, the sympathies of the Service were with him, not with Gambier, for one was a battle-scarred hero of Trafalgar, the other, a 'dry land' Admiral, seldom at sea. For Harvey had sailed alongside the *Victory*, his ship the famous Fighting *Temeraire* (98) so shot up that it was rendered incapable of carrying any sail, its tally of dead forty-seven, of wounded seventy-six. Of the *Temeraire*'s 'most noble and distinguished' part in the battle, Collingwood wrote to Harvey, 'Nothing could be finer. I have not words in which I can sufficiently express my admiration of it'.[92] Harvey was duly granted a place of honour at Nelson's state funeral, standing at the foot of the bier.

These were the circumstances that brought Gambier little credit and the question of Harvey's past record entered into the Court Martial itself. At the time of Trafalgar, Gambier was in office as First Naval Lord at the Admiralty (his term ran from 15 May 1804 to 9 February 1806) and Harvey testified that, following the battle, Gambier 'had received him very coldly'[93] and that he had felt 'neglected for his former services'.[94] As Harvey painted the picture, it was the case of a patriot ill-rewarded. A veteran of Trafalgar could not be permitted to linger in disgrace and although Harvey was never to go to sea again, eight months after the sentence of dismissal he was reinstated in his full rank.*

The second strand inimical to Gambier was Cochrane's complaint that during the attack itself he received inadequate support from his Commander-in-Chief; and he let it be known that sitting as MP for Westminster he would oppose any Vote of Thanks to Gambier for the Basque Roads victory. Alerted to this, Gambier thought it politic to call for a Court Martial to clear his name. Cochrane had solid grounds for taking this stand. Gambier was well-known as a master of indecision and he regarded Cochrane's fireships as 'a horrible mode of warfare'.[95] According to Michael

---

* This was not a unique event. In 1811, Captain Lord William Fitzroy was sentenced 'to be dismissed from the command of his ship and struck off the list of the Royal Navy' for the offence of putting the Master of his ship in irons. But helped by the Prince Regent, Fitzroy gained the recommendation of the Admiralty Board for his reinstatement ('restoration' was the term) and ended up in 1855 as an Admiral of the White. The procedure for obtaining restoration was described in a letter to the *Naval Chronicle* presenting this as an instance of social injustice, since when the Master was tried on a charge of 'Contempt' for Fitzroy, his sentence of dismissal put restoration out of the question, since it carried the further condition that he be 'rendered incapable of service again as an officer' (xxvi. 397-98).

Lewis, this event caused 'a split in the Navy between "pro" and "anti-Gambiers".'[96] Although Gambier was vindicated at the subsequent Court Martial, a swung trial,* his reputation as a seaman was further dented and he already carried the opprobrium of only having served at sea for five and a half years in the period between his first commission as a Lieutenant in 1777 and his becoming a Rear-Admiral in 1795. To harp on this was unfair. In the earliest major engagement of the war, 1 June 1794, Gambier's ship, the *Defence* (74), had been the first to break the French line-of-battle and had taken a heavy battering. Howe had praised his gallantry and George III had wanted to reward him with a peerage.** But by 1809, it was a memory that had faded; and Gambier's disfavour came to a head in 1810 when George refused to accept his nomination by Perceval for the First Lordship – Perceval himself being an Evangelical Prime Minister. Well-informed, the King replied that Gambier's appointment 'would not be a popular one with the Navy, in which his professional abilities are not held in the highest estimation'.[97]

With this picture before us, we can readily understand why Francis should have looked to other 'friends' and why, in late 1806 or early 1807, he again sought the help of Moira, seemingly a powerful voice, since he was now in the Government as Master-General of the Ordnance, an appointment he had accepted on the understanding that his recommendations for honours and office should be attended to. But unknown to Francis, Moira's patronage was overstretched. Not only was he serving as a channel for applications from the Prince of Wales, but Moira's demands for his own candidates were, according to Aspinall, 'on a more extensive scale than his office and his seat in the Cabinet warranted.'[98] Not surprisingly, his 'interest' on behalf of Francis proved ineffective. As one biographer has put it, Moira 'was apter at promises than performances'.[99] Instead of a 'good Frigate', Francis was landed with the *St Albans* (64) with the mundane task of trooping and convoying.

If Francis felt overlooked, it was a sense of neglect and injustice that rankled for many years. In 1844, he wrote a short letter to O'Byrne, the editor of the forthcoming *Naval Biographical Dictionary*, updating his entry in Marshall's *Royal Naval Biography* and explaining his thirty years of idleness: 'That I have not served at Sea since 1814 is not from want of inclination or application, but have had no influence of a political or family description to back my pretensions'.[100]

Charles fared no better. He watched his contemporaries at the Naval College racing to their Captaincies: Thomas Brodie and Roger Curtis in four

---

* The President, Admiral Sir Roger Curtis, and Admiral William Young were both friends of Gambier, appointed by the Ministry to ensure that Cochrane's challenge would not succeed.

** Gambier's uncle, Sir Charles Middleton, then a member of the Admiralty Board, pointed out that it was unthinkable to ennoble a mere Post-Captain over the heads of the six untitled Flag-officers who also took part in the action.

years; Philip Broke in three and a half years; Duncumbe Bouverie in two and a half years; Charles Pierrepoint in one and three quarter years. His own advancement was on a different track. A Commander after seven years, it was another five and a quarter years before he reached the rank of Captain. Family had much to do with it. Pierrepoint was heir to the Viscountcy of Newark and the Earldom of Manvers; Curtis was the eldest son of Admiral Sir Roger Curtis; Bouverie's elder brother, William, was a Whig politician, MP and 3rd Earl of Radnor; Broke came from an old and well-connected family of better pedigree than Sir Walter Elliot could ever lay claim to. And the *Endymion* (44), in which Charles served as First Lieutenant from May 1803 to Autumn 1805, was commanded by the Hon. Charles Paget, fifth son of the Earl of Uxbridge, whose rise from Lieutenant to Captain was accomplished in the space of ten months. That Charles was left behind comes as no surprise. Thanks to Gambier, he moved from the *Scorpion* in 1795. But no promotion came his way. His real patron, Sir Thomas Williams, only reached Flag rank in 1809 and was in no position to help Charles until his appointment as Commander-in-Chief at the Nore in 1811. He then took Charles into the *Namur* as his Flag Captain, a modest appointment but the best he could do.

It is inconceivable that these setbacks and disappointments were not discussed openly within the family circle. The naval thread in Jane's letters to Cassandra makes it clear that the sisters were knowledgeable in these matters of appointment and promotion, and the part that patronage and interest played in advancing, or failing to advance their brothers' careers. In this sense, it was a highly political household, fired by Mr Austen's *nous*, informed by the sailor brothers themselves, and later enlarged with the news and views that came in from Henry Austen's growing network of naval and military contacts. But unseen, within the circle of the family and their friends, was a private world of communication between the sisters. Conducted by Jane – we know nothing of Cassandra's side – it was the vision of a humorist, treating news as news, respecting its consequences yet devouring it as material for the writer's art, even when it touched the fortunes and misfortunes of the sailor brothers. We see this in January 1801. On the first day of the new year, the Act of Union of Great Britain and Ireland became law. It was celebrated by the Navy with a round of promotions; and, with the commissioning of additional ships-of-the-line, came fresh appointments too. At this moment, Frances was without a ship, having been superseded in his command of the *Peterel*, and was still making his way slowly back to England from the Eastern Mediterranean. Jane writes of these matters to Cassandra:

What a surprise to him it must have been on the 20th of Oct:ʳ to be visited, collar'd

& thrust out of the Petterell by Capt:ⁿ Inglis! – He kindly passes over the poignancy of his feelings in quitting his Ship, his Officers & his Men. – What a pity it is that he should not be in England at the time of this promotion, because he certainly would have had an appointment! – so everybody says, & therefore it must be right for me to say it too. – Had he been really here, the certainty of the appointment I dare say would not have been half so great – but as it could not be brought to the proof, his absence will be always a lucky source of regret.[101]

Francis' situation is described with sympathy and understanding – but sympathy edged with wry amusement and playful mockery, a joke that could be shared with Cassandra alone and shown to no-one else, least of all to Francis himself.

The story of William Price's commission in *Mansfield Park* is treated here in Chapter Eight. However, there is a curious passage in the novel which could very well be a by-product of the disappointments of Francis and Charles and their complaints at this. It comes in Chapter Six of Volume III. William Price, having just been commissioned a Lieutenant, is keen to show himself at Mansfield in his new uniform,

> had not cruel custom prohibited its appearance except on duty. So the uniform remained at Portsmouth, and Edmund conjectured that before Fanny had any chance of seeing it, all its own freshness, and all the freshness of its wearer's feelings, must be worn away. It would be sunk into a badge of disgrace; for what can be more unbecoming, or more worthless, than the uniform of a lieutenant, who has been a lieutenant a year or two, and sees others made commanders before him? So reasoned Edmund.[102]

Where does this 'conjecture' come from? It is credited to Edmund. But nothing in the novel suggests that Edmund has any knowledge of naval matters or insight upon the feelings of young officers. And there is no call for him to ventilate such an expression of bitterness or cynicism. Indeed, such feelings are wholly out of character. Edmund's cast of mind is in the very opposite direction. His speculations lead him to think the best of people and he is not the person to indulge in resentful fantasies. My own belief is that these reflections on the 'badge of disgrace', a uniform 'unbecoming' and 'worthless', are the author's own and originate in Jane Austen's recollection of her brothers' frustrations of long ago. Francis and Charles had both suffered that very indignity of being Lieutenants 'a year or two' and of being passed over and of seeing others of their generation 'made commanders' long before them.

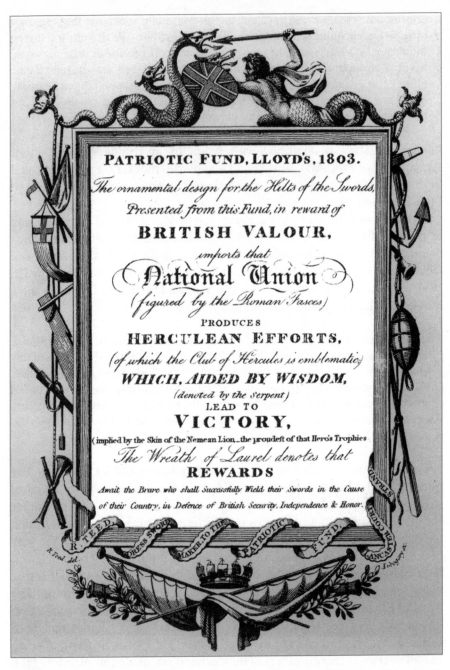

The label inside the lid of a Patriotic Fund sword-box explaining the classical motifs features in the decoration of the hilt and the 'REWARDS' which 'Await the Brave'. In Roman times, the laurel wreath sufficed. But in 1803, Lloyd's was ready to award trophies of high value, or their equivalent in cash, as preferred. (*By courtesy of Lloyd's of London*)

6

The Rewards of Success:
Prize Money, Honours and Promotion

'Your Profession has its' douceurs to recompense
for some of its' Privations'

Jane Austen to Francis, 3 July 1813

When Francis wrote to Mary Gibson complaining that he had missed the
'good Prizes', 'pecuniary advantage' and 'emolument', and the 'professional credit' of Trafalgar, he was enumerating the entitlements which
sailors felt to be their due. While they prayed to be preserved 'from the
dangers of the sea, and from the violence of the enemy', they also prayed
that they might 'return in safety to enjoy the blessings of the land, with the
fruits of our labours', in this instance, the 'fruits' of victory – a sentiment
which Jane Austen puts in the mouth of her prize-rich hero, Captain
Wentworth: 'I have been used to the gratification of believing myself to
earn every blessing that I enjoyed. I have valued myself on honourable toils
and just rewards.'[1]

The 'just rewards' of Trafalgar conveyed the gratitude of the nation.
Although only four out of the eighteen captured ships survived the storm
that followed the Battle, the others having escaped or sunk, as Collingwood
overruled Nelson's order that all captured vessels should be anchored,
nonetheless, exceptionally, Parliament voted prize-money of £320,000 to be
distributed round the Fleet. Added to the prize-money, this brought each
Captain over £3300, with lesser sums to the lower ranks. As was customary
for a major victory, honours were bestowed upon the Flag-officers and
Captains, and a representative body of junior officers received promotion,
the scale and level scrupulously graduated in accordance with Nelson's
'worth, with the importance of the achievement which he had died consum-
mating' (as William James expressed it in the *Naval History* of 1826),[2] and
with the recipients' rank and responsibility. All the Flag-officers and
Captains received commemorative gold medals. These were highly regarded
because sparingly awarded. Only five actions prior to Trafalgar had been
deemed of sufficient merit to justify their award.* Moreover, they were a

recognition of merit uncontaminated by patronage or interest (see Appendix 3).

Collingwood, Nelson's Second-in-Command, was promoted from Vice-Admiral of the Blue to the Red and created a Baron, with a grant of £2000 a year, to be continued after his death as a pension of £1000 to his widow and £500 a year to each of his two daughters.** The Third-in-Command, the Earl of Northesk, was promoted from Rear-Admiral of the White to the Red; and, already a peer, Northesk was honoured with the Order of the Bath, by far the most prized of the orders of Knighthood, since it was restricted in number and reserved for the military as a recognition of valour and success.[+] Hardy, Nelson's Flag-Captain, was made a Baronet. In the system of 'general promotions' following a major victory, chosen Lieutenants were promoted

---

* In all, there were eighteen Gold Medal actions for the entire period of the war:

> Lord Howe's victory, 1 June 1794.
> Battle of Cape St Vincent, 14 February 1797.
> Battle of Camperdown, 11 October 1797.
> Battle of the Nile, 1 August 1798.
> Recapture of the *Hermione*, 25 October 1799.
> Battle of Trafalgar, 21 October 1805.
> Sir Richard Strachan's victory, 4 November 1805.
> Battle of San Domingo, 6 February 1806.
> Brisbane's capture of Curaçoa, 1 January 1807.
> Capture of the *Thétis* by the *Amethyst*, 10 November 1808.
> Capture of the *Badere Zaffer* by the *Seahorse*, 6 July 1808.
> Capture of the *Furieuse* by the *Bonne Citoyenne*, 6 July 1809.
> Capture of Banda Neira, 9 August 1810.
> Hoste's victory off Lissa, 13 March 1811.
> Capture of the *Rivoli* by the *Victorious*, 22 February 1812.
> Capture of the *Chesapeake* by the *Shannon*, 1 June 1813.
> Capture of the *Etoile* by the *Hebrus*, 27 March 1814.
> Capture of the *President* by the *Endymion*, 15 January 1815.

** There was some uncertainty about how Collingwood was to be rewarded. See the Duke of Northumberland's sharp comment to Colonel McMahon (the Prince of Wales' Private Secretary), 10 November 1805: 'Pray what is to be done for Collingwood? Or is all his merit in the late victory to be drowned in the tears shed for Lord Nelson' (Aspinall, 1968, v. 275).

[+] Such was its kudos that after the Battle of St Vincent (1797), Nelson put in for a KB as his reward, rather than the Baronetcy which, as an untitled Commodore, leading a Squadron, he could expect. By a twist of fate, Nelson's KB insignia – a large decorative star upon a broad scarlet ribbon – provided a French sharp-shooter at Trafalgar with an unmistakable target. But the high prestige of the KB was dented in 1815, when the Order was opened up for the conferring of victory honours and divided into three classes. All surviving holders of the KB became Knight Grand Cross (GCB); those newly appointed could be made GCB or one of the lower grades: Knight Commander (KCB) or Companion (CB), the honour which Francis received at this time. Sir William Hoste, who commanded the *Amphion* at Trafalgar, complained at the wide distribution of the Order: 'Men who never saw a shot fired in real earnest: they obtained this Honour by *interest*, which being known, it lowered its value', whereas '*Medals for Service*' were worthy: 'no Medal could be obtained but for real service' (Farington *Diary*, 3 August 1816, xiv. 4883).

Commander or Captain, depending on their seniority, the size of the vessel in which they were serving and whether or not they had taken over command of their vessels during the course of the action. Similarly, representative Midshipmen were promoted Lieutenant: four from the *Victory*; three from Collingwood's ship, the *Royal Sovereign*; two from Northesk's, the *Britannia*; and one each from all the other ships-of-the-line and frigates. And the Lieutenant who brought Collingwood's despatches with news of the victory was made a Commander on his arrival in England.*

The greatest honours and rewards were reserved for the dead hero and were so designed that his name should be remembered down the generations. The Earldom customarily granted to a victorious Commander-in-Chief went to his brother William, who became Earl Nelson of Trafalgar and Merton. To ensure its survival, 'failing heirs male', the title could descend down the female line. It was also decreed that the successive holders of the title should use the name Nelson in perpetuity. As landed property was traditionally regarded as essential to the dignity and standing of a peerage and as William, a clergyman, was a man of humble means, to enable him to live up to the style of the Nelson peerage he was granted the enormous sum of £90,000 for the purchase of an estate with an annuity of £5000 for him and his successors. Further grants of £10,000, later increased to £15,000, were voted to each of his sisters and a pension of £2000 to the widowed Lady Nelson.

The scale of the honours and rewards showered upon the Nelson family was unprecedented. They were the desserts of a heroic drama, itself unprecedented. They memorialised a great naval hero – 'the greatest of our own, and of all former times', as Southey put it.[3] But we can also detect the alloy of politics. Pitt saw this as an opportunity to exploit the public mood, a chance for his Ministry to share in Nelson's hour of glory. The Duke of Northumberland, one of the Prince of Wales' circle, remarked on this to Colonel McMahon, 'I suppose Ministers hold up their heads again & talk big after this naval victory'.[4]

The Lloyd's Patriotic Fund was equally attentive to Nelson's family and the officers of the Fleet. Vases to the value of £500 went to the widowed Lady Nelson and the new Earl, and to Collingwood; a £300 vase to Northesk; £100

---

* The number and level of such promotions was watched and debated jealously throughout the service. An amusing instance involved Thomas Cochrane. Commanding a brig, the *Speedy* (14), in 1801, in an action of 'extreme brilliance', he captured a Spanish frigate of 32 guns. As Laughton records it, Cochrane's own promotion to post rank came 'after a very unusual delay . . . but his request for the promotion of Mr Parker, the lieutenant of the *Speedy*, was met with the reply from Lord St Vincent, then first lord of the Admiralty, that the small number of men killed on board the *Speedy* did not warrant the application . . . Cochrane had the impudence to answer that there were more casualties on board the *Speedy* in this action than there were on board the *Victory* at St Vincent, for which his lordship had been made an earl and his first captain a Knight' (*DNB*, 1887, xi. 166).

swords to the surviving Captains and Commanders; cash sums of £100 to Lieutenants, Captains of Marines and other officers 'severely wounded'; £50 to those 'slightly wounded'; and to petty officers, £40 to those 'severely wounded' and £25 to the 'slightly wounded'.[5]

This elaborate tariff of honours, promotion, pensions, trophies and cash payments was a measured response to the magnitude of the victory and the heroism of the hour; and Francis would have been able to judge the precise order of 'professional credit', 'emolument' and 'pecuniary advantage' to which both he and Rear-Admiral Louis would have been entitled had the *Canopus* occupied its designated position in the Order of Battle. What made this loss all the more difficult to bear was the knowledge, confirmed with the passing of the years, that of all the great naval successes, Trafalgar was honoured as the supreme and decisive victory, its veterans marked out and revered. To have been 'One of Nelson's Captains' at Trafalgar was a distinction beyond gift, purchase or patronage.

Moreover, Francis could have made good use of the money that followed Trafalgar. Since 1804 he had been engaged to Mary Gibson and according to Jane, in August 1805, was 'in a great hurry to be married',[6] a step she encouraged him to take. Lack of funds, however, held him back.*

In part, this was a consequence of his father's death in January 1805. The widowed Mrs Austen and her two daughters were left with a combined income of only £210 a year. So Henry, the businessman of the family, stepped in at once, arranging with James and Edward that together the three of them would contribute a further annual sum of £200. Telling Francis of these arrangements on 27 January (the day after their father's burial), Henry explained that as this income of 'a good 400 pounds per ann' was sufficient there was no need to take up Francis' offer of £100 a year; nor indeed for Francis to 'abridge' himself 'of any part of your own modicum – I know of what you are capable – And when you have taken a Galleon, you shall keep a carriage for my Mother if you choose'.[7] As a Navy Agent, Henry knew the exact level of Francis' 'modicum'. His light-hearted mention of a 'Galleon' touched on every sailor's dream, a Spanish treasure-ship sailing home from South America. This was a fantasy fresh in everyone's mind, as it was in Henry's, since four such ships had been intercepted as recently as October 1804 conveying treasure to the value of over a million pounds from Montevideo to Cadiz, intended, as it was supposed, for Napoleon's support.

However, literally overnight, the situation changed. A day after Writing his 'Galleon' letter, Henry heard from Francis that he had just been transferred from the *Leopard* (50) to the *Canopus* (80), the move from a 4th rate

---

* See Appendix 4: Francis Austen's Financial Problems, 1805–08.

to a 3rd rate bringing an increase in pay from £182 10s. 0d to £237 a year, plus allowances which doubled this figure. Henry wrote to congratulate him:*

> Your letter received this morning has given us all the sincerest pleasure in the intelligence which it conveys of the improvement of your present situation & approaching prospects – We all heartily wish you joy of the *Canopus*, which I see is an 80 Guns Ship, & which I calculate will nett you £500 per Ann.[8]

Now Henry felt able to put Francis down for an annual contribution of £50. Two days later, James added his congratulations, ending his letter with a glance towards Francis' future in the *Canopus* and beyond, to his newly-opened prospects of marriage:

> Adieu my dear Brother. May Health, Success & Honour attend you during your Absence; & may you have a speedy return & reap the reward which your Principles & Exertions deserve in the enjoyment of Domestic Comforts & the Society of Her who can best make your Home comfortable to you
> Yours ever most Affectly
> James Austen.[9]

But as we know the 'Success & Honour' of Trafalgar were to pass Francis by, and his marriage was to be a further year and a half a away. These setbacks we can put down to the general run of mischance. Nonetheless, strange as it may seem, Francis' appointment to the *Canopus* was a mixed blessing. While it brought him the improvement in pay which came with a higher-rated vessel, it also brought him into Nelson's Fleet and with that any chance of taking a 'Galleon' vanished.

When he was appointed Commander-in-Chief of the Mediterranean Fleet in 1803, the conviction had grown upon Nelson that the defeat of Napoleon was to be achieved by his total 'annihilation' at sea. This was his aim in the pursuit of Villeneuve to the West Indies, in 1805; his 'Plan of Attack' had a 'precise object, that of a close and decisive Battle' with as 'little manoeuvring' as possible.[10] In other words, not the traditional method of attack for a major engagement as laid down in the Admiralty *Fighting Instructions*, where the opposing fleets would be strung out in two parallel battle-lines many miles long, firing broadsides at a distance before approaching one another in a series of elaborate manoeuvres. Nelson's tactics were wholly different: close engagement achieved as rapidly as possible, cutting through the French line with the sole aim of destruction. During the months before Trafalgar, this

---

* In 1797, Eliza de Feuillide, Henry's wife-to-be, with a private income of her own, described his army pay of £281 as 'a comfortable Income' (*Austen Papers*, p. 168).

sense of purpose hardened. By October, his mind was clear. As he wrote to George Rose (Paymaster General and close friend of himself and Pitt) appealing for the reinforcement he needed to deliver a crushing blow: 'it is, as Mr Pitt knows, annihilation that the Country wants, and not merely a splendid Victory of twenty-three to thirty-six, – honourable to the parties concerned, but absolutely useless in the extended scale to bring Buonaparte to his marrow-bones: numbers only can annihilate'.[11] Three days later, he expressed the same purpose to Collingwood, his Second-in-Command: 'We have only one great object in view, that of annihilating our Enemies, and getting a glorious Peace for our Country'.[12]

To achieve this, for the coming battle he devised a two-pronged Plan of Attack which involved cutting off and surrounding sections of the opposing line of ships: 'I shall go at them at once, if I can, about one-third of the line from their leading ship . . . I think it will surprise and confound the enemy . . . It will bring on a pell-mell battle, and this is what I want'.[13]* This was the Plan that Nelson revealed to his senior officers, Louis and Francis Austen among them, on 30 September. The *Canopus*, Francis writes, was to be 'fifth ship from the van' i.e. in the group alongside the *Victory* leading one prong of the attack, a position in which he supposes they would have their 'share' of action.[14] The extraordinary impact of this meeting Nelson described to Emma Hamilton:

> when I came to explain to them the 'Nelson touch', it was like an electric shock. Some shed tears, all approved – 'It was new – it was singular – it was simple!'; and, from Admirals downwards, it was repeated – 'It must succeed, if ever they will allow us to get at them! You are, my Lord, surrounded by friends whom you inspire with confidence.'[15]

This same certainty of thinking stood behind Nelson's reply to Moira.[16] That a Captain in search of a frigate was after prize-money was not a cynical assessment, but a truism accepted throughout the Navy. So low was an officer's pay,[17] even a Captain's, that prize-money was the only route to wealth. Nelson accepted this motivation in others, just as he recognised it in himself. Nonetheless, during 1804, Nelson's conviction hardened. Only one objective could stand, a single, decisive engagement. In August, he wrote from the *Victory* to Sir Alexander Ball, the Governor of Malta, an old campaigner who had served with him in the Mediterranean and the Battle of the Nile: 'I am keeping as many Frigates as possible round me; for I know the value of them

---

* This idea came from the *Essay on Naval Tactics* (1790) by John Clerk, who argued that the indecisiveness of so many naval battles was the consequence of keeping to lines of battle and that the solution lay in breaking the line and so achieving a 'mêlée'. Both Collingwood and Nelson knew the *Essay* (Laughton, 1907, iii. 398).

on the day of Battle: and compared with that day, what signifies any Prizes they might take?'[18] Three weeks later he wrote again to Ball, reporting on those frigates which were dispersed around the Mediterranean: 'If I had them, I do assure you not one of them should go Prize hunting: that I have never done . . . I expect my Prize-money is embarked in the Toulon Fleet'.[19] It was the French Fleet in Toulon he was waiting for.

This is the train of thought in which Nelson's studied warning to Moira is to be placed, that 'A frigate would have been better calculated to have given Capt. Austin a fortune' but that under his command Captain Austen can look forward to heroic if less profitable action against a fighting foe, 'a French 80 gun ship'; and that 'nothing is to be got except the French fleet should put to sea'. In short, service under Nelson at this moment demanded a total dedication to the decisive annihilating battle in which money-making would play little part.

There is no hint of reproof in Nelson's reply. The principle of prize-money was well understood. It was the Admiralty's system for sharing out the spoils of war, originally designed (according to the Cruizer and Convoy Act of 1708) 'for the better and more effectual encouragement of the Sea Service' 'adding to the encouragement of the captors and the terror of the enemy', as a Marine Dictionary of 1815 has it.[20] It was regarded as the fairest and most straightforward way of rewarding success and for ensuring that sailors at sea, both officers and crew, gained some recompense for putting their lives at risk. Sailors, as much as anyone else, were worthy of their hire, and since the pay was so low, a share of prize-money they reckoned as no more than their due, 'the fruits of our labours' quoted in the opening paragraph of this chapter, the 'fruits' entreated of God in one of the 'Forms of Prayer To Be Used at Sea', specifically 'in his Majesty's Navy every day'.[21] To-day, this argument may sound mercenary, a contamination of the high ideals of patriotic duty and service to King and Country. But there was no reason for Nelson's navy to suffer pangs of conscience over a practice long established and officially administered. As a contemporary commented in 1805, for all the high-flown talk of 'disinterested patriotism' and the 'love of glory' as 'the main springs of military character . . . it would be romantic and absurd' to deny the truth of 'the proverbial remark, that a Spanish war is the best means of manning our navy'.[22] Lord Cochrane – one of the most successful of prize-winning frigate Captains – reflected bluntly in his *Autobiography*: 'Whatever may be the ideas of modern statesmen' [he was writing in 1859],' prize money formed then, as it will ever form, the principal motive of seamen to encounter the perils of war.'[23]

Nor, when one was speaking of the sea, was money-making regarded as an ignoble motive. In this respect, naval ideology was determined by Britain's position as an island nation. Control of the seas was essential to its survival, to its trading prosperity and to its expansive ambitions. The classic statement of these views was sounded in the grandiloquent maxim of Sir Walter Raleigh:

> for whosoever commands the sea commands the trade; whosoever commands the trade of the world commands the riches of the world, and consequently the world itself.[24]

An understanding reflected in the Preamble to the Naval Discipline Act of that period: 'It is on the Navy, under the good Providence of God, that our wealth, prosperity, and peace depend'.

A century later, in 1707, Lord Haversham pointed to the mutual interests of trade and the navy and their partnership in creating and sustaining Britain's greatness:

> Your fleet and your trade have so near a relation, and such a mutual influence upon each other they cannot be well separated; your trade is the mother and nurse of your seamen; your seamen are the life of your fleet, and your fleet is the security and protection of your trade, and both together are the wealth, strength, security and glory of Britain.[25]

In times of war, the commercial contract between the Navy and its mercantile patrons was out in the open. The City merchants wanted a well-manned Navy and were prepared to pay for it. At the outbreak of the Long War, the City supplemented the Royal Bounty for volunteers (£5 for an Able Seaman, £2 10s. od. for an Ordinary Seaman, £1 10s. od. for a Landsman) with £2 for an Able Seaman and £1 for an Ordinary Seaman; and in 1794 the Lord Mayor opened a subscription for additional bounties, steps which many seaport towns followed. The contract was confirmed at the highest levels: witness Nelson's letter to Sir William Anderson, the former Lord Mayor of London, thanking the Court of Common Council for their congratulations following the Battle of the Nile: 'assure them, it shall be the business of my life, to act in the manner most conducive to the prosperity of the City of London, on which depends that of our Country'.[26] The City's response was equally business like: 'Do you find Victories, and we will find rewards', the Lord Mayor assured him.[27] But for the Battle of Copenhagen in April 1801, this was a bargain the City failed to keep.* From the nation, Nelson received a Viscountcy (although, to his continuing protests to Addington, the Prime Minister, and St Vincent, the First Lord, no commemorative medal was struck). From the City, Nelson had his tariff of expectation: for himself a

---

* The Fleet commander was Admiral Sir Hyde Parker, with Nelson Second-in-Command and Rear-Admiral Graves Third. However, as Nelson records, 'The Thanks of Parliament went only to Sir Hyde's conduct in *planning*, not for the *fighting*' of the Battle (Nicolas, 1845, v. 21 and note).

'Sword'; for his next-in-command, Rear-Admiral Graves, 'the Freedom in a Gold Box', and material 'Thanks' for the 'Officers' and 'Men'. Nelson's argument was the familiar one: the City 'exists by Victories at Sea', and that without naval protection the prosperity of 'the first commercial City in the world' would be lost. He had delivered his 'part of the honourable contract', whereas the City's 'promise' of 'rewards', 'a promise made by a Lord Mayor in his robes and almost in the Royal presence', was left unfulfilled.[28]

Nelson had good reason to feel offended and defrauded on his own behalf and that of his officers and men. The gift of Honorary Freedoms, complete with Freedom boxes in gold or silver, and commemorative Swords of Honour, to a specified value of one hundred or two hundred guineas, was the currency of City 'rewards' and the measure of its gratitude.* To be ignored or underpaid was to be insulted and in September 1802 Nelson wrote privately to the Lord Mayor, following an invitation to dine with him, explaining that until his 'brave Companions' of Copenhagen were honoured by the City, no such invitation could be accepted.[29] It was a threat that Nelson stood by. Having received an invitation in November to the Guildhall dinner for Lord Mayor's Day, he sent a further refusal to the Lord Mayor Elect; and wrote again, two weeks later, declaring himself to be the 'natural guardian of the character of the navy, army and marines who fought and so profusely bled under my command that day.'[30]

The strongest representation of the City's 'shipping interest' was through Lloyd's, its concerns neatly encapsulated in 'Ships, Colonies and Commerce', the motto it adopted for the Jubilee of George III in 1809. The Lloyd's 'subscribers' included men of commerce, trade and finance – insurance brokers and under-writers, ship-owners, merchants and other investors attracted into the insurance market by the boom in war-time shipping premiums and the vast profits they generated. One effect of the war was to bring insurance business from all over the world into London and by the Jubilee year the level of risk covered annually at Lloyd's was running at £100 million. The subscribers had an enormous stake in the security and success of the British merchant fleet and this was reflected in the large sums of money paid to senior naval officers either in cash or trophies of high value, with lesser sums to seamen and their families. In the early stages of the war, before the Peace of Amiens, news of an important naval victory was the signal for the subscribers to start an *ad hoc* whip-round: over £21,000 was raised for the Glorious First of June in 1794, £52,000 for Camperdown in 1797, £38,500 for

---

* Of the thirty-five swords presented by the City between 1797 and 1816, twenty went to naval commanders, eleven to army chiefs; and during that same period twenty-six Freedoms were naval, eleven army. See *London's Roll of Fame* (1884), McAleer (1981) and Southwick (1983).

the Battle of the Nile in 1798 and £15,500 for Copenhagen in 1801. When the war recommenced in 1803, these efforts were channelled into the Lloyd's Patriotic Fund designed 'to animate our defenders by sea and land' by 'granting pecuniary rewards of honourable badges of distinction, for successful exertions of valour or merit'.* The public at large was invited to subscribe and much was made of the Fund's democratic spread and 'Common Cause': 'the Mite of the Labourer combining with the Munificent Donation of the Noble and the Wealthy' to 'inspire our Seamen, our Soldiers and our Countrymen at large' and 'impress on the minds of our Enemies the appalling conviction *That the Energies of this great Empire are irresistible, as its resources are incalculable*'.[31] Thus the trumpeting. In reality, the bulk of the donations came from Lloyd's itself and its leading members, those 'Sons of Commerce' celebrated by Dibdin, the popular balladist, for their 'magnificent act' which by the end of the war had raised £630,000.** Both the City Corporation and the Lloyd's Patriotic Fund were given to high-minded statements about their patriotic and humanitarian objectives; and their award of pensions to the wounded and bereaved can be regarded as good works in the national interest. Yet within the disbursement of their charity was a high degree of self-interest. The bulk of their support went to Flag-officers and Captains in the form of cash payments and valuable trophies, material inducements to stick to the meritorious but otherwise unprofitable task of protecting trade. In the language of Nelson and the Lord Mayor, these were the 'rewards' for services rendered in keeping the sea-lanes open, the convoys secure and the trading and mercantile world at a high level of prosperity.

The activities of Lloyd's and the City Corporation gave rise to a chorus of congratulation and self-congratulation. With a war to be financed, the civic virtues of commerce and enterprise gathered a patriotic light. Moreover, Lloyd's could claim to make a direct contribution to the war effort, maintaining close relations with the Admiralty, advising on the organization of the convoys, their ports of assembly and sailing dates and, more important still, sharing the inflow of intelligence, political as well as maritime, which came in from the captains of merchantmen and its port agents throughout the world. Inevitably, there were those unpersuaded by the Lloyd's rhetoric of charity and patriotism. At the end of 1805, Captain Francis Beaufort wrote in his

---

* See Appendix 2: The Lloyd's Patriotic Fund Awards.

** These words come in the opening verse of the song 'The Subscription at Lloyd's', in *Britons Strike Home: A New Entertainment* (1803) by Charles Dibdin Snr: 'If the world ever saw a magnificent act,/That time might on adamant write,/Sons of Commerce 'tis yours – that mankind shall attract – /Astonishment mixed with delight'.

Britons Strike Home, the motto on the Lloyd's Fund seal, was taken from *Bonduca* (Boadicea), the historical tragedy by John Fletcher (c. 1619): 'Britains, strike home, revenge your country's wrongs!/Fight and record yourself in Druid's songs'.

private Journal

> Any body of men, much less Tinkers and haberdashers, presuming publicly to reward the army and navy is I think very wrong. Still, while they conferred their freedoms in gold boxes it was bearable . . . when they give swords, however, it is *impious*. What, a taylor, for instance, giving an Admiral a Sword! . . . But what will you say when they at last have dared to offer money, MONEY to officers!! .. Now indeed may our troops and sailors be called mercenary! And now may the French epithet of a nation of shopkeepers be justly applied to us.[32]

St Vincent complained of what he called a 'mischievous system of rewards . . . which is held out to the navy as giving greater encouragement than the government of the country'.[33] In 1807, the *Naval Chronicle* entered the debate, quoting Lord Howick (First Lord from 16 July to 29 September 1806) that the Patriotic Society exerted a 'fatal influence', whereas an anonymous correspondent took the opposite view, representing the Government as ungenerous and unrewarding.[34] Another vociferous critic was Cobbett. From the very inception of the Lloyd's Fund, his democratic instincts were alerted, his sense of justice offended. Was the Fund, as it claimed, operating disinterestedly on behalf of the nation? Or was it not, as Cobbett felt, a socially divisive instrument, setting the 'shipping interest' against the 'landed interest' of the 'Nobility, Gentry and Clergy' and unconstitutional, too, in usurping the function of the Crown as the source of national honours and awards[35] – a charge also levelled by other critics at the activities of the Corporation of London.[36] As the years passed, Cobbett's denunciation of the Lloyd's Fund – 'this offspring of craft, selfishness and ambition'[37] – was no less caustic. Lloyd's itself he saw as a 'little government', 'a formidable rival .. . in the affections of the Navy and Army'.[38] He derided its awards, its 'gaudy trinkets, and useless decorations' and compared the value of the 'swords, and other expensive rewards' presented to the Flag-officers and Captains with the cost of the pensions awarded to the bereaved families of the common sailors.[39] Lloyd's and its Fund he viewed as a creation of 'the commercial system'[40] and a voracious consumer of national wealth. This criticism struck home. In 1809, following Wellington's victories in Spain and Portugal, involving heavy casualties, the presentation of Vases and Swords ended and the resources of the Fund were turned wholly to relieving hardship.

Whatever the justice of Cobbett's position, and whatever the state of the economy at large, the City was undeniably a scene of prosperity on an amazing scale. On the one hand, the country bore the cost of waging war, with military expenditure calculated to be running in 1811 at 16 per cent of Britain's national income, the same level as in the War of 1914–18. The Navy

Estimates rose from £5,500,000 in 1793 to £12,500,000 by 1800 and at the close of the war were approaching £19,000,000. Army expenditure rose at a similar pace: from about £10,000,000 in 1793 to £18,000,000 by 1800 and £39,000,000 in 1815. And following Trafalgar and the failure of his invasion plans, Napoleon opened up an economic offensive, blockading European and neutral trade with Britain and its colonies. Yet throughout the war, Britain's trade shows a steady increase. In 1794, imports were running at about £38,000,000 a year. By 1806, the figure was £55,500,000 and by 1814, nearly £72,000,000. Export and re-export figures show an equally striking rise: in 1794, £32,000,000; by 1806, £51,000,000; and by 1814, nearly £66,000,000. There was rejoicing at a profitable war: 'Our commerce had flourished, our wealth had increased, our possessions had multiplied . . . War, the curse of every other nation, had to Great Britain been a comparative blessing'.[41] This was Viscount Hamilton addressing his fellow-peers in 1808. And in 1810 an American observer, John Quincy Adams, could see that Napoleon's blockade, far from confining British trade, was sending it world-wide in search of fresh markets in North and South America and the West Indies; and directing it into neutral vessels and neutral ports:

> the Continental system, as they called it, and as they managed it, was promoting to the utmost extent the views of England; was, instead of impairing her commerce, securing to her that of the whole world; and was pouring into her lap the means of continuing the war, just as long as her ministers should think it expedient.[42]

An important component in this trading situation was the licensing system by which enemy trade, largely French, was permitted within British ports. In 1810, no less than 18,000 licences were issued. Indeed, this licence-trade was encouraged, with convoying provided. As the *Naval Chronicle* observed, by early 1812 this Continental trade was 'unusually free and active', with licences reported to have been issued 'to every French port'.[43]

The City fathers, the subscribers at Lloyd's and the Directors of the East India and other trading Companies dispensed their 'rewards' lavishly. It was money well spent. For his victory at the Nile, the East India Company voted Nelson the sum of £10,000, the Turkish Company presented him with plate and the City gave him a richly decorated Sword of Honour. Sir John Jervis received a similar sword for his victory off St Vincent. Its 'shell' (wrote the Lord Mayor) 'will have two views of the action enamelled, and I hope to your satisfaction. The hilt will have your ship with her name encircled with diamonds, the City Arms and your own all enamelled and executed, I hope, to your taste'.[44] To Francis Austen, modest rewards for the safe-guarding of East India Company convoys; and for the victory at St Domingo, a £100 Vase from the Patriotic Society of Lloyd's.

In the dividends of naval service, it was the Flag-officers, above all the Commanders-in-Chief, who could expect to be most richly rewarded. The line of benefactors was long and few Admirals escaped their favours. Ready at hand were the City fathers, the Directors of the Chartered Companies, the subscribers of Lloyd's and the Crown itself with pensions, honours, promotions, profitable appointments and naval sinecures at its disposal; and further down the line were the councils of mercantile and trading towns outside London – Bristol, Liverpool, Norwich and others – with Freedoms and their groups of traders waiting with their gifts.

But even the humblest of seamen and the youngest of Lieutenants could dream of winning riches, could hope to reap their reward in prize-money, the 'golden harvest' of the sea. Tales of fortune were the staple of seamen's talk – and of the officers too. On board the *Inconstant* (36), a frigate cruising in the Mediterranean in 1797, Betsey Wynne, the Captain's wife, was amused to hear the officers' fantasising. With news of two Spanish frigates convoying 'a valuable prize . . . The Officers are building castles in the air and think already they have taken (with the Inconstant alone) the two frigates and their prize. Indeed nothing amuses me so much as to hear them, they are in expectation of getting immense riches'.[45] The average prize value of a merchantman was about £2500 and privateers produced about half that figure. But the officers of the *Inconstant* had greater prizes in mind, such captures as the *San Iago* in 1793 carrying specie to the value of nearly one million pounds, of which £50,000 went to the Commander-in-Chief of the Mediterranean Fleet, Lord Hood, £30,000 to each of the four Captains in the Squadron, and lesser sums to the lower ranks of officers and men. And in 1799 the capture of two Spanish treasure-ships off Cape Finisterre brought the Admiral over £81,000, over £40,000 to each of the four Captains, over £5000 to each of the sixteen Masters and Lieutenants, £2470 to each of the 33 Warrant Officers, £790 to each of the 103 Midshipmen and Petty Officers and to each of the 894 ordinary seamen the sum of £182.[46] In this distribution, each Captain's share represented his pay for over 300 years and a seaman's pay (of £12) for fifteen years. The discrepancy was enormous. It remained an on-going complaint of

THE

Bermuda Gazette,

And WEEKLY ADVERTISER.

No. 1105.   SATURDAY, APRIL 13, 1805.

SPANISH WAR
Now or Never.
WANTED,
SEAMEN and STOUT LANDS-
MEN
To compleat the Crew of His Majef-
ty's Sloop of War the
INDIAN,
Of Twenty Guns,
CHARLES JOHN AUSTEN, Efq.
Commander.

THE INDIAN is the
fineft and moft beautiful
Man of War ever built, and
her conftruction puts her faft
failing beyond a doubt. Therefore
plenty of Spanifh Doubloons and
Dollars will fall to the lot of all thofe
fpirited Young Men who come forward
without delay and repair on board the
faid Sloop now fitting alongfide of Mr.
Goodrich's Wharf, in St. George's.

N. B. There are a number of Petty
Officers births vacant, who are five fhare
Men.

Grog and Frefh Beef every day at
twelve o'clock.
GOD SAVE the KING,
AND
Succefs to the TIGHT LITTLE ISLAND.

Charles Austen's advertisement to crew the *Indian*. But the appeal was not sufficiently tempting and the crew had to be completed by impressment. Bermuda was not the only 'Tight Little Island'. It was a phrase Charles borrowed from a popular song by Charles Dibdin Jnr describing Britain's security and fastness.

As to the quality of the *Indian's* 'construction' and its 'fast sailing', this was not mere boasting. Bermuda sloops, built of cedar, which was lighter, more durable and stronger than oak, were renowned for their weatherliness and speed and were reputed to be the fastest vessels afloat.

the lower-deck and came up as one of the eight articles of grievance at the Mutiny at the Nore in 1797; and it was a recurrent topic for cartoonists.* The division of prize money was on a scale specified in the Cruizer Act (1708) renewed at the beginning of each war:

	before 1808	after 1808
		Shares
The Captain (or Captains)	3 eighths	2 eighths
Captains of Marines and Army, Sea Lieutenants, Master and Physician; equal shares in	1 eighth	1 eighth
Lieutenants of Marines and Army, Secretary of Admiral, Principal Warrant Officers, Master's Mates, Chaplain; equal shares in	1 eighth	1 eighth
Midshipmen, Inferior Warrant Officers, Principal Warrant Officer's Mates, Marine Sergeants; equal shares in	1 eighth	4 eighths
The rest: equal shares in	2 eighths	

before 1808 Flag Officers: one of Captain's eighths (Flag-eighths)
after 1808   Flag Officers: one-third of Captain's share

When there were two Flag Officers on station, the division was 2 : 1 between the senior and junior; when three, the division was 2 : 1 : 1. Commodores and the Captains of the Fleet ranked with junior Flag Officers for this purpose.

The review of 1808 was vigorously resisted by the Captains. It reduced their share by one-third, passing it on to the Midshipmen and others on that level. Lord Cochrane told the House of Lords that this 'diminution of the prize money by recent regulations' was the principal reason for his leaving the service.[47] However, the key issue for the Captains was the regulation which remained unchanged, i.e. that in any capture the value of the prize was shared amongst all the vessels in sight of the action and furthermore that a specified part of the Captain's share went to the Flag-officer commanding the Fleet or independent Squadron to which he belonged. This put a premium on having

---

* Illustration 21 is a cartoon by William Heath in 1805, 'Equity or a Sailor's Prayer before Battle: Anecdote of the Battle of Trafalgar'. It shows an officer addressing a sailor praying over a gun: 'Why Starboard! how is this at prayers when the enemy is bearing down on us; are you afraid of them?' 'Afraid! – No! I was only praying that the enemy's shot may be distributed in the same proportion as the prize money, the greatest part among the Officers.' One bystanding tar says to his companion: 'Why don't you sing Amen to that, Tom'.

a 'roving commission', that is cruising independently, under orders directly from the Admiralty, which is why the pipe-dream of the officers in the *Inconstant* was that they should capture their prizes 'alone'. In these circumstances, the Captain's share came to him undiminished. This was Cochrane's situation in 1805. Melville, the First Lord, gave him permission to cruise for a month off the Azores under Admiralty orders. Such was his catch in prizes – the *La Fortuna* alone carried 300,000 dollars (about £75,000) – that his frigate, the 'Flying' *Pallas* (36), returned with a new nickname, the 'Golden' *Pallas*. However, the Port Admiral at Plymouth, from which the *Pallas* had sailed, had rewritten the Admiralty orders and issued them under his own authority, a trick which enabled him to claim one-third in Cochrane's share of the winnings.

The workings of the prize-system created much ill-will. The Prize-courts were slow in operation and their bill of expenses could seriously reduce the awards. The letter of the law, voluminous at it was, left many grey areas and loose ends. Disputes could wind their way for years through the Admiralty and Civil Courts. *Nelson* v. *St Vincent* ground on from 1799 until November 1803, Nelson attempting to recover £20,000 in Flag-eighths that St Vincent had collected as Commander-in-Chief of the Mediterranean Fleet at a time when in reality he was on leave in England and Nelson, his Second-in-Command, was in direct charge of the Fleet. In private Nelson complained vigorously: 'My Commander-in-Chief runs away with all the money I fight for . . . But damn me if I let any man swindle me out of my property whilst he is at his ease in England . . . I have only *justice, honour,* and the custom of the service on my side; he has *partiality, power, money* and *rascality* on his'.[48] In the event, 'the custom of the service' prevailed and the Court of Appeal found in Nelson's favour, a verdict reported prominently in the *Naval Chronicle.*[49]

Nelson was equally indignant when, in 1804, the boundaries of his Mediterranean station were reduced, giving Sir John Orde a separate station west of the Straits of Gibraltar, with orders to place his Squadron at the approaches to Cadiz, across the path of the annual Spanish treasure fleet approaching from South America. This, as Nelson described it, was the 'golden harvest' Orde was sent to reap – a step in Pitt's strategy for bringing Spain (neutral, but supporting France) into the war.[50] The treasure fleet was captured, its cargo of copper, tin, silver and gold valued at over a million pounds, and Orde and his Captains were rich overnight. Nelson felt robbed: 'he is to wallow in wealth whilst I am left a beggar',[51] a complaint that rumbled on in his letters for many months, the note of bitterness unrestrained: 'I should have been a very rich, instead of a poor man, if Lord Melville had not given the Galleons to Sir John Orde', he wrote to his sister in May the following year.[52] His one consoling thought was that the 'liberal-minded' Melville would see justice was done and 'oblige me in some other way, in giving me something for some of my relations' (this would be by way of appointments and sinecures). In this same letter Nelson clambers to a high-minded and moral foothold, assuring Davison, his prize-agent, that 'my spirit is above riches, and nothing can shake my firm resolution to do my duty to my Country'.[53]

In 1810, this whole episode was taken up by Coleridge as a glaring example of unfairness to the seamen as well as to Nelson and his officers, their proper reward for years of unremitting service stolen from them:

> Year after year, the same dull duties of a wearisome Blockade, of doubtful Policy – little if any opportunity of making Prizes; and the few Prizes, which accident might throw in the way, of little or no value – and when at last the occasion presented itself which would have compensated for all, then a disappointment as sudden and unexpected as it was unjust and cruel, and the cup dashed from their lips! – Add to these trials the sense of enterprizes checked by feebleness and timidity elsewhere, not omitting the tiresomeness of the Mediterranean Sea, Sky, and Climate . . . It was indeed an unexampled circumstance, that a small Squadron should be sent to the Station which had been long occupied by a large Fleet, commanded by the Darling of the Navy, and the Glory of the British Empire, to the Station where this Fleet had for years been wearing away in the most barren, repulsive, and spirit-trying service, in which the Navy can be employed!*

The consequence of blockading upon naval morale was also spelt out by Richard Lovell Edgeworth in his *Essays on Professional Education*. When there was the 'hope of prize money, or of sharing the fund at Lloyd's . . . the nation is safe',

> but when England shall have shut up all the ships of the world in their respective ports, the hopes of prize money must sink; the funds at Lloyd's will fail; and the British empire may perhaps find too late, that no mercenary rewards can supply the place of military enthusiasm, and the love of glory. It would be vain, it would be impossible, to educate youths to military professions, unless they were afterwards to have reasonable hopes of being rewarded in proportion to their labour and their deserts. – How nobly Nelson thought and wrote on these subjects![54]

---

* This passage comes in a long biographical sketch of Sir Alexander Ball, Captain RN, the Civil Commissioner of Malta, its governor, whom Coleridge had served in 1804–05, first as his private Secretary and then, from January to September 1805, as Acting Public Secretary in the civil administration, one step below Ball himself. So this 'digression' (as Coleridge calls it) on Nelson was written out of a close and knowledgeable interest in the circumstances. Coleridge wrote the Ball biography for *The Friend*, his own 'Literary, Moral and Political Weekly Paper', where it appeared in the issue for 15 March 1810.

The inherent problem in the prize system, to which no solution was ever found, was the potency of its attraction *away* from war: the fact that fortunes were to be made not in the pursuit of the enemy's warships but in the search for his treasure-ships and richly-laden merchantmen, those galleons that Henry wished for his sailor brother. The lucky ones were the Captains of fast, 'good' or 'crack' frigates cruising independently within striking distance of the shipping lanes, whereas Captains on ships-of-the-line enjoyed few opportunities and fewer still if they were on close blockade, a duty which was dangerous and unrewarding. And since, in the years leading up to Trafalgar and beyond, successive Ministries had settled for a strategy of containment involving the Channel, North Sea and Mediterranean Fleets, blockade became the predominant duty, a hardship Francis knew all too well. That there was a loss of prize-money was recognised. St Vincent advised Grenville, First Lord of the Admiralty in 1806, that for Commanders in the Bay of Tangiers on a duty 'very arduous and unproductive in prize-money, promotion might be held out as the reward of meritorious conduct in the performance of it'.[55]

To a lesser degree, the same problem arose with freight money, the payment made by individual merchants and trading companies for the safe conveyance in naval vessels of coin, bullion, plate or jewels. This was permitted under naval regulations and the ship's Captain was entitled to a payment of 1 per cent or 2 per cent of freight value, a sum which he kept to himself, or shared with his officers and crew; and the great attraction of this payment was enough to keep ships loitering around the freighting ports, such as Lisbon, away from their proper duties.

The Admiralty did its best to introduce correctives, with inducements encouraging Captains towards battle engagement. Honours and promotion were not awarded for the capture of civilian ships, only for service in action against naval vessels and money was to be made by the capture of enemy ships-of-war. Providing that they were serviceable, these vessels could be purchased by the Navy Board and added to the British Fleet, as 450 were during the course of the war. The purchase price was based upon a valuation of the hull, weaponry, masts, equipment and naval stores; and a 32-gun frigate could raise about £16,000. But only the greatest of Fleet victories could be expected to approach 'galleon' levels. After the Battle of the Nile – considered by some naval historians to be the most decisive victory of the war – the hull of the *Franklin* (renamed *Canopus*) was purchased by the Navy Board for £30,000, five other French vessels realised £87,000, and the total of £117,000 was distributed amongst the Fleet according to the prize-money scale. In addition, Nelson successfully put the case to Spencer, the First Lord, for the value of the three prizes which he was forced to abandon and set fire to, following orders from St Vincent to sail immediately, thus depriving his Squadron, by his estimate, of a further £60,000. As he argued in his letter, 'if an Admiral is, after a victory, only to look after the captured Ships, and not distressing the Enemy, very dearly indeed does the Nation pay for the Prizes'. (Possibly Nelson had a specific instance in mind. Following his success at the Glorious First of June in 1794, Howe was criticised for being so concerned with the security of his prizes – which produced £213,000 – that he failed to drive home his advantage to the full, with the possible destruction of further French ships). Nelson went on to point out that 'An Admiral may be amply rewarded by his feelings and the approbation of his superiors, but what reward have the inferior Officers and men but the value of the Prizes?'[56]* In fact, just as the pursuit of prizes could distort a Fleet action, so, at a lower level, the ordinary seamen could look after their own interests by attempting to disable rather than sink enemy ships. To do this, gun-crews tended to aim high, attempting to cut down the sails and rigging, rather than aiming shot at the hull line which would lead to holing and sinking, and the possible loss of a prospective prize.

Collingwood put the same argument to Barham after Trafalgar. Due to the bad weather, of the original eighteen vessels captured, only four remained. As a consequence 'the usual reward to the Captains, arising from the sale of prizes, is almost all lost by the wreck and destruction of the ships . . .'.[57] And, Nelson-like, he wrote privately to his sister, pointing to the injustice of this situation: 'The loss of the ships so hardly won should not be the loss of those poor creatures who laboured so to win them, but of the Nation'[58] (an injustice recognised in the Parliamentary award of £320,000). For himself, although not a rich man, Collingwood felt 'amply rewarded' (as he told his sister) by the King's 'approbation' and the Barony conferred upon him. More, in the form of prize-money, he did not look for: 'The times require that all should exert themselves for their country, and while I can see at all, I will not lose sight of that'.[59]

However, such selfless sentiments are rare. Vice-Admirals, such as Collingwood, enjoying a pension of £2000 with their Barony,** could afford

---

* A small but significant additional inducement was 'head money' (sometimes called 'head and gun money'), a payment of £5 for every member of the enemy crew on a captured ship, distributed on the same basis as prize-money.

** Pensions were annuities, awards paid for many occasions and contingencies: in Nelson's case, £923 from the Admiralty 'for loss of one arm and one eye' and a £2000 Exchequer Pension for his success at the Battle of the Nile, as he set down in a statement of 'Income and Property' (Hibbert, 1995, p. 312). Collingwood's pension was to enable him to live up to the dignity of his new peerage. He feared, nonetheless, that his 'rank, so far above my fortune, will subject me to a thousand embarrassments' and that there was 'no chance of making a fortune at sea' as French and Spanish shipments were being transported in the neutral safety of American vessels (letter to his sister, 1 January 1806, quoted in Hughes, 1957, p. 169).

to place patriotism above reward. But for the service as a whole, prize-money came as a fitting recompense for hardship and danger. When pangs of conscience arose, it was not because prize-money carried mercenary or less than honourable associations. Jane Austen could view it as a wholly desirable objective for her brothers. The source of Captain Wentworth's £25,000 is unquestioned and he comes blessed in its possession. Nonetheless, problems did arise. Early in the war, for example, some enterprising officers fitted out ships as privateers and ran them as a business sideline alongside their ordinary naval duties. And towards the end of the war, under the influence of Evangelical thinking, there was some criticism of the vast and disproportunate gains which prize-money could bring. The continuing point of friction, however, was the conflict between matters 'private' and 'public', between the self-interested concerns of a profit-seeking frigate Captain and the orders of the Admiralty or his Commander-in-Chief. This was Francis Austen's situation from the moment he joined the Mediterranean Fleet in 1805 and was placed within Nelson's single-minded strategy of 'annihilation', a 'public' objective allowing no room for such a 'private' occupation as speculative cruising.

This distinction, familiar throughout the Navy, entered the vocabulary of naval families. Charles' wife, Fanny Palmer, connected it with the condition of being a sailor's wife: 'You well know the uncertainty of Naval people, & that their private arrangements must yield to public duty; indeed I find there is little use in planning . . .', she wrote in 1814, a few months before her death.[60] 'Private' interests were allowed their place but had to give way as 'public' need arose, an issue upon which the Admiralty was prepared to be surprisingly accommodating and ready to explain at some length. This is illustrated in an exchange of letters in March 1797 between Edward Pellew, then enjoying that most desirable of all situations, command of a detached frigate-Squadron on a profitable station, and Spencer, the First Lord. Pellew feared that he would be removed from his Squadron, operating out of Falmouth on the Western Approaches, to be put under the orders of Lord Bridport, Commander-in-Chief of the Channel Fleet, and called upon to join the in-shore Squadron blockading Brest. He wrote to Spencer pleading poverty. Spencer answered that with regard to prize-money

> Your Station from the opportunities it frequently affords of meeting with objects of Pursuit and Capture, has ever since I have been at the Board been looked upon by all the Officers in the Navy, as the most desirable in my appointment, and accordingly scarce a day pafses that I have not some application or other from Officers to be placed upon it; to all these applications I make it an invariable Rule to return the same answer, namely, that the particular destination of Ships can only be determined by Considerations arising out of the exigencies of the publick

Service, and not from any of a more private Nature, and I really do not know (if I could with propriety change your Station or destination on any grounds other than publick ones) where I could employ you with a better chance for your gaining Emolument as well as Distinction and Credit. As to cruizing more at large nothing can be more pernicious, as you well know; the War with Spain has now been long enough made publick to put them on their guard, and that harvest therefore is pretty well over.[61]

Spencer's letter was dated 14 March. Pellew, unabashed, wrote back on the 18th requesting a station which covered 'the coast of Portugal, with the circuit of the Azores, Canaries, and Cape de Verd',[62] these Spanish and Portuguese possessions to be found between latitudes 10° and 40° and undoubtedly the best stretch of sea for the rich 'harvest' he was after. Spencer replied on 28 March with exemplary patience and courtesy, once again raising the 'Necessity' of public service and pointing to the change in French naval tactics, their 'small Squadrons' forming into a 'large Body' which, in turn, called for the British 'detached Squadrons' to take their place in an 'enlarged' Channel Fleet.

As to a more profitable cruizing ground, I really do not know how that is to be found for as I said in a former Letter the whole of that Question depends on an uncertainty, and I believe on looking back it will be seen that the greatest Prizes which have been made in most Wars have been fallen in with from accidental Circumstances rather than any forethought for the Purpose, which I am inclined to believe most frequently ends in Disappointment.[63]

Spencer's mention of 'uncertainty' and 'accidental Circumstances' betrays a landsman's ignorance. Pellew, like any experienced frigate Captain, could have corrected him. There was little 'uncertainty' and 'accidental' circumstance to their success and a very considerable exercise of 'forethought' and 'Purpose'. It was the Captain's calculated report of such successes that could carry the air of 'uncertainty', not the event. Pellew, like other successful frigate Captains – his wartime earnings from prize-money, convoying and freight-money amounted to over £300,000 – made it his business to know where best to loiter and lie in wait and how to match his sailing tactics with Admiralty cruising instructions and his records with Admiralty expectations.

A professional First Lord, such as St Vincent, would have answered Pellew shortly and sharply, having in mind, as thoughtful commanders did, the harsh experience of those officers and their men on blockading and other duties similarly unprofitable. Before the Trafalgar vote of £320,000, Collingwood had written to his wife about 'the poor seamen', 'shabbily' treated, 'who fought a battle that set all England in an uproar, and all the poets and painters at work' without receiving 'one sixpence of prize-money'.[64] Fittingly, Nelson provides the last word on this matter, writing to his wife in similar vein after the capture of Toulon in 1793:

> I believe the world is convinced that no conquests of importance can be made without us; and yet, as soon as we have accomplished the service we are ordered on, we are neglected. If Parliament does not grant something to this Fleet, our Jacks will grumble; for here there is no prize money to soften their hardships; all we get is honour and salt beef.[65]

Jane Austen was able to regard the getting, and missing, of prizes with a humorist's eye. 'The Endymion has not been plagued with any more prizes', she wrote to Cassandra in 1801, perhaps echoing the easy-going manner of her brother Charles.[66] From what we know, his prime concern was the lives of his men, not making money. Late in 1808, when sailing out of Bermuda (as Jane reported the event to Cassandra) Charles took 'a small prize . . . a French schooner laden with Sugar, but Bad weather parted them, & she had not yet been heard of . . .'.[67] Charles feared the vessel and its cargo lost. The 'real misfortune', he wrote to Cassandra, was not this but losing 'the lives of twelve of my people, two of them mids,'[68] the prize-crew he put on board to bring the vessel home.

It would be comforting to suppose that Francis too was able to reconcile himself to the loss of a 'golden harvest'. But from what we know of his character and situation, that seems unlikely. As far as the records go, overall his prizes brought in no more than a few hundred pounds, a slight tally for someone at sea for much of the war – although it is worth calculating this in modern terms, multiplying by a factor not less than forty; and worth remembering that the £30 Charles received in 1801 as his share of a captured privateer, with the expectation of £10 more, was sufficient for him to be laying out 'the produce'[69] in the gold chains and topaz crosses he sent to Cassandra and Jane.

It was during Francis' command of the *Peterel* in 1799-1800 that most of his small success came: £200 from his share of specie found on a fishing boat and head-money from several French ships,[70] a meagre return for the capture and destruction of over forty enemy vessels. But Admiral Richard Hall's comment sets these figures in an understandable light: 'Time and again the records show the destruction of such prizes, usually by burning, with the comment "not worth sending in".'[71] Beyond these small amounts, we know only the fact that Francis received a share (unspecified) in the capture of four vessels at St Domingo in 1806; and his earnings from convoying and freighting far exceeded the total of his prize-money.

However, these earnings, from the East India Company, came at a later period, in 1808–09, when Francis was on escort duty to India and China, and his need for money had arisen some years before, since it was on reaching the rank of Captain that an officer's financial burden increased sharply. A Lieutenant's pay in the 1790s was £5 12s. od. a lunar month, £7 if on a First or Second Rate, while a Captain's pay was on a scale rising from £8 8s. od. a lunar month on frigates of the Sixth Rate, up to £28 on a First Rate, recognising that not only were the Captain's responsibilities heavier on a larger vessel, so too were his expenses. These increased with the size of the ship, for there was a larger number of fellow-officers to entertain; and if sailing in a Squadron or Fleet, with fellow-Captains and Flag-officers, the food and wines, the glasses and silverware were expected to be to a higher standard. And for himself, the Captain had to find smarter uniforms and a presentable cabin outfit and furnishings. Moreover, a Captain was expected to provide his own navigational instruments, his chronometer (which alone could cost as much as £80),* spyglasses and charts and other items needed for running the ship. So it was that promotion could put a Captain in debt and in this case prize-money was regarded not as a bonus but as an essential, if chancy, part of his income. For this reason, there was such an outcry in 1808 when the Captains lost one-third of their prize share. Although they had the benefit of the improved pay-scale introduced in 1806, according to Dillon's reminiscences, the consequence was that 'the Captains, generally speaking, left off laying tables, as their pay would not admit of their doing so. The Prize Money, such as it was – and which fell to the lot of very few – made up in some cases for the expenses to which the Captains were liable'. But 'Many ruined themselves in keeping up the respectability of the profession'.[72] Francis himself encountered this problem in 1808, in transporting a Brigadier General and two of his staff officers in the *St Albans* from England to Portugal, He applied to the Admiralty for 'some remuneration for the Expence' of accommodating them at his 'Table' for a period of four weeks. The Admiralty calculated that 'the sum of One Hundred and Fifty Pounds would be a proper remuneration for Captain Austen for this service'.[73]

This background helps us to understand why Charles was forced to adopt such economies in housing his family on board the *Namur*. Cassandra antici-pated this problem in 1811 when, after an absence, by her reckoning of almost seven years, he returned to England with his wife and two daughters: 'There must be always something to wish for, and for Charles we have to wish for rather more money. So expensive as every thing in England is now, even the necessaries of life, I am afraid they will find themselves very, very poor'.[74] Six months later, Cassandra was able to report on Charles' venture into his

---

* Captains sailing out of Portsmouth could claim one from the Naval Academy, as long as the small stock lasted.

'aquatic abode', 'a scheme' which at first had filled his mother and sisters with misgivings. However, she was happy to say that Charles and Fanny 'have found their residence very tolerably comfortable and it is so much the cheapest home she could have that they are very right to put up with little inconveniences'.[75]

Eighteen months further on, in the Autumn of 1813, neither Charles' patience nor his purse could stand any more of life in an anchored ship, economical as it might be. By this time, his wife wrote, he was impatient to be at sea once again, on active service and 'in the way of making a little Money while there is an opporty'.[76]

Another financial hardship that Francis encountered was half-pay for those periods when he was without a ship.* More than just the cut in pay was the loss of any opportunity to benefit from freight-money and convoying, not to speak of prize-money. The *Naval Chronicle* made the inadequacy of half-pay a public issue, remarking in 1805 that the rate for a Captain 'will not allow him to support his station in life'[77] and many officers with no other source of income were compelled to live as economically as Charles chose to do on the *Namur* and as the Harvilles are depicted in *Persuasion*, in their confined winter quarters at Lyme, far from the smart society of Bath and London and quite unable to follow the Crofts in renting a country-house. There was no call for Jane Austen to explain the source of the Admiral's wealth. Her readers were familiar with the riches to be won from Flag-eighths. As to Francis himself, on half-pay in the final years of the war, through the kindness of his brother Edward he and his family were able to stay at Chawton House when there was no tenant in occupation; and when the House was let, they moved to modest lodgings, a cottage near Alton.

A further blow was the collapse of Henry's bank in 1816. We know from Mrs Austen that her son Francis was 'so much the loser' that for three years he was unable even to make his usual remittance of £100; and when he was in a position to do so, in 1819, she 'declined it, on account of his large and increasing family' – by then numbering eight, with a further child expected in a few week's time.[78] Charles, too, with no savings from prize-money to call upon, was unable to keep up his annual payments to her following the loss of the *Phoenix* in 1816. Out of favour with the Admiralty, he was left, with his three children, to survive on his half-pay.

---

* So-called, it was slightly above half full pay. The rates for a Captain ran at £128 to £220 a year before 1814; after 1814, £190 to £270, the level of pay in line with seniority on the Captains' List.

7

Politics and the Navy: The Popham Poem

'A Gallant Commander . . .
For Promptitude, Vigour, Success, does he stand'

Jane Austen 'On Sir Home Popham's
sentence – April 1807'

Following their marriage in July 1806, Francis and Mary Austen ('Mrs F.A.' as she was known in the family) took lodgings at Southampton where they were joined in October by Mrs Austen, her two daughters and Martha Lloyd, 'making one family with his mother and sisters', as Francis put it in his 'Memoir', 'a plan equally suited to his love of domestic society and the extent of his Income which was somewhat restricted'.[1] Southampton was popular with naval men for its proximity to Portsmouth. Although its heyday as a spa-town lay in the past, it was still visited by the occasional 'family of distinction' during its season, from July to October, and enjoyed sufficient patronage to support a respectable list of amenities and attractions: two theatres, a pump room, two sets of assembly rooms, Botanic Spa Gardens and several sea-water baths, together with circulating libraries, a subscription news-room, good shops and three banks. An ancient fortified seaport, with medieval and Elizabethan buildings, and remains worthy of an antiquary's interest, Southampton's more recent improvements had seen the High Street paved and lighted, and patrolled by watchmen for its entire length of three-quar-ters-of-a-mile. It was a road along which the ladies could stroll at their leisure and in safety, as Fanny Knight did one Summer's evening in 1807, noting in her diary that 'Aunt Jane & I walked in the High Street till late'.[2] Altogether, Southampton retained the character of a quiet provincial town and, for the Austen ladies, it made a relaxing change from the more demanding social round of Bath, the city they left, Jane Austen wrote to Cassandra, 'with what happy feelings of Escape!'.[3]

Visiting Southampton in 1812, Mary Russell Mitford found it a 'lovely spot which combines all that is enchanting in wood and land and water, with all that is "buxom, blythe and *debonair*" in society'. It held 'an attraction inde-pendent even of its scenery in the total absence of the vulgar hurry of busi-ness or the chilling apathy of fashion. It is, indeed, all life, all gaiety, but it has an airiness, an animation which might become the capital of Fairyland.'[4]

This is a Southampton touched with the wand of enchantment. The 'narrow, dirty lanes' encountered by a visitor the year before[5] and the 'bad smells of the bye streets' and the 'putrescent quagmires' left by the sea, the experience of an American visitor in 1810,[6] are passed over unobserved. Daily life in lodgings also carried a more mundane reality. With Cassandra at Godmersham for the winter, Jane was left to take charge of the domestic arrangements: 'the torrents of rice puddings and apple dumplings',[7] she recounted to her sister; Mrs F.A.'s pregnancy faintings, which usually followed 'a hearty dinner';[8] and the entertainment of their guests when brother James, his wife and seven-month-old Caroline came to stay – James with his taste for boiled leg of mutton, 'underdone',[9] and his tiresome habit of 'walking about the House & banging the Doors, or ringing the Bell for a glass of Water', behaviour she found disappointing in 'so good & so clever a Man'.[10]

Life at Southampton moved at an easy pace. Nonetheless, Jane found that their 'acquaintance increase too fast'. Francis was recognised by Admiral Albemarle Bertie, a distant relation by marriage. 'To the Berties are to be added the Lances, with whose cards we have been endowed.' Paying their call, the Austen ladies 'found only Mrs Lance at home, and whether she boasts any offspring besides a grand pianoforte did not appear. She was civil and chatty enough, and offered to introduce us to some acquaintance in Southampton, which we gratefully declined.'[11] Other naval men in the town included Captain Edward James Foote (a friend Francis first met on service in the East Indies), whose little daughter was entertained with 'the Treasures of my Writing-desk drawer',[12] and Captain Edward-Walpole Browne, local commander of the Sea Fencibles, introduced to the Austens by Sir Thomas Williams (Charles' patron) who lived nearby at Brookwood.

What lightened the early months in lodgings was the prospect of moving into a more permanent home at No. 2 Castle Square, a fashionable quarter not far from the High Street and well away from the town's 'Stinking Fish', which Jane Austen had mentioned in 'Love and Freindship'.[13] According to Jane Austen's nephew, James Edward Austen-Leigh, who remembered the place well, No. 2 was 'a commodious old-fashioned house' with a fine walled garden, one side of which was bounded by the ramparts of the medieval city wall commanding views across Southampton Water southwards to the Isle of Wight and westwards to the New Forest. 'The top of this wall was sufficiently wide to afford a pleasant walk, with an extensive view, easily accessible to ladies by steps. This must have been a part of the identical walls which witnessed the embarkation of Henry V before the battle of Agincourt...'.[14]

Preparations for the move were well-advanced by February 1807, with

Francis and Mary wishing Cassandra to return from Godmersham 'in time to help them in their finishing purchases' and threatening, in her absence, wrote Jane, to 'chuse everything in the stile most likely to vex you, Knives that will not cut, glasses that will not hold, a sofa without a seat & a Bookcase without shelves'.[15] Then there was the pleasurable task of putting the garden in order, the shrubs to improve along the gravel walk, with syringa and laburnum ('for the sake of Cowper's Line'[16] – 'Laburnum, rich / In streaming gold; syringa, iv'ry pure', *The Task*: 'The Winter Walk at Noon'); and currants and goose-berry bushes for the border under the terrace wall.

Inside the house, 'The alterations & improvements . . . advance very prop-erly, & the Offices will be made very convenient indeed'.[17] Beds for the family and garret-beds for the servants were being constructed and 'the Window-Curtains, sofa-cover, & a carpet to be altered'.[18] Francis joined in the prepa-rations, 'making a very nice fringe for the Drawingroom-Curtains'.[19] By this time, the third week of February, Jane could report to Cassandra that they were 'envied in our House by many people, & that the Garden is the best in the Town'.[20] For Francis, it was a period 'of tranquil enjoyment' in which 'the winter glided rapidly away', such a state of domestic happiness, he wrote, 'that he had ceased to expect and almost to wish for professional employ-ment'.[21]

However, he was to enjoy Castle Square only briefly. The move there was made on 5 March and two weeks later, to his surprise, he was appointed to the *St Albans* (64) for convoying duties to India and China. As a return to active service, this command was welcome. Yet it was disappointing, nonetheless, since the First Lord of the Admiralty had promised Lord Moira that Francis should 'have the first good Frigate that was vacant',[22] an undertaking never fulfilled.

In these early months at Southampton came a remarkable document, Jane Austen's terse and epigrammatic lines 'On Sir Home Popham's Sentence – April 1807':

> Of a Ministry pitiful, angry, mean,
> A Gallant Commander the victim is seen;
> For Promptitude, Vigour, Success, does he stand
> Condemn'd to receive a severe reprimand!
> To his Foes I could wish a resemblance in fate;
> That they too may suffer themselves soon or late
> The Injustice they warrant – but vain is my Spite,
> *They* cannot *so* suffer, who never do right. –[23]

The circumstances were these. On 6th March 1807, a Court Martial was convened on board the *Gladiator* at Portsmouth for the trial of Captain Sir Home Riggs Popham. Popham was charged with having withdrawn his Squadron from the Cape of Good Hope in April 1806, leaving the Colony unprotected, in order to carry a military expedition to Buenos Aires with the aim of liberating the provinces of the Rio de la Plata from Spanish rule – all this without orders from the Admiralty. At the end of a trial lasting five days, the Court sentenced Popham – who was hoping for an honourable acquittal – to be severely reprimanded. (This was the heaviest of the lenient sentences, with cashiering, reduction in rank and loss of seniority higher in the scale, and moderate reprimand or admonition below.)

While these facts are clear enough, virtually everything else about the poem is elusive. Why Jane Austen felt such contempt for the 'Ministry' which set the trial in motion and why she championed their victim, the 'Gallant' Popham, there is no clue whatsoever in the Austen records. With the sole exception of George Holbert Tucker, who gives a single paragraph to the circumstances of the trial,[24] biographers of Jane Austen, old and new, have chosen to ignore the poem; and the only discussion on the literary front comes in the brief notes to David Selwyn's 1996 edition of the collected poems.[25] This is surprising, for in Jane Austen's meagre output of verse – about twenty pieces are known – the Popham poem is the only example of satire on a public event, the kind of ferocious little squib (in the tradition of Pope and Swift) which commonly appeared in the press on contentious political issues and personalities. Alongside Jane Austen's other writing, it stands alone, an anomaly. No more than a trifle, it burns with indignation, a document (if we want to look at it in this light) which upsets any notion of Jane Austen's indifference to the battle-ground of public life and the to-and-fro of political debate.

R. W. Chapman is the only scholar to have put forward an explanation for the poem, suggesting that Jane Austen's 'interest might be personal' since 'Popham lived at Sonning, Berkshire, where her aunt's husband Dr Cooper was Rector'.[26] However, as Dr Cooper died in 1792, this requires us to suppose that Jane Austen was sufficiently moved to write a poem on behalf of one of her uncle's parishioners of many years before. This seems unlikely, especially for someone who was not a ready versifier and whose poetry is only concerned with family affairs. More to the point, there is no evidence that Popham, or his family, ever lived at Sonning, which is near Reading. Where he did settle, in 1804, was at Sunninghill, at the other end of the county, near Windsor, and it looks as if Chapman simple confused the two place-names. Nor does the Popham end provide any help. When the late Hugh Popham was preparing his ancestor's biography in the 1980's he came across no reference to any Austen (or Austin) in Popham's official correspondence – where, unfortunately, the search has to end, since none of his private letters appear to have survived.[27]

Readers will by now have gathered that we are left in the dark. What it was that fired Jane Austen to write such a stinging attack on Grenville's Ministry and such a heartfelt championing of Popham, its victim, is a complete mystery. The historian is faced with that least happy of choices: silence or speculation. Yet the Popham/Austen question is so intriguing that I have had no hesitation in choosing the second route and I hope readers will accept this single apology for the construct of fact, supposition and guesswork which follows.

To some extent Jane Austen's poem may have been fired by party feeling. For although the Austens were not a political family, they were staunch Tories, unwavering in their support of Church and Crown, the Anglican supremacy in religion to be defended as vigorously as the royal prerogative in affairs of state. Grenville's Ministry, however, was a Whiggish assembly. Its aims included curtailing the influence of the Crown and extending the power of the Commons, with Catholic Emancipation as an early objective. Twenty years earlier, it was the Foxite-Whigs who had brought about the trial of the Austens' friend and benefactor, Warren Hastings, for whom Jane retained a lifetime's respect.* On that occasion the family was quick to show its support. Cousin Philadelphia Walter (a daughter of Mr Austen's half-brother) called on Mrs Hastings in town, shared her box at the opera and visited the trial, where she sat from ten to four, having 'the satisfaction of hearing all the celebrated orators, Sheridan, Burke & Fox . . . [who] was highly superior to either as we cd. distinguish every word, but not to our satisfaction as he is so much against Mr Hastings whom we all here wish so well'.[28] Of these three 'old' Whigs bent on prosecution, Fox and his devoted friend Sheridan, one of the managers of the impeachment, survived to serve in Grenville's Ministry.

Hailed by its supporters and derided by its opponents as 'The Ministry of all the talents, wisdom, and ability of the country', it was a government formed in February 1806, after Pitt's death, from the followers of Grenville, Fox and Addington. From the outset, the 'Talents' followed an unpopular course. Long out of office, Grenville at once set about rewarding his followers, most of all the Grenville family, with profitable positions, sinecures and pensions, to the point of public scandal, arousing a barrage of criticism in the press.

* In 1813, on the publication of *Pride and Prejudice*, Jane told Cassandra, 'I am quite delighted with what such a Man writes about it . . . I long to have you hear Mr H's opinion of P. & P. His admiring my Elizabeth so much is particularly welcome to me' (15 September, *Letters*, pp. 218–221). Fanny Burney and Hannah More both thought highly of Hastings.

With Fox set on making peace with France, and others in the Cabinet bent on aggressive policies, the Ministry's handling of the war was bungling and muddled. On the home front, three issues in particular added to their unpopularity. First came the Budget of March 1806. Its principal measure was an increase in the Property Tax (a re-named Income Tax) from 6 1/4 per cent to 10 per cent (two shillings in the pound), plus a reduction in the level of tax exemption, a removal of the allowances for children and a requirement that the tax should be paid in full with any exemptions to be reclaimed afterwards. Unwelcome as these measures were in themselves, they also carried a strong whiff of hypocrisy, coming from a party which in opposition had bitterly attacked a similar increase proposed by Pitt. Now it was the turn of the Talents to taste (as Grenville put it) 'a general sourness and discontent' 'among the middling classes',[29] together with a savaging from Cobbett and Gillray.

A second contentious move in the Spring of 1806 was the group of reforms designed by Windham, the Secretary for War, to improve the terms of service, the pay and the pensions for the Regular Army. In the course of introducing his Motion to Parliament, Windham took the opportunity to air an old complaint of his against the Volunteers, a locally-raised part-time defence force, describing it as a costly encumbrance. He announced his intention of reducing the various Volunteer allowances and privileges, and the exemptions from militia service. The move was ill-judged. In the early stages of the war, the Volunteers were little more than a rich man's hobby. But under the threat of invasion, the membership increased; and by 1804, at the height of the invasion scares, it stood at 380,000. Strong in *esprit de corps* (camaraderie for the rank-and-file), it was a largely autonomous organization, run by the local gentry as a social as much as a military activity. Service with the Volunteers was an act of conspicuous patriotism. Its officers held the King's commission and wore the King's uniform. It was a contribution to the war effort which could be made without stirring far from one's parish or neighbourhood; and it satisfied an appetite for military prestige and the glamour of weaponry and public parades. Although the official line was to discourage 'useless and ornamental dress',[30] the officers rapidly succumbed to 'Scarlet Fever',[31] indulging themselves in costly regimentals, uniforms often extravagant and impractical, with sashes and cross belts, and head-dress of every description, including cocked hats, helmet hats with turbans of scarlet silk or moleskin, and bearskins decorated with cockades, gilt ornaments, badges and feathers, with bonnets for the Highland Volunteers – a plumage sufficiently splendid to inspire Ackermann's equally splendid volume of colour-plates (his first), *The Loyal Volunteers of London* (1798–99), illustrated by Rowlandson, its eighty-seven plates expensively heightened with silver and gold.

Volunteer finery was displayed on every possible occasion – at drills, inspections, field days and general musters, and exercises, camps, ceremonial reviews, drum-head services, troopings-of-the-colour, and the celebration of royal birthdays and great victories, such as St Domingo, when the Volunteers would volley *feu-de-joie* as a contribution to the civic rejoicing, events fully reported in the town and country press.

Nor was this solely a male preserve. Windham succeeded in offending the ladies too. Their contribution was to organise subscriptions, sew flags and banners, present the Volunteer colours and make up the admiring throng. Ladies' magazines celebrated the patriotic show, featuring full-page plates of the most colourful Volunteer garb. And Volunteer assemblies, especially those involving the Volunteer elite, the Yeomanry cavalry regiments, were society events to which the ladies flocked. At Stowe Park, in October 1803, Betsey Fremantle (the wife of Captain Fremantle RN) observed that 'All the neighbourhood was there and the sight of the ground and concourse of people was charming'. In the late Autumn weather, the ladies had the comfort of a marquee from which to watch the Volunteers 'go through their different manoeuvres'.[32]

However, Windham trampled on these local enthusiasms and sensibilities. He withdrew the Inspecting Field Officers, regulars who provided a backbone of military expertise to the Volunteer organization. By his account, the Volunteers were no more than a rabble, useless against the enemy, the very purpose for which Pitt had encouraged their formation at the beginning of the war. 'It was', Windham told the Commons, 'a most dangerous error in judgment to suppose that, because a body of men appeared well to the eye, or made a tolerable show upon a parade, that they were, on that account, to be relied upon as effective soldiers'.[33] Or, as he put it more pithily, in a flight of mockery for which he was never forgiven, they were 'painted cherries which none but simple birds would take for real fruit'.[34] This was flatly contradicted by the reports of the Inspecting Field Officers from all over the country. In 1803–04, Volunteer units were found 'fit to be joined to Regular Troops'.[35] In the opinion of Lord Cornwallis, Master-General of the Ordnance and a soldier or long experience, 'no man, whether civil or military, will persuade me that 300,000 men, trained as the Volunteers at present [December 1803] are, do not add very materially to the confidence and to the actual security of this country'.[36]

Finally, there was the measure which brought the Ministry down in March 1807, a concession towards the Irish Catholics enabling them to hold commissions in the armed services, including staff rank in both the Army and the Navy, even when they were not on the Irish establishment. At first, this proposal seemed acceptable to the King. But then he put his foot down, not only against this measure, but against any discussion whatsoever of the Catholic question. He stood by the letter of his Coronation Oath, solemnly given, and to his mind sacred, inviolable and constitutionally binding, 'to the utmost of' his 'Power' to 'maintain the Laws of God, the true Profession of the Gospel, and the Protestant Reformed Religion Established by Law'.[37] In his eyes, even to raise the Catholic question was to threaten the Crown: 'He must be the Protestant King of a Protestant country, or no King' were his words to Lord Eldon, Chancellor of the next Ministry under Portland.[38]

George's fears and the intransigence with which he held to his Protestant duty may, as some historians have suggested, be a symptom of clinical mania.[39] Yet the mass of the people were firmly behind George in his declared role as the guardian of the established order and in the General Election of 1807 the Tories were quick to profit by this, taking up as their slogan the street-cry of 'No Popery!'.

These were issues to which Jane Austen and the household at Southampton would have been alert, issues of national import. Devout Anglican families recoiled at the hint of Rome, and the threat to the Volunteers struck at loyalties across the land. In the winter of 1797, Bonaparte's Army of England was encamped along the Channel coast. In pursuance of the Defence of the Realm Act, passed in April 1798, the Government called for detailed returns of the manpower available and Mr Austen was able to report that thirty-five men of the parish of Steventon were willing to serve. The Volunteer lists for Hampshire, Berkshire and Kent are studded with the names of the Austens, their family connections and friends. In Kent, brother Edward was to become senior Captain of the East Kent Volunteer Cavalry; his brother-in-law, William Deedes, Colonel of the South Kent Volunteers; Thomas Papillon, elder brother of John (Rector of Chawton from 1801), Major in the South Kent Volunteer Cavalry; Samuel Egerton Bridges, commissioned Captain in the New Romney (Duke of York's Own) Regiment of Fencible Cavalry, and later Captain in the Denton Volunteer Cavalry; Sir Edward Knatchbull, Lt. Colonel Commandant of the Provender Yeomen Cavalry; Stephen Lushington, Captain Commanding the Chislehurst and Footscray Volunteers. In Hampshire, James Holder of Ashe Park offered to raise a Volunteer company from the Parishes of Ashe, Dean, Dummer, Harrington and Steventon, recommending George Lefroy and William Digweed as Lieutenants, a proposal supported and signed by (amongst others) James Austen, then Curate of Steventon. James, although not a Volunteer himself, was very active in the cause, helping to recruit almost a hundred in Steventon and the neighbouring parishes, and subscribing £10 towards the formation of a local Company. In Berkshire, Fulwar Fowle – once a student of Mr Austen's at Steventon Rectory and a member of St John's, the Austens' Oxford college, and an elder brother to Tom, Cassandra's fiancé – was proud to serve as Lieutenant Colonel Commandant of the Kintbury Infantry Company (Rifle) of the Berkshire Volunteers. Fowle, the Vicar of Kintbury, was known to the King himself as 'the best preacher, the best officer and the best rider to hounds in all my royal county of Berkshire'.[40] And his younger brother Charles served with equal distinction as Major Commandant of the Hungerford Volunteer Infantry. These patriots – clergymen* and landowners alike – were stung by criticism of their service, however buffoonish it might seem to Windham. This was not lost upon the ladies. News of the Volunteers occupied their family letters and our best insight upon Volunteer activities during the invasion scare of 1803–04 comes in the correspondence of Jane Austen's oldest and closest friend, Mrs Lefroy, and her sons George and Edward.[41] It is here, for example, that we learn of the Lord Lieutenant of Hampshire's disapproval of cler-gymen holding commissions, which is probably why James Austen, for all his activity in helping to raise the local Company at Steventon, took no part in its running. So we can be certain that Windham's comments were taken badly at Southampton, particularly at the time when James was staying as a guest.

Two further Government decisions struck directly against the Austen family itself, steps which seem to justify Jane Austen's description of the Ministry as 'pitiful, angry, mean'. The first involved James's father-in-law, General Edward Mathew. A distinguished soldier, in 1783 he became George III's First Equerry and in the same year was favoured by the King with the Governorship of Granada and command of the Leeward Islands. By some bureaucratic oversight, on Mathew's second tour of duty the royal confirma-tion of his salary was never obtained; consequently, it was not ratified by the Exchequer. As a result, in 1792 the General was presented with a bill for £11,000, that being the amount drawn, without the King's authority, as his Governor's salary. At the time of Mathew's death in December 1805, the bill remained unpaid and an application was made to his estate for £24,000, the original sum plus compound interest, for which payment in full was now required by the Grenville Ministry. Unfortunately, no appeal was possible to the King as his memory had failed.

This held serious consequences for James, whose first marriage, in March 1792, was to Anne Mathew, the General's daughter. The young couple began

---

* Although in 1798 the Archbishops of Canterbury and York 'urged members of the clergy from taking up arms in the most dire circumstances' (Collins, 1998, p. 198), they were not forbidden to bear arms by Canon Law or by any other Church regulation of recent date. The French Revolutionaries were seen as atheists and enemies of God and in that light the Long War was regarded as a religious war in which the clergy were justified in playing their part – in the Volunteers, a purely defensive role.

married life on an income of £300 (£400 was an income upon which a single woman could live comfortably): £200 came from the four church livings and curacies James had collected plus an allowance of £100 Anne received from her parents. On the strength of this and future expectations, they lived in some style and beyond their means, with a pack of harriers and a carriage for Anne. At Anne's death in May 1795, the General transferred her allowance to James, to be used for his granddaughter Anna's upkeep and education. But these payments ended with the General's death in December 1805. The funds set aside by the Mathews for Anna were swallowed up in the Exchequer demand, which also took a further £3500, this being the balance of the £7000 settlement made by Anne's mother at the time of her daughter's marriage.

According to Anna's third daughter, Fanny, the Exchequer claim 'was a great anxiety to the Austens'.[42] James himself felt 'vexed and outmanoeuvred'.[43] Moreover, he was still troubled by the death of his first wife. This could explain why Jane found her brother such difficult company at Southampton. With straitened financial circumstances, economies were necessary and even threatened his sporting pursuits. As Jane reported to Cassandra, 'Mrs J.A. does not talk much of poverty now, though she has no hope of my brother's being able to buy another horse *next* summer'[44] – this at a time when James was reduced to one. While this measure of economy may sound modest,* it shows that he was under a decidedly unwelcome pressure. For, like his brothers, James had been encouraged by his father to enjoy field sports. He had hunted since childhood and grew up to become a thorough sporting parson for whom a hunter was essential. Nor was the hunt a mere recreation. It was probably the most important social gathering of the neighbourhood, a focal point and bond for the local gentry which secured the clergyman's standing in company with the Squire and other local landowners. Valuable introductions followed as a matter of course. Twenty years earlier, in *The Loiterer* – a weekly journal which James and Henry launched at St John's College, Oxford** – James had made this very point: 'For nothing is more certain than a good shot has often brought down a comfortable Vicarage, and many a bold rider lept into a snug Rectory'.[45+] The proof of this

---

* In addition to the cost of the horse, and its feed and maintenance, the reckoning had also to include a progressive tax on saddle or carriage horses of around £3 for one horse, and around £4 for each of two horses and so on. There was also a tax of £12 for four-wheeled carriages, less for smaller vehicles.

** A thorough-going Tory paper, *The Loiterer* ran for sixty issues from 31 January 1789 until James' departure from Oxford in March 1790. Its contributors included the Austen brothers and other St John's men, with one letter, signed Sophia Sentiment, attributed to Jane.

+ In *Persuasion*, The Rev. Charles Hayter, without a parish of his own, is keeping a living warm for a young man under age. His prospective brother-in-law, Charles Musgrove, deplores the fact that Hayter is not a sporting parson and is failing to exploit this opportunity for meeting a landowner who could propose him for a living.

lay in James's own good fortune. His presentation, in 1791, to the Vicarage of Sherborne St John was the gift of William Chute, the founder in 1790, and Master of the Vine Foxhounds, an introduction which came about through their hunting together in North Hampshire. So if James and his wife now troubled the Southampton household with their grousing about horses, we can see why allowance was made.

The second instance of the Ministry's 'pitiful' meanness was in the treatment of Francis in his pursuit of a frigate. The family hopes now lay with Lord Moira, Master-General of the Ordnance, a Cabinet post giving him direct access to Thomas Grenville, the First Lord. Understandably, the Austens were optimistic. In effect, the military adviser to the Cabinet, Moira carried a further line of interest as leader of the Carlton House Party in Parliament and the Prince of Wales' representative in government. On Pitt's return in May 1804, there was talk of Moira, who was then serving as the Army Commander-in-Chief in Scotland, taking a place then on offer to him in the Cabinet. 'At a very dignified and numerous meeting of political parties, the Prince had declared his backing: that Moira and I are one, we have but one heart and one fate through life between us.'[46] A remarkable pledge of support to make in public, it was remembered by everyone present. So to outsiders, it would appear that any application that carried Moira's support would surely be successful and the Austens had every reason to suppose that with such weighty interest at work, Francis would soon have his frigate, a command to which he was anyway entitled by merit and had only missed two years earlier through the misfortune of Nelson's death and the confusion following Trafalgar. But unknown to the Austens, Moira's credit with the Admiralty, and elsewhere, was wearing thin. A sympathetic memorialist noted this circumspectly: 'he permitted the proverbial rapacity of his Whig friends, and the incessant importunities of the multitude who lived on his generosity, to deprive of some appointments, not strictly Military indeed, those who were said to have reasonable pretensions to them'.[47] Melville got to the point more shortly: 'I suspect Lord Moira totally overrates his influence in any quarter.'[48] For many years Moira had been advancing his own applicants through the interest of the Prince and when at last he gained office himself, in February 1806, with direct Ministerial access, the floodgates opened. His demands came thick and fast, so many and so pressing that scores with 'reasonable pretensions' were passed over, among them Francis Austen. It was a failure which could only strike the family, unaware of the true situation, as a show of ministerial spite. This, together with Windham's assault on the Volunteers and the pursuit of General Mathew's salary, serves to explain the note of personal animus we can detect in the poem's opening line.

In view of the family's experience, it is no surprise that Jane Austen should feel so strongly about the Grenville Ministry. On the other hand, why she took up Popham's cause and bestirred herself to write a poem on his behalf is not so obvious. Strictly speaking, by the time of the Court Martial his guilt was already established and the purpose of the hearing was to enable him to present his side of the case and for the Court to decide upon an appropriate sentence. However Popham might represent the circumstances, in mounting the expedition to Buenos Aires there was no doubt that he was acting without Admiralty orders. The Ministry regarded him as a loose cannon, an insubordinate naval commander to be made an example of: in the words of Thomas Grenville, the First Lord, 'to show the navy we are as attentive to them as to demand subordination from them'.[49] He decided 'to confine the charge to the one simple and undeniable proposition, viz, that being ordered to carry a force for the Cape and for India he had no justification for going a buccaneering to Spanish America'.[50] Moreover, writing on the first day of the trial, he felt confident that the President of the Court, Admiral Sir William Young, would control proceedings from the Admiralty point of view.*[51]

A letter from Admiral Collingwood to Captain Fremantle, a member of the Admiralty Board, provides us with a strictly professional naval judgment on these events. At sea at the time (16 March 1807), Collingwood was unaware of the verdict:

> I suppose we shall hear soon what has been the result of the court martial on Sir Home Popham. I believe you know my sentiments on that subject: if officers who are sent on a service allow themselves by a prospect of success in another quarter to be diverted from it and leave their proper station exposed, it will be difficult to find a reason which can justify it, success in his undertaking will not. But it has been told me that Sir h.p. has been led to that attack on the Spanish settlements by private instructions, which he received from Mr Pitt and Lord Melville, but that ought to be known by the board before this time. If people are to follow their own imaginations the Minister loses his direction of the state.[52]

In the Navy there could be no sympathy for an officer who departed so flagrantly from his orders, a departure not even made palatable by success (as Nelson's blind-eye subterfuge had carried the day at Copenhagen), for the Buenos Aires adventure ended ignominiously with the surrender of the British forces. We have no record of Francis' views on this matter. But the Popham case was a *cause célèbre* and would have been the topic of conversation in naval households, at Castle Square as much as anywhere else, and we can guess that Francis, a stickler for naval procedure, took the same professional line as Collingwood. Francis' log-books and Admiralty correspondence are those of

---

* The Admiralty line against Popham is documented in Appendix 9.

1. Jane Austen: the 'Andrews' engraving made in 1869 from a sketch of her sister by Cassandra. A niece commented that 'though the general resemblance is not strong', 'there is a *look* which I recognise as *hers*'.

2. The topaze crosses purchased for Jane and Cassandra by Charles in 1801 and paid for out of his share of the prize-money for the capture of a privateer.

3. Francis Austen, miniature 1796, in his uniform as a Lieutenant.

4. Francis Austen, about 1806, in his uniform as Captain. Alongside the St Domingo medal is the badge of the CB (Military) painted in at a later date.

5. Francis Austen in the full-dress uniform of Vice-Admiral painted soon after his promotion at the time of Queen Victoria's Coronation in June 1838.

6. Sir Francis Austen, about 1863–65, when he had attained the rank of Admiral of the Fleet.

7. Fanny Palmer, the first wife of Charles Austen, married in Bermuda in 1807, died in 1814.

8. Charles Austen, about 1810, in the uniform of a Captain.

9. Charles Austen, in the early 1840s, in the uniform of a Captain. He wears the star of the CB (Military).

10. Charles Austen, about 1850, in the full-dress uniform of a Rear-Admiral.

11. Scene of action between the English frigate *Unicorn* (32), in which Charles Austen was serving as a Lieutenant, and the French frigate *La Tribune*, 8 June 1796.

12. The *Bermuda* (16), a Bermuda-class sloop, sister-ship to the *Indian* which Charles commanded 1805-10 (reconstruction painted by Derek Gardner, Bermuda Maritime Museum).

13. The *Canopus* (80). Francis Austen was Flag Captain 1804-06.

14. The *Winchester* (52) seen in 1830. The engraving is dedicated to Charles Austen, Flag Captain 1828-30, and the ship's officers.

15. The Ramparts at Portsmouth where Mrs Price took her Sunday walks and Henry Crawford conducted Fanny Price in *Mansfield Park*. The lithograph by James Calcott dates from about 1840. But the scene would be as in Jane Austen's day, save for the wooden semaphore signal tower on the right (built 1822).

16. Portsmouth Point in 1800 by Rowlandson. From carousing, drunkenness and petty thieving, to tender farewells, this scene catches every mood of the town's crowded life, its eyes always to the ships and the sea.

17. Home Riggs Popham, a portrait probably engraved soon after his promotion to Captain in 1795. He was then in his middle thirties.

18. (*left*) Horatio Nelson, *c.* 1797 by Lemuel Francis Abbott.

19. (*right*) Emma, Lady Hamilton, Emma Hart, as she was then, *c.* 1785 by George Romney.

20. Charles Middleton, Admiral Lord Barham, First Lord of the Admiralty, 1805-06.

21. A seaman at Trafalgar, praying that the enemy's shot be distributed in the same proportion as the prize money, with the greater part going to the officers.

22. The Point of Honour' by George Cruikshank, 1825. A seaman, bound to a deck grating, is about to be flogged, when the real culprit announces himself, addressing the Captain.

an officer punctilious in observing orders and equally scrupulous in recording any departure from the letter of his instructions. One such occasion arose later that year.

In charge of the St Albans, he was ordered by his Squadron commander to proceed to Beerhaven (an anchorage on the north side of Bantry Bay in south-west Ireland) and escort five East-Indiamen to the Downs. However, as he explained to the Admiralty, hearing from another Captain that the East-Indiamen were actually elsewhere, in Crookhaven (thirty miles away), 'I therefore judged it to be consistent with the spirit of my orders to proceed thither instead of going to Beerhaven'. The procedure was laid down. Every order received was recorded and reported on in meticulous detail, if not by the Captain himself, by the Captain's Clerk acting on the Captain's instructions and copies were made of all documents and official communications. The summary of these particular orders and events fills several pages of Francis' official letter to the Admiralty written on his arrival at Spithead on 1 January 1808.[53] Officers bred in a tradition in which obedience to orders was the life and soul of the service,* imbued with a respect, as Francis puts it, for 'the spirit' as well as the letter of their orders and driven by training and habit to explain and justify any departure, would have no time for the barrage of evasion and special pleading that Popham laid down in his defence.

But Jane's attitude is startlingly different. The Popham of her poem is not a disobedient sailor but a victimised hero – as if she swallowed his story hook, line and sinker, betraying a gullibility quite foreign to the Jane Austen of the letters and the novels. There, we see a writer whose view of human nature is wholly unillusioned and a part of whose genius lay in revealing the deceptions and self-deceptions of John Thorpe, Willoughby and Henry Crawford, all men in the Popham mould.

The puzzle deepens when we consider Popham's character. He was a man of great ability and varied talents – a linguist, an able speaker in Parliament, a skilful pamphleteer, with a keen political sense and in military matters a near-genius, bubbling with schemes and wheezes to defeat the enemy and smiled on and supported by Tory politicians for his perennial optimism. He was recognised as the expert in what we now call combined operations, coordinated action involving the Army and Navy together in landings from troop-ships and barges, often with supporting fire from the naval vessels. In such 'conjunct expeditions', it was vital to have a recognised and accepted chain of command (disputes between senior officers of the two services were all too common) and for the embarkation and landing to take place to a strict sequence and timing to maintain the tactical formations in which the engage-

---

* The importance of this subject in the public mind can be judged from Southey's Life of Nelson (1813): see Appendix 7.

ment was to be fought, and with an eye upon winds and tides, the natural hazards to any sea-borne operation. In controlling such complex arrangements Popham was a master of diplomacy as well as of logistics.

During the Long War, Popham enjoyed a record of success and it was partly out of his experience in Flanders in 1793–94, involving land-and-sea manoeuvres, that he conceived the idea of the Sea Fencibles. In 1798 he proposed to the Admiralty the 'Outline of a Plan' for the 'Auxiliary Defence of the Coast of England against invasion',[54] a Plan which was adopted and within whose line of defence Nelson and Francis Austen were to serve during the invasion scares either side of the Peace of Amiens.

Popham was also known throughout the Navy for his creation of a highly effective code of flag signals, his *Telegraphic Signals or Marine Vocabulary* devised in 1800, published in 1801 and adopted by the Admiralty and issued to ships-of-the-line in 1803. Individual words and frequently-used commands, as much as a sentence long, could be announced by a single flag. Nelson was so impressed by the practicality of the system that in September 1805, before leaving England for the last time, he twice visited the Admiralty to ensure that copies of the *Marine Vocabulary* were supplied to the entire Mediterranean Fleet. On 19 October, Captain Henry Blackwood wrote home to his wife, 'At this moment we are within four miles of the Enemy, and talking to Lord Nelson by means of Sir H. Popham's signals'.[55] This 'talking' was the news that the Combined Fleet had put to sea. On the day of Trafalgar itself, 'Popham's signals' were used to transmit Nelson's final message round the Fleet.* The system proved so successful throughout the Navy that when, in 1811, Popham issued an improved version, extending his original code, it was immediately adopted by the Admiralty for the Navy's exclusive use.

Nonetheless, despite all his abilities and successes, Popham was suspect, regarded as a maverick too clever by half, a rogue, artful and dodgy; something of a charlatan, 'clever but incurably plausible'; 'gentlemanlike and insinuating'; 'a *damned* cunning fellow';[56] 'a pleasant man but a *dasher*'[57] – as we would say, cutting a dash with more show than substance. His explosive devices – early forms of mines and torpedoes known as 'catamarans', or, to the sailors, 'infernals' – were seen as mere '*charlatanerie*,'[58] himself as a 'Naval quack'.[59] And his defects of character – as they were seen – were matched by his failure to achieve the standing of a true tar or tarpaulin,** the

---

* Nelson's original intention was to begin his signal with 'England confides . . .'. But he was advised that 'confides' would require eight flags, whereas 'expects', already in Popham's code, only required one. Nor was 'duty' in the code-book – presumably because naval life was so deeply imbued with the idea that it was taken for granted. That word too had to be spelt out in single alphabetical flags. This historic message was then followed by the Telegraphic Signal No. 16: 'Engage the Enemy more closely'.

** 'Tar' lasted many years – and Queen Victoria delighted to refer to her sailors by this name.

force of the word brought out in the *1811 Dictionary of the Vulgar Tongue*, where 'Tarpaulin' is defined as 'A coarse cloth tarred over: also figuratively, a sailor'.[60] For an officer this would mean an education in the long, hard knockabout school of life at sea, his professionalism won through years of seamanship and promotion through successful command under fire. Although Popham's start was sound enough – he entered the Navy in 1778 and became a Lieutenant five years later – his career then departed from conventional lines. In 1787, he took leave of absence for two years to pursue his own trading ventures; and failing to extend his leave, was struck off the Lieutenants' list. When he was reinstated, in September 1793, his appointment was not to a ship but as an Agent of Transports to the British Army in Flanders under the command of the Duke of York. A correspondent reported to the Admiralty that Popham's appointment 'makes much noise at Ostend – the employ he has been in has raised it – he's very clever, knows almost everything . . .'.[61] For Popham was a familiar figure at Ostend. It was the base for his commercial operations in the East Indies and the China trade, and from India, he could operate (as he noted) 'without interruption or restraint'.[62]

His major venture, and disaster at this time, was the *L'Etrusco* bringing back from China a cargo of porcelain, tea, cotton cloth and medicinal gums and extracts valued at £50,000, in which his share was one-third. In addition, it carried his own private cargo of silk, fans, clocks, paintings and other luxury goods of high value. *L'Etrusco* reached Ostend safely in July 1793, having evaded pirates, privateers, ships of various navies and Revenue cutters on the long voyage home, only to be boarded by an armed party from a British frigate anchored nearby and seized, rightly or wrongly, as a Prize of War. Popham was to contest this seizure through the courts for fifteen years until, in 1808, his plea ended up as a set of parliamentary Papers laid before the House of Commons. In this same year an action for debt arising out of the first of his trading ventures, dating back to 1789, was heard in the Court of King's Bench.

Litigation runs as a strand through Popham's life. It kept alive the memory of his early duplicities and frauds, the trading illicitly under false names, false colours and false nationalities, with claims and counter-claims of ownership and indebtedness – altogether a web of deception and uncertainty which was exposed to examination through the courts, widely reported and made much of by his enemies.

Even his successes were tainted. In Flanders, his effectiveness in arranging transport for the British forces won him the patronage of the Commander-in-Chief, the Duke of York. With royal support, promotion came fast: from Lieutenant to Commander in November 1794, with charge of Inland

Navigation in Flanders. Four months later, further promotion from Commander to Captain (following a personal letter from the Duke to the First Lord of the Admiralty). These promotions were resented by officers serving at sea and won him an apt nickname, 'the Duke of York's Admiral', while the *Naval Chronicle*, which regarded itself as the upholder of solid professional values and traditions, described Popham as the first of a new breed, the 'Naval Officers of science',[63] more at home on land than sea. Distrust of Popham extended far into the Admiralty itself, with damaging consequences. For example, early in 1798 he proposed an ambitious expedition to demolish sluice gates and a lock on the Bruges-Ostend Canal. This would prevent the movement of French invasion barges along a secure inland route.

It was a sound operation for which Popham was ideally equipped. From his time in Ostend, he knew this to be a vulnerable point on the canal system and he possessed the skill and experience needed for the detailed planning and control of an operation deploying both land and sea forces. The Secretary for War, Henry Dundas, was won over by Popham's obvious expertise, his solid planning and infectious optimism. Others followed, among them General Sir Charles Grey, commanding the South-Eastern District; William Huskisson, the Under-Secretary for War; and Evan Nepean, the Admiralty Secretary. Against his better judgement Spencer, the First Lord, was persuaded to give Popham naval command of the operation, with predictable consequences. The 'jealousies of the *Under* Lords' was Popham's explanation – accurate, as it turned out – for the source of his difficulties.[64] Little support was forthcoming from the junior, professional members of the Admiralty Board, least of all from the junior Sea Lord Rear-Admiral Sir William Young (who was to preside, nine years later, at his Court Martial). Popham was allocated an inadequate ship and crew; at one point, an attempt was made to divert him to Ireland; and the operation was fatally delayed. The sluice-gates, his main target, were destroyed – but the troops were unable to get back to their ships in time and the military force surrendered. Spencer was right to anticipate the root of these problems, as he did in a secret letter to Dundas, before the expedition set sail:

Dear Sir, – Feeling the force of the arguments which have suggested themselves to Sir Charles Grey on the subject of Captain Popham's having the command of the expedition, I have endeavoured, though not without considerable difficulty, to make such an arrangement as will allow of it, and I think you may venture to set Sir Charles at ease on that point. I cannot, however, avoid showing that in these matters I shall, with all possible disposition to concur in making the joint services that may be undertaken go on well, be under the necessity of protesting against this peremptory sort of nomination of *naval* commanders by land officers, as well as against the kind of appeal upon the subject which I perceive has been made on this occasion by Captain Popham to Sir Charles Grey. Captain Popham should remember that he is a very young captain,* that he never commanded a ship-of-war of any description (as far as I know) in his life; and I am not without apprehensions that his being placed in the command of a squadron on this occasion may give great disgust and offence to the profession who are sufficiently irritable in these matters.[65]

Nonetheless, despite these problems, Popham stayed in the good books of the Tory politicians. Too valuable to be dispensed with, he was sent on several missions, part-commercial, part-political: to Russia in 1799 (where he received his Knighthood from the Czar); to the Gulf States, including Aden, in 1800; and, in 1802, to establish a commercial treaty with the Arab states. This last mission gave an opening to his naval enemies, led by St Vincent, First Lord of the Admiralty. Popham was charged with profiting personally for 'the most enormous and profligate' expenditures in the repair of his flagship, the *Romney* (50).[66] This was on the basis of figures supplied by Benjamin Tucker, a protégé of St Vincent, at one time his Private Secretary, now Junior Commissioner on the Navy Board's Committee of Stores. To secure a platform for his defence, Popham entered Parliament and as a result of his performance in the Commons, and some well-judged pamphleteering, won himself the hearing of a Parliamentary Select Committee. In 1805, he was cleared of all charges – but not before a smear campaign had been mounted and a scurrilous pamphlet, suspected to be the work of Tucker, circulated amongst the officers of his Squadron. The *Naval Chronicle* put it aptly: 'his character was whispered away'.[67] In the process, quantities of mud were thrown, some of which stuck and provided lasting ammunition for his enemies. And the accusations remained from long ago – that he was a cheat, no officer and gentleman, but an upstart trader on his own behalf bringing dishonour to the service.

From all we know, it seems clear that a more or less systematic vendetta, inspired by St Vincent – 'a dragon who destroyed those with whom he disagreed' – and carried into effect by Tucker, was conducted against Popham within the highest reaches of the Admiralty and beyond.[68] In Parliament St Vincent led his own Whig grouping known as Lord St Vincent's Party, 'so inveterate against Sir Home Popham' that the Commons was persuaded not to 'give him a Vote of Thanks for the Conquest of the Cape of Good Hope....'.[69] According to the diarist Joseph Farington, Charles Grey, the First Lord of the Admiralty until the end of September 1806, shared St Vincent's 'envy & malignity' towards Popham;[70] and, on the evidence of the Court Martial *Report* maliciously annotated by Tucker (see Appendix 9), it

---

* a very young captain'; referring not to Popham's age (he was now 35) but to the fact that he was junior in terms of appointment.

seems that Thomas Grenville, Grey's successor as First Lord, if not active in this campaign, was certainly party to it.

In the long run, what secured Popham was his military genius, his own political wits, his Tory supporters, his air of conviction and his incorrigible optimism. Jane Austen found her publisher, John Murray, 'a Rogue of course, but a civil one'.[71] Popham was that too, and amusing into the bargain. Fortunately, we have a contemporary sketch which brings him to life. It comes in the recollections of Lieutenant Colonel Fletcher Wilkie, who served in Popham's ship as Lieutenant of Marines on the expedition which regained the Cape of Good Hope in January 1806, three months before Popham led the further expedition to South America:

> I should certainly say that he was not what is called one of Nelson's sailors – neither was he what another Navy man of some celebrity has been named, 'a soldier on board ship,' – the nearest thing I can imagine was a diplomatist afloat. He had led a sort of miscellaneous life – had been employed on gunboat service, forwarding pontoons, and such duty, under the Duke of York, in Holland – who ever afterwards remained his friend; he was then concerned in some private trade – the less said of that the better; at length he was appointed to his present command. He possessed what the Scotch call a good deal of *cleverality* – was very conversant with the details of landing and embarking troops – had made considerable improvements, and given greater scope to the code of telegraphic signals – could run up the repairs of a ship, to make them cut a respectable appearance in the annual expenditure – and could plunder an enemy's dockyard in the most complete and scientific manner. In his manners and address he was gentlemanlike and insinuating – and his powers with the pen need not be doubted, as they got him from between the horns of a dilemma, perhaps more awkward than ever was previously encountered by any public man. Amongst his own officers he was very popular – he took them always wherever there was a prospect of prize-money – and everything in the shape of promotion, that fell at all within his power, he gave to the squadron. To do him justice, also, as regarded ourselves, he spared neither trouble nor expense to ensure the health of the troops. We had fruit served out in abundance both at Madeira and Bahia – and at the latter place he bought the entire cargo of a ship loaded with London porter, which was served without discrimination to all hands. We had roomy ships, great attention to cleanliness – and all these combined brought us to the Cape in the most perfect health. I shall mention, as an instance, the regiment to which I belonged myself. We embarked 903 rank and file from Cork, and landed 901 at the Cape – one man having died of consumption, and another detained on board by accident. I question if, in any other of the most favoured situations in the world, the result would have been equally good, out of a body of 900 men thus confined for six months on board ship.[72]*

---

* The statistics for disease at this time show that Popham's attention to hygiene and the health of his men achieved an extraordinary level of success.

This account reveals how much the detail of Popham's career – his ups and downs, his shady deals and shaky reputation – was familiar to naval men, and on what solid ground stood his name for humanity and practical concern for his crews. A mixture of rumour, gossip and fact, the Popham story would have been well-known to Francis Austen and to the household at Castle Square at the time of the Court Martial.

Six months earlier, in September 1806, a wave of popular enthusiasm had greeted the news of Popham's success in the capture of Buenos Aires. The *Hampshire Chronicle*, a Southampton paper, reported that on 12 September the despatches had passed through Winchester on their way to London; and its issue of 22 September reprinted the text of the despatches from the *Gazette*, including Popham's report to the Admiralty, 'congratulating' (in his own words) 'their Lordships on His Majesty's forces being in full possession of Buenos Aires and its dependencies; the capital of one of the richest and most extensive provinces of South America', a capture offering 'peculiar advantages' 'To the commerce of Great Britain . . . as well as to the active industry of her manufacturing towns.' With a further stroke of news management, Popham also sent open letters to the Mayors and Corporations of the principal trading and manufacturing centres – London, Liverpool, Bristol, Manchester, Birmingham and Glasgow – extolling the rich prospects in South America for British commerce and industry. As he anticipated, the letter was reported to the nation at large. Six months before, on 1 March, church bells throughout the country had celebrated his success in seizing Cape Colony from the Dutch – although St Vincent had successfully prevented a Parliamentary vote of thanks; and in April, the Committee of the Lloyd's Patriotic Fund had awarded him a £200 Vase. Now, once again, he was hailed as the hero of the hour. The Lloyd's Committee took the lead, resolving on the very day the South American news was received in London that Popham should receive another £200 Vase for 'gallant and disinterested conduct in this successful and important enterprise'.[73] Two weeks later, on 2 October, the City of London signified the approval of the commercial and financial communities, conferring on Popham and Beresford, the Army Commander, *in absentia*, Honorary Freedoms of the City and 'Swords to the value of Two Hundred Guineas', citing 'their very gallant conduct and very important services rendered . . . at once opening a new source of commerce to the manufactures of Great Britain, and depriving her enemy of one of the richest and most extensive colonies in her possession'.[74]

A more precise gloss is given in the *Morning Post*: 'The drooping spirit of commerce is wonderfully revived . . . Every speculative mind is engaged in preparing adventures for that market.'[75] For although Napoleon's

Continental Blockade was not yet in place, manufactured exports had suffered a sharp drop and home consumption was at a low ebb. By Order in Council, Buenos Aires was declared a part of His Majesty's dominions and thus open to trade. So South America was seen as a godsend, a market on which to unload goods standing unsold in Britain's warehouses, including such unlikely items as top hats, pianos and light-weight stays.

Popham also made great play with the hoard of specie seized from the Royal Treasury at Buenos Aires, over a million dollars, which he shipped on the first vessel to England, arranging, as a grand stunt, the ceremony with which it was to be transported from Portsmouth to London. On 18 September, *The Courier* reported this remarkable procession.

> Thirty sailors, dressed in the same uniforms as when they attacked the Spaniards on shore, have it under their charge, preceded by a brass field-piece, which they intend to fire a salute with, on their entrance into the principal towns on the road. The Royal Marine band played several martial tunes, at the head of the wagons; which were decorated by the Spanish flags taken at Buenos Ayres, and three British colours, with R.B. on them, meaning the Royal Blues, the corps of Seamen that landed being so called by Sir Home Popham.[76]

In London, the crowds turned out to pull the train of waggons through the streets to the Bank of England and Popham was blessed as a national benefactor, praised as a military hero and hailed as a man of enterprise with the interests of the country and its citizens at heart. Although (as Farington reports) there was an 'evident intention' on the part of the Ministry 'to do something unfavourable to Him', their opponents had plans of their own 'to increase His popularity & render the Ministry cautious of what they might do'.[77]

But there was no silencing Cobbett. Unswayed either by popular feeling or ministerial policing, his *Weekly Parliamentary Record* kept up an independent and determinedly sceptical commentary: 'The capture of this colony has, it is said, "filled the commercial world with joy". Not me!';[78] and he went on to question its benefit to the people of England. Its rule and upkeep, he prophesied, would be a further burden on the taxpayer; sentiments he promptly repeated the following week; and in later issues he was to quote extensively from the reports, despatches and letters of Beresford and Popham, including Popham's letter of 6 July 1806 announcing to the Admiralty Secretary, William Marsden, the capture of 'the capital of the richest and most extensive provinces of Spanish America'.[79] Cobbett described Popham's 'circular letter' as 'highly reprehensible',[80] ridiculed the presentation of the Lloyd's vase and attacked the shipping of Popham's personal booty, his 'plunder'.[81]

By the end of the year, the Ministry felt sufficiently sure of its ground to follow up Cobbett's line of attack. On 19 December, Lord Howick (recently, as Charles Grey, First Lord of the Admiralty, now Foreign Secretary) delivered a Parliamentary onslaught (fully reported in *The Times*), revealing that he was one of the first in government to seek Popham's recall, and attacking the whole expedition, 'conduct' he considered 'highly reprehensible, and a subversion of all discipline and government'. Howick then turned to 'the fatal influence of that Patriotic Society at Lloyd's, which is held out to the Navy as giving greater encouragement than the Government of the country'.[82] This was a speech close to Cobbett's heart, and duly reported in his *Parliamentary Record*,[83] and taken up at some length four weeks later, when he pointed out that Popham was a pawn in a larger political battle. The official criticism of the Lloyd's Fund was a controversy awakened, he suggested, by 'a reward to an officer disliked by the ministers' and the opposing views of the *Courier* and the *Morning Chronicle* represented 'a battle between the anti-ministerial and the ministerial newspapers'.[84]

These, and other views, were summarised in the *Annual Register* for 1807, which spoke of the expedition as having 'originated in a spirit of rapacity and plunder'[85] and cast Popham as the villain of the piece, manipulative, a man of 'very plausible eloquence'.[86] Had he ever 'been placed in a situation to have a single shot fired at him? . . . yet by a dextrous management of newspapers, he came to be called, by his numerous partisans, the *gallant* captain, the *gallant* commodore, the *gallant* Sir Home Popham'.[87] Cliché it might be. Yet along with Popham's other admirers – including the Patriotic Fund at Lloyd's and the Corporation of the City of London – Jane Austen too was happy to follow convention and hail him as 'Gallant Commander', even though the expedition's victories had been easily won and its success short-lived. Within two months of their first victory, the British troops were routed, forced to surrender and driven into captivity. News of this dismal fiasco only reached London after Christmas. But long before that the decision was made to recall Popham. The order went from the Admiralty on 28 July 1806 to be received by Popham at the beginning of December. He arrived at Weymouth on 16 February 1807, and was arrested and charged four days later.

By this time the country was split. You were either against Popham, as a rash and disobedient adventurer, a self-publicist of tarnished reputation, fit (according to some) to be shot; or for him, as a quixotic seaman patriot of daring and enterprise, made the scapegoat of a failing Ministry and the victim of naval jealousies. If we trust the poem, Jane Austen had no doubts. Her faith remained unshaken. For her, Popham stood as the touchstone of 'Promptitude, Vigour, Success', a belief difficult for anyone to sustain without some understanding of the man himself, his flaws and weaknesses.

But how could she have known Popham so well? And why did she rouse herself to take his part so vigorously in a poem which belonged to her private life and which was addressed, as it seems, only to herself and the family?

To these questions there is no firm answer. Nothing has come to light to establish a direct connection between Popham and the Austens, let alone with Jane in person. But turning to the realm of possibilities, we have the coincidence of naval service. Both Popham and Francis were in the East Indies at the same time, followed the same routes and visited the same places. There exists the possibility of their having met. All we can do at this point is to rehearse the facts in the hope that some day letters or memoirs will turn up to tell us what really happened.

Popham first arrived in India in 1787, having obtained two years leave of absence from the Navy, as he explained, 'to follow my private affairs . . . a Marine Enterprise from Ostend to the East Indies' and to improve his professional skills of 'Practical Astronomy and Marine Surveying'. On his arrival at Calcutta, these 'skills' were soon put to good use. At the request of Lord Cornwallis, the Governor-General, he undertook 'a survey of Laccam's Channel and Harbour'[88] at the mouth of the Hooghly, on the sea approaches to Calcutta, a task which won him official thanks. Soon established in Calcutta society, he married the daughter of a Captain in the East India Company's military service, remaining in India until the end of 1788 when he returned to his trading base at Ostend.

In July 1790, Popham left Ostend for a second visit to India and we next hear of him in the Spring of 1791 when his ship was contracted by the East India Company to supply their forces engaged in skirmishes with Tippoo Sultan on the Malabar Coast. On the way to Bengal, L'Etrusco was caught by the South Westerly monsoon and carried Eastwards across the Bay of Bengal to 'the Company's New Settlement on the Prince of Wales Island in the Streights of Malacca',[89] known today as Penang. While his ship was being repaired, Popham occupied his time profitably, conducting a wide-ranging survey of the island.* This included an account of its climate and produce, and an assessment of its suitability as a naval base and the prospect that Penang 'might become the magazine of all western trade, while London should become the emporium of the whole Oriental commerce'.[90] This vision, fired by Popham's mercantile spirit, never came about. But the survey did produce something of substance. Popham made use of his nautical expertise and carried out extensive hydrographic exploration of uncharted waters.

---

* The survey was published in London in 1799: *A Description of Prince of Wales Island, in the Streights of Malacca with its Real and Probable Advantages to Recommend it as a Marine Establishment.*

This led him to an important discovery, the existence of 'a South Channel between the Island and the Malayan Coast',[91] a route of sufficient depth to allow the passage of merchantmen. This meant that ships bound for China could now avoid the longer route round the northern tip of the island, in the face of the monsoon; and to demonstrate the value of his discovery, in the Summer of 1792, having returned to Penang, he piloted a fleet of East Indiamen and local vessels through this new southern route, arriving in Canton in September and returning to Europe in 1793 with a valuable cargo.

These activities coincided with the period of Francis' service in the East Indies. In 1791, Francis was in the *Perseverance* off the Malabar coast when the *L'Etrusco* arrived with supplies of rice and grain; and, under Commodore Cornwallis, he paid several visits to Prince of Wales Island, the earliest of these in January and February 1790. With his own particular interest in hydrography and the making of charts, Francis could not have been unaware of Popham's pioneering work in these waters; and as a chart of the newly-discovered South Channel was published in Calcutta in 1792, Cornwallis may have taken advantage of this route. So if their paths did cross, it is here and in Calcutta that Francis and Popham would have met. The European population of the island was minute, fewer than twenty in 1788 and not much larger in the years following. In Calcutta was another small grouping, the society immediately around the Governor-General. According to his own report, Popham was treated favourably by Lord Cornwallis, by whom he was 'graciously and kindly received';[92] and in the circle of the Governor-General Francis – first as a 'young gentleman' and later as a Lieutenant under the patronage of his Commodore, the Governor-General's brother – could have met him.

Popham was a striking and memorable figure, and the diarist William Hickey thought that his activities were worth recording.[93] Both of them had attended Westminster School and regular Westminster dinners were held in Calcutta for its old boys. (At such a dinner in 1801, Popham was a guest-of-honour and Hickey took the chair as the Senior Westminster present.) If the supposition of a meeting between Popham and Francis is correct, Francis' letters home would surely have carried some mention of him, some account of his reputation as a man of enterprise and achievement. If so, we have the possibility that it was through Francis that the Austens first heard about Popham, and that whatever interest Jane subsequently took in his fortunes had its beginnings here in the early 1790s.

A less welcome encounter with Popham may have occurred in the Autumn of 1804, when Francis was serving in the *Leopard* (50), Admiral Louis' Flagship at the head of a powerful Squadron cruising off Boulogne. It was here that

Napoleon had assembled a large flotilla of invasion craft. The Government, concerned at this build-up, was receptive to any scheme for their destruction and Popham came up with a characteristically ingenious proposal. This was to send in water-tight containers packed with explosives set off by means of a clockwork timer. These 'catamarans', as they were known, can be regarded as a primitive form of torpedo, according to the *Naval Chronicle*, 'resembling . . . a large coffin.'[94] To sailors imbued with the traditions of the 'wooden world', it sounded a madcap idea and met with suspicion and resentment throughout the Channel Fleet, especially among those weather-hardened veterans blockading Brest and Rochefort and riding out the winter gales off the French coast. Melville, First Lord of the Admiralty, who witnessed the attack, was fully aware of these rumblings and set out an uncompromising Admiralty position to Lord Keith, Commander-in-Chief of the Channel Fleet. It was recognised that Popham – not only the inventor of the weapon but the organiser of the attack – 'is an object of envy with some, of jealousy with others, but as he is attempted to be run down, it is the duty of the Government to run him up'.[95] Support at this level was needed since the attack, on 3 October, was unsuccessful; four fire-ships and five catamarans were expended for the destruction of a single barge.

Francis' own verdict is set down in his Memoir:

> Captain Austen was present at the attempt made to destroy the enemy's flotilla at Boulogne by means of vessels loaded with combustibles which were to be exploded by clockwork machinery and which totally failed from the impossibility of directing the vessels with any tolerable precision to the object intended to be assailed. This horrible mode of warfare seems scarcely justifiable in principle (amongst civilised nations) short of self-preservation and perhaps its entire want of success may have been a fortunate circumstance for England who could not have expected to be the only power to use such machines and whose shipping would be constantly liable to similar attack with much greater facility from the exposed situations of the anchorages then used.[96]

While his analysis of the failure of the attack is straightforward, Francis' objection to the catamarans 'in principle' requires a brief elucidation. An attempt to destroy an enemy without risking any injury oneself, as this device seemed to allow, transgressed the rules of war. In the language of the time, weapons such as this, 'employed in the darkness and silence of night, against a helpless and unsuspecting enemy', 'ought never to be resorted to'.[97] We may call this Quixotic but it was a sentiment still surviving in naval circles from the days of chivalry. Francis may have communicated his views to the Austen household at Bath, or reported them personally during the few weeks' leave he enjoyed between quitting the *Leopard* and joining the *Canopus*, mocking

POLITICS AND THE NAVY: THE POPHAM POEM

the inventor and condemning his devices. On the other hand, it is questionable whether Francis would have conducted his mother and sisters into
matters so technical. So Popham's name may have passed unmentioned at
this time.

However, strange to say, the possibility of a link between Popham and the
Austens is very much stronger around circumstances which appear, at first
sight, to be quite remote: these arise out of Popham's support for the South
American liberation movement, a sequence of events which begins in August
1803, when Popham offered his services to Francisco de Miranda, the
Venezuelan patriot; and it concludes with the expedition to Buenos Aires and
his Court Martial. What could connect these events with the Austen family is
the involvement, firstly, of Lord Moira, Francis' patron and heavily in debt to
Henry Austen, and secondly, the involvement of Henry himself, in a speculative financial role. Such a scenario would point to a strong family interest in
the success of Popham's enterprise and go some way to explain Jane Austen's
concern for his fate.

Miranda, a self-exiled Venezuelan, known as General Miranda from his
service with the French Army, had been badgering British Ministers since
1783 for support in mounting an expedition to liberate his own country and
other parts of Spanish America. Turned down by North and Fox, in 1790 he
brought the same scheme to Pitt. Although Pitt expressed caution, Miranda's
hopes were kept alive. He was on the government pay-roll with an annuity of
£200 and found encouragement when, from time to time, talks were
resumed. He managed to enlist influential support, including Addington,
Dundas, the Foreign Secretary, George Canning, Nicholas Vansittart, a
young Tory politician who was to become Chancellor of the Exchequer, and
Grenville – although in time Grenville became disenchanted and by 1804 no
longer trusted him. Burke, his liberal feelings stirred, also backed Miranda's
aim of emancipating South America.

Popham brought fresh vigour to Miranda's campaign. In the military
sphere, he provided credibility, the recognised expertise to carry through
such an ambitious land-and-sea operation. Popham also added weight on the
political front. He enjoyed the confidence of several members of the government, the most important being Dundas. A long-term ally of Pitt, Dundas
wielded considerable power through his control of the Scottish vote in the
Commons. With the return of Pitt's Ministry in May 1804, Dundas (now
Lord Melville) came into office as a powerful First Lord of the Admiralty. One
member of the Campbell clan, Lord John, writing that same month to
another, had no doubt on the matter: 'Dundas is the man who gives away
everything. He rules Pitt, and is thus the first man in England.'[98]

If we are to believe his critics, Miranda was not unlike Popham – a soldier of fortune, a contraband trader and an adventurer at large, duplicitous when it suited him. However, history remembers him, fittingly and very precisely, not as The Liberator of Venezuela (a title reserved for Simon Bolivar) but as *El Precursor* (The Forerunner). This was the endeavour that sustained him through the many years of waiting on ministerial favours. Popham's motives were quite different. As an ingenious tactician and deviser of schemes, he was taken by the challenge of Miranda's great enterprise. Moreover, it was an enterprise leading to boundless wealth, for him personally and for his country. The prize, as he saw it, was trading and commercial riches, the opening up of a vast new market for British goods; and beyond that, the fabled El Dorado of Peru's silver and Mexico's gold. These were treasures which loomed large in the public imagination and with some reason: from Spanish South America came three-quarters of the world's supply of silver at this time; and, save for a minute quantity from the Guinea Coast of Africa, all the world's gold.

Miranda's second partner was Alexander Davison, Nelson's prize-agent, banker, and manager of his financial affairs. Davison's main source of income was his business as a government contractor, supplying the Army with barracks stores and equipment, everything from boots and tents to candles and coals, a trade from which he took a double profit, charging the government the buyer's commission of 2 1/2 per cent on goods which he supplied out of his own warehouses (a malpractice for which he was convicted in 1808, after ten years at it, serving twenty-one months in Newgate). His part in Miranda's scheme was to find the ships, supplies and funds.

When he first joined up with Miranda in 1803, a few months ahead of Popham, Davison offered to secure three or four vessels for the expedition provided that the government would agree to equip a man-of-war and cover his expenses should the attack on Venezuela fail. Popham, with a surer grasp of the military implications, soon upped this modest requirement. In November 1803, he addressed a paper to Charles Yorke (the Home Secretary) with an extended shopping-list: a regiment of infantry, two companies of artillery and two squadrons of dismounted cavalrymen. Popham also argued for a second expedition to be mounted against Buenos Aires. Quite apart from its possible strategic importance in future military operations, Buenos Aires was a tempting prize. The seat of the Royal Treasury, the principal route to Spain for Peruvian silver, the headquarters for the largest Spanish merchants, the main city for the *intendencias* (provinces) of Spanish South America, and the commercial heart of its trade.

Over the coming months, further ambitious and wide-ranging schemes were drawn up, involving ever more ships, larger forces and the prospect of liberation for wider areas of Spanish America. There was a setback when

Addington, the Prime Minister put an end to government support. But on Pitt's return to office in May 1804, discussions were reopened, culminating in meetings between Popham, Melville and Pitt in October. To set these discussions on a positive course, Popham, with Miranda's help, drew up a comprehensive plan and overview, his Memorandum of 14 October.[99] This laid out the economic, political and military advantages to Britain if Spanish South America was freed, not by military conquest but by selective occupation at strategic points along the Atlantic and Pacific coasts, exploiting the supposed readiness of the people to rise against a 'tyrannical Government' – an over-optimistic assumption on Miranda's part. Such steps, Popham argued, if taken promptly, would pre-empt any French ambitions in the area. Denying Spain its supplies of gold and silver would not only channel these vast riches to Britain, it would also put an end to Spain's support of France, with dire consequences for Napoleon. Moreover, Spain would be deprived of its hard-wood and a source of its seamen,leaving its navy, the third in Europe, disabled. This was his line of argument. Popham went on to outline the course of the operation and detail the land and sea forces required. Trinidad would be the staging-post for landings along the north-eastern coast, including the primary objective, Caracas, the capital of Venezuela, where Miranda felt certain of finding support. 'The next point from Europe must certainly be Buenos Ayres', requiring 'a force of three thousand men'. As to immediate action, the Memorandum concluded, this should be the despatch of Miranda to Trinidad to prepare the ground without further delay.

The note of urgency at this point reflects Miranda's impatience to get started. He regarded his arrival in Trinidad as the trigger to the whole enterprise, since it was from the West Indies that he proposed to contact sympathisers on the mainland and agree with them the detailed plans for the Caracas insurrection. It was a voyage for which he had been long prepared. A ship was ready to move at short notice. Only an official go-ahead was needed. But this never came. For all their readiness to listen and their sympathy and support, both Pitt and Melville remained cautious, doubly so in the face of this Memorandum.* The scope, ambitions and demands of the grand design carry all the marks of Popham's optimistic and inventive mind. Its rhetoric of high promise and rapid reward is the work of the skilled pamphleteer:

> The idea of conquering South America is totally out of the question, but the possibility of gaining all its prominent points, alienating it from its present European connexions, fixing on some military position and enjoying all its commercial

* At the Court Martial, Popham laid the Memorandum before the Court as part of his evidence in defence, submitting, on grounds of public policy, that it should not be read out. So it was not disclosed, nor was it subsequently published with the trial documentation.

advantages can be reduced to a fair calculation, if not a certain operation; the nerve and spirit which such an enterprize would give to this country if successful are incalculable, the riches that it would bring in, the new sources that it would open for our manufactures and navigation both from Europe and Terra firma [South America], and from Asia to the Pacifick are equally incalculable and the popularity and stability that it would give any Government that undertook it may be estimated from the preceding propositions with the additional satisfaction of knowing that some accounts must be received of the result of its first operation in three months after it sailed from England.

We can imagine how seasoned politicians viewed bait as bare-faced as this. And the document as a whole betrays a *folie des grandeurs* driven by Miranda's dreams and Davison's rapacity. Melville's belief in Popham was stretched to breaking point. According to Miranda's notes on the meeeting, Melville was encouraging, saying 'that although the plan was vast and apparently complicated, yet, in his opinion there was nothing in it which was not practical and sensible in relation to the whole.'[100] Privately, however, Melville was sceptical. Having in mind the shortage of troops, the complexities of such a long-distance operation and, above all, the risk of driving Spain into a deeper alliance with France, he observed to Moira that 'it is scarcely possible to figure a more wild idea as applicable to the present times'.[101] And Melville was particularly well-placed to judge the practicability of Popham's scheme. Four years earlier, as Secretary for War, he had urged on his cabinet colleagues the importance of South America. However, what he then argued for was neither 'conquest or colonization' but 'the acquisition of the South American market' for British 'manufactures and commerce' and the establishment of 'commercial stations', including 'the River Plate.'[102]

Although the approaches to Ministers and the papers presented were confidential or marked 'secret', Miranda's general intentions were well-known. Since the breakdown of the Peace of Amiens in May 1803, with the expectation of an imminent declaration of war on Spain, the possibility of an attack on Spanish America, in some form or other, had been widely canvassed in political and commercial circles. A recognisable lobby came into being. This included merchants and City men alongside politicians, military and other public figures. Popham and Davison, of course, were at the heart of this campaign, providing its leadership, while on the fringes of this network, standing to one side, is the figure of Moira. As an intimate of the Prince of Wales and his political representative, Moira kept his distance from Miranda. But Miranda's associates he knew well.

Popham he first met in Flanders in 1794 with the Duke of York's forces. A successful General himself and a veteran of Bunker's Hill, Moira had appreciated Popham's military gifts. Beyond this, he detected the mind of a politician

and judged that the young officer would make a serviceable courier and intermediary in the confidential affairs of his royal master. Moira must have
reported back before the end of the year and Popham's name crops up in
correspondence from Major-General David Dundas writing to the Prince
from Holland in November 1794, referring familiarly to 'Popham' as having
repaired a bridge and the presence of 'Popham's sailors' at 'Nimeguen'.[103]
Later, it served the interests of the Carlton House party to have Popham's
support in Parliament. Moira attempted, without success, to find Popham a
seat in 1801 – not suspecting that his worldly-wise protégé was looking after
his own interests at the same time, seeking the 'protection' of Dundas (as he
put it) 'in directing me through the rugged path of politics'.[104] Nonetheless,
the connection with Dundas and other Tory politicians proved no embarrassment to Popham in his dealings with Moira, which flourished over these
years, its intimacy maintained. It was this connection which emboldened
Popham to write to the Prince of Wales from Buenos Aires in July 1806, ten
days after its capture and before the defeat of the British forces, prematurely
announcing the success of the expedition, pointing to the 'great commercial
productions & capabilities' of this, 'the richest Province of South America',
'the channels it offers for a very extensive consumption of every British
manufacture', and soliciting the Prince's help in persuading the Government
to send out reinforcements so that the operation could be extended. In this
letter, Popham names Moira as his 'very particular friend'.[105]

The nature of Davison's relationship with Moira is less clear. What we can
say is that Moira felt sufficiently obliged to him to go out of his way in
offering support and patronage, even after his disgrace in 1804, when Davison
was sentenced to twelve months in the Marshalsea for bribery at a
Parliamentary election. (Nelson's bitter comment was that Davison had been
'duped', that he had ignored 'a friend's caution . . . He would only consult
Lord Moira and such clever folks . . .').[106] As Master-General of the Ordnance
in Grenville's Ministry, Moira gave Davison the office of Treasurer of the
Ordnance; early in 1806, he backed Davison for a Baronetcy, an award
successfully opposed by Grenville and Fox; and at Davison's trial in 1808,
Moira testified in his defence. Was it friendship or obligation? Probably the
second. Moira was careless with money, chronically in debt, on his own
account and on behalf of his master, while Davison was a money-man,
anxious to make his way in society and prepared to pay for it. Loans* or gifts
may well explain why Moira and the Prince of Wales patronised the extravagant parties staged at Davison's town house in St James's Square.

As far as Davison was concerned, Miranda'a Liberation movement was an

---

* We know, for example, that in July 1809, on jewels deposited as security, Davison lent the
Prince of Wales over £11,000.

opportunity for investment. As a first step, in return for the promise of his help,* he had already negotiated trading concessions with Miranda.* Miranda was joined by Popham from much the same motive. Moira also regarded the South American scheme as a money-making venture and it was a project which both he and Davison continued to promote, with Melville's encouragement, until Miranda eventually set sail in August 1805.

Having at last found help from sympathisers in the United States, Miranda reached the coast of Venezuela in April 1806 and persuaded Rear-Admiral Sir Alexander Cochrane to protect his landing from interference by sea and to ship him a limited range of supplies, all this in secret and, at first, unauthorised by the Government. At this time, Moira was known to Admiral Cochrane as one of Miranda's 'warm friends' in the Ministry.[107] With Davison now installed as Treasurer of the Ordnance, Moira tried to persuade his Cabinet colleagues to authorize full and official support, but with no success.

In supporting him financially, Henry Austen would certainly have known of Moira's involvement and it would have been quite in character for Henry to have offered backing for Miranda's scheme, in the expectation (like Davison) of an eventual return. Henry's brothers and sisters, investors in his banking and Agency activities, would have watched these events with close attention, probably with concern as well. Ambitious for wealth, Henry shared the entrepreneurial and risk-taking propensities of Popham and Davison and in money matters was daring, even foolhardy, with a train of sureties and investments in which members of the family were heavily committed.**

Francis, indeed, had a double concern – as a partner in Henry's Agency and as a sailor, for whom the opportunity of action off the Atlantic and Pacific coasts of South America would have been a welcome alternative to the long stretches of blockade duty which followed from Britain's strategy of containment. Not everyone in the Navy shared Nelson's single-minded dedication to this task; nor did they so roundly reject the excitements and rewards of 'buccaneering expeditions', a position put forcefully in Nelson's letter to Moira in the Spring of 1805 (part of this letter has already been discussed in relation to Moira's support for Francis, see above, page 90):

> As I know nothing of what is going on in the expedition way, I can't say that I approve or disapprove, but a blow struck in Europe would do more towards making us respected and of course facilitate a peace than the possession of Mexico or Peru, of both which I am sure we are perfectly ignorant of the disposition of the

---

* Armies were enormous consumers of leather and as a government contractor, Davison would have been well aware of the great flow of hides that passed through Buenos Aires, approaching 1,500,000 a year. More widely, leather was a raw material of prime industrial use, occupying the place later taken by rubber, plastics and elastic metals.

** See Appendix 8.

inhabitants, and least of all I hope we shall have no buccaneering* expeditions. Such services fritter away our troops and ships when they are so much wanted for more important occasions and are of no use beyond enriching a few individuals. I know not, my dear Lord, if these sentiments coincide with yours, but as glory and not money has through life been your pursuit, I should rather think that you will think with me that in Europe and not abroad is the place for us to strike a blow which should make the Corsican look aghast even upon his usurped throne.[108]

It appears that Moira's original (missing) letter to Nelson aired the idea of a Miranda-style 'liberation' expedition and that Moira placed this immediately alongside the suggestion that Nelson should give Francis a frigate – as if, in Moira's mind, the two were associated. Indeed, they would be if Henry Austen, and through Henry's Agency, Francis too, were involved in backing the Miranda-Popham operation, an enterprise in which Moira's own finances were also bound up.

If these suppositions are correct, the Austens had a direct interest in the recent ups and downs of Popham's career, an interest sufficiently close, and sufficiently knowledgeable for Jane Austen to produce this angry squib at the finish of the Court Martial. The trial proceedings were reported at length in the provincial and London press and the Austens would have followed the accounts in the Southampton papers, the *Hampshire Chronicle* or the *Hampshire Telegraph*, both of which, catering for a heavily naval readership, had in the past made a good deal of Popham's exploits at the Cape and Buenos Aires, and now gave considerable prominence to the trial proceedings.**

Popham exercised his 'cleverality' to the full. His three 'friends to assist in the Defence' were chosen with care.[109] One was John M'Arthur, also a money-maker, who had joined Popham in one of his trading ventures twenty years earlier. M'Arthur was also a sea lawyer, the acknowledged expert in Courts Martial law and procedure, and the author of the standard work, the *Treatise of the Principles and Practice of Naval and Military Courts Martial* of 1792. On the second day, Saturday 7 March (the first having been spent in lodging the charges against him), Popham succeeded in having the hearing suspended until the Monday following. This, he claimed, was needed to allow him time to prepare his defence, in view of 'the variety of new documents and

---

* Nowadays, the word has a jolly, adventurous ring. In Nelson's time, it carried the far less congenial association of ruthless piracy.

** Reporters were permitted to attend the Court Martial but no press coverage was allowed until its conclusion. The level of public interest and the trial's heavy political overtones ensured that the reports were given ample space and that the trial itself was a matter of fierce debate between the pro- and anti-ministerial papers. A full account, running to around 20,000 words, appeared in the *Naval Chronicle* (1807), xvii. 209–42.

papers most unexpectedly introduced into the charge'. In fact, as it was pointed out by the Court, the only addition had been 'a list of papers intended for the support of the charge'.[110] But the Court, not to be wrong-footed, allowed Popham his adjournment.

As the central plank of his defence, Popham argued that the expedition to South America was not, as the prosecution maintained, a rash adventure, an opportunist move, ill-conceived, taken on the spur of the moment and wholly unauthorized, but an operation long considered, carefully planned – the Memorandum was introduced as evidence of this – and carried out with Ministerial knowledge and approval. Popham represented himself as a patriot sailor. In proceeding 'upon this long projected expedition' and in fulfilling 'a favourite object with Mr Pitt', he was doing what he felt to be 'my duty, for the interest of my country'. As to having 'left the Cape exposed to attack and insult', he rejected that outright, with praise deftly turned to the military commander: 'through the well-known zeal, ability, and judgment of Lieutenant-General Sir David Baird, the Cape of Good Hope was placed in a state of the most perfect security'.

Popham also rejected outright the charge that personal greed was the driving force, 'that sordid, instead of honourable motives operated to induce me to undertake this expedition,'[111] and he pointed to 'instances where captured property, to the value of several million dollars, had been restored to its settler owners'.[112] What the Court did not know, however, was that Popham had promised Baird a share in the immense sums he hoped to gain during the operation. This was the *quid pro quo* for Baird's military force – 700 men of the 71st Highland Regiment, some dismounted light dragoons and six field-pieces – supplied to Popham for the River Plate attack. On 6 July 1806, with over one million dollars on its way to England, and the expectation of much more, Popham wrote to Baird that 'if we can get our property fairly out of here, I think you will be fifty thousand pounds richer than the last time you shook me by the hand'.[113] As to exceeding his orders or, rather acting without any at all, Popham came out with a list of naval heroes, including St Vincent at Tenerife and the 'illustrious' Nelson in pursuit of Villeneuve to the West Indies and back (in which Francis had taken part in the *Canopus*), all of whom, he claimed, had acted with 'discretion'. And as Popham argued to the Court, 'Officers, having commands like his, could not be fettered by the literal tenor of the orders usually given. A command like that was, from its very nature, discretionary, and the word discretion was of very comprehensive meaning'.[114] By this, he was referring to the word's double sense as given in Johnson's *Dictionary*, 'wise management' and 'uncontrolled and unconditional power'.

But the counter-evidence was unambiguous and secure against Popham's tactics. When Melville was asked by the Admiralty Counsel, Thomas Jervis (a second cousin of St Vincent), whether Popham was 'appointed to any command, authorising him to attack any part of South America', he answered shortly, in a manner which prevented any 'discretionary' hair-splitting: 'Certainly not, in the proper sense of the word'. The Court, too, was alert to Popham's tricks. At the opening of the fourth day, Tuesday 10 March, the President warned him against continuing to flood the trial with 'wholly irrelevant' letters and documents and putting 'wholly irrelevant' questions to the witnesses; and he asked him to 'confine' himself to 'plain facts' and not protract 'the proceedings'.

On the fifth day, Popham decided to call no more witnesses and close his defence. He confined himself to a short speech. In its brevity, its moment of swelling rhetoric and its allusion to *Othello*, the defender of the Venetian state, it was, in its way, shrewdly aimed:

> I here close my defence; and I throw myself upon the wisdom and justice of this Honourable Court; my feelings and my character have suffered severely, but I trust to your judgment to relieve the one, and to rescue the other. If I have, in the exercise of my zeal, exceeded the strictest bounds of discretion, I hope it will be evident, that I have been actuated solely by a desire to promote the honour, the interests, and the glory of my country; and if, in the prosecution of these great objects, aided by my gallant followers, and fostered by the superintending hand of Providence, it has been my good fortune to be put in possession of the two capitals of two quarters of the globe, I trust it will be found, upon a close examination of my defence, 'that the very head and front of my offending hath this extent – no more!'*

To conclude the trial with these two lines was a theatrical stroke; and flattering, too, to the thirteen members of the Court, crediting them with a familiarity with the 'trial' scene in which Brabantio charges Othello with seducing his daughter by witchcraft.** Othello answers that he has 'married' her: this is the 'extent' of his guilt; and in the lines which follow, he presents himself as a simple soldier, a man of 'feats of broil and battle', the teller of 'a round unvarnished tale', 'Rude' of speech, 'little blessed with the soft phrase of peace', transparent in his honesty – just as Popham represents himself

* Different sources report this speech with slight variations. The version here follows the *Naval Chronicle* (January–June 1807), xvii. 242.

** That the Court would know *Othello* is not so unlikely as it seems. It was a much performed play with some memorable Othellos and Iagos, Kean's and Kemble's amongst them. Noble and affecting, Othello was a romantic tragedy much to the period's taste and was especially popular amongst naval men. When Francis visited Gibraltar in October 1805, at the time of Trafalgar, it was put on by officers of the garrison. And articles and reports in the Navy's professional journal, the *Naval Chronicle*, are larded with quotations from Shakespeare, *Othello* included.

now.[115] Whether it was for the strength of his case, the effectiveness of its presentation, or as evidence of weighty consideration, the Court pondered its verdict for nearly five hours before finding the charges proved.

What Jane Austen made of the trial is expressed in her poem. Popham defended himself with spirit and style; he presented his case persuasively; and to someone not in possession of the full facts or disinclined to credit them, his defence was convincing. She may have been amused, too, seeing in him the outline of a 'Shakespearean' Henry Crawford. She may also have remembered the other sides to Popham's character: not just the rogue and adventurer but also the humane commander described in Colonel Wilkie's recollections. And she would certainly have known about the forces of prejudice – Admiralty, naval and political – which time and again had sought to bring him down. Following the trial, Farington reports the commonly accepted view: 'It is thought that the Court Martial upon Sir Home Popham cd. have done no other than they did; but the malignity of the Admiralty & the Administration are manifested to the people.'[116] And equally clear to Jane Austen. 'On Sir Home Popham's Sentence' is all in one her tribute and her protest, modest, private and heartfelt, and if the suppositions of this chapter are correct, deeply grounded in the life of the Austen family.

The Court Martial verdict was popular and taken as an acquittal – a slap in the face for the 'Talents', and a vote of approval for the enterprise and commercial spirit of Jane Austen's 'Gallant Commander'. The *Hampshire Chronicle* for 16 March carried the day-by-day details of the trial; and its column of 'London' news opened with a report of the reception which met Popham on leaving the Court, to be

> greeted by a great number of Naval and Military Officers. An immense crowd of people waited his landing at the Sally Port, where the Provost-Marshal's carriage attended his arrival; the crowd chiefly consisted of persons belonging to the Navy, and the inhabitants of the town. They had prepared to take the horses from his carriage, in order to draw him home, but he avoided this mark of attention, and walked through the town, amidst the loud acclamations of the populace, to the house of Captain Madden; he was saluted by all ranks of people as he passed. The bells soon after rang a merry peal.

Popham was irrepressible. On the afternoon of 18 March, he bounced back in London with a visit to Lloyd's Coffee-house, to be greeted by the merchants and underwriters with 'Long live the Hero of La Plata!'. To the three hearty cheers he responded with a short speech, of which a mocking satirical version appeared in *The Times* the following day. Two days later, on 21 March, *The*

Times printed a letter from 'An Old Subscriber' at Lloyd's, expressing his concern that there were still people set on vindicating Popham and protesting against his visit to the Subscription Room 'on the very day a rumour of an immediate change in Administration was circulated' – a rumour of substance, as it turned out, since within the week the 'Talents' were out and the Tories, under Portland, were back.

The most judicious comment on this train of events – from the attack on Buenos Aires to the Popham reception at Lloyd's – is to be found in the *Universal Magazine*. Identifying Popham as the man of the hour, its March issue features him twice, under 'Biographical Sketches' and the 'State of Public Affairs'. Whilst critical of the South American venture, the *Universal* regarded the prosecution as a political trial inspired by a faction and commented that 'a more popular acquittal certainly never took place'.[117] Yet it went on to observe that in the precise wording of the sentence, 'severely reprimanded', 'the term severely is here very expressive, and was very properly introduced, to abate the confidence with which the accused justified his conduct . . . and we read with surprise, that the condemned' should have visited Lloyd's to be 'received with cheers of acclamation'.[118]

The Court Martial was no set-back to Popham's career. A month after the verdict, he was given a small Squadron 'to cruise off the Continent . . . with a Roving Commission';[119] and three months later, in July, he was appointed Captain-of-the-Fleet to Gambier who was leading the expedition to Copenhagen.* His appointment, thought to be a recommendation by the Duke of York, his former commander in Belgium and Holland and now Commander-in-Chief of the Army, provoked a storm of protest. Three of the senior Captains in the Fleet – Samuel Hood and Richard Keats, both Commodores, and Robert Stopford with (respectively) nineteen, eighteen and seventeen years seniority to Popham's twelve – formally presented their grievances to Gambier: their 'extreme sorrow and concern' at being placed in a position of 'inferiority' to him.[120] Admiral Sir Charles Pole saw it as an 'injudicious and disgraceful appointment', objecting not only to Popham's lack of seniority but to his character, an issue picked up by the press. While some papers, including the *Sun* and the *Courier*, supported his appointment,

---

* This appointment raises the question – did Popham share Gambier's Evangelical enthusiasms? One indication is in the *Hampshire Telegraph* (4 March 1805). This reprints the 'Exhortations and injunctions' he issued 'to the ship's company of his Majesty's ship *Diadem*' (64), to which he was appointed in December 1804. The *Telegraph* comments that 'The excellent discipline preserved by this intelligent officer, on board the ship immediately under his command, is unusually spoken of and admired . . .' and it commends the 'Exhortations' as deserving 'the imitation of every commanding officer'. Among these is a prohibition on swearing or 'blackguard expressions' and an injunction to the crew to 'behave themselves devoutly at church-service . . . as becometh brave Seamen and good Christians'. More details of the booklet can be found in Popham (1991), p. 135.

others, including the most influential, the *Morning Chronicle*, turned on him: 'as a Naval Officer [he] ranks very low indeed . . . nobody ever heard of him, but in his own vapouring dispatches' etc, etc.[121] But Popham proved his critics wrong. His long experience of combined operations was put to good use and he had knowledge of the area, having served in Vice-Admiral Archibald Dickson's Copenhagen operation in 1800. Gambier's confidence in Popham was rewarded and in his final Despatch the Admiral could speak of this without fear of contradiction:

> I feel it my duty to make a peculiar acknowledgement of the aid I have derived from Sir Home Popham, Captain of the Fleet, whose prompt resources, and complete knowledge of his profession, especially of that branch which is connected with the operations of an army, qualify him in a particular manner for the arduous and various duties with which he has been charged.[122]

And for Popham, there was the added satisfaction of being one of the three British signatories to the Articles of Capitulation for the Town and Citadel of Copenhagen.

The operation could be counted a success, inasmuch as it secured the Danish fleet from the French. But it provoked an angry and prolonged debate. The attack was vilified as shameful and discreditable. With no declaration of war, Copenhagen was under bombardment for three days, and extensive fires led to the death of almost two thousand civilians. George III called the assault 'a very immoral act',[123] throughout Europe Britain was execrated, and in the Commons and Lords the debate rumbled on, day after day, filling the columns of Hansard. The *Monthly Magazine*, a Unitarian journal, was scathing, characterising Gambier as 'that *evangelical* admiral who in his public dispatches piously thanks divine Providence for the security with which he pillaged the fleet and arsenals of a neutral city'.[124] Nonetheless, the Motion for a formal Parliamentary Vote of Thanks – usual on the occasion of a great victory – put to the House of Lords by Hawkesbury (the Home Secretary) and seconded by Moira, was gained, despite vigorous opposition. Gambier got his peerage and Popham duly made his appearance in the Chamber, acknowledging the tribute 'with a gracious, and mercifully short, speech of thanks'.[125] Promotion and honours followed: Rear-Admiral of the White in 1814, KCB in 1815, Commander-in-Chief of the West Indies, 1817–20. From this last appointment he returned in bad health and died at Cheltenham on 11 September 1820. He was buried at Sunninghill, where his memorial stands to this day.

The last words on Popham were, inevitably, mixed, recalling his scrapes and scandals as well as his achievements. The conclusion to the *Gentleman's*

Magazine obituary is worth quoting: 'Perhaps Sir Home has not left one Officer behind of his own age who has seen more service, or been employed in more important affairs.'[126] A more searching verdict comes from Moira, written not at the time of Popham's death but in 1814, at a moment when his financial probity was once more in question. This was regarding an inflated claim made by Popham for the cost of entertaining Moira, Governor-General designate of Bengal, and his considerable suite, on carrying them out to the sub-continent. Moira is addressing the Prince of Wales' Private Secretary in a confidential letter:

> I should grieve to have Sir Home placed in an unfavorable light, because, with all those injudicious tricks by which he has entailed a host of enemies on himself, there is essential good in him. He has great professional skill, much readiness of resource, & indefatigable activity in working on any subject which attracts his fancy.[127]

The immediate outcome of Popham's Buenos Aires expedition was a mood of national euphoria. For Grenville, the premature news of success conjured up the prospect that 'all Spanish America' might 'fall into our hands' within a year.[128] Popular feeling was for action. There was pressure too from merchants and manufacturers. From the seat of government it seemed the very moment to depart from Britain's successful but unexciting strategy of containing Napoleon's Fleets in blockade, a 'defensive system of warfare',[129] and strike a popular, decisive and profitable blow in the New World, thereby scotching France's transatlantic ambitions. Four thousand troops were sent at once to reinforce Beresford and two further expeditions were mounted for a great pincer operation. From the East, there was to be launched the conquest of Mexico; from the West, the liberation of Chile and an onwards march across the Andes to join forces with the British Army in Buenos Aires – a grandiose, Popham-like scheme scuppered by news of the Buenos Aires defeat. The forces were re-routed and by the Spring of 1807 more than thirteen thousand front-line troops were *en route*, or already camped among the swamps of the River Plate. These new forces met with no more success than Beresford's original contingent. It was another story of heavy losses, capitulation, withdrawal and departure. Again, Moira's verdict is worth quoting:

> For our expulsion from the river of la Plata, I only grieve for the loss of so many valuable lives, and of reputation. Our possession would have been a drain on our wealth and population, and would have yielded neither revenue, nor commercial profit in return.[130]

This is an accurate assessment. But Moira's wisdom was after the event. In a vacillating Cabinet, his had been one of the voices most persuasive in rallying support for the South American adventures.

In this story of high ambition and dismal failure, Popham was vindicated on one point at least. Events showed that the people of Buenos Aires were ripe for change and the blow he struck at the Viceroyalty set these forces in motion. Spanish rule was never effectively re-established in the city. Over the next few years the country's own liberator emerged, José de San Martín, and an independent Argentina came into being.

Although in the long term his cause succeeded, Miranda himself met a tragic end. He enjoyed a few months of glory early in 1812 as leader of the first revolutionary government of Venezuela. But at the end of July, thought to be a traitor, he was handed over by Bolivar to the Spanish royalists and taken to Cadiz, where he died in prison in 1816. The liberation movement continued under Bolivar and in 1819, a year before Popham's death, he proclaimed the independence of the former Spanish colonies of Colombia, Ecuador, Panama and Venezuela, creating the confederation known as Gran Colombia. Ten years later, Venezuela broke free, setting forth as an independent republic.

Remote as these events are from Jane Austen, they nonetheless impinged upon the family. From his two-and-a-half years in the *Aurora* Charles brought home three precious mementoes: a salver presented by his officers and crew, a snuff-box from 'the Young Gentlemen' and a naval sword carrying this historic inscription: 'Presented to Captain Charles John Austen R. N., commanding HMS Aurora at the city of the Caracas, 1st March 1827 by General Simon Bolivar the liberator of his country as a mark of esteem.'[131] We have no record that Charles rendered any personal service to Bolivar; and we can guess that the sword was presented to him, the senior naval officer at Caracas, as a token of gratitude for Britain's continuing support for Bolivar's political ambitions. At this time, Bolivar faced a deep crisis. A breakaway party was attempting to take Venezuela out of the Gran Colombia confederation, of which Bolivar was President. In this power struggle, the support for Bolivar visible in the British naval presence was crucial, and civil war was was averted. Further support for Bolivar came the following month, when Charles returned, carrying with him a passenger of signal importance, Alexander Cockburn, His Majesty's Envoy Extraordinary to the Colombian States, a diplomat sent from London to strengthen Britain's ties with an area of South America judged worthy of cultivation and alliance.

Charles entered fully into the social and diplomatic life of the capital. He was well-liked and the British Consul in Caracas, Sir Robert Ker Porter, a personal friend of Bolivar, regarded Charles with respect and affection, noting his attendance at dinners and excursions, and writing in his *Diary* of 'the gallant Capt', 'one of the most worthy naval personages in Command in this quarter'.[132] By a freak of history, twenty years later, Francis too was to play a similar part in Venezuelan affairs. During that country's crisis in 1848, he travelled from the moorings of his Flagship, the *Vindictive*, at La Guara, overland to Caracas, to offer support to the President and 'exchange assurances of friendly relations' (Hayward [2000], p. 17).

To return to Jane Austen herself, it may seem surprising that we can make a reasonable guess at her own views on British ambitions in South America. But we do have a basis for this in a book she was reading enthusiastically in January 1813, an *Essay on the Military Policy and Institutions of the British Empire* by an army Captain, Charles Pasley. It sounds an unlikely volume for Jane Austen to borrow from the local reading club, the Chawton Book Society. Indeed, as she told Cassandra, it was 'a book I protested against at first but which upon trial I find delightfully written & highly entertaining . . . The first soldier I ever sighed for; but he does write with extraordinary force & spirit'.[133] Pasley's subject was Britain's place on the world stage, looking far into the future. His imperialist polemic was robust and advanced with 'a certain easy ruthlessness' (as Geoffrey Carnall remarks),[134] and with an attractive stylishness too: 'War we cannot avoid, and in war we cannot succeed by merely displaying the valour, unless we also assume the ardour, and the ambition of conquerors.'[135] It was not surprising that expansionist patriots should respond with enthusiasm, Jane Austen among them. According to *The Times* (which published a lengthy, two-part review, reprinted in the *Gentleman's Magazine* in February and March 1811), the book 'excited greater attention among the higher classes of Political Readers in the country than any since the time of Mr BURKE'.[136] Alongside Jane Austen, these 'Readers' included Southey, who concluded his long review-article in the *Quarterly* lauding the book as 'one of the most important political works which has ever fallen under our observation'.[137] Other admiring readers were Walter Scott and the Wordsworths, both Dorothy and William, who read the *Essay* 'with instruction and pleasure',[138] and were sufficiently caught up in its argument to open a correspondence with Pasley. One of his most attentive readers was Coleridge, with whom he had been on friendly terms since their time together on Malta in 1804–05, when they worked together on a paper briefing the Governor on policy options towards Egypt; and reviewing the book in *The Courier* he was glad to be able to recommend his friend's 'admirable essay'.[139]

A forward-looking military strategist, Pasley had considerable experience with the Royal Engineers as a siege-and-explosives expert in Europe (and eventually became their Colonel-Commandant and a full General in 1860). At this moment, he warned,

> the British nation is placed in a situation of danger, to which its past history affords no parallel – menaced with destruction by a much superior force, which is directed by the energy of one of the greatest warriors that has appeared . . . nothing but our naval superiority has saved us from being at this moment a province of France.[140]

Such a tribute to her brothers' service was calculated to win Jane Austen's heart from the outset. Turning to Britain's global future, Pasley saw an end to Britain's naval superiority. With France, Spain and Holland ranged against us, Britain could not expect to retain 'the empire of the seas' indefinitely.[141] Our land forces were now powerful enough to fight a major campaign on mainland Europe. Not only Sicily (already under British occupation) but the whole of Italy should be annexed and Egypt too. He looked to colonies on a 'great scale',[142] to a 'martial policy' carrying the 'noble enterprise' of a land war into Europe,[143] and concluded that Britain's 'wisest, safest, and most effectual' way 'of defending our country' is 'by attacking and destroying all its enemies'.[144] As to Spanish America, he took the Buenos Aires operation as a prime example of half-measures. The expeditionary force was too small to succeed, 'much less to conquer and to establish itself on both sides of that vast peninsula by acting in two corps, as was at first proposed [a pincer attack from Chile and the Rio de la Plata] – the most gigantic enterprise, that was ever perhaps chalked out by the government of any country, for such a handful of men to effect by force of arms'.[145]

Later editions of the *Essay* (two in 1811, one in 1812) – and it is one of these later editions that Jane Austen may have seen – developed this expansionist line of thought. If Jane Austen's admiration for Pasley's 'extraordinary force & spirit' was stirred by this overriding argument, we can take it that she would have viewed a British presence in South America with approval – Popham's venture included.

One last question remains. Did Popham himself ever see Jane Austen's poem? Much as one would like to think so, the sober answer must be no. No copy was found among his papers, nor any reference to it. So we must assume that the 'Gallant Commander' passed unaware of this witness to his good name, a ringing testimonial from someone whose heroes were few and chosen with care.

On the other hand, Popham would have found a crumb of satisfaction elsewhere – in Wordsworth's *Poems* of 1807, a collection which gathers poetry of nature and imagination alongside a group of 'Sonnets Dedicated to Liberty', verse stirring and patriotic, and addressed to the nation at this critical hour. Popham's eye could have been caught by the last of these, 'November 1806'. On the 21st of the month, Napoleon issued the Berlin Decrees, intended to destroy Britain by a total blockade of its overseas commerce and communication. A month earlier, Prussia, Britain's last remaining ally, had been defeated at the Battle of Jena and the country now seemed to stand alone, a challenge that Wordsworth asks his readers to confront with resolve and a grim and sombre rejoicing – provided, he concludes, that we can trust 'those who rule the land', the very question to be raised, since those rulers were none other than Grenville's 'Talents', their time running out:

> We shall exult, if they who rule the land
> Be men who hold its many blessings dear,
> Wise, upright, valiant; not a servile band,
> Who are to judge of danger which they fear,
> And honour which they do not understand.

Accusation rather than question, and Popham, Jane Austen and many others would have cheered Wordsworth with one voice.

Cassandra Austen's comic medallion portrait of Henry V in Jane Austen's 'The History of England' (1791). The face is that of a young man (Francis, then seventeen, or Charles, twelve?) in a quasi-Captain's uniform with a hefty sailor's cue or pigtail. (*British Library*).

PART II

NAVAL FACT AND
NAVAL FICTION

'Adm[1]. Foote – surprised that I had the power of drawing the
Portsmouth-Scenes so well.'

Opinions of Mansfield Park

In December 1800, Mr Austen chose to give up his parish and retire to Bath. He
was then sixty-nine. With a mildly hypochondriac wife, and husbands to be
found for his unmarried daughters of twenty-five and twenty-seven, it seemed
a practical and far-sighted step to take, of benefit to all the family. According to
Francis, reminiscing fifty or sixty years later, Mr Austen felt too 'incapacitated
from age and increasing infirmities to discharge his parochial Duties in a
manner satisfactory to himself'.[1] Whatever his reason, the decision was made
without discussion and came with no warning. On hearing the news, Jane
Austen is said to have fainted on the spot. For all its splendid crescents, its
amenities and amusements, its theatres and its fashionable society, Bath was no
exchange for the Rectory at Steventon and the Hampshire countryside which,
so we are told by Caroline Lefroy, her Aunt 'thought . . . must form one of the
joys of heaven'.[2] Some pale reflection of her loss is carried in *Mansfield Park*, in
the sadness of Fanny Price, exiled in the 'bad air' and 'bad smells' of her
confined home at Portsmouth, deprived of 'all the pleasures of spring' with its
'liberty, freshness, fragrance and verdure' and 'the animation both of body and
mind, she had derived from watching the advance of the season . . .'.[3]

Jane put up a brave front. Only days after this unwelcome news, she was
already building a comedy for herself, writing in the guise of a sentimental
heroine in an epistolary novel:

> I get more & more reconciled to the idea of our removal. We have lived long
> enough in this Neighbourhood, the Basingstoke Balls are certainly on the decline,
> there is something interesting in the bustle of going away, & the prospect of
> spending future summers by the Sea or in Wales is very delightful. – For a time we
> shall now possess many of the advantages which I have often thought of with Envy
> in the wives of Sailors or Soldiers. – It must not be generally known however that I

am not sacrificing a great deal in quitting the Country – or I can expect to inspire no tenderness, no interest in those we leave behind.[4]

Like these service 'wives', she jokes, they will now have the freedom to shift from lodgings to lodgings, a wandering existence she was to witness in the life of Mary Gibson (Francis' wife) and which she depicted in the sea-port years of Mrs Croft in *Persuasion*. But the reality was far different, no joke at all.

The move took place in May 1801; the family furniture and Jane's piano and her books were dispersed. The effect of this change was disastrous. Her writing came to a halt. The previous decade had been highly productive. The late 1780s and early '90s had seen three volumes of childhood writing, the *juvenilia*, and then, between 1795 and 1800, the first three novels: 'Eleanor and Marianne', a novel-in-letters, later rewritten as *Sense and Sensibility*; 'First Impressions', the first version of *Pride and Prejudice*; and 'Susan', which, years later, became *Northanger Abbey*.

This creative period brought to an end, what followed was eight years with nothing to show except some occasional verses and the opening section of 'The Watsons' – an uncharacteristically cheerless story, with a distressed heroine in a bleak setting and written with little trace of humour. This novel was soon abandoned, probably over the Winter of 1804–05, when she suffered a double blow in the deaths of her father and Mrs Lefroy, her closest friend.

For much of this time, in company with her mother and sister, Jane Austen endured an itinerant existence in a succession of lodgings and temporary homes – five addresses in Bath, a city she left 'with what happy feelings of Escape!',[6] two at Southampton, a stay in Clifton, holidays in South Coast and West Country resorts alternating with visits around the family and to friends in London and the Home Counties. As we read in the letters of this period, such a varied scene was rich in material for a novelist of manners, and there is a note of forced cheerfulness in her letters. But all too often the company was 'stupid', the parties 'intolerable'[7] and even family visits offered no guarantee either of stimulus or relaxation. Her brother Edward's home, Godmersham Park, where she would stay for months at a time, was the place to 'shake off vulgar cares & conform to the happy Indifference of East Kent wealth'[8] with its 'Elegance & Ease & Luxury'.[9] Yet it brought the indignity of being the dependent relative in grand surroundings with servants to be tipped and the embarrassment of being 'sunk in poverty',[10] as she laughed it off to Cassandra. Life '*a la* Godmersham'[11] could also be oppressive, with an endless succession of visitors to be received and entertained – 'They came & they sat & they went',[12] she wrote laconically of one morning's procession. In 1808 Edward's wife, Elizabeth Bridges, died and in a motherless family of eleven children the services of a visiting aunt were in constant demand and the precious moments of 'happy solitude'[13] became few and far between. Added to this, the in-laws were prickly. Anna Lefroy tells us that with the Bridges of that period 'A little talent went a long way . . . & *much* must have gone a long way too far.'[14] It was a rootless, wandering and ultimately unproductive experience, with no end in sight. Without stability and emotional security, Jane was unable to get down to the business of writing. Moreover, her ambitions were frustrated. In 1797, the publisher Thomas Cadell had refused to consider 'First Impressions'; and Richard Crosby failed to bring out 'Susan', which he had accepted in 1803, advertising the novel for immediate publication.

At a deeper level, her creative powers were numbed by private grief. The story of Jane Austen's emotional relationships, what the *Memoir* describes as the passages of 'romance',[15] is shadowy and what details have found their way into the family records are imprecise and conflicting.[16] The weight of report (rather than evidence, since there is no hint in Jane Austen's surviving letters) suggests that between 1801 and Autumn 1804, the one such close friendship which could have led to marriage – variously with an army officer, a naval officer or a clergyman – was terminated by the suitor's death.

Her will to write seems to have been restored only in the Summer of 1809 when Edward provided his mother and sisters with a cottage on his Hampshire estate at Chawton, a small village on the London-Winchester road, close to the country town of Alton.

The promise of a secure and settled home was a prospect of delight which Jane wanted to share with Francis (then on his way to China in the *St Albans*), writing him a verse-letter from Chawton in July, ending on this happy note:

Cassandra's pen will paint our state,
The many comforts that await
Our Chawton home, how much we find
Already in it, to our mind;
And how convinced, that when complete
It will all other Houses beat
That ever have been made or mended,
With rooms concise, or rooms distended.
You'll find us very snug next year,
Perhaps with Charles & Fanny near,
For now it often does delight us
To fancy them just over-right us. –[17]

Soon after moving in, Jane Austen looked over her manuscripts with a view to revision; and probably with Henry's advice, she turned her mind to the business of finding a publisher. At some point in the Winter of 1810–11, *Sense and Sensibility*, no longer a novel-in-letters, was submitted to Thomas Egerton, who agreed to take it on a commission basis.* Its acceptance, and publication in October 1811, meant a great deal. For too long an amateur, finding an audience only within the family, at the age of thirty-five she could at last regard herself as a real writer, a professional author, on the way to reaching the reviewers and the public at large. Her long pent-up energies were freed and in February 1811, soon after this first success, she set to work on *Mansfield Park*, to be followed in rapid succession by *Emma* and *Persuasion*, these three great novels completed in the space of five and a half years, up to August 1816, twelve months before her death.

Jane Austen opened a new tradition in English fiction, the so-called 'modern' novel as it was defined by Sir Walter Scott reviewing *Emma* alongside *Sense and Sensibility* and *Pride and Prejudice* in 1815. Un-romantic, un-sentimental and un-Gothic, its stories were set in 'the current of ordinary life', a fictional world in which the reader meets 'a correct and striking representation of that which is daily taking place around him'. For Scott, this degree of domestic realism called to mind 'the merits of the Flemish school of painting. The subjects are not often elegant, and certainly never grand; but they are finished up to nature, and with a precision which delights the reader.'[18] The realism, or verisimilitude of the 'modern' novel is not, in Jane Austen's hands, an imitation of life, but an effect of art – 'Life being all inclusion and confusion, and art being all discrimination and selection', as Henry James described art's 'sublime economy'.[19] In the words of Conrad, this is the 'economy' which creates 'a form of imagined life clearer than reality'.[20] Jane Austen's methods of 'discrimination and selection', and her creation in the novels of this 'imagined life', are techniques and effects that later novelists have never ceased to admire and imitate and critics to analyse and explain. For this reason, Chapters 8 and 11 are narrowly focussed. They concentrate on Jane Austen's creative use of the *naval* facts and experiences taken from her own considerable fund of naval knowledge and from the lives of her sailor brothers and elsewhere** to form the 'imagined life' of her naval characters and the

* This was a standard arrangement at the time. The author was responsible for the cost of paper, printing and advertising, expenditures which were deducted from the sales receipts out of which the publisher also took a commission of 10%. The author was liable for the shortfall if the sales income failed to cover the costs of production, etc. As it worked out, Jane Austen took a profit of £150 on the first edition of *Sense and Sensibility*, the 750 or 1000 copies selling out in under two years.

** For example, in September 1814, she wrote to Martha Lloyd, who was then staying at the home of Captain James Deans-Dundas RN in Bath, asking her to pass on her compliments 'to your Friends. I have not forgotten their parti[cular] claim to my Gratitude as an Author' (2 September 1814, *Letters*, p. 274). As *Mansfield Park* was published in May 1814, it seems that her thanks were for naval advice.

circumstances of their careers. Such a limited approach, restricted as it is to
the naval content of these novels, can convey little or nothing of Jane Austen's
wider achievement in these works. On the other hand, this narrow 'naval'
focus serves to bring out at least one of Jane Austen's artistic principles, that
of restricting herself to areas with which she was familiar. In advising a novel-
writing niece, she could have been speaking to herself:

> we think you had better not leave England. Let the Portmans go to Ireland, but as
> you know nothing of the Manners there, you had better not go with them. You will
> be in danger of giving false representations. Stick to Bath & the Foresters. There
> you will be quite at home.[21]

This advice – simple, straightforward and eminently practical – embodies
Jane Austen's own procedure. Restrictive as it might be for other writers, it
was a discipline within which her own imagination, 'quite at home', was at
liberty to expand. Long stays at Godmersham were preparation enough for
the country-house world of Mansfield Park and what it was like to be treated
as the poor relation; and her own visits to Portsmouth stand behind the
squalid and oppressive realism of the Price household. In these worlds apart,
the novelist could feel herself equally 'at home', just as she could feel at ease
with Wentworth and the naval household at Lyme Regis and, very differently
circumstanced, with these same officers moving in the smart society of Bath.
These were the territories of experience in which her imagination found
inspiration and freedom.

Lieutenant

8

Mansfield Park: The Young Lieutenant

'The Portsmouth girls turn up their noses at any one who has not a commission. One might as well be nothing as a midshipman.'

Mansfield Park, vol.ii, ch. 7

Mansfield Park is Jane Austen's most ambitious novel, a work in which she offered her public something weightier than *Pride and Prejudice*, less 'entertaining', she told Francis,[1] but more substantial in its treatment of religion and morality and providing a more varied social landscape than she had attempted before; and going further, too, in exploring the sexual aspects of 'guilt and misery'.[2] Treating the manners and social culture of the day, specifically 1810–13,* it was designed by Jane Austen as a 'condition of England' novel, a commentary on the moral and religious health of the gentry, both its decadence and its sources of strength, and, like the nation at war, its chance of pulling through. If we call it a novel with a purpose, its design upon the reader is distinctly social and religious. As Marilyn Butler has pointed out, 'It can be no accident that so many of the social issues taken by the Evangelicals – the abolition of slavery, clergy non-residence and pluralism, family prayers, an over-secular system of education for girls as for boys – are touched on, usually to be supported by either Edmund or Fanny.'[3]

Jane Austen's method of being 'quite at home' with the naval content of *Mansfield Park* was to stay on dry land, bringing her sailor-hero, William Price, back to England to recount his war-time exploits – the gist of them, not the detail – to an admiring family circle at his uncle's country house; and as his sister Fanny is the centre of the novel's observation and experience, and his most attentive and fervent admirer, William's naval career is seen largely from a sister's point-of-view, a position which Jane Austen was able to fill

---

* The main action of the story runs from the autumn of 1810 to the summer of 1813, a period very close to the time Jane Austen was actually at work on the book, between February 1811 and July 1813. Although no dates are given in the text, there is a strict and very detailed internal chronology which enables us to work backwards and forwards in the story from a central marker: Fanny's possession, in chapter 16, of a volume of Crabbe's *Tales* (the full title is *Tales in Verse*) soon after its publication in September 1812. Despite this exact indication, editors and critics continue to propose a variety of mis-datings – among them 1803–06, 1805–07, 1808–10. A detailed consideration of the chronology and its historical implications is given in Southam (1995).

naturally and with complete understanding from her own experience. Like her young heroine, she knew all too well the pains of separation and the anxiety of having her brothers at sea for years on end.

The careers of her sailor brothers meant that Jane Austen was also 'quite at home' with a story of naval ambition. For this, the family was the natural setting, since a sailor's extended family was a crucial factor in his progress, opening the possibility of naval and political connections, and the benefits these could bring in advancing his career. In this respect, Francis and Charles seemed to be fortunate from the very beginning. Products of the Naval Academy at Portsmouth, they were classed as 'College Volunteers', a privileged category whose commissions were assured by Admiralty order. Beyond that stage, their early postings and their search for promotion owed much to Mr Austen's resourcefulness and the friendship of Warren Hastings and the effectiveness of other family connections. The scheme of *Mansfield Park* involves an entirely different scenario. Jane Austen gives William Price an anxious and uncertain future. He has to make his way with no interest or patronage to call upon and a father who only stirs himself for his newspaper and his grog. This was at the very time, historically, when competition for commissions was at its height – a commission being, not as it is today, an appointment to commissioned rank, but an appointment to fill a Lieutenant's vacancy on a named vessel. The rapid expansion of the Navy in the early years of the war meant that by 1812 – the very year Midshipman Price returns to England – a log-jam had built up throughout the system. So many Lieutenants were already in post that vacancies were becoming more and more difficult to find. This left stranded an increasing number of 'young gentlemen', almost two thousand of them, having 'passed for Lieutenant', satisfying the Admiralty Board with the necessary certificates, years of service and examination, waiting for commissions to arrive. In many cases, these never came. The sight of 'passed' Midshipmen in their twenties and thirties, soured with waiting, was a frightening prospect for young hopefuls of nineteen and twenty. As William puts it, bleakly and bluntly, to be a 'poor scrubby midshipman'[4] is to be 'nothing'.[5] In the circumstances of 1812, for a Midshipman without 'interest', 'promotion' – a step 'long thought of, dearly earned and justly valued' – comes (as Jane Austen describes it) not as an expectation but a 'blessing'.[6]

This statement of William's predicament is reached in volume 2, following his arrival at Mansfield.* Until this point, more than half-way through the

---

* *Mansfield Park* was originally published in three volumes. I have kept to this volume and chapter numbering because Jane Austen had the volume division in mind in the writing of the story and structured its drama and climaxes accordingly. These volume divisions are retained in the Oxford edition used here. In modern editions, chapters 19–31 form volume 2 and chapters 32–48 volume 3.

novel, Fanny Price occupies the centre of the story and William is held at the margins. His career is reported intermittently and in the lightest detail. On William's first going to sea, Edmund Bertram comforts Fanny, telling her 'such charming things of what William was to do, and be hereafter, in consequence of his profession';[7] and Fanny later informs Mary Crawford 'of his profession and the foreign stations he had been on'.[8] But these professional 'things' remain unelaborated and the 'foreign stations' unnamed. For the seven years of William's service all we learn is that the last four at least have been passed under Captain Marshall* of the *Antwerp* in a Squadron operating in the Mediterranean, that he was treated very kindly by the ship's chaplain and that (Francis-like) he writes to Fanny regularly and at length. We are left to fill in the rest for ourselves: which amounts to saying that the early career of Midshipman Price runs along familiar lines. What Jane Austen makes individual is the bond between brother and sister and the burden of 'misery' that falls on Fanny during the years of his absence at sea.

> Once, and once only in the course of many years, had she the happiness of being with William. Of the rest she saw nothing; nobody seemed to think of her ever going amongst them again, even for a visit, nobody at home seemed to want her; but William determining, soon after her removal, to be a sailor, was invited to spend a week with his sister in Northamptonshire, before he went to sea. Their eager affection in meeting, their exquisite delight in being together, their hours of happy mirth, and moments of serious conference, may be imagined; as well as the sanguine views and spirits of the boy even to the last, and the misery of the girl when he left her.[9]

While the naval thread of *Mansfield Park* opens on a poignant note, the arrival of Mary Crawford in chapter 6 introduces a perception of the Navy which is wholly different. Whereas Fanny's heart is fixed fondly on her Midshipman brother, Mary's 'acquaintance' is with 'Admirals'. 'Of the inferior ranks', she announces, 'with an air of grandeur', 'we know very little'. 'Post Captains may be very good sort of men, but they do not belong to *us*.' The only recommendation she sees in the 'profession' is 'if it make the fortune, and there be discretion in spending it',[10] views which pass unchallenged. Fanny and Edmund listen in silence, preoccupied as they are by the revelation of Mary's life with Admiral Crawford and her scathing remarks on the 'circle' of Admirals gathered at her uncle's home, these commanders memorable not for their great victories or deeds of valour but for 'their bickering and jealousies' over 'their flags, and the gradation of their pay'. This is

---

* Almost certainly a private reminder for the family of Francis' service as Midshipman in the *Perseverance*, among whose officers was a Lieutenant Marshall.

fertile ground. From Admiral of the Red to Rear-Admiral of the Blue, including the Vice-Admirals Red, White and Blue, there were nine different grades, each with its distinguishing flag, its mast of display, and its rate of pay and allowances. But what really upsets her listeners is Mary's comment on the Admirals' behaviour and morals, whatever is bitterly insinuated in her notorious pun on those '*Rears*' and '*Vices*' of which she saw 'enough'.[11]

No doubt it was a common enough joke in naval families. In 1801, Jane Austen passed a very similar comment in describing to Cassandra a 'stupid' whist party in Bath, at which she observed a Miss Langley, 'like any other short girl with a broad nose & wide mouth, fashionable dress, & exposed bosom'; and, next to Miss Langley, Henry Stanhope, recently promoted *Rear*-Admiral, 'a gentlemanlike Man, but then his legs are too short, & his tail too long'.[12] Her pun – the Admiral's 'tail' refers both to his prominent backside and his naval queue or pig-tail, sported by sailors of the old school – was a family joke, Stanhope being a distant cousin, a joke that Jane Austen confines to the privacy of a letter for her sister's eyes only. However, the question arises whether Jane Austen has given Mary Crawford nothing more than a joke in poor taste, a mild and facetious pun – the Admirals' 'Rears' and 'Vices' of rank, backsides and bad behaviour – or something more gross, an allusion to sodomy; this, alongside rum and flogging, said to be one of the navy's trio of vicious traditions.* Bridget Brophy,[13] Park Honan and others have interpreted the pun in this light, Honan noting that in 1798 sailors on Francis' ship, the *London*, were flogged for this 'unnatural crime', the sentence recorded in the ship's log;[14] and the editor of the 1996 Penguin Classics edition tells us that this 'rather filthy joke draws attention to the Royal Navy's war-time reputation for homosexual activity.'[15]

Offences of this kind were reported in the press and there is no reason to suppose that anyone – Jane Austen or her readers – was unaware of their occurrence. As evidence that Jane Austen knew about homosexuality and was prepared to joke about it, both Bridget Brophy and David Nokes point to the 'sharade' in the 'History of England',[16] where the friendship between James I and his favourite, Robert Carr, Earl of Somerset, gives us the answer *carpet*. Allowing, for the sake of argument, that the Brophy/Nokes interpretation is correct, nonetheless there remains a world of difference between a private joke of 1791 and what, in 1814, Jane Austen, or her publisher, would commit to print.

The freedoms of the eighteenth-century did not survive long into the next; and, where they did, certain limits remained. *The Post Captain* (1805) by John

---

* Before the First World War, Winston Churchill, a reforming First Lord of the Admiralty, was criticised by a senior officer for 'one of his proposals on the grounds that it was against naval tradition'. Churchill replied, 'Don't talk to me about naval tradition. It's nothing but rum, sodomy and the lash' (quoted in Gretton, 1968, p. 2)

Davis, the best-known comic novel 'of Naval Society and Manners' of the period, belongs to the robust tradition of Smollett and makes great play of sexual *double-entendre* latent in naval slang and terminology. But within this coarseness the niceties are observed. No risqué jokes are placed in the mouths of women and there is not a hint of homosexuality in the book.

In the space of two years, between the first and second editions of *Sense and Sensibility* (1811 and 1813), in response to the stiffening propriety of the time, the mildest of jokes about 'a natural daughter'[17] was removed either by Jane Austen or by the publisher, Thomas Egerton, who 'praised' *Mansfield Park* in particular for its 'Morality',[18] and on commercial grounds, if no other, he would never have permitted such an outrageous joke from Mary Crawford or anyone else. Sodomy was a taboo topic in mixed company and it is unthinkable that it should appear in respectable fiction, let alone in a novel by a lady. This, we should remember, was a time when the standards of public taste were being set by the Evangelical physician Thomas Bowdler, his four-volume *Family Shakespeare* (1807) designed for reading in the home, omitting the 'indelicate' and 'indecent', anything indeed which could 'raise a blush on the cheek of modesty' or offend the 'virtuous mind' (Preface, pp. vi-vii); when Byron, in 1811, observed that 'In such an age, when all aspire to taste;/The dirty language, and the noisome jest,/Which pleased in Swift of yore, we now detest' ('Hints from Horace', lines 393–95); a moment when Byron also felt it wise to reorientate his affections in Cantos One and Two of *Childe Harold's Pilgrimage*, published in 1812, removing all reference to his 'beloved playmate' and the 'boyish minions of unhallowed love'.[19] Reticence and aversion also dictated what could be said in the professional literature. Reporting a court martial for sodomy in 1807, the *Naval Chronicle* spoke of 'the horrid and abominable crime which delicacy forbids us to name'.

With these guidelines before us, we can understand that while Edmund finds Mary's joke indecorous and tasteless, at worst, offensive, he detects nothing gross, nothing wholly outrageous. 'It is a noble profession'[20] is the best response he can summon, a reply meant to put an end to the discussion. But, as we are to discover, the words ring hollow. The honour of the profession lies in the future, with William, not with the Navy of Admiral Crawford and his cronies, a group of half-pay officers circulating between London and Bath. In an earlier chapter Jane Austen has already provided us with the Admiral's scandalous history: 'a man of vicious conduct', after his wife's death he brought 'his mistress under his own roof'.[21] This, and no more, is the transgression and style of behaviour that lies behind the '*Vices*' of Mary's pun.

So, although both Edmund and Fanny catch a lurking indelicacy in Mary's language, neither react as if some unspeakable indecency has struck their ears. Fanny, it can be argued, is simply unaware, protected by her innocence. But Edmund, a product of Eton and Oxford, cannot be supposed to share his cousin's ignorance of the world. Yet when he discusses Mary's conversation in the following chapter, he goes no further than to find it 'not quite right' and 'very indecorous',[22] while Fanny's astonishment is not at Mary's pun as such but at her speaking so freely and so lightly of the Admiral's private life.

Jane Austen gives Mary Crawford one further naval intervention in volume 1. This comes a week or so later, in chapter 11, when Mary questions Edmund's vocation. Entering the Church, she suggests, is all too easy, and can be done without further thought when there is a family living ready to step into. Fanny rallies to Edmund's defence, offering military parallels:

> 'It is the same sort of thing,' said Fanny, after a short pause, 'as for the son of an admiral to go into the navy, or the son of a general to be in the army, and nobody sees any thing wrong in that. Nobody wonders that they should prefer the line where their friends can serve them best, or suspects them to be less in earnest in it than they appear.'[23]

Adroitly, Mary turns Fanny's example to her own advantage.

> 'No, my dear Miss Price, and for reasons good. The profession, either navy or army, is its own justification. It has every thing in its favour; heroism, danger, bustle, fashion. Soldiers and sailors are always acceptable in society. Nobody can wonder that men are soldiers and sailors.'[24]

For Mary Crawford, these professions are socially acceptable, professions that anyone would choose. The unspoken question remains – if not for the easy income, who on earth would choose the Church? The example of her brother-in-law Dr Grant – in her eyes 'an indolent selfish bon vivant'[25] – leads her to condemn the clergy in general for 'indolence and love of ease',[26] a charge which Edmund resists, not without a slightly malicious dig at Mary's past:

> 'Where any one body of educated men, of whatever denomination, are condemned indiscriminately, there must be a deficiency of information, or (smiling) of something else. Your uncle, and his brother admirals, perhaps, knew little of clergymen beyond the chaplains whom, good or bad, they were always wishing away.'[27]

At the mention of 'chaplains', Fanny's thoughts turn to her brother:

> 'Poor William! He has met with great kindness from the chaplain of the Antwerp,' was a tender apostrophe of Fanny's, very much to the purpose of her own feelings, if not of the conversation.[28]

Jane Austen's readers would have understood from this that the *Antwerp* (an invented name) was a man-of-war. Although Chaplains were on the nominal roll for all ships of 20 guns and upwards, in short supply they were usually only to be found on third-rates of 74 guns and above. In referring, through Edmund, to the Admiral's intolerance of naval Chaplains, Jane Austen was also calling on a deeper level of familiarity with naval life and traditions. She was alluding to a matter which was singularly delicate and contentious at this time, something which she would certainly have picked up from Francis. An officer of Evangelical leanings, he would have resisted the prejudice of Flag Officers of the Admiral Crawford school. His Chaplains would have found themselves made welcome in a 'praying' ship.

The heart of the problem lay in reconciling the work of the Chaplains with conditions on a fighting ship. At a practical level, would they be in the way? Could they stand the sight of blood? Nelson's solution, when leading an attack on the French flotillas at Boulogne in 1801, when British casualties were expected to be heavy, was to leave his Chaplain behind. And it was this same Chaplain, Alexander Scott, who described the scene below decks at Trafalgar as 'like a butcher's shambles' and who found the sights and smells unbearable.[29] There were also matters of conscience. As one Chaplain put it, how was he to 'act and speak as becomes the promoter of "peace and good-will towards men"' 'amidst preparations the most complex and ingenious for the purpose of plundering and murdering his fellow-creatures'.[30]

Barham achieved a minor success in carrying Evangelical principles forward in the 1806 *Regulations and Instructions Relating to His Majesty's Service at Sea*, a complete revision of the *Regulations* of 1731. The responsibility of Captains to ensure regular public worship at sea was emphasised and, for the first time, the Chaplain's duties were outlined. He was to set a good example, to instruct 'the young gentlemen' and ships' boys in 'the principles of the Christian Religion', 'to hear them read, and to explain to them, the Scriptures and the Church Catechism' (which is where William would have had contact with the Chaplain and met his 'great kindness'), to conduct the Sunday Service and to attend the sick and dying.[31]

Nonetheless, despite this strong backing, Chaplains continued to meet with hostility. Brian Lavery cites the experiences of Edward Mangin, Chaplain of the *Gloucester* (74) in 1812. He

> perceived that 'nothing can possibly be more unsuitably or more awkwardly situated than a clergyman in a ship of war; every object around him is at variance with the sensibilities of a rational and enlightened mind'. He found that visiting the sick was worse than useless: 'The entrance of the clergyman is, to a poor seaman, often a fatal signal.' He saw that his 'constant efforts to rebuke the seamen, etc. for profane swearing, and intemperate language of every kind' had no effect. He

found employment in conducting Sunday service, when the men behaved 'with utmost decorum', and in burying the dead, a common enough occupation on a man-of-war. 'To convert a man-of-war's crew into Christians,' he wrote, 'would be a task to which the courage of Loyola, the philanthropy of Howard, and the eloquence of St Paul united, would prove inadequate,'[32]

To complete the picture, Sunday at sea was this Chaplain's despair, 'observed more as a day of revels than worship',[33] with drunkenness prevailing. While Jane Austen did not feel it was her business to look into this area of conflict, nor to make it a matter of discussion amongst her characters, nonetheless, this lightest of allusions would have been quite enough to alert her navally-informed readers, reminding them of Admiral Crawford's generation of sea-dogs, many of whom regarded the Chaplain as an encumbrance, and of the different climate now prevailing. Under the premiership of Spencer Perceval (November 1809 to May 1813), a fervent Evangelical Tory, and with a sympathetic First Lord (Charles Yorke, May 1810 to March 1812), Evangelical groupings in Parliament and the Admiralty succeeded in raising the status of Chaplains. In 1812, a Chaplain-General to the Fleet was appointed, Chaplains' pay and conditions were improved and all vessels were issued with Bibles, New Testaments, Books of Common Prayer and Psalters for the use of the crews.

In proposing these changes to Parliament, Yorke drew attention to the Chaplain's inferior position. As ordained clergymen, Chaplains were, as Edmund points out, 'educated men'.[34] Yet they were not ranked as commissioned officers, having only warrants, and were paid at the same rate as ordinary seamen, a salary of less than £12 a year, with the demeaning addition of a groat (4d.) for every member of the crew. Not surprisingly, Yorke explained, 'few men could be found willing to fill those situations; in fact for the immense number of ships in Commission there were only 39 Chaplains' (as against the 282 vessels in service entitled to carry them).[35] Francis' patron, Lord Gambier, took a leading part in introducing these measures and himself proposed the new level of annual pay of £150, while Yorke's recommendation to Parliament was that the offices of Chaplain and Schoolmaster be combined, with a commensurate level of pay.

A vastly more important Evangelical cause, perhaps their proudest single achievement, was the outlawing of the slave trade. This is a subject Fanny Price raises at the family gathering to hear Sir Thomas's account of his stay at the Bertram plantations in Antigua. But her question on the 'slave trade' – still a burning issue at the time of *Mansfield Park* – is received in 'such a dead silence!' that she stops there and then.[36] After a twenty-year campaign, abolition became law in 1807. Yet the trade was so profitable that it continued to flourish, illicitly, even in the face of further legislation in 1811 making the offence a felony punishable by transportation (up to fourteen years), rather than subject merely to a fine, as before, It was a cause in which the Evangelicals continue to lobby both the Admiralty and the Government. William Wilberforce, the leading parliamentary Abolitionist, urged Yorke to 'clear the coast [of West Africa] by a thorough sweep',[37] and members of the Evangelical Clapham Sect, the 'Saints', had the ear of Perceval.

The effectiveness of their continuing campaign can be seen in some of the key appointments. For example, Captain Edward Columbine, a director of the Africa Institution, which joined Abolitionist and Evangelical interests, was charged in 1808 with taking a Commission of Enquiry to the West Coast of Africa to investigate the British settlements there and the best methods of suppressing the slave trade; and he went on to be appointed Governor of Sierra Leone, a colony established specifically to provide a home for freed slaves. And the officer commanding the enforcement Squadron sent to the West Coast of Africa in 1811, Captain Frederick Irby, was claimed by the Evangelical Abolitionists as 'a man of our own choice',[38] the words of Zachary Macaulay.

Enforcement was largely a matter of interception at sea. Tactically, this was a problem, since the Navy was principally engaged with the containment of the French and Dutch fleets around the naval bases of Europe, and the West African Squadron in 1811, consisting of no more than five ships, was inadequate to do the job. Legally, there were problems too. The Navy was only authorised to act against vessels of British ownership with slaves actually on board. It was a difficult task in which both Francis and Charles were involved, often to their frustration. One such occasion was recalled by Francis:

> Chaced a ship which proved to be a Portuguese bound for Rio Janeiro. She had on board 714 slaves of both sexes, and all ages. She appeared to be about 300 tons!! And in those days the St Albans was compelled to let the craft proceed on her course.[39]

The exclamation marks convey his revulsion at discovering a human cargo packed into a ship of this size. Even by the standards of the day, the figures are horrific. We have a measure of this in the legislation of 1799, which set a limit of 400 for a cargo of slaves; and in the previous year, when the trade was unregulated, the largest slaver arriving in the West Indies, the *Elliot* of 371 tons, carried a cargo totalling 505. So the sight of 714 on a vessel of 300 tons was nothing short of a nightmare.

It was on another voyage in the *St Albans* that Francis observed on St Helena that 'slavery however it may be modified is still slavery'. He wrote of 'the harshness and despotism which has been so justly attributed to the conduct of land-holders or their managers' in the West Indies and went on to record his regret 'that any trace of it should be found to exist in countries dependent on England, or colonised by her subjects'.[40] These, of course, are the views of a confirmed Evangelical, far in advance of his times, for the British emancipation of slaves was not achieved until 1833.

On the question of the slave trade, naval thinking was totally divided, almost schizophrenic. On the one hand, for a century and a half the maintenance of the 'colonial system', notably the protection of the West Indies and its trade – slaves coming in and sugar exported – had been seen as one of the Navy's prime duties. This was a commerce in which the British had been 'the world's greediest and most successful traders',[41] claiming as of right the full force of naval protection as major contributors to the nation's wealth. No mercantile venture was more profitable than the 'triangular' trade carrying British manufactured goods to Africa, to be traded for slaves transported on the Middle Passage across the Atlantic to the West Indies and America, the empty slave-ships then bringing sugar, tobacco and rum back to Europe. It was also believed that the West Indian fleets, including the slavers, were a 'nursery' of seamen, a deep reserve of trained and experienced sailors to man the Royal Navy in time of war. Nelson was brought up in this tradition, having first visited the Caribbean in 1771, as a boy of twelve, serving in a West Indian merchant ship, and in the Navy he returned to the West Indies again in 1777 and 1782. He regarded Jamaica, the largest and most productive of the British sugar islands, as the jewel in the crown, to be guarded at all costs, together with the slave trade itself, a commerce to be protected. Wilberforce's Abolitionist campaign was 'meddling'[42] and Nelson was delighted to tell Collingwood of a parliamentary defeat for Abolition in 1796.[43] While Nelson saw himself as a defender of the slave trade, standing firm in a just cause, his critics thought otherwise. At the height of the Abolitionist campaign in Parliament, he explained his position to a Jamaican trader, a friend of thirty years standing. It was a letter which, according to the Monthly Repository, revealed Nelson in his true colours, as 'An outrageous abettor of the slave trade'.[44] Nelson declared himself forthrightly:

> I was bred in the good old school and taught to appreciate the value of our West Indian possessions, and neither in the field nor the Senate shall their just rights be infringed, while I have an arm to fight in their defence, or a tongue to launch my voice against the damnable doctrine of Wilberforce and his hypocritical allies.[45]

The 'value of our West Indian possessions' was well understood. They provided no less than 80 per cent of Britain's income from its overseas investments. And correspondingly, the 'good old school' had roots which extended far into British society. Few families of any wealth or property were without West Indian connections or investments. Amongst those in the Austen circle were their cousins the Hampsons, the Walters and the Leigh Perrots, and their wider acquaintance included the Holders (of Ashe Park), the Beckfords (of Basing Park) and the Wildmans (of Chilham Castle, near Godmersham). Mr Austen himself was for many years a trustee of a plantation, in none other than Antigua, the source of the Bertrams' wealth in *Mansfield Park*, and the plantation-owner, James Langford Nibbs, was godfather to James Austen. Even amongst the Austens, slavery and the slave trade was accepted, or at least tolerated, as legitimate 'property', both personal and national, and as a necessary source of income.

But amongst naval officers who had encountered the evils of the trade at first hand, there were views quite contrary to Nelson's 'good old school'. In fact, the origin of the Abolitionist movement can be traced to a naval 'conversion' experience. This occurred in 1759 when Captain Charles Middleton (as he was then), commanding the *Arundel* (24), met the *Swift*, a slaver from Bristol, in which an epidemic was raging. The *Arundel*'s surgeon, James Ramsay, did what he could for the sick. Soon after, he left the Navy, was ordained, and dedicated himself to improving the treatment of slaves in the plantations of St Kitts, where he remained for nineteen years. In 1781, he came back to England, at the invitation of Middleton, to take up the living of Teston in Kent, Middleton's country seat. Together with Lady Middleton, a moving spirit in the cause, Ramsay and Sir Charles made Teston a gathering-ground for like-minded reformers – the 'Testonites', Hannah More called them – including Thomas Clarkson, the historian of the slave trade. Encouraged by Lady Middleton, Ramsay brought out the first statement of the Abolitionist cause to be argued wholly on first-hand evidence: *An Essay on the Treatment and Conversion of African Slaves in the British Sugar Colonies*, 1784. That same year, Middleton entered Parliament, and two years later, Sir Charles and Lady Middleton set about persuading Wilberforce to undertake the leadership of the parliamentary campaign.

It was in a household of such Evangelical zeal and activity that the young James Gambier was brought up by his Middleton aunt and uncle. A friend and supporter of Wilberforce, he joined him in 1799 as a founding member (and Vice-President) of the Church Missionary Society, a strictly Evangelical enterprise and kept in Evangelical hands to distinguish the Society from similar bodies, the London Missionary Society and the Society for the Propagation of the Gospel.[46] In 1812, Gambier became its President.

The Abolitionist campaign, before and after 1807, was shot through with politics – parliamentary, naval and religious, an overlapping of interests neatly illustrated in the circumstances surrounding the appointment of

Middleton (now the seventy-nine-year-old Lord Barham) as First Lord of the Admiralty in May 1805. Pitt's Ministry was in difficulties at this time. The previous First Lord, Melville, had resigned in April under the threat of parliamentary censure and impeachment,* and Pitt needed to secure what alliances he could, including the support of Wilberforce and his following among the Abolitionists and Evangelical MPs. As Creevey remarked, Barham's appointment placed 'a superannuated Methodist at the head of the Admiralty to catch the votes of Wilberforce and Co now and then'.[47]

These larger issues Jane Austen makes no attempt to capture, although Francis may well have reported on matters so close to his own feelings and faith. What Jane Austen communicates through the 'dead silence' at Mansfield Park is that, at this time, the autumn of 1812, the 'slave trade' was still a topic too close to the bone for a plantation-owning family to discuss freely and openly. If the same taboo prevailed within sections of the Austen family, at least the two sisters could speak of it in their correspondence. At the time she was working on *Mansfield Park*, Jane laughingly confessed to Cassandra that Clarkson, the author of *The History of the Abolition of the African Slave Trade* (1808), was among the writers with whom she had once been 'in love'.[48]

The two naval scenes in chapters 6 and 11 of volume 1 serve Jane Austen's purpose principally in advancing the characterisation of Mary Crawford as someone hard-boiled, bitter, unillusioned and cynical. In less dramatic fashion, these scenes also link the Navy and the Church as professions, the routes along which the two heroes of the novel, William and Edmund, make their way. This is a theme continued in volume 2, where their *professionalism* is explored.** Edmund, in prospect a parish priest with Evangelical ambitions, keen to undertake his work and conscientious about the performance of his duties, no absentee cleric, but a resident clergyman, attending to the needs of his parishioners; William, with all the promise of becoming a young officer of the new school, knowledgeable in his profession and a friend to religion. The difference between the two is that while Edmund talks about the professional he hopes to be, William, in his line of service, for all his youth, already is a professional.

---

* Melville was accused of 'gross irregularities' in the handling of Government funds during his period as Treasurer of the Navy (January 1784 to June 1800).

** Jane Austen first took up this question in *Sense and Sensibility*, where Edward Ferrars reviews the professions he might have followed: the Church, the Army, the Navy and Law. But he is aimless, has no vocational call, seeing them only as means to 'employment' and 'independence' (pp. 102–03). This current of thought is explored in Richard Edgeworth's *Essays on Professional Education* (1808; 2nd edn 1812) and in Maria Edgeworth's *Patronage* (1814), a novel which (drawing on her father's book) tells the stories of young men pursuing careers in Law, Medicine, Diplomacy, Military Service and the Church.

William comes to Mansfield in chapter 6 of volume 2. The event is carefully placed in the dramatic ordering and tempo of the novel. Following the high comedy of Sir Thomas's unexpected return from Antigua, the instant abandonment of *Lovers' Vows*, the dispersal of the cast and a period in which Sir Thomas resumes his place as head of the family, William, newly arrived, becomes the centre of attention, the hero of the hour, with tales of war to tell and called upon by his uncle to tell them: his voyages in the Mediterranean and to the West Indies, the 'horrors' of shipwrecks and engagements,[49] 'the imminent hazards, or terrific scenes',[50] 'every variety of danger which sea and war together could offer.'[51] *

The effect is lively and striking. Yet Jane Austen keeps the recital at a marked level of generality. In William's reporting of these 'hazards' and 'scenes', nothing is eye-witness or participant. The telling is indirect. 'I' is absent. Abundantly present is the circle around William, his naval reality registered from person to person: Fanny, for whom William is the brother 'so long absent and dearly loved';[52] Sir Thomas, who observes 'a young man of an open, pleasant countenance, and frank, unstudied, but feeling and respectful manners',[53] who listens to the young sailor's 'clear, simple, spirited details with full satisfaction – seeing in them the proof of good principles, professional knowledge, energy, courage and cheerfulness – every thing that could deserve and promise well';[54] and, for the occasion, even Lady Bertram is roused from inertia, 'could not hear of such horrors unmoved, or without raising her eyes from her work to say, "Dear me! how disagreeable. – I wonder any body can ever go to sea".'[55]

Lady Bertram's response is comic and fully in character. Around Henry Crawford, Jane Austen weaves a deeper comedy. Since Shakespeare, the civilian stirred by tales of war has been a stock figure in English plays and novels and Crawford stands squarely in this tradition. But Jane Austen transcends the convention. Beneath the excited bravado lies a conscience – and Crawford being Crawford, a conscience shallow and momentary. For an instant he glimpses himself as the civilian shamed, the gentleman of leisure discomfited by a reminder of his unpatriotic idleness. This vignette of self-recrimination is short-lived. With scarcely a pause, he resumes his habits 'of fortune' and returns to his 'command', a landlubber's sporting 'command' of 'horses' and 'grooms':

* For the first readers of *Mansfield Park*, the dangers of the sea were recent history. In 1811, returning from the Baltic, the *St George* (98) and the *Defence* (74) were wrecked in the winter storms. Of the ship's company of the *St George* only six out of 850 survived; of the *Defence's* crew of 530 only twelve. Three days later, on 25 December, came a further loss – the *Hero* (74), only twelve surviving out of over 500. Together, these three disasters were accounted the worst naval catastrophes for over a hundred years.

He longed to have been at sea, and seen and done and suffered as much. His heart was warmed, his fancy fired, and he felt the highest respect for a lad who, before he was twenty, had gone through such bodily hardships, and given such proofs of mind. The glory of heroism, of usefulness, of exertion, of endurance, made his own habits of selfish indulgence appear in shameful contrast; and he wished he had been a William Price, distinguishing himself and working his way to fortune and consequence with so much self-respect and happy ardour, instead of what he was!

  The wish was rather eager than lasting. He was roused from the reverie of retrospection and regret produced by it, by some inquiry from Edmund as to his plans for the next day's hunting; and he found it was as well to be a man of fortune at once with horses and grooms at his command.[56]

At the opening of this chapter 6, Jane Austen introduces a fresh impulse to the story. This is Crawford's decision – having time on his hands – 'to make Fanny Price in love with me'.[57] His pursuit becomes the sustaining dramatic strand for the central section of *Mansfield Park*. It also serves as a major device in the plotting of the novel, linking this element of the story to the advancement of William Price, a sequence which leads to Fanny's banishment from Mansfield and her return to the family home in Portsmouth, where Crawford's wooing, now a serious attachment, is continued.

  From the very beginning, Crawford's courtship takes a naval route. He rushes to be the first to bring Fanny news of the *Antwerp*'s return from the Mediterranean. But this she knows, having already received a letter from William himself, 'a few hurried happy lines, written as the ship came up the Channel, and sent into Portsmouth, with the first boat that left the Antwerp, at anchor, in Spithead'; whereas Crawford has to rely on a belated source of information, the 'ship news' in 'the paper esteemed to have the earliest naval intelligence' (of the daily newspapers this would be the *Morning Post*; of the weeklies, the *London Gazette*).[58] We might wonder if such circumstantial detail is necessary to the story. But this is the kind of meticulous and authenticating accuracy which the sailor brothers and their naval colleagues would be looking for and which would be appreciated by the Austen family at large, remembering their own anxious concern for news of the brothers' comings and goings.

  What upsets Crawford's plan for flirtation is the arrival of William and the sight of Fanny blooming in her brother's company; 'the warm hearted, blunt fondness of the young sailor' answered by Fanny's sparkling eyes and glowing cheeks.[59] For the first time, Crawford sees her not as a pretty girl, a mere plaything, but as a woman, capable of love; and he falls for her himself. Infatuated – for that is the extent of it – he presses forward with a series of attentions and favours calculated at loading Fanny with a burden of 'obligation', an indebtedness with which he hopes to bind her in affection and gratitude.

These springs of action are tightened within the compass of chapter 6, which concludes with Crawford's second indirect act of courtship, his lending William a hunter, with 'obligation' in view, a purpose which Jane Austen underlines. Only when William returns safely (thanks to his experience of 'horsemanship in various countries . . . the scrambling parties in which he had been engaged, the rough horses and mules he had ridden' – details which could very well derive from accounts by letter or word-of-mouth from Francis or Charles) could Fanny 'be reconciled to the risk, or feel any of that obligation to Mr Crawford for lending the horse which he had intended it should produce'.[60]

Fanny's coming-out ball – an idea planted in Sir Thomas's mind on over-hearing William's wish to see his sister dance – provides the opportunity for a further step in Crawford's scheme. Fanny's jewellery consists of an 'almost solitary ornament', an 'amber cross'. A present from William, brought back from Sicily, it must be worn. But a gold chain was 'beyond his means' and all she has to hang it on is a humble 'bit of ribbon',[61] unworthy of the gift and the occasion. Crawford learns of the problem, buys a necklace and, by way of 'trick' and 'confederacy',[62] gets his sister to pass it off as a gift from her, a mere 'trifle',[63] as her story goes, given to her by Henry some years earlier. Although Fanny is troubled by doubts and scruples, she eventually accepts the gift at face value. But Jane Austen sets poetic justice to work. The necklace proves too large for the ring of the cross; so, instead, Fanny uses a chain offered by Edmund; and, worn together, all three – the cross suspended from the chain, and the necklace on its own – become the adversative emblems of true love and false friendship:

> and having, with delightful feelings, joined the chain and the cross, those memorials of the two most beloved of her heart, those dearest tokens so formed for each other by every thing real and imaginary – and put them round her neck, and seen and felt how full of William and Edmund they were, she was able, without an effort, to resolve on wearing Miss Crawford's necklace too.[64]

Charles Austen, and other members of the family, would be delighted at such a notable working-up of the topaze crosses and gold chains sent to Jane and Cassandra in 1801: his gift of jewellery now answered with a gift of literature.

Crawford's fascination with Fanny and William – their warmth and flow of feeling and their responsiveness to one another – casts him in the voyeuristic role of watcher and listener; and when the game of speculation breaks up (in chapter 7), leaving the brother and sister on their own, he turns his chair to overhear their conversation: William's complaint at being no more than a Midshipman and Fanny's attempts to cheer him up with the suggestion that

Sir Thomas will come to his rescue, will 'do every thing in his power to get you made'.[65] From this moment, Crawford sees his opportunity to set a truly compelling trap of 'obligation' – by getting his uncle, Admiral Crawford, to use his 'interest' on William's behalf. Since no Flag Officer would risk his reputation by recommending someone unknown, this means arranging a meeting for the Admiral to judge if Midshipman Price is really officer material. Even then, there is the task of persuasion, not an easy matter. As Mary Crawford tells Fanny much later – turning the screw of 'obligation' yet further on her brother's behalf – 'The Admiral hates trouble, and scorns asking favours; and there are so many young men's claims to be attended to in the same way'.[66]

Conveniently for Crawford's scheme, William is due to return to Portsmouth at the end of his fortnight's leave and is happy to accept the offer of a lift to London and an invitation to dine with the Admiral. As any Midshipman would, William appreciates the value of such a meeting: 'in likening it to going up with dispatches' he 'was saying at once every thing in favour of its happiness and dignity which his imagination could suggest'.[67] (The point here is that an officer returning to England with the official despatches reporting a great victory at sea would be honoured with promotion or a commendation, or be otherwise rewarded, sometimes financially, as the representative of the victorious Fleet.) Like his nephew, Sir Thomas sees the worth of this opportunity: William's 'introduction to Admiral Crawford might be of service. The Admiral he believed had interest' – an understanding which passes Fanny by.[68] Ignorant of these matters and thus unsuspecting, she takes Crawford's offer of a lift to be a genuine act of kindness, saving her brother an awkward change of coaches and a tiring journey.

Jane Austen's chronology over this period is unfailingly precise. William arrives at Mansfield on 9 December; Fanny's coming-out ball is on the 22nd; on the 23rd William leaves in the company of Crawford; and twelve days later, on 4 January (at the opening of chapter 13, the final chapter of volume 2), Crawford returns, announcing to Fanny, somewhat theatrically, in two staccato sentences, 'He is made. Your brother is a Lieutenant.' Fanny's ignorance of what has been going on is confirmed: 'doubt, confusion and felicity' is 'the progress of her feelings' as, one by one, she reads the three letters, just arrived with that morning's post, handed to her by Crawford:

> The first was from the Admiral to inform his nephew, in a few words, of his having succeeded in the object he had undertaken, the promotion of young Price, and inclosing two more, one from the Secretary of the First Lord to a friend, whom the

Admiral had set to work in the business, the other from that friend to himself, by which it appeared that his Lordship had the very great happiness of attending to the recommendation of Sir Charles, that Sir Charles was much delighted in having such an opportunity of proving his regard for Admiral Crawford, and that the circumstance of Mr. William Price's commission as second Lieutenant of H. M. sloop Thrush,* being made out, was spreading general joy through a wide circle of great people.[69]

A feat of style, this sustained sentence communicates the formality of the process by which 'interest' is set to work, its studied politeness, its circuitousness and the turning of its mechanism as 'Sir Charles', the Admiral's intermediary, almost certainly a Minister, perhaps a member of the Cabinet, gets his recommendation to the First Lord. 'Young Price' carries the personal tone of the Admiral's patronage. Then come the hypocrisies of procedure: that all these steps are accompanied with 'happiness' and 'delight', concluding with the blank presumption that Mr Price's commission 'was spreading general joy through a wide circle of great people', a social falsehood behind which stands the simple fact that Mr Price is a nonentity, unknown in any 'circle' other than that of his own family, from which 'great people' are notably absent – not unlike the Austens themselves when Francis and Charles entered the Navy. What drives this home is William's appointment to a sloop, a ship of between ten and eighteen guns, the humblest of vessels, which offered none of the opportunities for prize-money and distinction to be enjoyed in frigates or ships-of-the-line, into which a candidate with powerful interest might expect to be commissioned.

It is worth noting the place of 'the Secretary of the First Lord' in this business. He was not a mere functionary but, like Benjamin Tucker, a confidant personally appointed by the First Lord, often an experienced senior Captain and a necessary friend at court. When, in 1817, Dillon sought command of an 'active frigate', after sending in his application to the First Lord, 'I now felt it necessary to consult Lord Melville's Private Secretary, who received me with marked attention, and told me that he thought I might have the command of a fine frigate if I would only apply'.[70] Dillon's case, as a Captain of some standing, is quite different from William's. But Jane Austen's sure grasp of Admiralty procedures stands behind the youngster's *sotto voce* comment that he would 'rather find' Mr Rushworth, now newly-married to his cousin Maria Bertram, 'private secretary to the First Lord than any thing else'.[71]

Crawford hurries on, explaining to Fanny his impatience with the time the business has taken, the 'difficulties from the absence of one friend, and the

* Larger sloops carried two Lieutenants.

engagements of another',[72] his uncle's delight in William and his exertions on William's behalf, and his own reluctance to say anything of this until his uncle's 'praise should be proved the praise of a friend' (in the terminology of 'interest', only someone who oils the wheels successfully is to be called a 'friend').[73] Fanny expresses her sense of obligation and Crawford duly asserts his claim: 'that every thing he had done for William was to be placed to the account of his excessive and unequalled attachment for her'.[74] His 'moral taste'[75] deserts him and, free from scruples, he loads this 'obligation' with a proposal of marriage. The irony is evident: the fates of brother and sister are intertwined: William's success is won at the cost of Fanny's future. Crawford's 'Kindness to William' leaves Fanny 'more obliged' to him 'than words can express'.[76] On this divided note – the brother happy and commissioned, the sister assailed and distressed – Jane Austen brings the second volume to a close.

The early chapters of volume 3 provide no respite. The net of 'obligation' is drawn more tightly and Fanny's ordeal continues. Sir Thomas charges her with '*ingratitude*' (Jane Austen's italics convey the loading of his accusation),[77] and Crawford appears before her as the suitor to whom, on William's behalf, and in all conscience, 'gratitude' is due, a conclusion reached with rhetorical flourish and a sense of climax:

> He was now the Mr Crawford who was addressing herself with ardent, disinterested, love; whose feelings were apparently become all that was honourable and upright, whose views of happiness were all fixed on a marriage of attachment; who was pouring out his sense of her merits, describing and describing again his affection, proving, as far as words could prove it, and in the language, tone, and spirit of a man of talent too, that he sought her for her gentleness, and her goodness; and to complete the whole, he was now the Mr Crawford who had procured William's promotion!
>
> Here was a change! and here were claims which could not but operate. She might have disdained him in all the dignity of angry virtue, in the grounds of Sotherton, or the theatre at Mansfield Park; but he approached her now with rights that demanded different treatment. She must be courteous, and she must be compassionate. She must have a sensation of being honoured, and whether thinking of herself or her brother, she must have a strong feeling of gratitude.[78]

The first five chapters of volume 3 show Fanny at her strongest, her 'heroism of principle' deeply searched as she stands up successfully to Crawford's badgering and her uncle's armtwisting.[79] But Sir Thomas sees a further opportunity with William's arrival at Mansfield on ten days' leave – 'the happiest of lieutenants because the latest made'.[80] Having found no success with moral blackmail and bullying, Sir Thomas changes tack, sending Fanny back with her brother to stay for a time at Portsmouth, a stiff dose of discomfort calculated to soften her up for a further approach from Crawford.

Within the overarching drama of 'obligation' (which continues until chapter 11) comes a secondary drama of disappointment, the dashing of Fanny's expectations when she returns to Portsmouth and is with her own family once again, after an absence of nine years, and her further hopes of seeing William in his naval habitat, and of visiting the *Thrush* and the dock-yard in his company, hopes buoyed up by her brother's eagerness even before the journey home is begun:

> It would be the greatest pleasure to him to have her there to the last moment before he sailed, and perhaps find her there still when he came in, from his first cruise! And besides, he wanted her so very much to see the Thrush before she went out of harbour (the Thrush was certainly the finest sloop in the service). And there were several improvements in the dock-yard, too, which he quite longed to shew her.[81]

These happy anticipations extend far into the future as William daydreams of heroism, promotion, prize-money and rural retirement:

> Of pleasant talk between the brother and sister, there was no end. Every thing supplied an amusement to the high glee of William's mind, and he was full of frolic and joke, in the intervals of their higher-toned subjects, all of which ended, if they did not begin, in praise of the Thrush, conjectures how she would be employed, schemes for an action with some superior force, which (supposing the first lieu-tenant out of the way – and William was not very merciful to the first lieutenant) was to give himself the next step as soon as possible, or speculations upon prize money, which was to be generously distributed at home, with only the reservation of enough to make the little cottage comfortable, in which he and Fanny were to pass all their middle and latter life together.[82]

As Fanny discovers, this is a precious moment lost all too soon. On their arrival, Portsmouth closes in, not only the painful reality of her family but the naval reality of duty and its demands. The *Thrush* has left harbour prema-turely, to anchor out at Spithead. With the rush to get William into his uniform and collect his gear, the house is in uproar and Fanny's arrival barely noticed.

Our last sight of William is in his Lieutenant's uniform, parading before the family, 'looking and moving all the taller, firmer, and more graceful for it'. Fanny breaks down, sobbing 'out her various emotions of pain and plea-sure'. But pulling herself together, she soon recovered herself: and wiping away her tears, was able to notice and admire all the striking parts of his dress* – listening with reviving spirits to his cheerful hopes of being on shore some part of every day before they sailed, and even of getting her to Spithead to see the sloop.[83]

But none of this happens. The exigencies of the service take over and Fanny's hopes are dashed.

Before the week ended, it was all disappointment. In the first place, William was gone. The Thrush had had her orders, the wind had changed, and he was sailed within four days from their reaching Portsmouth; and during those days, she had seen him only twice, in a short and hurried way, when he had come ashore on duty. There had been no free conversation, no walk on the ramparts, no visit to the dock-yard, no acquaintance with the Thrush – nothing of all that they had planned and depended on. Every thing in that quarter failed her, except William's affection. His last thought on leaving home was for her. He stepped back again to the door to say, 'Take care of Fanny, mother. she is tender, and not used to rough it like the rest of us. I charge you, take care of Fanny.'
      William was gone.[84]

The last words sound a note of finality: 'William was gone', twice repeated, is the tolling bell. William's 'affections' reminds us of his place in the thematic structure of the novel, as the figure of 'fraternal love', a bond that Jane Austen places above all others, even above 'the conjugal tie' and which she celebrates at some length both early in the story,[85] when as a youngster William says goodbye to Fanny before going to sea for the first time,[86] and on his return to Mansfield seven years later.[87] It was for this that Nina Auerbach called their relationship 'the vivid heart of the book',[88] while the philosopher Gilbert Ryle cast William as the 'real hero of the story', seeing 'their brother-sister love' as 'the paradigm against which to assess all the others. Fanny's love for her cousin Edmund had begun as a child's love for a deputy – William.'[89]

William's part in the novel is now concluded and beyond this point there are only two perfunctory references: when Henry Crawford calls on the Prices, 'They talked of William, a subject on which Mrs Price could never

* This refers to a very recent innovation. By the uniform regulations announced in the *Gazette* on 28 March 1812, to take effect in August, Lieutenants were now given a single epaulette, worn on the right shoulder, and a distinctive Navy button, newly-introduced, with a crown above an anchor. The other 'striking parts' of William's dress would include his 'new' cocked hat and 'uniform waistcoat' (p. 381); his sword-belt, worn across the chest; his buttoned cuffs; his cotton-net pantaloons; and his high Hessian boots, fashionable with tassels and gold-twist edging (if William's money ran to these decorative extras). These changes were celebrated by verses in the *Naval Chronicle*: 'Lines on The Change of Uniform' included a reference to 'The Epaulet, – badge proud and fair!' (July–December 1812, xxviii. 335)

tire',[90] and, on the last page, we hear, somewhat remotely, of his 'continued good conduct, and rising fame'.[91]

In one of the most powerfully-drawn episodes of *Mansfield Park*, William's departure leaves Fanny unsupported and painfully exposed to the shock of homecoming. Jane Austen draws the scene in the Price household, a combination of squalor and vitality, with – what is for her – a low-life realism almost Dickensian in its grim humour. The forceful presence of this chaotic family is a *tour de force* found nowhere else in the novels. Within this 'abode of noise, disorder, and impropriety',[92] the presiding figure is Mr Price, Lieutenant of Marines, Fanny's experience of him compressed into a few sentences:

> On her father, her confidence had not been sanguine, but he was more negligent of his family, his habits were worse, and his manners coarser, than she had been prepared for. He did not want abilities; but he had no curiosity, and no information beyond his profession; he read only the newspaper and the navy-list; he talked only of the dock-yard, the harbour, Spithead, and the Motherbank;* he swore and he drank, he was dirty and gross. She had never been able to recal anything approaching to tenderness in his former treatment of herself. There had remained only a general impression of roughness and loudness; and now he scarcely ever noticed her, but to make her the object of a coarse joke.[93]

We hear nothing of these jokes. But we can guess what they were: jibes at Fanny's refined manners and cultivated speech and at her revulsion, however well-concealed, at her father's habits and at conditions in the family home. A shy product of Mansfield, she is a sitting target for his abuse, a scapegoat as it were for the gulf between the prosperity and dignity of the Bertrams, with Sir Thomas a Member of Parliament, and the poverty and dishonour of the Prices. This is something that comes across as powerfully today as it did for the readers of *Mansfield Park* in 1814. They would see in Mr Price the Navy's darker aspect, a living reminder that, in the words of Southey, its 'ways ... are as little ways of pleasantness as its paths are paths of peace'.[94]

On the other hand, there is a problem for modern readers in placing Mr Price socially and in terms of his 'profession'. How was it that a man 'without education, fortune, or connections' could become a Lieutenant of Marines in the first place?[95] Why was his marriage to Frances Ward, as we learn in the opening pages of the novel, a clandestine affair, a marriage so disgraceful as to put her beyond the pale? And what is his professional standing vis-à-vis his

---

* The Motherbank, just west of Spithead, was the anchorage for merchant-ships awaiting the formation of convoys and naval escorts.

son, now a naval Lieutenant? These are matters of information and interpretation which editors of *Mansfield Park* have left untouched, and not surprisingly, since the Marines aspect presents a historiographical problem.

Although the duties and organisation of the Marines are well documented, naval historians have had little to say about the social and professional standing of Marine officers. To date, the fullest account is to be found in *The Social History of the Navy, 1793–1815* (1960) by Michael Lewis. According to Lewis, Marine officers 'were always regarded' 'both navally and socially' as 'officers and gentlemen',[96] a view supported in more detailed evidence presented by other historians.[97] But Mr Price – 'gross', 'dirty' and foul-mouthed – is a world away from Lewis's gentlemanly specimens and, in this light, he remains an unexplained and inexplicable anomaly.

The modern image of the Marines – the Royal Marines, as they became in 1802 – is of an elite force, highly-trained and with a reputation for missions of daring and adventure. This was not the case in Jane Austen's day. Under Admiralty control, the Corps of Marines, largely composed of sea-going infantry, was seen as a subordinate and inferior branch of the Navy. However effective the Marines might be in action, providing small-arms fire at close quarters and in amphibious operations, nonetheless they suffered an inescapable disadvantage. Seamen knew their trade, were at home on board ship, in their element at sea, whereas fairly or unfairly, Marines were regarded as ignoramuses, 'idlers' they were called, no more than landlubbers afloat, in the sailors' phrase, 'neither flesh, fowl, nor good red herring'. At sea, their duties were essentially static. They stood as sentries on guard at the Captain's door, at the ward-room, the spirit-room and the powder-magazine and, while food was cooking, at the galley door. During the night, marine sentries were stationed at the large guns. With bayonets fixed, they provided a show of uniformed authority at floggings (in Illustration 22 we see them lining the quarter-deck, overlooking the scene); and at the threat of mutiny, with muskets loaded, they formed a protective line across the quarter-deck, standing between the Captain and officers and a rebellious crew. When called upon, they might play a seaman's part, taking a hand at the capstan, working the pumps, or making up a gun crew; and they might join a boarding-party to provide covering fire for the crew-men armed with cutlasses. But however honourable and meritorious their service might be (and St Vincent spoke of their 'honour, courage' and 'loyalty'),[98] amongst sailors their stupidity was legend, a standing joke. To a tall story, the disparaging riposte was 'Tell it to the marines'; or, as John Davis has it in *The Post Captain* (1805), 'You may tell that to the marines, but I'll be d–d if the sailors will believe it'.[99] Hardly surprising that a small volume of *Advice* by a former Marine officer should ask, querulously, 'Then who the d—l would be a M——E?'[100]

Amongst the ordinary seamen the Marines were also disliked for the part they played in enforcing the Captain's authority, a role that cut them off from the body of the crew and which was underlined by their military uniforms, weapons and separate quarters. For the ship's officers, it was more a matter of contempt than dislike. Marine officers were their inferiors – professionally, socially and in rank. Whereas a newly-commissioned naval Lieutenant, such as William Price, would have served a sea-apprenticeship of not less than six years, a Marine Lieutenant might be little more than a raw recruit and completely unprepared for life at sea. Commissions were obtained by nomination, employing 'interest' with the First Lord. Applicants were interviewed to establish their suitability to hold a commission. But this procedure was undemanding and only called for details of their birth, family, education and height. Having 'passed the Board', candidates were then sent to one of the three Marine Divisions at Chatham, Portsmouth or Plymouth, to see in the first few days if they were physically capable of drilling and handling a sword. Once 'off the adjutant's list', candidates, some as young as fifteen, received their commissions to a specified Company of Marines.[101] It comes as no surprise to find that in Grose's 1811 *Dictionary of the Vulgar Tongue* a 'Marine Officer' is defined as 'An empty bottle: marine officers being held useless by the seamen'.

With such modest entry requirements, commissions in the Marines were eagerly sought. Apart from the sons and relatives of marine officers, who could look forward to preferential treatment, it was a career for those who could find nothing better, for orphans, for example, with the backing of a patron, or those who might otherwise be destined for a shop or counting-house;[102] and it provided a convenient berth for Midshipmen unable to get commissions in the Navy. Yet beyond the point of entry, it was not an attractive career. Promotion, by seniority, was slow and for most officers there was a ceiling at the rank of Captain. Above that, the officers of field rank (Major, Lieutenant-Colonel and Colonel) numbered no more than forty-five. The three highest posts – the General of Marines, the Lieutenant-General and the Major-General – were a naval monopoly and invariably filled by Admirals. Below them came four 'Blue Colonelcies', awarded to distinguished Captains high on the seniority list yet not sufficiently high to achieve Flag rank. It was a sinecure bringing handsome pay without duties, an appointment to which Nelson was gazetted in 1795 and Francis Austen in May 1825. (He retained the appointment until his promotion to Flag rank in July 1830). To rub it in, the rate of pay enjoyed by 'Blue Colonels', £700 a year, was higher than that of regular Marine Colonels. Moreover, in rank, Marine officers were at a disadvantage, since they were subordinate to naval officers (a naval Lieutenant ranked with a marine Captain); and, while at sea, they were subject to naval discipline and command. By the Navy's standards hardly officers and often scarcely gentlemen, they were treated accordingly.

The Admiralty tried to rectify this in the *Regulations and Instructions* of 1808. The wording of the newly-added section for Marines serving at sea tells its own story:

> The Marine Officers are upon all occasions to be treated, as well by the Captain of the Ship as by all other officers and people belonging to her, with the decency and regard due to the commissions they bear: and though Lieutenants of Marines share in prizes only with Warrant Officers of Ships, upon consideration of their different sea-duty, yet it is not intended to degrade their rank; and they are, while they do their duty, to be considered and treated in all respects as a Commission Officer should be.[103]

The need for such protective *Instructions* can be gauged from the literature of the period. To quote Northcote Parkinson, marine officers, with 'less to do than perhaps anyone else on board' were 'always represented as dividing their time between gluttony and sleep'[104] and were accordingly depicted as men of bulk and appetite, the Sergeants ever ready to loosen their sashes 'for ground-tier stowage'.[105] The opportunity for such humour was abundant. Marine detachments, running to a quarter or a fifth of a ship's complement, were carried on all but the very smallest vessels. Sloops and gun brigs of ten guns would have fifteen marines; frigates of twenty-four guns, a marine Lieutenant and twenty-nine men; and so on up to first rates, with upwards of 100 marines, headed by a Captain and two Lieutenants.

In February 1812, when Jane Austen was a year into the writing of *Mansfield Park*, Christopher Hely Hutchinson, the maverick MP for Cork, a man of wide military experience with the British and allied armies, put the Marines' 'serious grievances' before the House of Commons, describing the ways in which its officers were disadvantaged and challenging the House – did the Corps deserve 'to be so distinguished from the rest of the navy?'[106]* Hutchinson's case was just, well put and unanswerable. However, in its existing form, the Corps provided a convenient area for Admiralty patronage. Accordingly, the First Lord, Charles Yorke, an effective parliamentary orator, cobbled together a defence of the *status quo* and the House rejected Hutchinson's call for an 'inquiry'.

---

* A long-standing complaint was that Marine officers, promoted by seniority, stood at a disadvantage both to Army officers, who gained their promotion by purchase, and to Navy officers, promoted (up to Captain) on merit. To rectify this, a system was introduced by which Marine officers could be promoted by brevet rank. This was a promotion in name only. It was temporary and carried no increase in pay.

For our purposes the parliamentary discussion serves as a useful summary of the disadvantages under which the Marines suffered. Jane Austen would have heard of these matters from Francis and Charles, and she also followed the curious story of a neighbour, Earle Harwood, a younger son of the Harwoods, an old Hampshire family, for many generations the squires of Deane, where Mr Austen was Rector for over thirty years, latterly with James' assistance as curate. Earle first tried his luck as a coal-merchant. Finding no success in that trade, he then turned to the Marines and was commissioned in 1796 at the age of twenty-three. After service at home and overseas he reached the rank of Captain. Some unexplained scandal surrounded his wife. Jane exchanged gossip and speculation with Cassandra. In October 1798, a year into the marriage, old Squire Harwood and his wife were still refusing to see her; she was to be allowed to visit them at Deane on condition that

> she continued to behave well for another Year. – He was very grateful, as well he might; their behaviour throughout the whole affair has been particularly kind. – Earle & his wife live in the most private manner imaginable at Portsmouth, without keeping a servant of any kind. – What a prodigious innate love of virtue she must have, to marry under such circumstances! –.[107]

Two months later Jane reported to Cassandra the news of Earle's appointment to a prison ship at Portsmouth – this would be a hulk housing French prisoners-of-war – where he was to live on board with his wife, such was their poverty. The gossip was that the new Mrs Harwood had a past to live down, and was of humble origin too:

> I cannot help thinking from your account of Mrs E. H. that Earle's vanity has tempted him to invent the account of her former way of Life, that his triumph in securing her might be greater; – I dare say she was nothing but an innocent Country Girl in fact. –[108]

A year-and-a-half later, Earle was once again 'giving uneasiness to his family, & Talk to the Neighbourhood' on account of a gunshot wound to the leg.[109] To the relief of his family, it was ascertained that the injury was accidental and not the result of a duel.

Earle Harwood died in August 1811. The circumstances of his marriage and career may have been in Jane Austen's mind when she sketched the history of Lieutenant Price ('disabled for active service'),[110] with a reversal of roles: for it is *his* background – *his* lack of 'education, fortune, or connections' – which renders him unacceptable to the Bertrams.[111] This is the 'very imprudent marriage', a clandestine marriage, which sets 'an absolute breach' between Frances Ward and her sisters, and leaves her to make her way in life as best she can, uninvited and unvisitable.[112]

Although Jane Austen tells us almost nothing about Mr Price's service career, the signs are there and the silences significant. A Lieutenant at the time of his marriage in the early 1790s, he is a Lieutenant still, in 1813, an evident failure, since the average rate of promotion was from Second to full Lieutenant within the first year, and to Captain seven or eight years later. His disablement might suggest a wartime injury. But Mr Price is noticeably silent about his time at sea. While he has served long enough to acquire a taste for grog – his 'rum and water'[113] – and to appreciate the efficacy of 'the rope's end'* and 'a little flogging'[114] – his prescription for the eloping couple, Crawford and Maria Bertram, now Mrs Rushworth – this may well have been pre-war service, for unlike his son he is given no scenes of action to recall nor heroic tales to tell. Nor, with a family of ten, aged between six and nineteen, could he have been at sea for long.

That Mr Price should make his home at Portsmouth fits his profession. With its protected Fleet anchorage at Spithead, its natural harbour and extensive dockyards, Portsmouth was the Navy's largest and most important base and served as the headquarters for one of three Marine divisions, its peacetime establishment of 3500 now much swollen. Rank-and-file marines were recruited and trained there. Housed in barracks while awaiting a posting (25,000 of the entire force of 35,000 were at sea), they were employed in guarding the dock-yards, and policing the streets, and provided a source of unskilled labour for dock-yard jobs and for the provisioning of vessels such as the *Thrush* in preparation for a voyage.

These explanatory details are the unwritten background. What Jane Austen chooses to focus on is the identity of Mr Price has created for himself as a fixated naval man, his horizons limited to naval matters and the world of Portsmouth:

> He did not want abilities; but he had no curiosity, and no information beyond his profession; he read only the newspaper and the navy-list; he talked only of the dock-yard, the harbour, Spithead, and the Motherbank . . .[115]

What these 'abilities' are, and what kind of man Mr Price could have been, becomes clear to Fanny a few weeks later, on the occasion of Crawford's visit and their encounter in the High Street. Far from leaving Crawford 'disgusted'

---

* To stop its unravelling, the end of a rope was bound up tightly with twine and could be used as a 'starter', a heavy and painful instrument of punishment. 'Starting' was given freely, sometimes on the order of an officer, sometimes not. Officially, amongst the petty officers, it could only be administered by the Boatswain's Mate. Typically, it was given for laziness or neglect on the part of a seaman. Unlike flogging, a highly ceremonial punishment, which was administered before the entire crew (to serve as a deterrent), 'starting', with a stick or rope's end, was given on the spot and not recorded in the ship's log-book. In 1809, 'starting' was prohibited.

and herself disgraced by his 'vulgarity', Mr Price rises to the occasion:

(as Fanny instantly, and to her great relief discerned), her father was a very different man, a very different Mr Price in his behaviour to this most highly-respected stranger, from what he was in his own family at home. His manners now, though not polished, were more than passable; they were grateful, animated, manly; his expressions were those of an attached father, and a sensible man; – his loud tones did very well in the open air, and there was not a single oath to be heard. Such was his instinctive compliment to the good manners of Mr Crawford; and be the consequence what it might, Fanny's immediate feelings were infinitely soothed.[116]

But this is not the everyday Mr Price, the man who walks into the story with a show of violence and the manners of a seaman, 'his own loud voice preceding him, as with something of the oath kind he kicked away his son's portmanteau, and his daughter's band-box in the passage',[117] greets his son, ignores Fanny and launches into his hurricane of news, inevitably thorough-going naval news, sailor-to-sailor, updating William on the latest movements of the *Thrush*.

The Thrush went out of harbour this morning. Sharp is the word, you see. By G –, you are just in time. The doctor has been here enquiring for you; he has got one of the boats, and is to be off for Spithead by six, so you had better go with him. I have been to Turner's about your mess; it is all in a way to be done. I should not wonder if you had your orders to-morrow; but you cannot sail with this wind, if you are to cruize to the westward; and Captain Walsh thinks you will certainly have a cruize to the westward, with the Elephant. By G –, I wish you may. But old Scholey was saying just now, that he thought you would be sent first to the Texel.* Well, well, we are ready, whatever happens. But by G –, you lost a fine sight by not being here in the morning to see the Thrush go out of harbour. I would not have been out of the way for a thousand pounds. Old Scholey ran in at breakfast time, to say she had slipped her moorings and was coming out. I jumped up, and made but two steps to the platform. If ever there was a perfect beauty afloat, she is one; and there she lays at Spithead, and anybody in England would take her for an eight-and-twenty. I was upon the platform two hours this afternoon, looking at her. She lays close to the Endymion, between her and the Cleopatra, just to the eastward of the sheer hulk.[118]

Only at this point, prompted by William, does Mr Price notice Fanny and greet her, off-handedly. But this is a moment's interruption. Instantly, he is

---

* The Texel was the most westerly of the West Frisian Islands and an anchorage for the Dutch Fleet commanding the mouth of the Zuider Zee. For the North Sea Fleet it was the key blockading station since the Texel Channel was the outlet for the main Dutch naval base at Amsterdam.

back in the man's world, the naval world, talking 'only to his son, and only of the Thrush' despite William's efforts 'to make his father think of Fanny, and her long absence' (no less than nine years!) 'and long journey'.[119] Jane Austen deepens this naval coloration two pages later, giving him a staccato 'burst' of seaman's language – at least, the toned-down literary version of tarpaulin talk, its roughest edges smoothed to the conventions of the contemporary ladies' novel.

> At a more than ordinary pitch of thumping and hallooing in the passage, he exclaimed, 'Devil take those young dogs! How they are singing out! Ay, Sam's voice louder than all the rest! That boy is fit for a boatswain. Holla – you there – Sam – stop your confounded pipe, or I shall be after you.'[120]

The comparison is apt. The boatswain's mates were the disciplinarians, the chasers and shouters on a ship, rousing the crew from their hammocks, driving the laggards on deck and keeping them to their tasks throughout the day.

The violence of Mr Price's language carried a particular significance for the Austens. As the *Memoir* tells us, Francis was 'a strict disciplinarian'. Yet 'it was remarkable of him (for in those days, at least, it was remarkable) that he maintained this discipline without ever uttering an oath or permitting one in his presence'.[121] This sets him apart, a rare bird. For although 'profane oaths, cursings' and 'execrations' were punishable by court martial under the Articles of War,[122] it was a hollow regulation. The reality of life at sea could not be more different. The point is well made in a letter to the *Evangelical Magazine* in 1807. Admittedly, this is a partial source. But the picture rings true:

> I was surprised by a visit from an old acquaintance of mine the other day, who is now an officer of rank in his Majesty's navy. In the course of conversation, I was shocked at the profane oaths that perpetually interrupted his sentences; and took an opportunity to express my regret that such language should be so common among so valuable a body of men. 'Sir (said he, still interspersing many solemn imprecations), an officer cannot live at sea without swearing; not one of my men would mind a word without an oath; it is common sea-language. If we were not to swear, the rascals would take us for lubbers, stare in our faces, and leave us to do our commands ourselves.[123]

A different form of 'sea-language' is contained in Mr Price's account of the *Thrush* leaving the harbour. Packed with detail, it offers a convincing pastiche of nautical expression and defines the narrow boundaries of Mr Price's mental world. The passage is also fascinating textually as the only place in

Mansfield Park where Jane Austen found herself at fault (one is tempted to say 'at sea') over matters of detail and obliged to make substantial changes for the second edition of 1816. These alterations can be followed in full in the Notes to the Oxford edition and are outlined here:[124]

First edition (1814)	Second edition (1816)
Line 2: *Alert* is the word	*Sharp* is the word.

Alert is to be on the look-out, standing by and ready for any sudden duty or emergency. All Mr Price wants to say is 'Be quick about it.' A case of over-egging the nautical pudding.

Line 6: I have been to Turner's about your *things*	your *mess.*

Things, although correct in itself as a naval/military term for equipment or belongings sounds indeterminate, flavourless and hence civilian, whereas *mess* is only a naval/military term. Strangely, its precise meaning remains unknown. Common-sense tells us that these are William's 'mess things' or 'mess kit'. A William Turner, merchant, likely to be a naval supplier, was listed in Portsmouth High Street in 1811. He also seems to have acted as agent, not actually supplying items but arranging for their supply.[125] Could, then, William's 'mess' be his private store of food and drink? Jane Austen knew of this Mr Turner of Portsmouth. In 1805, she suggested using him to forward a letter to Francis, then serving at sea; in 1809, he was employed to forward a rug to Charles in Bermuda;[126] and, in January 1815, Charles 'paid a bill at Turners for Corks'.[127]

Lines 17–18: she *was under weigh*	she *had slipped her moorings and was coming out*

Leaving Portsmouth Harbour for the anchorage at Spithead, the *Thrush* would not, strictly speaking, be '*under weigh*', i.e. having weighed anchor, since, within the harbour she would not have used her anchor but a fixed mooring buoy. If this sounds like splitting hairs, it is just the point of particularity that Francis, a precisionist, would have insisted on.

Line 22: I was upon the *point*	I was upon the *platform*

The famous Portsmouth Point, a promontory which served as the point of departure and arrival for much of the naval and civilian traffic to and from the ships in the Harbour and the Fleet (its busy scene is shown in illus. 16). Looking due north, this would give an excellent view into the Harbour. But as the *Thrush* sailed southwards out to her berth at Spithead, it would soon be lost to sight, hidden by the intervening houses, whereas the *platform* (mounted with cannon for challenging or saluting vessels entering the harbour), at the bottom of the High Street, provided an unimpeded view.

Lines 23–24: She lays *just astern of the Endymion, with the Cleopatra to larboard*	She lays *close to the Endymion, between her and the Cleopatra, just to the eastward of the sheer hulk.*

The *Thrush* would only take its position from a ship to the left of her (*larboard*, modern *port side*) when they were sailing in fleet formation 'line abreast' i.e. side-by-side. The *sheer hulk* was an old ship, no longer fit to go to sea, and used as a floating maintenance vessel and equipped with 'sheers' for the removal and fitting of masts and spars.

To this list of changes one more is to be added. Immediately after lines 23–24, William replies: 'Ha! ... *that's* just where I should have put her myself.' The second edition adds a further sentence: 'It's the best birth at Spithead.' Not a correction but a straightforward addition, which William contributes as an item of sailor's local knowledge and continues his father's enthusiastic tone for the rightness of everything connected with the *Thrush*.

While this last addition and the change to line 6 can be regarded as minor improvements which Jane Austen could have made on her own, the other four changes are corrections of error, of shortcomings of knowledge that would only be picked up by someone who was familiar with Portsmouth and the vocabulary of seamanship – and was moreover a sufficiently attentive reader to spot these errors and sufficiently close to Jane Austen to pass on advice. All this points to Francis. Family anecdotes draw him as a sea officer conscientious, correct and finicky to the last degree, just the man to fasten on his sister's nautical mistakes, however small. From July 1815, living with his young family at Chawton Great House, he would have had ample opportunity to advise her of these necessary changes before December, when she sent the corrected text to John Murray for the second edition. Overall, the evidence of these changes seems to suggest that in the writing of *Mansfield Park*, between 1811 and 1813, Jane Austen was happy to handle the naval part of the story herself, without needing to take advice from Francis or anyone else; and that it was only in this one passage that she got out of her depth. At that very time, Robert Southey was working on his *Life of Nelson*, and he referred to his brother Tom, a Captain, for just such advice. He admitted his nervousness: 'I walk among sea terms as a cat goes in a china pantry, in bodily fear of doing mischief, & betraying myself.'[128] For once in her life, Jane Austen neglected to advance with such caution. Where she did consult Francis (and, presumably, Charles as well) was about the use of their ships' names, three of the four mentioned in this 'Thrush' passage. These were *their* ships she felt, and not to be used without permission: and so, observing the proprieties, she wrote to Francis, who was then commanding one of the ships in question, the *Elephant* (74) on escort duties in the Baltic: 'And by the bye – shall you object to my mentioning the Elephant in it, & two or three other of your old Ships? – I *have* done it, but it shall not stay, to make you angry. – They are only just mentioned.'[129] This request was sent at the beginning of July 1813, with the novel just finished. Nine weeks later came Francis' permission. This letter has not survived. But we can infer its contents from the reply in which Jane takes up her brother's 'kind' (yet somewhat far-fetched) 'hint' that mentioning their ships might destroy her anonymity, an idea which she turns into a joke:

> I thank you very warmly for your kind consent to my application & the kind hint which followed it. – I was previously aware of what I sh^d be laying myself open to – but the truth is that the Secret has spread so far as to be scarcely the Shadow of a secret now – & that I beleive whenever the 3^d appears,* I shall not even attempt to tell Lies about it. – I shall rather try to make all the Money than all the Mystery I can of it. – People shall pay for their Knowledge if I can make them.[130]

As well as the family association, two of the ships enjoyed national fame: the *Elephant* as the vessel in which, in 1801, Nelson had placed the telescope to his blind eye; and the *Canopus* (80) (mentioned by William, two pages before), formerly the *Franklin*, a famous capture from the French at the Battle of the Nile. With Francis as Flag Captain, she sailed with Nelson's Mediterranean Fleet in 1805 and fought at St Domingo. The other two ships were not unknown; their exploits are recorded in Clowes.[131] But their real importance was for the Austens and their circle: the *Endymion* (44), particularly memorable to Jane and Cassandra as the ship in which Charles was sailing in the Mediterranean when he sent them the gold chains and topaze crosses, and in which he served no less than three times, twice under his patron, Sir Thomas Williams; and the *Cleopatra* (32), the ship he finally brought home in 1811, following his years on the North American Station. The *Thrush*, too, belongs to family history, for this is the *Lark* (16) in thin disguise, the vessel which Francis joined in March 1794 on his return from the East Indies and in which he sailed a year later, part of the Squadron bringing Caroline of Brunswick, the future Princess of Wales, from Cuxhaven to Gravesend, a duty which no doubt provided the young Lieutenant with a fund of royal anecdotes to entertain the family.

---

* *Mansfield Park* being her third novel to be published.

The *Thrush* passage looks to William Price's future, whether it is cruising westwards, to join the Channel Fleet, or eastwards to 'the Texel', where a large blockading Squadron was stationed. These were naval dispositions with which Jane Austen was familiar and which she places within the natural flow of Mr Price's talk as a knowledgeable 'old salt', an armchair sailor, delighted to be active in his son's preparations for sea.

This is as far as Jane Austen goes in conveying the sense of Portsmouth as a centre of naval operation, a gathering ground for the Fleet, its midway position on the coast providing a strategic point of command eastwards and westwards along the Channel. As for drawing the urban reality of Portsmouth, the old town and dockyard, Jane Austen's technique is much the same. Detail is sparing yet sufficient, largely contained within the narrative flow, and resting for its full effect upon the reader's familiarity with the town and its naval attachments. Although Portsmouth was not considered a resort or a place of fashion, following the visit of George III and royal family to review the Fleet in honour of Howe's victory of 1 June 1794, it attracted visitors in large numbers – many of them relatives and friends of naval men.

One such visitor was William Wilberforce, come to visit Captain Gambier (as he was then) and view the triumphant Fleet at Spithead with their train of French prizes. In his diary Wilberforce noted the spectacle at Portsmouth Point, the sailors' landing place after months or years at sea, a sight from which he recoiled: 'wickedness and blasphemeing abounds – shocking scene' (vividly rendered by Rowlandson).[132] Other tourists came throughout the year to see the array of ships and the celebrated wonder of this 'grand naval arsenal . . . the rendezvous and headquarters of the British Navy' (to quote a contemporary).[133] At naval reviews and other great occasions it was patronised by royalty, with high society in tow. And the King's official birthday celebrations in June, featuring a great naval display, drew sightseers from far afield, including friends of the Austens.[134]

Anyone who had entered Portsmouth by the London road would recognise the route along which Fanny and William approach the old town: through 'the environs of Portsmouth', where Fanny is impressed by 'the new buildings' (at Half Way Houses – present-day Landport – and Nelson Square) before 'They passed the Drawbridge' (reminding us that Portsmouth was a guarded and fortified garrison-town, protected by 'barriers',[135] bastions and ramparts and by a wide, water-filled moat) 'and entered the town', this being the old town, Portsmouth proper, contained within the area of the fortifications, with about 7000 inhabitants. This route brings them through the Landport or Town Gate and after a left and a right turn, into the north end of the High Street, a long, wide thoroughfare, from which they

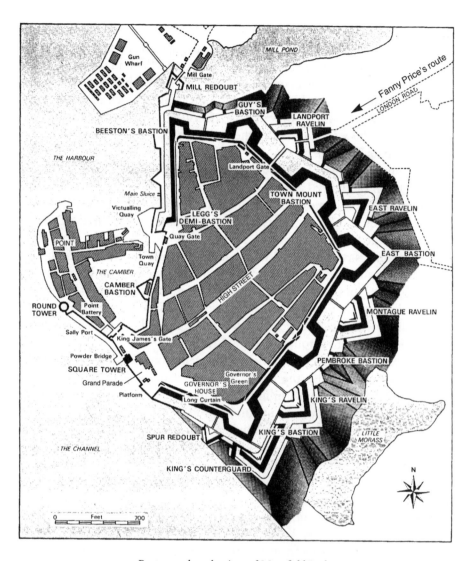

Portsmouth at the time of *Mansfield Park*

turn 'into a narrow street' and arrive at Mr Price's 'small house'.[136] Old Portsmouth was a warren of such lanes and alleys; some parts, according to a visitor in 1811, 'very narrow, dirty' and 'disagreeable'[137] and we can suppose that the Prices' home was in one of the lanes off the High Street and close to the Grand Parade – possibly Golden Lion or Fighting Cock or Little Penny Lane – as Mr Price says that to watch the *Thrush* he 'made but two steps to the platform'.[138] This would also place them close to 'the Sally port' (the landing-place for boats from the men-of-war),[139] from which William and his friend Mr Campbell, the ship's Surgeon, go out to the *Thrush*.

The arrival of Henry Crawford is the occasion for more details of naval Portsmouth. These come within the miniature comedy of Mrs Price's amazement at finding that a man 'so great and so agreeable', staying at 'the Crown'*
– an inn on the High Street, patronised by senior officers and, for that reason known as the Navy House – should not be calling on 'the port-admiral' (commanding all seamen and the ships in the harbour in commission) or 'the commissioner' (of the dockyard), 'nor yet' have 'the intention of going over to the island' (as the Isle of Wight was known locally), 'nor of seeing the Dock-yard',[140] a place Crawford has visited 'again and again' (a reminder of his naval connections through Admiral Crawford).[141]

Crawford soon finds himself there once again, conducted by Mr Price and chatting with him about the latest 'naval regulations' (these could be the changes to the Lieutenant's uniform, see above, p. 200) and debating 'the number of three deckers now in commission'.** In the dockyard itself, Mr Price is 'soon jointed by a fellow-lounger . . . come to take his daily survey of how things went on' and 'the two officers' become immersed in 'matters of equal and never-failing interest, while the young people sat down upon some timbers in the yard, or found a seat on board a vessel in the stocks which they all went to look at'.[142] (This would be a ship in the course of construction).

Scenes like this are commonly found in diaries, letters and travel journals of the time.[143] For the dockyards, eighty-two acres in extent and 'esteemed the largest and most superb in the known world',[144] were an attraction as popular with tourists as the great country houses. Considerably expanded over a period of fifty years, from the 1760s until the completion of the fire-proof Pay Office in 1811, the Portsmouth dockyards were famed for their mechanical marvels, with steam engines driving the metal mills and the saw

---

* Much improved over the twenty years since Jane Austen's maternal aunt, the formidable Mrs Lybbe Powys, stayed there in 1792. She enjoyed 'an elegant dinner' but found the Crown 'as dirty an inn as I was ever at' (Climenson, 1899, p. 268).

** These were men-of-war of the first and second rates, with three gun-decks and upwards of 90 guns; the figures for vessels in commission and those 'in ordinary', i.e. under repair or otherwise laid up, were regularly published, as a matter of general interest.

mills and powering the greatest wonder of all, the massive engineering equipment in the great Block Mills built in 1802–06, the first example in the world of machine-tools designed for mass production. By 1810, the forty-five machines were producing no less than 130,000 blocks a year for the pulleys and tackle needed on board ship to handle cables, anchors and the larger sails. (Almost certainly these were among the 'several improvements in the dockyard' which William had looked forward to showing Fanny.)[145] Viewing these developments was not just for the technologically-minded. When the Emperor Alexander and his sister, the Duchess of Oldenburg, toured Portsmouth during the victory celebrations of 1814, an observer noted that they 'occupied themselves in visiting the Dockyards, Machinery, Haslar Hospital [the naval hospital on the opposite side of the harbour entrance] – in short, everything worthy the notice of enlightened beings'.[146] And not far from the main gates could be found the Royal Naval Academy and the Commissioner's House. There was also the opportunity to see ships under repair and in construction (as Mr Price's party does) and to visit the *Victory*, already an established attraction.

The presence of Susan, 'all eyes and ears', restrains Crawford in his pursuit of Fanny. So at this moment of rest in a quiet corner of the dockyard, he is obliged to conceal his purpose under an entertaining recital of Norfolk affairs and, more pointedly, a 'well aimed' representation of himself as the good landlord, 'the friend of the poor and oppressed', lacking only 'an assistant, a friend, a guide in every plan of utility or charity'.[147] To Fanny's discomfort, Crawford continues in this suggestive line, until, on the way home, separated from the others, he is able to speak out, to tell her undisguisedly that 'his only business in Portsmouth was to see her',[148] a purpose which he takes up again the next day, joining the Prices on their way to church in 'the Garrison Chapel'.[149] Situated near the Grand Parade, it served the officers and men of Portsmouth Garrison. The Prices worshipped there presumably because it was both convenient and open to them as a naval family.

Following the service, Jane Austen leads her characters onto the Ramparts (see Illustration 15), another noted feature of visitors' Portsmouth. This is where Mrs Price takes her 'weekly walk', meeting her friends and enjoying a gossip. As distinct from their military and defensive function, the ramparts have their attractions, appealingly described in *The Portsmouth Guide* of 1775:

> The Ramparts are a beautiful elevated terras walk, of a mile and a quarter round, edged with elm trees, kept in the most regular order. From this eminence, the unbounded prospect of the sea, contrasted with the landskip, which the neighbouring country affords, forms one of the most striking variegated scenes imaginable. Indeed it has always been an object of the highest admiration to strangers,

and we may venture to say ever will be so, as long as the beauties of nature and art continue to merit our attention.[150]

Jane Austen's account of their walk – Crawford with Fanny on one arm, Susan on the other – is, for her, a rare passage of open-air description, evoking the atmosphere and influence of the seasons – a March day by the calendar, but 'April in its mild air, brisk soft wind, and bright sun occasionally clouded for a minute', 'the shadows pursuing each other', 'the ever-varying hues of the sea . . . dancing in its glee and dashing against the ramparts', a view which raises Fanny's spirits and to which both she and Crawford respond 'with the same sentiment and taste'.[151] What we notice immediately is the physical and emotional exhilaration (for the reader as much as for Fanny) of this 'two hours saunter' in the fresh air and 'bright sun',[152] with the wide views from the Ramparts, all this a liberation from the 'confinement' of the Price home, with its 'bad air' and 'bad smells',[153] the 'smallness of the rooms', 'the narrowness of the passage and staircase',[154] the 'little intermission of noise or grog'.[155] And on the naval side, we notice the severity of Jane Austen's restraint, the spareness of the impressionistic seascape: 'the effects of the shadows pursuing each other on the ships at Spithead and the island beyond' is all she allows us to see.[156] The spectacle which brings sightseers flocking to the Ramparts – the Solent alive with shipping, the sails billowing, the flags and pennants streaming in the wind, the thunderous salutes and the strains of martial music from the ships' bands – upon this vivid and colourful scene Jane Austen turns her back.

Beyond this point in the novel, for the remaining six chapters, the focus remains on the internal world of Fanny Price, her reflections on Crawford and the unfolding 'guilt and misery' of his liaison with Mrs Rushworth. Of William we hear little more; nothing of his cruise in the *Thrush* or his friendship with Mr Campbell, the ship's Surgeon,* 'a very well behaved young man' (Jane Austen's few words for him);[157] no more than an assurance, on the novel's last page, couched in the most conventional terms, of his future of 'continued good conduct, and rising fame'.[158] There is an amusing symmetry to the disposal of the Prices, an economy to the design. Susan is conveyed to Mansfield to take the place of Fanny – now Mrs Edmund Bertram – and young Sam, another Midshipman Price in the making, sails with William in the *Thrush*. Quiet as it is, this ending would be no disappointment to naval

---

* From 1808 onwards, Surgeons, qualified by examinations conducted at Surgeons' Hall, ranked with the Lieutenants. Their main skills were amputating and bleeding; as rum was the crude anaesthetic, little more was possible. For more difficult cases, if there was time and opportunity, the Surgeon was to consult the Fleet or Squadron Physician, a far superior grade of medical man. Even the smallest of sloops would also carry an Assistant Surgeon, formerly known as a Surgeon's Mate.

readers. For by the summer of 1813, when the story ends, British fleets enjoyed mastery of the seas. There were no great engagements to be fought, merely the routine duty of blockade to be sustained, troops to be ferried to the Continent, and across the Atlantic, a side-show, war with America. The heroism of the story remains with Fanny Price, secure and undivided.

As their ships were mentioned, the sailor brothers might well have offered their sister some special appreciation of the naval elements in *Mansfield Park*. So she must have been disappointed that they were unresponsive. Charles, aboard the *Namur* at Sheerness, was curt and to the point: 'did not like it near so well as P. & P. – thought it wanted Incident,' a comment duly added to the collection of 'Opinions of Mansfield Park' which Jane gathered from friends and relations and from further afield.[159] Francis was slightly warmer, delighting in Fanny and Mrs Norris. But he too had nothing to say about William Price and the profession they shared:

> We* certainly do not think it as a *whole*, equal to P. & P. – but it has many & great beauties. Fanny is a delightful Character! and Aunt Norris is a great favourite of mine. The Characters are natural & well supported, & many of the Dialogues excellent. – You need not fear the publication being considered as discreditable to the talents of it's Author.

Accepting his tepid praise in good grace, Jane gave Francis' 'Opinion' pride of place at the head of the collection, just as she did later with his 'Opinion' of *Emma*.[160] Other readers were more discerning, including her brothers James and Edward, who picked out the 'Portsmouth Scene'. Most gratifying of all, Admiral Sir Edward Foote expressed his surprise 'that I had the power of drawing the Portsmouth-Scenes so well.' This was true recognition, for Admiral Foote was then Second-in-Command at Portsmouth, and Jane Austen made his 'Opinion' the last but one in her collection.

Beyond these private 'opinions', there was no public comment. *Mansfield Park* went unreviewed, something which irked Jane Austen, since both *Sense and Sensibility* and *Pride and Prejudice* had been welcomed by the *British Critic* and the *Critical Review*, and when the *Quarterly Review* came out with Sir Walter Scott's memorable review-article, praising these first two novels and *Emma*, the latest, while not even mentioning *Mansfield Park*, she complained to John Murray, the *Quarterly's* publisher, at its total omission, expressing her disappointment 'that so clever a Man as the Reveiwer of *Emma*, should consider it as unworthy of being noticed.'[161]

---

* 'We' because Francis was then staying with his family at Chawton House.

Afterword

A stray naval figure, mentioned only once in *Mansfield Park*, and otherwise unaccounted for, is 'old Mrs Admiral Maxwell' (p. 387), the godmother of Mary, the Price daughter who died when she was aged about six or seven and is fondly remembered by Fanny. It could have been that in an earlier version of the novel Admiral and Mrs Maxwell played a part in the story, of which this single unexplained reference is the sole remnant.

Admiral

9

Nelson – Heroism, Honour and Dishonour

'I am tired of Lives of Nelson, being that I never read any'

Jane Austen to Cassandra, October 1813

By the time *Mansfield Park* was published, in May 1814, Jane Austen's author-ship was an open secret. As she wryly observed to Francis during the previous year, it was a 'Secret . . . spread so far as to be scarcely the Shadow of a Secret now'.[1] The blame fell on Henry. Proud of his sister and moving in society, he was irrepressible, incapable of silence. Jane's irritation gave way to amuse-ment. To Francis, whose confidence could be trusted, she was prepared to make a joke of it. Serving in Baltic waters on the tedium of convoy duty and commanding a difficult and unruly crew, he was glad to receive one of his sister's long and entertaining letters, to hear about her spreading fame and to share her thoughtful and reflective moments:

> Henry heard P. & P. warmly praised in Scotland, by Lady Robt Kerr & another Lady; – & what does he do in the warmth of his Brotherly vanity & Love, but immediately tell them who wrote it! – A Thing once set going in that way – one knows how it spreads! – and he, dear Creature, has set it going so much more than once. I know it is all done from affection & partiality – but at the same time, let me here again express to you & Mary my sense of the *superior* kindness which you have shewn on the occasion, in doing what I wished. – I am trying to harden myself. – After all, what a trifle it is in all its Bearings, to the really important points of one's existence even in this World! –[2]

The novels were read at every level of polite society, even amongst members of the Royal Family, including the Prince Regent and his circle. In 1812, the Regent's daughter, Princess Charlotte, a sixteen-year-old, was touched by the magic of *Sense and Sensibility*, fancying herself a second Marianne Dashwood 'in *disposition*', with 'the same' streak of 'impru-dence'.[3] Yet another of Henry's indiscretions, perhaps the most momentous of all, carried the 'secret' back to the Princess's father at Carlton House. Seriously ill in October 1815, Henry was attended by a number of doctors, including Matthew Baillie, one of the Court physicians. During his recovery, Henry boasted of Jane's authorship and Baillie, with 'very intimate access to the Prince Regent', reported this back to his royal master, adding that the novelist herself was staying in London. The doctor returned to Hans Place with gratifying news: 'that the Prince was a great admirer of her novels: that he often read them, and had a set in each of his residences'.[4] As a gesture of respect and admiration, the Regent directed his Librarian, the Rev. James Stanier Clarke, to call on her with an invitation to see round Carlton House and visit the Library there, a tour which could be freely made as the Regent was then leaving for the country. Moreover – a signal honour – he authorised Clarke to convey the message that she was at liberty to dedicate her next work to him without the usual protocol of seeking permission to do so.

This generosity on the part of the Regent was far from disinterested and we can guess that Clarke's instructions also included assessing whether this lady novelist would fit into the Prince's circle as a suitably entertaining and personable guest, for he enjoyed the company of artists and writers and men and women of attraction and wit. Evidently, she failed the test and no further invitation was forthcoming. Nonetheless, Jane Austen's visit, made on 13 November, together with what followed – the dedication of *Emma* to the Regent; her correspondence with Clarke; and the amusing 'Plan of a Novel' based upon Clarke's somewhat bizarre suggestions for her next work – compose one of the most fully-documented and amusing episodes in Jane Austen's life. The Carlton House story went round the family and was remembered as 'a little gleam of Court favor', a 'little burst of Royal Patronage'[5] to which the *Memoir* devotes an entire chapter, as being the most notable occasion on which her 'personal obscurity', her 'entire seclusion from the literary world',[6] was penetrated. It makes an entertaining story and no biographer has failed to relate the episode in detail.

Solemn, ceremonious and, in the manner of Court functionaries, deferentially courteous, Mr Clarke has been placed alongside Mr Collins in the line of comic clergymen. Yet Jane Austen judged him worthy of respect and in excusing herself from following the last of his suggestions – 'an Historical Romance, founded on the House of Saxe Cobourg'* – she felt confident of his sympathy and understanding.[7] Unusually forthcoming, she favoured him with a statement of her personal convictions as a novelist, in the words of David Nokes, her nearest approach ever to declaring a 'literary manifesto'.[8]

* A very timely and, as far as Clarke was concerned, self-interested suggestion, since he had just been appointed Chaplain and Private English Secretary to Prince Leopold of Cobourg who was then engaged to the Heiress Apparent, Princess Charlotte. Their marriage, on 2 May 1816, was seen as a love match. It was very popular with the nation, as well as politically expedient, and the author of such a novel would certainly be rewarded (as Jane Austen supposes) with 'Profit or Popularity', probably with both. (*Letters*, p. 312).

You are very, very kind in your hints as to the sort of Composition which might recommend me at present, & I am fully sensible that an Historical Romance, founded on the House of Saxe Cobourg might be much more to the purpose of Profit or Popularity, than such pictures of domestic Life in Country Villages as I deal in – but I could no more write a Romance than an Epic Poem. – I could not sit seriously down to write a serious Romance under any other motive than to save my Life, & if it were indispensable for me to keep it up & never relax into laughing at myself or other people, I am sure I should be hung before I had finished the first Chapter. – No – I must keep to my own style & go on in my own Way; And though I may never succeed again in that, I am convinced that I should totally fail in any other. –[9]

Jane Austen ends the letter on a note of remarkable warmth, signing herself 'Your very much obliged & very sincere friend'.[10] For although she laughed at Clarke's suggestions, taking them *verbatim* into her 'Plan' and ridiculing them, she also treated him courteously and seriously as a fellow-author, a man of 'Talents & literary Labours'[11] who offered her the use of his 'Cell',[12] his writing hideaway in London, a *pied-à-terre* in Golden Square with its own small library and servant. And she would have known of Clarke's reputation as the most prolific naval and maritime historian of the day and his standing as Nelson's official biographer, appointed by the Prince Regent.

Unfortunately, we have no details of the visit. Jane Austen's impressions of Carlton House – in such a letter as she would have sent to Charles, then chasing pirates in the Greek Archipelago – would make a fascinating account. A spectacular and palatial mansion, it was a treasure-house of splendid furnishings, paintings and *objets d'art*, with Sèvres china, Gobelin tapestries, elaborate clocks, marble busts and bronzes. Its magnificent interior was said to rival Versailles, St-Cloud and the Winter Palace at St Petersburg. Others, however, found its riches in excess, its opulence vulgar and overdone, betraying a 'tawdry childishness', a mere 'appetite for profusion'.[13] And on the lower floor its Gothic Library, approached by way of the majestic Grand Staircase, with its winding balustrades and great statues of Chronos and Atlas, lay within a breathtaking enfilade of State rooms extending for upwards of 500 feet. As we know from *Northanger Abbey*, such scale and ostentation were not to Jane Austen's taste, leaving her unimpressed and critical and suspicious of its moving spirit.* On the other hand, she would have felt quite at ease with the Librarian. Clarke was a ready conversationalist – Farington found him 'of a very vivacious disposition; in company a great

---

* See vol. ii, chs. 7 and 8, in which General Tilney conducts Catherine Morland on a tour of the Abbey and its grounds. While the General shows off his 'improvements' and modernisations with pride, Catherine is dizzied and overwhelmed by their proliferation and extent. As *Northanger Abbey* was revised during 1816, it is possible that these chapters carry some critical residue from the Carlton House visit.

talker' and would soon have established their common interest in naval matters.[14] He had served in the Navy, knew of her brothers Francis and Charles and was keen to present her with copies of his naval and maritime books. In the magnificent Ante-Room, he could point to the assembled portraits of Rodney, Keppel, St Vincent and Nelson, this quartet of naval heroes given pride of place. And, an amateur artist himself, Clarke could show his own modest paintings of men-of-war and engagements at sea. Two prized pictures derived from his first naval appointment in February 1795, as Chaplain in the *Jupiter* (50), the Flagship in which Caroline of Brunswick, the Princess of Wales Elect, was brought from Cuxhaven to Gravesend. He had taken the opportunity to make a rapid portrait of the Princess as well as a sea-view of the escorting Squadron, which included the *Lark* (16) carrying Lieutenant Francis Austen.

Clarke's Captain, the Squadron Commodore, was John Willett Payne, an outstanding sailor, decorated for his part in the Glorious 1st of June, 1794. When the royal mission was completed, Clarke followed Payne to the *Impetueux* (74) and saw action with the Western Squadron of the Channel Fleet from 1796–99, some of this time spent in the blockade of Brest. He showed the qualities of a true sailor in sticking this out. He was conscientious, too, in carrying through his duties as Chaplain and selected a group of his ship-board sermons for a volume published in 1798. Clarke was rightly proud of the book. It was, he wrote to Jane Austen, one of those 'I ventured to publish from being at Sea – Sermons which I wrote & preached on the Ocean' and which he wished to present to her following the visit to Carlton House.[15]

This early experience 'at Sea' was important to Clarke. It resurfaced in his suggestion to Jane Austen that in some future work she should take the figure of 'an English Clergyman' – Clarke held the living of Preston-cum-Hove – and, a further hint, that she should 'Carry' her 'Clergyman to Sea as the Friend of some distinguished Naval Character about a Court.'[16] This 'distinguished Naval Character' was his own former commander, Captain Payne of the *Jupiter* and *Impetueux*, the Court connection being with the Prince of Wales. During the 1780s and 90s, Payne had occupied a number of appointments in the royal household, including some years as Private Secretary and Auditor to the Duchy of Cornwall, the Prince's main source of income. Clarke was prompt to acknowledge Payne's support and patronage, dedicating *Naval Sermons* (1798) to this 'Brave, Zealous, And Sincere' officer. In 1800, Clarke contributed to the *Naval Chronicle* a lengthy 'Biographical Memoir' of Payne,[17] by then Rear-Admiral of the Blue, and three years later, on Payne's death in November 1803, a fulsome 'Obituary', noting that the funeral service, at St Margaret's Westminster, was attended by representatives of the Prince of Wales and conducted by the Rev. James Stanier Clarke, 'a particular friend of the deceased' and, thanks to his patron, a Chaplain of the Household to the Prince of Wales.[18]

Clarke's celebration of his patron went on in other places as well: before Payne's death, for example, in the dedication to *The Progress of Maritime Discovery* (1803) and afterwards, in his edition of *The Shipwreck* (1804), the poem by William Falconer – another of the books which Clarke wanted to send Jane Austen in 1815. These tributes are conventionally worded, with the expressions of gratitude customary from a beneficiary to his patron. Yet there must have been some sniggering in naval circles and amongst the Carlton House set, some amusement at the elevation of Payne as a paragon of modesty and virtue. For although 'Jack' or 'Jacko' was one of the Prince of Wales' closest and most trusted friends, he was also his *eminence grise* (as John Brooke describes him),[19] or, as the naval historian Laughton phrased it in the *DNB*, 'the associate of the prince in his vices and his supporter in his baser intrigues'.[20] In short, Payne served as his master's pimp or procurer, a trusted *factotum* with the job of paying off the Prince's discarded partners and settling with disgruntled husbands. A personal friend to Mrs Fitzherbert, he was employed as the Prince's go-between in patching up differences between them and was appointed by the Prince, together with Moira, to be her guardian and trustee.

As a womaniser, Payne was not far behind his royal master. His most notable liaison was formed, in about 1780, with Amy or Emy Lyon, a young prostitute of fourteen, who became one of the great beauties of the day, immortalised in a series of paintings and studies by George Romney (see Illustration 19), some of which hung on the walls of Carlton House. Passing from Payne to Sir Harry Fetherstonehaugh of Uppark and onwards to the Hon. Charles Greville, Amy, by now Emily, changed her name to Emma Hart, ending up, in 1786, as mistress to Greville's uncle, Sir William Hamilton, British Minister at the Court of Naples, whom she married in September 1791. She was twenty-six, Sir William sixty-one. Eight years later, she achieved her great and enduring conquest in Horatio Nelson.

Clarke was not unaware of Payne's murky background, in particular, his sordid employment with the Prince, and his biographical eulogies are masterly in evasion. In the 'Biographical Memoir' of 1800, Clarke employed his literary talents in erecting a graceful poetic screen, turning to Milton for the words in which to describe the early years of friendship between Payne and the Prince and the debauchery of their circle: 'these social days of "jest and youthful jollity" ',[21] a melodious and sanitising turn of phrase picked, appropriately, from *L'Allegro*, Milton's celebration of youthful 'delights'.[22]

However, at Carlton House in 1815 there was no call for Jane Austen to reflect on Clarke's shady associations or scandals from the Prince's past. In his private room, Clarke had his Friendship Book to hand (in which, it is said, he then dashed off a swift portrait of his visitor)* and could point to the works of his own authorship or editing. Prominent amongst these was a run of the *Naval Chronicle*, a monthly journal of professional history, biography and current record which he set up in 1799 together with John M'Arthur, Secretary to Admiral Lord Hood and, later, Nelson's Prize-Agent in the Mediterranean. Clarke's editorial work kept him close to naval events and naval careers. He knew of the promotions and marriages of the sailor brothers, recorded in the pages of the *Chronicle*. So was Francis' act of daring in the pursuit and capture of *La Ligurienne* in 1800, his report, from the 'Peterell, at Sea, March 22', given in full in Volume III.[23] And beyond the bound volumes of the *Chronicle*, Clarke could point to books of his own authorship – to his long pamphlet on Union with Ireland (1799); his bulky *Progress of Maritime Discovery* (1803), 750 pages in length; his three volumes of *Naufragia or Historical Memoirs of Ship-Wrecks* (1805, 1806); the *Life of Admiral Lord Nelson* (1809) in two massive volumes, written in collaboration with M'Arthur, followed in 1810 by a 700-page Abridgement; a *Sermon* (1811), preached at St Paul's, in which he took the opportunity to give thanks for the service at sea of his colleagues in 'the Clerical Profession';[24] and, newly-published, his *Life of James II*, drawn from the Stuart papers that the Prince Regent, respectful of Stuart history, had been at some pains to collect at Carlton House. It was an official work inasmuch as it was prepared by Clarke, at the 'Command' of the Regent, in his role as Historiographer to the King, a post to which he was appointed (at the Regent's insistence, and ahead of Southey) in 1812.[25]

This was yet another interest Jane Austen shared with the librarian. Inheriting Stuart loyalties from her mother's side of the family, the 'Loyal Leighs', since childhood she had kept the traditions alive, remaining a passionate supporter of the Stuart cause,[26] and Clarke undertook to send her a copy of the anticipated second edition of his James II biography. Acknowledging his visitor's special interest in naval matters, he may have drawn Jane Austen's attention to the Preface, in which he discussed the King's contribution both to naval administration and to Britain's strength at sea: the naval 'Principles and Maxims' which James 'established',[27] his thorough understanding of 'the whole business of the Admiralty'[28] and 'the essential and lasting service which James rendered this Country, in compacting and as it were building up its Naval Power . . .' – an assessment which is well-judged and has stood the test of time.[29]

Clarke's *magnum opus*, however, was not the *Life of James II* but his *Life of*

---

* For the detailed evidence, we have to await a forthcoming biography of Clarke, *A Clergyman Carried Off to Sea*, by Richard James Wheeler.

Nelson. (I call it Clarke's, since his was the original commission early in 1806 and M'Arthur was only called in later.) Designed as a monument to the nation's hero, it was carried through accordingly, in monumental style. Twenty-one pounds in weight, the two Imperial 4to volumes – 10³/₄" x 13¹/₂" – constitute a slab-like memorial 'of very stately bulk', according to the *Critical Review*.[30] Of 'unusual size' and 'inconvenient' shape, commented the *Gentleman's Magazine*, the work 'prepares the mind for something extraordinary'.[31] We have no reason to suppose that Jane Austen laboured through these volumes from cover to cover, although she could have seen copies at the homes of her friends. Captain Foote and Admiral Thomas Bertie, both living at Southampton, were on the list of subscribers, along with Warren Hastings and Sir Home Riggs Popham; and many copies went to book clubs and societies. In naval circles, the author's fame preceded the work itself. For Clarke was encountered travelling from ship to ship in pursuit of anecdotes and recollections to enliven the documentary record. The opportunity was too tempting: stories were concocted on the spot. We have an eye-witness account of occasions on which Graham Edward Lloyd, Captain of the *Vestal* (28), would spin his yarns. 'Clarke's eye would sparkle . . . he would lay down his half-eaten biscuit' and scribble away, to the amusement of his messmates. Gullible he may have been, yet Robert Steele, the Marine officer who recorded these scenes, did not underestimate Clarke. He saw him to be 'a fine, handsome man, with a simplicity and primitiveness of manner; at the same time, he was subtle, dextrous, and of this world.'[32]

For all their labour, and, under royal patronage, their privileged access to official records and family papers, the work of Clarke and M'Arthur was no masterpiece. M'Arthur is said to have supplied the facts, helped with the documentation and, having served with Nelson, contributed some recollections of his own, while Clarke provided the style. The result is an ill-digested mixture of direct quotation and encompassing narrative. Worst of all, Nelson is not permitted to speak with his own voice. Without warning, letters are cut, run together and altered. Sir Nicholas Harris Nicolas – the editor of what Carola Oman described as 'the Bible of the Nelson student',[33] the seven-volume *Dispatches and Letters of Lord Nelson* (1844–46) – put his finger on the editorial purpose behind this disastrous meddling. It was 'to exhibit' Nelson in 'fitting epistolary state; as if a Hero could never think, write, or speak naturally, but must always appear in full dress'.[34] The same principle is expressed in the work's dedication: that the materials, provided at the request of the Prince of Wales, 'should be furnished to form the history of a Life, which is to be held out as an example of Heroism and professional Talent to future generations.'[35]

In the Introduction, the exemplary and inspirational character of Nelson 'in full dress' is expounded to patriotic orchestration:

> The life of Horatio Nelson presents one of those rare examples of that early and ardent passion for true glory, which may induce men to excel in every branch of professional duty, and to preserve, through all the vicissitudes of public service, a stedfast reliance on the gratitude of their country.
>
> The following narrative will shew by what exertions the son of a private* clergyman obtained the highest rewards to which human nature can aspire, the applause of his contemporaries, and the veneration of posterity . . . he inspired his countrymen with such confidence in his integrity and abilities that they almost regarded his existence as essential to their own independence, and to the liberties of the civilized world.[36]

With such a fanfare, there was no fear that this ceremonial account would carry the reader too far into the scandalous areas of Nelson's private life – the entanglement with Lady Hamilton, the true identity of their daughter, passed off as their adoptive child, Horatia Nelson Thompson, and Nelson's desertion of his wife. It was on this understanding of delicacy and discretion that Nelson's brother, the first Earl, passed over letters in his possession, Clarke having undertaken to exercise his 'caution' and 'Honour' in handling them and offering Earl Nelson the opportunity of censorship.[37]

The Clarke and M'Arthur biography soon came under fire. William Gifford, the *Quarterly*'s editor, encouraged Southey to do a hatchet-job.[38] Little encouragement was needed. Southey had long suspected Clarke to be the author of an anonymous review of his own poem *Madoc* (1805), a review exhibiting 'manifest malice'.[39] Handed the opportunity, Southey now repaid in kind, picking off the primary author before turning to the biography itself. He ridiculed Clarke for a series of failed enterprises. His *Progress of Maritime Discovery*, originally announced as extending to 'seven ponderous quartos' (as Southey put it) was halted in the face of withering criticism after the appearance of volume one, and both the *Progress* and *Naufragia* displayed 'a mass of mock erudition'.[40] As to the *Life of Nelson* – 'the bulkiest work of its kind that has been seen in modern times' – Southey described it, quite fairly, as 'rather a work of reference than a biographical composition',[41] and then proceeded, in the remainder of his review, a further forty pages, to provide a sketch of just the 'biographical composition' he was seeking, its content drawn almost wholly from the work under review. But Southey's command of narrative and his ability to write lively and lucid prose left Clarke and

---

* 'private', a parish priest, as distinct from a clergyman such as Clarke himself, holding an official post as Domestic Chaplain to the Prince Regent. The one is seen as humble and modest, the other as eminent and well-funded.

M'Arthur far behind. John Murray, publisher of the *Quarterly*, had naval connections as Bookseller (meaning publisher) to the Admiralty and the Board of Longitude, and he spotted an opportunity. There were many lives of Nelson in circulation, but none of them a popular life, historically and biographically sound, and in Southey he saw his author. Southey was in agreement with Murray about the need for a good biography. '*All*' the existing ones, he maintained, were 'slovenly performances – there is nothing like a clear lucid narrative in them. I could make a good book and a useful one, and it would give me an opportunity of saying some things which I think worth saying and want a place for.'[42] He took the naval aspects seriously, obtaining from Croker plans of Nelson's principal sea engagements from the Admiralty records and consulting his brother Thomas, a serving Captain, on technical matters and nautical colour, sending him proofs for a final check; and he used the Preface to offer a brief statement of his purpose, a professional purpose, in writing the book:

> Many lives of NELSON have been written: one is yet wanting, clear and concise enough to become a manual for the young sailor, which he may carry about with him, till he has treasured up the example in his memory and in his heart. In attempting such a work, I shall write the eulogy of our great naval hero; for the best eulogy of NELSON is the faithful history of his actions: and the best history must be that which shall relate them most perspicuously.

In this, Southey was reflecting Murray's not uncommercial hope that it was to be 'such a book as shall become the heroic text of every midshipman in the Navy'.[43]

As a finishing touch, distinctively naval, Southey dedicated the book to John Wilson Croker, founder and Editor of the *Quarterly Review* and Secretary of the Admiralty, a writer qualified 'to decide upon its literary merits' and by his 'offical situation . . . qualified to appreciate its historical accuracy'.

The *Life of Nelson* was well received. The *Edinburgh Review* pronounced it to be 'spirited and honest' and deservedly popular.[44] Moreover, it cleared any lingering doubts about Southey's loyalty to King and country. Once, like Wordsworth and Coleridge, a friend of French Republican Liberty, he was now an advocate of Tory policies. He played down the fact that Nelson had never been a dutiful conformist favoured by the Establishment. In this respect, Southey succeeded in reclaiming Nelson as a patriot and national hero – a political stroke for which his reward soon came. The *Life* was published 1 May 1813. Five months later he was offered the Poet Laureateship, an honour which he was delighted to celebrate in the opening stanza of

'Carmen Triumphale for the Commencement of the Year 1814', a laureate piece running on for a further two-hundred-and-fifty lines in which the triumph announced was as much his own as his country's.

> In happy hour doth he receive
> The Laurel, meed of famous Bards of yore,
> Which Dryden and diviner Spenser wore,
> In happy hour, and well may he rejoice,
> Whose earliest task must be
> To raise the exultant hymn for victory,
> And join a nation's joy with harp and voice,
> Pouring the strain of triumph on the wind,
> Glory to God, his song, Deliverance for Mankind![45]

A reader of the *Quarterly*, Jane Austen would certainly have appreciated Southey's attack on the Clarke and M'Arthur biography. Whether or not she read his subsequent *Life of Nelson* is an open question. The single reference in her correspondence is in response to a letter in which Cassandra must have mentioned the book. So Jane now takes this up, dropping in a remark *en passant* as she jumps from topic to topic:

> No letter from Charles yet. – Southey's Life of Nelson; – I am tired of Lives of Nelson, being that I never read any. I will read this however, if Frank is mentioned in it. Here I am in Kent ... [etc, etc][46]

Frank was not mentioned. So if we take Jane's remark at face value, she may never have opened the book; and, beyond her connection with the Southey family,* there was no compelling reason for her to do so. During the triumphant decade from 1795 to Trafalgar, Nelson's exploits had been trumpeted, recorded at length in the official gazettes and newspapers, his prowess celebrated throughout the land and memorialised in a great outpouring of Nelsoniana – from statues, paintings, posters, prints and transparencies, verses, songs and ballads, commemorative china and stoneware, mugs, jugs and crockery, to tea-trays, pipe-bowls, ear-rings, pendants, pins and brooches, patch-boxes, fans, ribbons, vinaigrettes, shawls and head-gear. As

---

* As Jane Austen read and enjoyed Southey's poetry, we can guess that she followed his career with interest. Moreover, in 1808, Catherine Bigg-Wither, one of her closest friends, married Southey's uncle, Herbert Hill, soon to become Rector of Streatham in South London. Mr Hill paid for Southey's education at Westminster and Oxford and was regarded by him with deep affection: in Southey's eyes, Hill was 'always the man of letters' (quoted in Simmons, 1945, p. 90). There would have been some discussion of Southey's success when Jane Austen visited the Hills at Streatham early in April 1814. By that time, she was some way into the writing of *Emma*, which she began on 21 January, just two weeks after the opening stanzas of Southey's laureate piece, the 'Carmen Triumphale', had appeared in the *Courier*.

Lady Hamilton boasted, you could 'dress from head to foot alla nelson'.[47] Even Jane Austen surrendered to Nelson fever at his Victory of the Nile, sporting a borrowed, fez-like Mamalouc cap, 'all the fashion now', as she told Cassandra, 'worn at the Opera, & by Lady Mildmays at Hackwood Balls'.[48]

One could weary of Nelson the hero, and that would be a good enough reason, in 1813, for choosing to ignore Southey's *Life*, or, at least, making a game of it. But there were other issues, too. Nelson, the slave of passion, the adulterer living openly with Lady Hamilton, and Lady Nelson an abandoned wife, remained a scandalous story. The cuckold Sir William, an elderly anti-quarian and connoisseur, the plump and comely Emma caught in striking 'Attitudes', and the virile seaman, were still remembered as irresistible targets for Rowlandson, Isaac Cruikshank, Gillray and others, their caricatures ranging from ridicule and the mildly suggestive to the downright indecent. Emma's chequered past – her passage from Mrs Kelly's bawdy-house to the Temple of Health* and her succession of illustrious protectors – was common gossip.

At the time of Emma's marriage to Sir William, setting the lead for polite society, Queen Charlotte refused to receive her at Court; and when, in November 1800, the Hamiltons returned to England with Nelson in tow, Lady Spencer, the First Lord's wife, straitlaced and censorious, set the mark of Admiralty disapproval firmly against her.

On the precise relationship between Nelson and Lady Hamilton, public opinion was divided. Some trusted Nelson's word that their love was platonic. This was the view that Southey promoted in 1813. With not a glance at Emma's past, he drew a woman noble and inspiring, worthy of a hero's devotion: 'a woman whose personal accomplishments have seldom been equalled, and whose powers of mind were not less fascinating than her person';[49] a woman capable of creating heroes. Southey kept Nelson's famous words for his final chapter: ' "Brave Emma! – Good Emma! – If there were more Emmas, there would be more Nelsons" '.[50] Their love, he concluded, was manifold. 'Acutely human,' an 'undisguised and romantic passion', it was also spiritual. 'A portrait of Lady Hamilton hung in his cabin; and no Catholic ever beheld the picture of his patron-saint with devouter reverence'.[51]

Yet there was no way of disguising the fact that Nelson's 'infatuated attach-ment . . . totally weaned his affections from his wife'.[52] For Southey, this act of desertion, not adultery, was the onus of Nelson's offence:

---

* 'where the Scottish charlatan James Graham gave his lectures on procreation and charged £50 a night for couples to enjoy the pleasures of his "Great Celestial State Bed" on which might be conceived perfect babies "as even the barren must do when so powerfully agitated in the delights of love"' (Hibbert, 1994, p. 83).

Farther than this, there is no reason to believe that this most unfortunate attach-ment was criminal:* – but this was criminality enough, and it brought with it its punishment. Nelson was dissatisfied with himself; and therefore, weary of the world.[53]

Only once did Southey, the self-styled 'faithful historian', feel called upon 'to pronounce a severe and unqualified condemnation' of Nelson's 'public' conduct. This was for permitting the execution of Admiral Prince Francesco Caraccioli, the head of the Neapolitan Navy, who deserted the King of Naples to serve the French. Nelson ordered the execution to be carried out swiftly, precluding any opportunity for an appeal or reprieve, an act of injustice which Southey blames upon his liaison:

> Doubtless the British admiral seemed to himself to be acting under a rigid sense of justice; but to all other persons it was obvious that he was influenced by an infatu-ated attachment, – a baneful passion, which destroyed his domestic happiness, and now, in a second instance, stained ineffaceably his public character.[54]

Whatever remained uncertain about Nelson's relationship with Emma, whether it was adulterous and in the full sense *crim. con.*, seemed to be confirmed beyond doubt with the appearance of *The Letters of Lord Nelson to Lady Hamilton* in 1814. The two volumes, published anonymously, were put together by James Harrison, an impoverished journalist befriended by Lady Hamilton, using correspondence stolen from her. Croker, writing in the *Quarterly Review*, called it 'a shameless record', indignant not at Nelson's behaviour but at the invasion of his privacy, 'the prostitution of so noble a name'.[55] Others, however, were outraged by what the letters disclosed. Frances Lady Shelley recalled the occasion when Nelson, having taken communion before leaving England for Trafalgar, faced the priest hand-in-hand with Lady Hamilton and solemnly testified: ' "Emma, I have taken the Sacrament with you this day, to prove to the world that our friendship is most pure and innocent, and of this I call God to witness!" '. According to Lady Shelley, these latest letters exposed the sacred declaration as nothing less than 'horrible sacrilege!' and Nelson himself as a hero betrayed by his 'private life':

> And this is the man whom Southey holds up, as a model for all sailors! True, his public life is worthy of our highest admiration. If only it were possible to draw a

---

* Southey's 'criminal' carries the specific meaning of *sexually* adulterous, a usage familiar to the readers. An action of *crim. con.* (criminal conversation i.e. intercourse) would be taken by an aggrieved husband against his wife's lover to recover damages. In common law, their intercourse was an act of trespass on the husband, his wife being an item of his 'property', enabling him to claim 'damages for being deprived of the aid and comfort of the society of a wife' (*Annual Register, 1814, 1815,* 'Appendix to Chronicle', pp. 298–99).

veil across the private life of that great hero! Alas! a veil is often necessary, in the domestic history of the world's greatest men.[56]

Lady Shelley was not alone in voicing her disappointment and indignation. While the *Edinburgh Review* accepted that the letters were 'the matter of history, and must pass as such into the records of the age', it deplored the revelation at length of these 'odious details':[57] Nelson's 'culpable disregard of domestic ties', his 'neglect, approaching to cruelty, of one to whom he was bound by honour, as well as religion, morality, and law, to cherish'.[58] This, in short, was 'The notorious fact of Lord Nelson's domestic misconduct to his wife . . .'[59] Although Jane Austen could boast to Cassandra at having 'a very good eye' for an adulterer,[60] her views on deserted wives were heartfelt and left no room for laughter. She followed the tribulations of the Princess of Wales sympathetically. When the Princess, aided by the Whig lawyer Henry Brougham, wrote to the Regent in January 1813 – protesting, as a wronged mother, at the cruel limitations recently placed on her access to Princess Charlotte – because the Prince refused to give an answer, the Princess's friends released her letter to the *Morning Chronicle*. It was reprinted in the *Hampshire Telegraph*, where Jane Austen would have seen it, on 15 February, and on the following day she wrote to Martha Lloyd:

> I suppose all the World is sitting in Judgement upon the Princess of Wales's Letter. Poor Woman, I shall support her as long as I can, because she *is* a Woman, & because I hate her Husband – but I can hardly forgive her for calling herself 'attached & affectionate' to a Man whom she must detest – & the intimacy said to subsist between her & Lady Oxford is bad. – I do not know what to do about it; – but if I must give up the Princess, I am resolved at least always to think that she would have been respectable, if the Prince had behaved only tolerably by her at first. –[61]

Jane Austen regarded the Princess's misfortunes with amusement and sympathy. Caroline's intimacy with Lady Oxford, undesirable as it was, had its entertaining side. Jane Harley, Lady Oxford, was famously free with her favours; as Flora Fraser puts it, a woman 'whose love of Radical men was as great as her love of radical causes . . . Her children were by so many different fathers that they were known as the "Harleian Miscellany", after a celebrated collection of seventeenth-century manuscripts'.[62] Not (as we follow Jane Austen's line of thought) suitable company for a Princess with a far from untarnished reputation herself. But amusement is not the tone of Jane Austen's final reflection. Since the very beginning, in 1795, Caroline's marriage had been a history of humiliation and rejection played out in public.

This, too, in a minor key, was the story of Fanny Nelson's marriage. Hurtful reports of her husband's behaviour with Lady Hamilton in Palermo begain filtering back to London in the Spring of 1799. Naval friends warned both Nelson and Emma Hamilton that nothing could stop people talking, that their characters were at risk and that there were 'enemies' ready to place the worst construction on behaviour which to Lady Hamilton might seem perfectly innocent. By mid-November, the scraps of scandal found their way into the press. Reporting the appointment of Keith to take command in the Mediterranean and Nelson's expected return to England, *The Times* of 14 November was heavily allusive.

> *Perfidium ridens Venus & Cupido!*
> These perfidious Gods have in all time spread their smiling snares for the first of mankind. Heroes and Conquerors are subdued in their turn. Mark Anthony followed Cleopatra *into the Nile*, when he should have fought with Octavius! and laid down his laurels and his power, to sail down the *Cyndnus* with her in the dress, the character and the *attitudes* of Venus. What will not the eye effect in the bosom of a Hero?[63]

attitudes gave the game away; and they turned up again on 28 November. 'By a false point in one of the morning Papers, the admirable attitudes of Lady HAM-T-N are called Admiral-attitudes'.[64] When Nelson eventually reached London, in company with the Hamiltons, a year later, the cartoonists set to work, reviving the stories of Emma's past and mocking at Sir William's blindness, real or affected, at the entanglement of Nelson and his wife. Soon after this, Fanny received her dismissal and the *ménage-à-trois*, now with the addition of the infant Horatia, settled at Merton in the Autumn of 1801.

The painfulness of Fanny Nelson's situation was not abated by Nelson's death. Trafalgar provided Lady Hamilton with a platform upon which to base her claims, made repeatedly and in public, for support by the nation. On the morning of Trafalgar, Nelson had called upon Captains Hardy and Blackwood to witness the 'last Codicil' to his will. In this document, prepared some time before, he recited Emma's various 'services' to the country in advancing British interests at the Neapolitan court, services hitherto unrewarded, and he now solemnly declared Emma 'a Legacy to my King and Country', leaving his 'adopted daughter' too, to 'the country's beneficence'.[65] It was a 'Legacy' sanctified as a dying wish made to the *Victory*'s Chaplain: 'Remember I leave Lady Hamilton and my Daughter as a Legacy to my Country'.[66] But the trumpeting of his last wishes grated. 'When shall we have done with Lord N.'s latter will and test., and "my dear friend Lady H."?' protested Charles Kirkpatrick Sharpe, a well-known 'character', who saw Nelson as 'suffering . . . under cartloads of eulogy'.[67]

For nine years, until her death in January 1815, Emma pressed her claims for payment. She was supported in this by some of Nelson's friends. But his brother, the first Earl, would do nothing; the King, in his moments of sanity, had no time for the claims of an adulteress; and while the Prince of Wales offered words of sympathy, he passed on her appeals to the Ministry. In February 1813, she addressed Viscount Sidmouth, the Home Secretary, confronting what she called 'the black' infamy cast upon 'herself and Nelson'.

> Lord Nelson was not more brave than he was honourable and noble minded: wou'd it be either to have a criminal intercourse with the adored wife of his bosom friend.

Moreover, she argued, presenting an elaborate serial alibi, there would have been no opportunity, either in Italy or England, for such an act of *crim. con.* to have taken place. So the Ministers should no longer be 'fearfull of bringing forward the consideration of my memorial' for 'remuneration'.[68] But they remained firm in their refusal, maintaining that Lady Hamilton had been provided for by Sir William and that Nelson had been misled about her supposed services in Italy. Petitions and memoranda continued to flow: to Prime Ministers, to the Prince Regent, to the Admiralty Courts. Money was raised by the sale of Merton* and precious mementoes of Nelson. Her protectors of thirty years ago – Fetherstonehaugh and Greville – came to her rescue. But, living far beyond her means, Emma was arrested twice in 1813 and forced to stay within the 'rules' – the designated area for debtors – of the King Bench Prison. In July 1814, she fled to Calais to escape her creditors. Six months later, she died.

Like the running warfare between the Prince and Princess of Wales, the intimate affairs of Lady Nelson, the Hamiltons and Nelson himself made a fascinating scandal and public interest was fuelled by a succession of biographies. The earliest of these was *The Life of Lord Nelson* (1806) by James Harrison. This was a blatant piece of special pleading, commissioned by Emma herself, advancing her claim to a government pension. Although the Clarke and M'Arthur biography was primarily the hero's life, it nonetheless awakened further curiosity about Horatia's parentage. Admiral Sir Henry Dillon (then a Captain) recollected one such discussion at Portsmouth that same year. It was, Dillon says, a 'discussion . . . I shall never forget':

> The subject of conversation turned upon Nelson and Lady Hamilton. Who was the Father of Horatia? That was the question that could not be easily solved. I

---

* Nelson settled Merton Place on Emma in trust for Horatia. This included the furniture and the seventy acres of adjoining land. It was sold in 1810, the entire property and effects fetching £14,700.

maintained that Lady Hamilton was the Mother. [Captain James] Macnamara denied it in the strongest terms, and was rather heated on the occasion. I told him that I had no intention of disputing the case, but that I should reserve my own opinion. Time proved that I was right.[69]

Wider and equally heated controversies were stirred up in 1814 and 1815, firstly with the publication of the intimate letters of Nelson that Harrison had stolen from Emma. In the following year appeared the anonymous *Memoirs of Lady Hamilton*, a malicious and scandal-mongering biography. Its unnamed author was Francis Oliver, who was extremely well-informed, having served first as Sir William Hamilton's secretary, then as Nelson's and finally as Emma's, until she dismissed him in 1807. Having also acted as a courier between Nelson and Emma, and occasionally looked after Horatia, Oliver was in a position to take his revenge with damaging revelations about her private life. A mixture of fact and fiction, the *Memoirs* remains the source for much of the mischievous gossip about Emma's earliest days in London, the years she spent in the care of her protectors, her life with Sir William and the depravities of the Neapolitan court.*

How closely Jane Austen followed the cross-currents of the Emma-Nelson story, we have no idea. But the broad outlines, amusingly highlighted in the satirical prints, were common knowledge and the Austens had the benefit of being on the naval network, a channel along which service rumours and gossip travelled freely. During the entire period of Nelson's deepening relationship with Emma, from early 1799 until their departure from Italy in mid-1800, Francis was attached to the Mediterranean Fleet and on one occasion in May 1799, carried despatches to Nelson at Palermo itself, the scandalous heart of the affair. We cannot suppose that Francis was so discreet that no hint of these matters entered his letters home, or so tight-lipped as to say nothing on his return to Steventon in the Autumn of 1800. Nor that Charles, who also served in the Mediterranean during this time, would have failed to report a naval scandal quite so startling and intriguing. It was a classic situation of the warrior entrapped by siren wiles. As a well-read fellow-Admiral wrote to Nelson, viewed from England, he seemed a slave to passion, in the language of medieval romance, a 'Rinaldo in the arms of Armida', requiring 'the firmness of an Ubaldo, and his brother Knight, to draw you from the Enchantress'. Admiral Goodall next quoted a Latin tag, what he called pointedly, yet with tact, his own 'maxim': 'Cupidus voluptatum, cupidior gloriae' (Much as I seek pleasure, I seek glory more).[70] To the dismay of his naval

---

* An important account of Nelson, his image as 'an embodiment of patriotism in action' and a 'source of public virtues' is to be found in Fulford (1999).

brethren, it was advice Nelson chose to ignore. Admiral Keith, now his Commander-in-Chief in the Mediterranean, wasted no words: 'Lady Hamilton had had command of the Fleet long enough.'[71]

Nelson had style and a certain waspish humour that the Austens would have enjoyed. Witness his report to Collingwood of his off-hand reception by the King on his return from the Continent in November 1800 with the Hamiltons: 'His Majesty merely asked him if he had recovered his health; then turned to General —— and talked to him near half an hour in great good humour. It could not be about *his* success.'[72] But in whatever light Nelson's conduct was discussed among the Austens, the betrayal of his wife was an infamy which could not be ignored, excused or laughed away. A clerical family, the Austens were religious. They regarded the ties of marriage as sacred, binding and morally accountable. How seriously Jane Austen took these questions is evident in *Mansfield Park*. In the novel's drama of marriage, infidelity and adultery, the lurking villain of the piece, the prime source of infection is an Admiral. Jane Austen's language is unequivocal and damning. It is his 'vicious conduct'[73] which 'corrupted'[74] his wards, the next generation of Crawfords, to whom the 'contagion' has spread.[75] It is his home in Mayfair – into which the Admiral's mistress was installed soon after his wife's death – which provides such 'a bad school for matrimony'[76] and in which 'a bad domestic example' is set.[77] It is to him that Henry Crawford owes his 'corrupted mind'[78] and Mary Crawford her shallow cynicism, her 'perversion of mind'.[79] Of the Crawford brother and sister, Jane Austen might say, as she did in 1817 of another scandal-wracked family: 'What can be expected from a Paget, born & brought up in the centre of conjugal Infidelity & Divorces'.[80] But not all Admirals were Crawford-Nelsons, their feet of such basely human clay. Some, it could be boasted, enjoyed lives of lasting happiness in marriage, and there could be naval 'circles' quite free of 'Rears' and 'Vices'. These exemplary domestic scenes Jane Austen was soon to draw in *Persuasion*.

Afterword

By a strange quirk of circumstance, some years after Jane Austen's death the
Austen and Nelson families became linked in marriage. Following Nelson's
death at Trafalgar, his clergyman brother William received the title as first
Earl. In 1828, his wife the Countess Nelson died. Having lost his only son,
Viscount Trafalgar, the Earl was still determined, at the age of seventy-one, to
produce an heir and he proposed to a widow of twenty-eight, Hilaire, the
third daughter of Admiral Sir Robert Barlow. After refusing his offer several
times, she accepted him and they enjoyed six years of (childless) marriage
until the Earl's death in 1835. Two years later, the Dowager Countess Nelson
remarried. Her third husband was Jane Austen's nephew George, the second
son of Edward (Austen) Knight, of Godmersham Park in Kent. The couple
travelled widely on the Continent until the Countess's death in 1857. George
Knight died ten years later.

'my dear little George',[81] '*itty Dordy*', as he spoke of himself,[82] was a particular favourite of Jane Austen's and is mentioned frequently in her letters. He
was born in 1795 and educated at Winchester, Oxford and Dresden. As a boy
of thirteen, 'his eagerness in everything reminds me often of his Uncle
Henry,'[83] Jane wrote to Cassandra in 1808, a prescient insight, since, like
Henry, he turned out to be a man of many enthusiasms. He toyed with the
idea of taking Holy Orders, tried a career at the Bar, but, with an ample
allowance, he was able to travel widely on the Continent and had no need to
work.

His one public achievement was on the cricket field. A leading amateur,
representing Hampshire, Kent and All England in the 1820s, and an influential member of the MCC, he was famed as 'a very hard hitter indeed' and
played an important role in the revival of round-arm bowling, a much-
disputed area of the game:

> Then there's Knight – gallant Knight!. . . .
> As a bowler first-rate, as a bat far from vile,
> And he bowls in the new march of intellect style.[84]

This last line refers to the contribution he made to the theory of this bowling
style in letters to the *Sporting Magazine* in 1827 and his proposals for a change
in the laws.

Lord Brabourne saw his Uncle as something of a gentleman drifter, 'very well informed, agreeable, a pleasant companion, and always popular with his nephews and nieces', 'one of those men who are clever enough to do almost anything, but live to their lives' end very comfortably doing nothing'.[85] Today, George is best remembered as the reader of *Mansfield Park* who, Jane noted, was 'interested by nobody but Mary Crawford'.[86] His literary memorial is a parody on 'The Temple of Delight', a little poem by his uncle Henry singing the praises of Godmersham. In response, George, probably about fifteen at the time, addresses his hunting dog, Pincher:

> Gentle Pincher, cock thy tail,
> Open is the door to thee;
> Enter, & there ne'er shall fail
> Mirth & Hospitality –
> Partridge bones, & Pork shall charm thee
> Mutton shall with Veal unite;
> Sterling Beef shall then inform thee
> How domestic Dogs can find
> All the savings, which combined
> Make the Temple of Delight –[87]

Perhaps it was his literary Aunt Jane who inspired the youngster to this deft and cheeky little joke.

10

Emma: England, Peace and Patriotism

'Such is the Patriot's boast, where'er we roam;
His first, best country, ever is at home.'

Oliver Goldsmith, *The Traveller or A Prospect of Society* (1765) reprinted
at the head of the *Naval Chronicle*, vol. 28, July–December 1812

How I bless my stars I am of that dear little island, under a government
like ours. When I see other countries and other people, I am not only
proud of being an Englishman, but feel a sort of superiority, which is in
no other manner to be accounted for than its being common to all
Englishmen, and is inherent in them.

Captain William Hoste (*Amphion*, 32) in the Adriatic,
writing home to his father, 24 September 1809

Before accepting the Poet Laureateship in September 1813, Southey asked if
the official duty of producing Odes for Royal birthdays and New Years might
be modified. Could he not be permitted, instead, to write on any great
national occasion or event, just as the spirit moved him? His promoter, John
Wilson Croker, the Secretary of the Admiralty, replied that although it was
'not for us to make terms with the Prince Regent',[1] he could pass on a discreet
enquiry to that effect. However, as he pointed out, Southey should have no
difficulty in composing his first Ode, for the New Year of 1814: 'You can never
have a better subject than the present state of the war affords you'.[2] Since
mid-1812, the balance of the land war in Europe had swung in favour of the
Allies, and as recently as October 1813, with the 'Battle of the Nations' at
Leipzig – a decisive engagement which drove the French back across the
Rhine – the final phase of the war had opened. With victory in sight, Southey
could launch his inaugural Ode on a triumphant note: England's leading part
in the war, the defeat of France (now taken for granted), and what stirred him
most deeply, an end to Napoleon's blood-stained tyranny, a subject which he
had touched upon in the *Life of Nelson*, with an indignant outburst, a truly
'purple' passage, at the Emperor's 'enormities',

> those crimes which have incarnadined his soul with a deeper dye than that of the
> purple for which he committed them; – those acts of perfidy, midnight murder,

usurpation, and remorseless tyranny, which have consigned his name to universal execration, now and for ever.[3]

With the Laureateship as his authority and the Ode as his platform, Southey could give vent to his feelings. 'Vengeance' called for nothing less than Napoleon's 'Death' and France stood 'Disgraced . . . to all succeeding times'. For the politicians, this poetic rant was a triumphalism too far. Croker called Southey to order, reminding him that the Ode was an official perfor-mance and that diplomacy was called for. The Laureate needed to keep his eye on the settlement of the post-war world and France's readmission to the concert of Europe. With France in the future a 'friendly power', asked John Rickman,* 'can you stay in office this Carmen remaining on record?'[4] Reluctantly, Southey acted on these warnings. At some cost to his feelings, the most vengeful sections, what he called the 'maledictory stanzas',[5] were removed and incorporated into a new and unacknowledged poem, the 'Ode Written during the Negociations with Buonaparte', published anonymously in *The Courier* for 3 February and, with some slight changes, in *The Times* for 21 April 1814.

For Southey, his Laureate Ode was now 'spoilt',[6] no longer, as he told Rickman, a 'Carmen Triumphale', but an emasculated 'Carmen Castratum'.[7] The truncated version is tactful; the closing lines speak of 'France restored'; and Southey consigned his fulminating to the notes, where he reminded his readers of the unspeakable 'cruelties', 'atrocities' and 'abominations' perpe-trated by French troops on their retreat from Portugal. Ignoring Allied sensi-bilities, he also left unrestrained his exultant celebration of England's heroic stand, at times a solitary stand, throughout the length of the Long War:

> O England! O my glorious native land!
> For thou in evil days didst stand
> Against leagued Europe all in arms
> array'd,
> Single and undismay'd,
> Thy hope in Heaven and in thine own
> right hand.
> Now are thy virtuous efforts overpaid,
> Thy generous counsels now their
> guerdon find, . .
> Glory to God! Deliverance for
> Mankind!

---

* Like Croker, Rickman bridged the worlds of literature and politics. A familiar figure in the Southey-Coleridge-Wordsworth circle, he was Clerk to the Speaker of the House of Commons.

The anticipated 'Deliverance' was soon to come. On New Year's Day, 1814, the Ode was published and by 21 January, when Jane Austen began *Emma*, the Allied armies had entered mainland France – Blucher across the Rhine and Wellington through the Pyrenees.

By the end of March the Allies were at the gates of Paris and on 6 April Napoleon abdicated. Two days later, the news reached Chawton. Up at the Great House, Fanny Knight recorded the 'glorious news of Buonaparte vanquished and dethroned',[8] an event celebrated a month later by illuminations at Alton and a public supper for the parish poor. Soon, with Napoleon exiled to Elba, the Army and Navy began to wind down. Francis returned from the Baltic; Charles found his duties lightened on the *Namur* and expected to settle down with his family on shore; and the country prepared to welcome the Allied leaders for the Victory celebrations in June, an occasion that Jane Austen greeted with mock impatience, wishing them 'all away'.[9] In September, half-way through *Emma*, she was advising a novel-writing niece that '3 or 4 Families in a Country village is the very thing to work on', 'such a spot as is the delight of my life'.[10] Six months later, at the end of March 1815, her own matchless portrait of village England was complete.

Strictly speaking, *Emma* falls outside the compass of this book. A land-locked story, it has no naval content whatsoever. Idyllic and pastoral, its mood of high comedy and good humour is as far from the shadows of war as could be. Coming as it does between *Mansfield Park* and *Persuasion*, *Emma* can be regarded as an interlude, a playful interruption to the naval sequence, a gentle teasing of the sailor brothers with a heroine who has never glimpsed the sea and whose father declares it to be 'rarely of use to any body'.[11] Its 'use', when this does come up, has nothing to do with Britain's naval strength but belongs to a little side-comedy involving the competing claims of 'South End' and Cromer as 'sea-bathing places'[12] – something Charles would have enjoyed, since he took his family to Southend in the Summer of 1813. When a 'ship' enters the story, it is not one of Britain's 'wooden walls' but the answer to a charade clue, 'the monarch of the seas!'.[13]

Nonetheless, despite these apparent disqualifications, *Emma* calls for some discussion here. It is the only novel in which Jane Austen examines the ideas of Englishness and patriotism, values which (we are left to assume) are implicit to the motivation of William Price and Captain Wentworth. For while we hear much in *Mansfield Park* and *Persuasion* about the professional ambitions of these sailors, their appetite for glory and wealth, their zeal and sense of duty, their patriotic sentiments remain unspoken. In *Emma*, however, 'patriotism'[14] is held up for our inspection and the traditional enmity of England and France is played out in the antipathy between George

Knightley, a gentlemanly John Bull, and the Frenchified Frank Churchill. By Jane Austen's time, these national stereotypes were well-established and easily evoked. The tradition of the Frenchified Englishman went back over a hundred years, its origins in Restoration drama; and John Bull, an early eighteenth-century creation, figured prominently in the entertaining war-time commentary provided in popular songs and broadsides and the caricatures of Isaac Cruikshank, Rowlandson and Gillray and a host of minor political cartoonists. These were familiar images, close to hand: John Bull, the archetypal Englishman of bull-dog breed, four-square and solid, cudgel at the ready, a ferocious guardian of English virtues and values and rampantly Francophobic; the *quasi* French-Monsieur Englishman artful, devious, glib and deceitful, a foppish, rootless creature of frivolity and fashion.[15]

Among Jane Austen's contemporaries, the novelist who comes closest to representing these national types in the social sphere is Maria Edgeworth, whose writing she knew and admired. During 1814, while at work on *Emma*, she read *Patronage*, Edgeworth's latest novel, with its Frenchwoman of 'vivacity, ease, polish, *tact*, and *esprit de société* ranged against 'the solidity of understanding, amiable qualities, domestic tastes, and virtues of an Englishwoman'. Or, as Mary Crawford puts it succinctly in *Mansfield Park*, to win her brother in marriage, when 'English abilities' have failed, the 'address of a French-woman' is called for.[16]

Edgeworth draws a clear line between 'French manners' and 'English morals':

> French ease, gayety, and politeness; English sincerity, confidence, and safety [the security that comes from acting wisely]. – No *simagrée* [affectation, pretence], no *espionage*, no intrigue political or gallant.[17]

The use of French words was enough in itself to suggest that artifice was afoot and Jane Austen herself exploits this device towards the end of *Mansfield Park*, where the odour of sexual scandal hangs in the air. Mary Crawford dismisses her brother's escapade with Maria Bertram as nothing more than 'a moment's *etourderie*' (thoughtlessness) and in a newspaper report it becomes 'a matrimonial *fracas*.'[18]

Patronage also has a contrasting pair of brothers, nicknamed '*French* Clay' ('an Englishman aping a Frenchman') and '*English* Clay' ('a cold, reserved, proud, dull looking man . . . Everything about him is English'),[19] broadly corresponding to the contrast Jane Austen draws between Churchill and Knightley. This is not to suggest any direct influence. By the time Jane Austen came to *Patronage*, *Emma* was already half-written and would anyway have been shaping in her mind since the middle of 1813, when she finished work on *Mansfield Park*. The similarity in theme and characterisation belongs to the long-established tradition of French and English types; and that both Edgeworth and Jane Austen chose to take up the subject of Anglo-French differences at this particular moment is no coincidence. It arises from the historical situation. In prospect was an end to the Long War and the emergence of a peace-time society, circumstances calling for a new understanding of national traditions and identity.

Similarities between Edgeworth and Austen also arise from a common fund of vocabulary and phrasing for this subject. Towards the end of *Emma*, when enlightenment dawns, Emma sees the course of deception which Churchill and Jane Fairfax have practised on Highbury as a 'system of secrecy and concealment',[20] 'a system of hypocrisy and deceit, – espionage and treachery',[21] summoning up Edgeworth's picture of French 'intrigue political or gallant' and with a direct echo in 'espionage', a word recently arrived in English and still regarded as heavily French. Through these associations of language, Jane Austen attaches 'nationalities' to Knightley and Churchill, a process which begins in chapter 18, the final chapter of volume one. Knightley lectures Emma on Churchill's dereliction, his failure to visit Mr Weston on the occasion of his second marriage, a 'duty' 'which a man can always do if he chuses . . . not by manoeuvring and finessing, but by vigour and resolution'.[22] 'Manoeuvring' came into English in the 1780s as a term for the tactical disposition and movement of troops and ships. It was only a short step from warfare on land and sea to the battlefield of society and Jane Austen was soon using the word – in *Lady Susan* (*c.* 1793–94) and in her letters and novels – to describe scenes and situations where women scheme and manipulate for advantage, usually in money or marriage. In 1809, *Manoeuvring* gained particular prominence as the title of one of Edgeworth's *Tales of Fashionable Life*. This is the story of the tricks and devices of Mrs Beaumont, a fortune-hunting, marriage-making mother, its essence echoed in Mary Crawford's view of marriage as 'a manoeuvring business',[23] a cynicism fostered by her experience of Admiral Crawford's household. However, in Knightley's attack on Churchill, 'manoeuvring' stands in a moral vein, as an activity inimical to 'duty', to 'vigour and resolution', a meaning exactly caught in one of Nelson's letters, where he criticises a Danish commander for quitting his ship in the heat of battle, leaving his men to struggle on: '*Here* was no manoeuvring: *it was* downright fighting, and it was his duty to have shown firmness . . .'.[24]

The Frenchness of Churchill's unmanly behaviour is also signalled by his 'finessing', a *finesse* (in Johnson's *Dictionary* treated as a French word) being a trick or stratagem; and Knightley uses the word again towards the end of the novel, representing Churchill as self-deceived, trapped in a web of double-dealing: 'his own mind full of intrigue, that he should suspect it in others. – Mystery; Finesse – how they pervert understanding!'.[25]

The process of linguistic labelling is carried a stage further when Knightley sizes up Churchill's 'smooth, plausible manners' with definitions which are explicitly nationalistic:

'. . . your amiable young man can be amiable only in French, not in English. He may be very "aimable", have very good manners, and be very agreeable; but he can have no English delicacy towards the feelings of other people: nothing really amiable about him.'[26]

The contrast here is between French veneer, the art of pleasing, the 'l'aimable' which Lord Chesterfield so impressed upon his son as a means of social ingratiation, leading to social advancement, and the solid worth of English 'really amiable', by Knightley's definition – a meaning lost to us today – a quality of thoughtfulness and consideration for others.*

With Churchill's arrival, in volume two, the national contrast is taken further. Somewhat in the mould of Henry Crawford, Churchill is a skilled practitioner of 'l'aimable', a man of 'gallant' gestures and acts of 'gallantry'. This is not the 'gallantry' of war, with its 'gallant' heroes, a language of citation with which the Austens were familiar in the *London Gazette* and the *Naval Chronicle*. Rather, this is the terminology of the dilettante art of courtesies and courtliness, the counters of deception in Churchill's 'systems' of 'secresy and concealment', his 'Disingenuousness and double-dealing', as Knightley calls it, his 'gallantry and trick',[27] all this alien to the depths of Surrey. It takes an English word to penetrate the facade. Emma realises that permitting Churchill the freedom 'to be gallant' towards herself – this is the French word, accented on the second syllable – 'must have had such an appearance as no English word but flirtation could very well describe'.[28] Whereas Knightley, like his brother, is a man of few words and 'nothing of ceremony'.[29] Their 'true English style', the 'style' of Stanley greeting Livingstone sixty years later, is not outward display but containment and reserve.** They greet one-another laconically with ' "How d'ye do, George?"

* I have not come across any discussion of these particular French and English cognates contemporary with Jane Austen. But doubtless such discussions did go on, since it was part of the categorising spirit of the age to examine and define synonyms and close synonyms, a verbal interest captured by Jane Austen in the titles of *Sense and Sensibility*, *Pride and Prejudice* and *Persuasion*, where the novels provide a dramatisation of these heavily nuanced terms. Going by Hazlitt's remarks in *Tate's Magazine*, July 1839, on 'the loftier English sense' of 'amiable', the difference in moral weight between 'amiable' and '*aimable*' had long been a matter of comment. Roger Gard offers an example of 'amiable' from Maria Edgeworth's *Ormond* (1817) (Gard, 1992, p. 242).

** This 'style' had various manifestations. John Wilson Croker, the Secretary to the Admiralty, used it in Parliament. Defending the Ministry's handling of the 1812 War with America, he explained that 'the British Government send orders to their naval officers, not couched in doubtful terms, but in the plain good old English style, that as the American government had assumed a menacing attitude, they should put in force their standing orders to sink, burn, and destroy their enemy's ships' (*Hansard*, 18 February 1813, col. 1045).

and "John, how are you?" burying under a calmness that seemed all but indifference the real attachment which would have led either of them, if requisite,
to do every thing for the good of the other.'[30] Knightley's proposal is delivered in a similar manner: 'in plain, unaffected, gentleman-like English'.[31]
'Not a gallant man', as Emma observes, but 'a very humane one',* and
Knightley's loan of his carriage to Miss Bates and Jane Fairfax is, in the same
vein, 'a case of humanity' and 'un-ostentatious kindness'.[32]

On one remarkable occasion, Jane Austen raises the comedy of the 'gallant'
Churchill and the ungallant Knightley to a level beyond comedy, transforming Knightley's gesture of 'unfinished gallantry' into an expression of
love, one of the rare instances where Jane Austen's comic vision joins comedy
and tenderness:

> He took her hand; – whether she had not herself made the first notion, she could
> not say – she might, perhaps, have rather offered it – but he took her hand,
> pressed it, and certainly was on the point of carrying it to his lips – when, from
> some fancy or other, he suddenly let it go. – Why he should feel such a scruple,
> why he should change his mind when it was all but done, she could not perceive.
> – He would have judged better, she thought, if he had not stopped. – The inten-
> tion, however, was indubitable; and whether it was that his manners had in
> general so little gallantry, or however else it happened, but she thought nothing
> became him more. –[33]

(Jane Austen invites the reader to supply the explanation for Knightley's
'unfinished gallantry'. Presumably, the thought strikes him that the kissing of
hands comes too close to Churchill's repertoire of the 'aimable'.).

By the end of the story, Knightley's reading of Churchill is confirmed. The
secret engagement to Jane Fairfax does indeed call for skilful 'manoeuvring
and finessing', a ready show of agreeableness towards the citizens of
Highbury, and an indifference towards other people's feelings, even, at times,
towards Jane Fairfax and Emma. Yet we may wonder that, in chapter 18, on
the evidence of Churchill's letter alone, Knightley can show such gusto in
attacking someone he has never met; that a report of Churchill's visit to
Weymouth – a staid and highly respectable resort, and for that reason
favoured by George III over many years for the holidays of the Royal Family –
should make him, in Knightley's words, a habitué of one of 'the idlest haunts

---

* Readers of Southey's *Nelson* would remember this word from the final chapter, where it is
pronounced as one of the hero's greatest attributes, an aspect of his selfless patriotism: 'All men
know that his heart was as humane as it was fearless; that there was not in his nature the slightest
alloy of selfishness or cupidity; but with perfect and entire devotion, he served his country with all
his heart, and with all his soul, and with all his strength; and, therefore, they loved him as truly and
fervently as he loved England' (pp. 244–45). On the morning of Trafalgar, his prayer was that
'humanity after victory' should be 'the predominant feature in the British fleet!' (p. 251).

in the kingdom'.[34]* The clue lies in the calculated placing of this scene at the close of volume one, a month ahead of Churchill's arrival. Knightley's scathing remarks are aimed at a creature of his own imagining, a construct (as Emma detects) of his prejudice, itself an entertaining mix of phobias, Francophobia and Frankophobia – a punning that Jane Austen would not object to and which, in its literary mode, *Emma* encourages, as a novel of riddles, conundrums and word-play.[35]

A deeper searching of language is conducted on 'patriotism'. The word occurs in volume two, chapter six (in modern editions chapter 24), the scene in which Churchill continues to bamboozle Emma, pretending that his stay in Highbury is to honour his father while his real purpose is the pursuit of Jane Fairfax, a deceit in which Churchill uses Emma as his stalking horse. To this end, he asks Emma to give him a guided tour. As they move from place to place – from his father's former house, to the cottage of his wet-nurse, and on to the Crown Inn – Emma brings the conversation round to Jane Fairfax: had he seen 'her often at Weymouth?'[36] Churchill is caught off guard and plays for time. 'At that moment they were approaching Ford's' (already known to us as 'the principal woollen-draper, linen-draper, and haberdasher's shop united; the shop first in size and fashion in the place'),[37] and he takes the opportunity to duck Emma's question, steering the conversation far from Weymouth:

> 'Ha! this must be the very shop that every body attends every day of their lives, as my father informs me. He comes to Highbury himself, he says, six days out of the seven, and has always business at Ford's. If it be not inconvenient to you, pray let us go in, that I may prove myself to belong to the place, to be a true citizen of Highbury. I must buy something at Ford's. It will be taking out my freedom. – I dare say they sell gloves.'
>
> 'Oh! yes, gloves and every thing. I do admire your patriotism. You will be adored in Highbury. You were very popular before you came, because you were Mr Weston's son – but lay out half-a-guinea at Ford's, and your popularity will stand upon your own virtues.'
>
> They went in; and while the sleek, well-tied parcels of 'Men's Beavers' and 'York Tan' were bringing down and displaying on the counter, he said – 'But I beg your pardon, Miss Woodhouse, you were speaking to me, you were saying something at the very moment of this burst of my *amor patriae*. Do not let me lose it. I assure you the utmost stretch of public fame would not make me amends for the loss of any happiness in private life.'[38]

---

* When Cassandra visited Weymouth in 1804, hoping to catch sight of the Royal Family, she could report neither idleness nor the dissipation of Brighton; nothing worse than that there was 'no Ice' in the town (Jane's letter of 14 September 1804, *Letters*, p. 92).

For a minute or two, Churchill's diversion works. Emma leaves her question about Jane Fairfax and falls in with his bantering tone. Amused and flattered by his inventive chatter, she imagines that they are playing the same burlesquing game and throws in 'patriotism' as her contribution to the joke. But Jane Austen's readers would have seen the joke as double-edged. Everyone remembered Johnson's notorious dismissal of 'Patriotism' as 'the last refuge of a scoundrel'. As Boswell goes on to explain, in the *Life of Johnson* (1791),* 'he did not mean a real and generous love of our country, but that pretended patriotism which so many, in all ages and countries, have made a cloak for self-interest.'[39] (Johnson is said to have had the politician John Wilkes in mind.) This is the very 'cloak' in which, with Emma's encouragement, Churchill wraps himself now, posing as an ardent Highburyite. Jane Austen's readers would also remember *The Task* (1785), a greatly admired and much quoted poem, in which Cowper reflected on the benefits of rural life. As to public affairs in the 1780s, he found the 'age of virtuous politics is past',

> Patriots are grown too shrewd to be sincere,
> And we too wise to trust them . . .[40]

a verdict that readers of *Emma* could comfortably endorse, seeing before them a 'patriot' Churchill.

Just as they occur in this passage, 'patriotism' and '*amor patriae*' (the love of one's country) are found together in the titles of books, pamphlets, poems and sermons, particularly during the period of the Long War when the Volunteers were to be enthused or national sentiments appealed to. But the terms were not wholly synonymous. 'Patriotism' carried a strong whiff of political expediency. All the factions, alliances and shades of Whig, Tory and Radical opinion wrapped themselves in the 'patriot' banner, from 'belligerents', the war-mongers, at one extreme to 'peacemongers' at the other. It is a word for which sailors could express a healthy contempt, as we see in the Journal of Captain Francis Beaumont, 1805:

> As for patriotism – ha! ha! that is a thing pretty nearly forgotten in this country, indeed the word itself would be equally so like any other unmeaning symbol or hieroglyphic were it not for a few members of Parliament who make constant use of it (the word, I mean) and for the pamphleteers who like long words to fill their columns.[41]

---

* Jane Austen writes to Cassandra of the purchase of the *Life* and 'Cowper's works' (probably the 6th edition of the poems, 1797, or the new edition, 1798). (Letter of 25 November 1798, *Letters*, p. 22). Moreover, we know from Henry Austen that his sister's 'favourite moral writers were Johnson in prose, and Cowper in verse'. ('Biographical Notice', p. 7).

'*Amor patriae*', coming from the classical world, conveyed a purer air. One tradition stems from Ovid. Exiled from Rome to the shores of the Black Sea, the poet wrote of his 'amor patriae ratione valentior' (a love of my country stronger than reason itself).[42] This was Ovid's impassioned response to a formal *consolatio* from his friend Rufinus, who argued that he should resign himself and make the best of his situation. Cowper alludes to this tradition in describing an exile in modern times:

> Methinks, I see thee straying on the beach,
> And asking of the surge that bathes thy foot
> If ever it has wash'd our distant shore.
> I see thee weep, and thine are honest tears,
> A patriot's for his country . . .[43]

In Canto Sixth of *The Lay of the Last Minstrel* (1805) Scott continued the Ovidian line, elaborating it into a poetical anathema, a ringing curse of high drama and sounding rhetoric:

> Breathes there the man, with soul so dead,
> Who never to himself hath said,
>   This is my own, my native land!
> Whose heart hath ne'er within him burn'd,
> As home his footsteps he hath turn'd,
>   From wandering on a foreign strand!
> If such there breathe, go, mark him well;
> For him no Minstrel raptures swell;
> High though his titles, proud his name,
> Boundless his wealth as wish can claim;
> Despite those titles, power, and pelf,
> The wretch, concentred all in self,
> Living, shall forfeit fair renown,
> And, doubly dying, shall go down
> To the vile dust, from whence he sprung,
> Unwept, unhonour'd, and unsung.

Richard Lovell Edgeworth used this passage to illustrate 'The love of our country' in the chapter 'On Military and Naval Education' in his well-known *Essays on Professional Education*.[44]

The Lay was very popular, by 1814 in its fourteenth edition, and so well known that Edgeworth's novelist daughter Maria could float these melodious lines (all sixteen of them!) into the mind of Caroline Percy, one of the heroines of *Patronage*, as her unspoken riposte to some offensively unpatriotic comments from 'French Clay', in which he declares his indifference 'whether England be called England or France . . . what is country – or, as people term it, their native land?'[45]

If we see the Ovidian *amor patriae* as a nostalgic, sentimental or romantic tradition, a very different heritage, political in character, stems from Book 6 of the *Aeneid*. Here, Virgil parades the early heroes of Rome. Among them is L. Junius Brutus, one of the founders of the Roman Republic. His sons plotted to restore the last King, the tyrant Tarquin the Proud, and were brought before Brutus, charged with treason. Placing country before family, Brutus sentenced them to death. Virgil's final comment (voiced through Anchises) makes the point of the story: 'vincit amor patriae laudumque immensa cupido' (the love of country and the boundless passion for renown will prevail).[46] This was regarded as one of the most telling episodes in the early Republic. Replete with human drama, it carried a powerful moral for modern times. It was held up as a shining example of civic probity, the triumph of public good over private interest and was a set-piece for schoolboy verse-exercises and for memorising and declamation. Jane Austen would have heard the passage many times, repeated by her brother and by her father's pupils at Steventon Rectory. Even youngsters at sea were reading Virgil under the tutelage of educated Chaplains. In the *Impetueux* (74), blockading Brest in 1804, Coleridge's young nephew Bernard was reading his two hundred lines of Virgil a day to the ship's Chaplain.[47]

Like any educated man, Churchill knows his Virgil too.* Taking his lead from Emma's joke about 'patriotism', he can feel confident of not offending her in pushing the joke further, with a 'burst' of Virgilian '*amor patriae*' which parodies the moral, turning it inside out.** As a customer at Ford's, he can 'prove' himself 'to be a true citizen of Highbury' and take out his 'freedom' (his legal qualification to enjoy the ancient rights of citizenship). On the other hand, he assures Emma, he is not a second Brutus: 'the utmost stretch of public fame would not make amends for the loss of any happiness in private life'.[48] In this roundabout way, Churchill tells Emma he is now ready (having had time to prepare an answer) to turn aside from the business of patriotic shopping and attend to her original question about his contact with Jane Fairfax at Weymouth. What follows is yet more masterly evasive-

---

* Brutus's story was common knowledge amongst the educated. Chapter XII of *Patriotism; or The Love of our Country: An Essay . . . Dedicated to the Volunteers of the United Kingdom* by William Friend (1804), entitled 'The trial of a son for treason – Patriotism of a father', treats the story as being so familiar as to require no names.

** In *Waverley* (1814), Scott was similarly prepared to place *amor patriae* in a half-ironic context, putting the Latin tag in the mouth of the Baron of Bradwardine, an honorable Scots patriot with a pedantic taste for legal jargon and classical quotation (iii. 24, p. 335).

ness and obfuscation as Emma is led further into his 'system of hypocrisy and deceit' and the comedy of deception deepens.

In identifying the particular quality of Knightley's patriotism, our best guide is Cobbett's *Rural Rides*, a collection of the reports he made in the 1820s from journeys undertaken to enquire into the state of the countryside.[49] He observed the signs of economic and social decline and the plight of the farming communities from county to county. Cobbett associated the rising levels of agricultural poverty and discontent with the arrival over the last twenty or thirty years of a new breed of land-owner, the war-profiteers (as he saw them) who were now displacing the traditional squirearchy, what he described as

> a resident *native* gentry, attached to the soil, known to every farmer and labourer from their childhood, frequently mixing with them in those pursuits where all artificial distinctions are lost, practising hospitality without ceremony, from habit and not on calculation . . .

This group he compared with the new class of *arriviste* and absentee land-owners:

> a gentry, only now-and-then residing at all, having no relish for country-delights, foreign in their manners, distant and haughty in their behaviour, looking to the soil only for its rents, viewing it as a mere object of speculation, unacquainted with its cultivators, despising them and their pursuits, and relying, for influence, not upon the good will of the vicinage, but upon the dread of their power. The war and paper-system [bank notes and bonds] has brought in nabobs, negro-drivers, generals, admirals, governors, commissaries, contractors, pensioners, sinecurists, commissioners, loan-jobbers, lottery-dealers, bankers, stock-jobbers; not to mention the long and *black list* in gowns and three-tailed wigs. You can see but few good houses not in possession of one or the other of these. These, with the parsons, are now the magistrates.[50]

It may seem odd that Cobbett should include Generals and Admirals on his black list. But he saw 'the labouring classes' as carrying the burden, paying 'the whole of the expenses of the Knights of Waterloo, and of the other heroes of the war', these gallant and high-ranking veterans enjoying their pensions, pay, lump sums and annuities, with 'wives and children . . . to be pensioned, after the death of the heroes themselves' – a memorable instance being the lavish distribution of grants, annuities, and pensions to the Nelson family in 1806, with the enormous lump sum of £90,000 going to Nelson's elder brother to purchase an estate worthy of his new Earldom.[51]

Cobbett would have hailed Knightley as a paragon, the living embodiment of his 'resident *native* gentry' and in Donwell Abbey, set in its estate, he would have identified a precious remnant, one of those 'few' remaining 'good houses'. Knightley is close to his tenants, for the parish of Highbury lies within the Donwell property. He is permanently 'resident', a fixture of the neighbourhood: in Marilyn Butler's words, 'seen in the novel much more continuously than he is heard':

> In the middle distance he is everywhere – conferring with Mr Elton about parish affairs, or with Robert Martin about farming; detected sending apples to Miss Bates, or asking for her errands when he rides to Kingston. Highbury gatherings are not complete without him; unlike Emma, he is always present when the Coles or Eltons entertain.[52]

A visit to London on business brings him hurrying back to 'his farm, and his sheep, and his library, and all the parish to manage'.[53] Running 'the home-farm at Donwell',[54] his everyday concerns are those of Cobbett's ideal, a proprietor 'attached to the soil'. His horses are for use on the farm, rarely to draw a carriage. He is ready to lecture Harriet Smith on 'modes of agriculture',[55] to discuss with Robert Martin 'shows of cattle' and 'new drills'[56] and to speak 'as a farmer' to his brother, reporting to John in fine detail 'what every field was to bear next year . . . the plan of a drain, the change of a fence, the felling of a tree, and the destination of every acre for wheat, turnips or spring corn'.[57] Jane Austen's readers would recognise this as the language of agricultural improvement, of scientific farming, a professionalism regarded as fashionable and public-spirited under the royal patronage of 'Farmer' George and officially sponsored by the Board of Agriculture.* To encourage self-sufficiency in the country's war-time food supplies, the Board commissioned a series of Agricultural Reports surveying farming practice county-by-county. The Report on Surrey, first published in 1809, with a revised edition in 1813, picks out land-owners like Knightley for special praise: 'several of the most considerable and respectable landed proprietors', those who 'reside generally on their estates' and 'introduce and patronise improvements have tended much to advance the agriculture of Surrey'.[58] The tenant at Abbey-Mill Farm, Robert Martin, is an educated yeoman-farmer who shares Knightley's progressive views and, pointedly, Jane Austen makes him a reader of the Agricultural Reports.[59]

The Surrey Report also remarked on the attractions of the country, its healthy 'climate' and 'the general beauty of its scenery'. It was these recom-

---

* Established in August 1793, the Board was set up to encourage scientific farming, e.g. stock-breeding, crop-rotation and manuring, machinery for seed-drilling, drainage systems etc.

mendations, together with its proximity to London, which made Surrey such a desirable location 'for the settlement' of 'commercial men' who had 'made their fortunes'. The process was familiar. In the face of a 'great demand for landed property of small extent', the few large estates were being 'broken down'.[60] Just as Cobbett and others observed, 'the resident *native* gentry' surrendered to the power of money; in Repton's bitter comment, 'the ancient hereditary gentlemen' joined in the 'eager pursuit of gain'.[61] Only sixteen miles from London (Jane Austen gives us this precise distance), in other hands Donwell would be an estate under threat. But Knightley is loyal to his heritage, intends that his patrimony should be passed on intact. Sensitive to the interests of the villagers, with their long-established common rights, he chooses not even to re-route a path running across 'the home meadows . . . if it were to be the means of inconvenience to the Highbury people',[62] a public-spiritedness which marks him out at the very time when land-owners were most heavily engaged in promoting acts of enclosure and blocking ancient rights-of-way.* Tall paling fences were raised, 'not to confine the deer but to exclude mankind', Repton observed.[63] Ferocious notice boards became a feature of the country scene: 'Spring guns and steel traps set here'. Travellers became trespassers. But not in Knightley's little corner of Surrey. Here, the 'rage for improvements' (to borrow the invective of *Rural Rides*) is contained and the old ways of paternalism and liberality prevail.[64] How high a value Jane Austen placed on these qualities we can judge from *Pride and Prejudice*, where the housekeeper's praise of Darcy at Pemberley – 'the best landlord, and the best master . . . that ever lived . . . affable to the poor', a man to whom 'his tenants' give a 'good name' – warms Elizabeth's heart towards him.[65] There is, however, an important difference. In *Pride and Prejudice*, Jane Austen does no more than name the qualities: in *Emma*, we glimpse the detail of what it actually means to be a landowner attached to his heritage and concerned with the welfare of his neighbourhood.

Jane Austen continues this process in the description of Donwell Abbey and its grounds. Long in the family, it is the product of generations of care. Its farming may be up-to-date. But neither the craze for landscape 'improvement' nor the pursuit of money has been allowed to ruin the estate. Retaining the formal style of the late seventeenth and early eighteenth century, it boasts an unspoilt 'abundance of timber in rows and avenues which neither fashion nor extravagance had rooted up'.[66] We are reminded of Rushworth's ambitions in *Mansfield Park*. Attracted by Repton's style of landscaping, he plans to improve 'the prospect' at Sotherton, opening up its views by removing the 'avenue',[67] a scheme that horrifies Fanny Price, stirring her to invoke the

---

* Parliamentary enclosures came in two bursts: in the 1760s and 70s and during the war, this second phase peaking in 1812–14.

famous lines from Cowper: 'Ye fallen avenues, once more I mourn your fate unmerited'.[68] But no such modernisation has disturbed the grounds of Donwell; they boast 'all the old neglect of prospect'. And the Abbey itself, ancient and unchanged, remains in 'its suitable, becoming, characteristic situation, low and sheltered'.[69]

'Characteristic'/'character' is a key term for practitioners of the picturesque, whether travellers, amateur artists or landscape gardeners. According to William Gilpin, the leading authority, the 'characteristic' 'situation' for an abbey, 'intended for meditation', is to be 'hid in the sequestered vale', just as Donwell is.[70] Unlike General Tilney's Abbey at Northanger, lavishly modernised and equipped with the very latest in domestic technology, Knightley's Donwell is, in the manner of ancient buildings, unshowy and lived-in,

> rambling and irregular, with many comfortable and one or two handsome rooms. – It was just what it ought to be, and it looked what is was – and Emma felt an increasing respect for it, as the residence of a family of such true gentility, untainted in blood and understanding.[71]

Owner and building alike, both are true to themselves and transparently and self-evidently 'right'. As Jonathan Bate comments,

> A place that was once consecrated to the spiritual good life, to the vertical relationship between humankind and God, it is now consecrated to the social good life: it has become an emblem of productive and harmonious rural being. Instead of being drawn upward to the heavens, the eye looks out horizontally to the well-ordered environment.[72]

Emma's impressions are reinforced by the wider 'view' across the valley, towards the curve of the river and Abbey-Mill Farm, 'favourably placed and sheltered',

> with all its appendages of prosperity and beauty, its rich pastures, spreading flocks, orchard in blossom, and light column of smoke ascending.[73]

No hint of social distress or disorder here, the scene is harmonious and satisfying, a consort of man and nature, a balance of 'prosperity' and 'beauty', a scene typically, and, in the voice of Jane Austen, emphatically 'English', a 'view' to be contemplated and reflected upon, providing food for thought,

> a sweet view – sweet to the eye and the mind. English verdure, English culture, English comfort, seen under a sun bright, without being oppressive.[74]

The 'culture' in question is neither abstract nor fashionable; patriotically weighted, it is the cultivation of agri*culture*, the land-use and practical improvement so much encouraged during the French wars; and 'comfort' comprehends such workaday features as good soil, a ready water-supply and fish-ponds ('the old Abbey fish-ponds' remain) for the kitchens, shelter from the wind and weather;[75] in short, as Repton explains, 'comfort' is for those, like the Knightleys past and present, 'willing to sacrifice the beauty of prospect for the more solid and permanent advantages of habitable convenience'.[76] Accordingly, while 'fashion' dictates that the fruit and kitchen-gardens be put at a distance from the house, at Donwell they remain comfortably adjacent and the 'pleasure grounds' are relegated to a further remove.[77]

There is an aesthetic dimension too; not Repton's 'beauty of prospect' but Gilpin's contention – here reaffirmed by Jane Austen – that England was just as worthy of painting as Italy. Occasionally, Gilpin would see aspects of Europe in English views. 'The whole scene makes a good Alpine picture',[78] he said, looking towards Box Hill (seven miles from Highbury). But his picturesque tours enumerate the qualities of scene which are distinctively English, the homeland's atmospheric skies and shadowed landscapes much to be preferred by the water-colourist to the harsh Italian light. Hence Jane Austen's sun 'bright, without being oppressive'. Within the Donwell demesne, Abbey-Mill Farm possesses a vernacular charm, its evocative 'column of smoke ascending' – signifying rural peace, prosperity and contentment – found in countless countryside drawings and paintings of the Constable school. As Gilpin pointed out, unlike 'the vast tracts on the continent', 'England . . . is a country only on a small scale' and 'more suited to human vision'.[79] So while fashionable chatter was of European landscapes and landscapists – Salvator Rosa for 'wildness', Claude for 'softness', Poussin for 'majesty' – the English painter's 'love of locality' was, in the words of Edward Dayes (an aesthetic 'Tourist' in the line of Gilpin), to be applauded as an expression of 'amor patriae',[80] an affectionate appreciation of one's native land for which Jane Austen's 'sweet view' is the descriptive and ideological counterpart.

The view to be cherished is the view at home, familiar and well-loved. Jane Austen's patriotic intent is undisguised. Who could remain unaffected by this 'English' scene? Frank Churchill, for one. Within a few pages, he declares himself 'sick of England'; 'would leave it tomorrow, if I could', he confides to Emma, promising her, indifferently, his souvenirs of a European visit: his sketches of 'Swisserland' 'to look at – or my tour to read – or my poem'.[81] These were the fashionable trophies, the treasured mementoes, glimpsing the sublime in Alpine vistas, in the wonder of glaciers and the grandeur of mountain peaks and passes, these foreign sights preferred to the comfortable and undramatic presence of the 'English' scene.

But the promise of these gifts leaves Emma unmoved. By this time they were common currency. Every traveller's album held amateur sketches and amateur poems; as for European tours, there were more than enough, an 'inundation',[82] a complaint echoed by the author of *Alpine Sketches* (1814) at the sight of 'Booksellers windows . . . already crowded with Wanderings, Trips, Tours, Visits, Sketches, and Guides.'[83]

Among the earliest readers of *Emma* Mrs Cage was someone after Jane's heart: 'delighted' with all the characters, she picked out Miss Bates as 'incomparable' and found herself transported: 'at Highbury all day, & I can't help feeling I have just got into a new set of acquaintance'.[84] But above all, there was the enthusiasm of her sailor brothers, both of whom put *Emma* at the top of their list. Francis, his judicious views given pride of place at the head of the 'Opinions' Jane gathered from her family and friends, 'liked it extremely, observing that though there might be more Wit in P & P – & an higher Morality in MP – yet altogether, on account of its peculiar air of Nature throughout, he preferred it to either'.[85] While Francis was able to enjoy *Emma* with his family in their cottage at Alton, Charles was in the Mediterranean slowly making his way home, following the loss of the *Phoenix*. He was in low spirits, caught up (as his diary records) in 'sad & melancholy reflections', dreaming 'of my lost & ever lamented Fanny and of our poor little ones!'.[86] He yearned for England. His copy of *Emma* (he wrote to Jane) 'arrived in time to a moment. I am delighted with her, more so I think than even with my favourite Pride & Prejudice',[87] reading it 'three times' during the passage home.[88] 'Three times' out of respect and affection for his sister's gift, no doubt. But 'three times' also for its evocation of village England in all its locality and parochialism, the flavour of its characters and community, things which must have meant so much to a sailor on the high seas. Did Jane Austen have this in mind herself? On learning that Charles, 'Poor dear Fellow!', had received 'not a Present!' on his birthday in June 1815, she joked about sending him 'all the twelve copies' of *Emma* 'which were to have been dispersed among my near Connections – beginning with the P.R. & ending with Countess Morley'.[89] If any gift could bring comfort to her brother in his remote situation, still grieving the death of his beloved wife, and carry the spirit of the English scene and English life, it was this. Highbury, to borrow the words of Herman Melville, 'is not down on any map; true places never are'.[90]

Afterword

a sweet view – sweet to the eye and the mind. English verdure,
English culture, English comfort, seen under a sun bright, without
being oppressive.

Emma, p. 360

Here, Jane Austen insists upon the Englishness of the 'view', its qualities observed in 'the mind' as well as by 'the eye', under an illuminating sun which is 'bright' but not 'oppressive'. This, as Jonathan Bate reminds us, is the 'temperate climate' of a 'liberal society' (Bate, 1999, p. 545) and a further chapter on *Emma* would treat the political significance of inherited estates, and the eighteenth and nineteenth-century conventions of discourse in prose and poetry relating features of the landscape and property to the moral and political state of the nation. Such geopolitical ideas were sharpened at the time of the French Revolution which threw into relief values of rootedness, tradition, ancient rights, patronage, hierarchy etc, identified as being quintessentially English and epitomised in Donwell, both the Abbey itself and its estate. For recent scholarly discussion see particularly Everett (1994), his valuable chapter 6, 'The View of Donwell Abbey'; Fulford (1996 and 1998); Bate (1999, 2000); Helmsinger (1997); Hunt (1992); Paulson (1982) and Williamson (1987).

11

Persuasion: The Righting and Re-Writing of History

Nelson was once Britannia's god of war,
And still should be so, but the tide is turn'd;
There's no more to be said of Trafalgar,
Tis with our hero quietly inurn'd;
Because the army's grown more popular,
At which the naval people are concern'd;
Besides, the Prince is all for the land-service,
Forgetting Duncan, Nelson, Howe, and Jervis.

Byron, *Don Juan* (canto i, octave iv)

Writing in September 1818, Byron announced this great sea-change in national sentiment at the very opening of *Don Juan*. It was a shift of loyalties that Jane Austen had observed as well; and in *Sanditon*, her last, uncompleted novel, begun early in 1817, the turning of the tide in favour of the Army, at the Navy's expense, is alluded to lightly. Mr Parker, Sanditon's speculative promoter, is keen to keep his new seaside resort abreast of fashion. He regrets using the name 'Trafalgar House' for his new home, 'for Waterloo is more the thing now', and Waterloo he is keeping 'in reserve', ready for a 'Waterloo Crescent' for visitors the following year.[1]

It was no mystery why Wellington had taken over as the nation's hero, why Strand Bridge, started in 1811, should be renamed Waterloo Bridge by Act of Parliament in 1816. Military success was fresh in memory whereas the great naval victories were events of the past. Since Trafalgar and St Domingo the naval record was tame and unmemorable, with no engagement of such magnitude and none to provide such a stirring brew of tragedy and triumph. In response to Napoleon's concentration of naval power, Britain's strategy at sea was one of containment. From Venice to Toulon, along the Channel ports, to Antwerp and the Texel, and northwards to the Baltic, the French fleets, growing in size,* were held in tight blockade, a policy which was

---

* Following Trafalgar and St Domingo, the French fleet was reduced to thirty-five ships-of-the-line. But 'Bonaparte flung himself into the task of out-building the Royal Navy'. By 1813 his fleet of ships-of-the-line had grown to eighty ready for sea, with a further thirty-five under construction, a total of 115. The comparable British total was 102 (Glover, 1973, p. 19).

successful but unspectacular. In the closing stages of the Long War, the great victories and battle honours were won on the mainland of Europe, the scene of Napoleon's final defeat. In these events, the Navy played a purely supporting role for the British and allied armies fighting near the coast. Beyond this, the Navy was also active in trade protection and control. But all this was routine and unexciting, certainly to the nation at large. In the words of the *Naval Chronicle*, by the Summer of 1814 the Army had 'overtaken the royal navy' 'in the race for glory'.[2] By how much was measurable: *The Aegis of England* (1817) by Maurice Evans, a Navy and Army Agent, listed *The Triumphs of the Late War as they Appear in the Thanks of Parliament*. Of the nineteen naval Triumphs, as many as fifteen were achieved up to and including Trafalgar, while in the remaining nine years of the war, only four were added. By comparison, the Peninsular campaign and Waterloo on their own, brought a total of eight Triumphs for the Army.

Inter-service rivalries and the disparagement of the Navy became a matter of Parliamentary debate in 1815–16. It arose from Castlereagh's proposal for a National Monument to be raised in gratitude for those 'heroes' who fell in the Battle of Waterloo: 'whether regarded in its moral, in its political, or in its military character, [it] was the greatest action which the British arms had ever performed'. Coming only eleven days after the Battle itself, it was hardly surprising the Castlereagh's rousing words should be answered by the House with 'Hear, hear!'[3] However, by the following February, Castlereagh had discovered the folly of such a one-sided gesture and, somewhat nervously, tried to set things right, proposing a similar Monument to express the nation's 'gratitude . . . for the services which had been performed by the navy during the late eventful war'.[4] He knew he was treading on thin ice and was careful to argue the case for equal treatment, urging Members 'to avoid any thing that seemed to cast but a shade of difference in favour of one service over the other'.[5] He pointed out that with a Monument each, 'The two professions could then stand in the view of posterity upon the same point of elevation', 'which would preclude the most distant suspicion of preference between the two services'.[6] The second of these statements he led up to with an elaborate explanation of the Navy's unspectacular, yet essential, role in the latter stages of the war. Castlereagh's presentation of the case was cautious and diplomatic. Nonetheless, the Member for Appleby, George Tierney, who regarded himself as a naval spokesman and, twenty years in Parliament, carried some authority, was unplaced and he put his complaint baldly: 'The services of the navy were last year forgotten, when a monument was voted to commemorate the victory of Waterloo'.[7] He was afraid that 'a partiality' might be 'manifested for one service to the prejudice of the other'[8] and suggested that the solution might be 'the erection of a church, in which the names of our naval and military heroes should be commemorated . . .'.[9] The debate rumbled on until June 1816 and a committee was charged with carrying matters further.

The Navy was itself highly sensitive to the question of its standing. Four years earlier, in July 1812, Vice-Admiral Sir Sidney Smith had written bluntly to Liverpool, the Prime Minister, advising him that having destroyed 'all opposition on the coasts of the four quarters of the globe', the Navy had 'worked itself out of employment' and was now left to play a supporting role to 'the Army in all its operations'.[10] It was not just that the Navy felt over-shadowed. More seriously, its prestige was badly dented in its latest theatre of action, the War of 1812 against America (touched on, for a moment only, in *Mansfield Park*).* In military terms, judged alongside the Napoleonic struggle, this was no more than a side-show. For the Navy, however, it ranked as a humiliating episode. Britain's mastery of the seas was challenged by an American force which consisted, at the opening of the war, of no more than eight frigates and twelve sloops. But the bare figures are deceptive. The American frigates were super-frigates, exceptionally powerful, utilising hulls the size of a British second-rate; and their navy as a whole was highly professional with valuable operational experience in fighting the Barbary pirates of North Africa.

Thinking of the Americans as disobedient children to be taught a lesson, to its dismay, the British Navy found itself out-sailed, out-manoeuvred and out-gunned. A historian of the period, Edward Baines, captures the shame of this reversal:

> At the moment when America ventured to declare war against the most powerful maritime state in the world, her own navy (if navy it could be called) did not include one single line of battle ship, and the utter annihilation of her frigates and smaller vessels was predicted in this country with a vaunting confidence that gave increased poignancy to the disappointment and disasters which Great Britain was doomed in the prosecution of her naval campaigns to endure.[11]

The first engagement, a single combat in August 1812, was ominous. It ended with the capture of the *Guerrière* (38) by the USS *Constitution* (44). For the Americans, it was a historic triumph. As Baines puts it, they celebrated

---

* Picking up a newspaper, Tom Bertram asks Dr Grant his 'opinion' of the 'strange business in America' (p. 119), this being the outbreak and early events of the war, 'strange' because the United States declared war on 8 June unaware (on account of the six weeks it took for the news to cross the Atlantic) that Britain had just dropped the root cause of the dispute. These were the Orders in Council which restricted American trade with Napoleonic Europe and authorised the searching of American vessels for British sailors. Since Sir Thomas Bertram's voyage home from Antigua was made in September/October 1812, he would have been at risk from the Americans as well as the French.

a victory achieved over the lords of the ocean – over those who till now had claimed that element as their own, and had driven from it all who dared to dispute their maritime rights and dominion.[12]

The loss of the *Guerrière* struck deep. Benjamin Haydon remembered 'dwelling' on the news for 'a whole morning, in sullen disgust. I felt as if I had been grossly insulted. I felt indignation & detestation at Dacres [the Captain] for not sinking [for not fighting to the finish] – such were the feelings of every one in the Kingdom'.[13] This is Haydon thirty years after the event, still complaining of the *Guerrière*'s surrender![14]

Years of superiority had bred the presumption of success. The popular reaction in Britain was one of disbelief and anger, while in government circles the loss was regarded as nothing less than a 'Naval disaster'.[15] *The Times* was scathing: 'Never before in the history of the world did an English frigate strike* to an American . . . Good God!'[16] With the country 'ridiculously sanguine and secure', it was a moment when 'Our navy was to drive the pigmy fleets of America from the Ocean', the *Edinburgh Review* reflected in 1814.[17] Instead, came news of defeat, a shock to the profession as well as to the nation. It monopolised the pages of the *Naval Chronicle*. The loss of the *Guerrière*, 'one of our stoutest frigates', was a disaster 'rare in our naval annals', an event that 'so far compromised' 'the character of the service' that lengthy explanations were called for.[18] Why was our American squadron not already reinforced? Why was a blockade not in place? (no easy task, given the extent of the American seaboard). With the threat of 'these immense frigates', 'further misfortunes' were only to be expected and they duly followed.[19] Two months later, in October 1812, the *Macedonian* (38) was shot to pieces and surrendered to the USS *United States* (44); and on 29 December, in the third frigate engagement, the *Java* (38) was taken by the USS *Constitution*. The next issue of the *Naval Chronicle* was dominated by these further disasters, regarded by one correspondent as 'a national disgrace'.[20] Letter after letter came in from sailors distressed by these losses and the editor announced the *Chronicle*'s endeavour 'to collect every document we could procure respecting The American Navy',[21] information which, it was hoped, could show the way to success.

Naval voices were heard in Parliament too. During the Commons debate of 18 February 1813, George Canning, with past experience as a Treasurer of the Navy and as a Minister for Foreign Affairs, attacked the Government for its unreadiness in the face of a long-expected war. Amongst the public at large, he sensed 'feelings of shame and indignation', a 'wholesome' indignation he called it,

---

* Striking was the lowering of a ship's colours, a sign of surrender.

which ought to be cherished and maintained. It cannot be too deeply felt that the sacred spell of the invincibility of the British navy was broken by those unfortunate captures: and however speedily we must all wish the war to terminate, I hope I shall not be considered as sanguinary and unfeeling when I express my devout wish that it may not be concluded before we have re-established the character of our naval superiority, and smothered in victories the disasters which we have now to lament, and to which we are so little habituated.[22]

In private, Canning would have heard the contempt and indignation of diplomats such as George Jackson, who felt that 'the conduct of the naval war against the Americans . . . would disgrace the sixth form of Eton or Westminster'.[23]

As further losses followed, the Navy's reputation sagged. The Earl of Darnley, an inveterate commentator on naval affairs, struck a chord of eloquent dismay: 'The charm of invincibility had now been broken' and the 'consecrated standard' of Great Britain 'no longer floated victorious on the main'.[23] Early in 1813, American privateers appeared off the coast of Portugal, capturing transports and supply ships, losses which led Wellington to complain bitterly at naval slackness and inefficiency, and gave the Army an opportunity to crow. The military historian Fortescue pointed to a 'dangerous hostility' between the services:

> Hitherto the Navy had always treated the Army with contempt; and its arrogance had been extravagantly heightened by its own glorious successes, and by the innumerable failures of the red-coats. Now the tables were turned. The Army was triumphant; the Navy was humiliated; and human nature asserted itself at once. 'I think,' wrote Larpent after recounting the news of the American victories at sea, 'I think the Army rather rejoice, and laugh aside at all this falling on the Navy, as they bullied so much before.'[25]

(Francis Seymour Larpent was Wellington's Judge-Advocate in Spain.)

Far from ending 'speedily', as Canning had hoped, the war wound on inconclusively for another two years, with actions off the Atlantic coast and on the Great Lakes and a series of raids aimed at destroying coastal towns, expeditions which included the capture of Washington and the burning of its public buildings, a vengeful policy which aroused considerable dismay in Britain. But the Admirals on the spot took a dim view of American resistance. Sir George Cockburn, blockading the central Atlantic coastline, was outraged at what he called the 'dastardly and provoking manner' in which the American citizens chose to defend themselves. They 'took every opportunity of firing with their rifles from behind trees or haystacks, or from the windows of their houses upon our boats, whenever rowing along the shore within their reach, or upon our people [the ordinary sailors] when employed watering'.[26] Cockburn's response was savage retaliation, setting fire to their homes and seizing their stores of food. The Commander-in-Chief on the North America station, Admiral Sir Alexander Cochrane, proved no less ferocious. In 1814, his orders to the Squadron Commanders 'required and directed [them] to destroy and lay waste such towns and districts upon the coast as you may find'. This was what he called 'retributory justice'.[27]

The American War proved costly for both sides and fruitless too. There was no victory. The United States failed in its ambition to seize Lower Canada; Britain made no conquests; and the Treaty of Ghent, signed in December 1814, amounted to little more than an agreement to stop fighting and return to the pre-war *status quo.*

These were events on which the Austens were well-informed through the sailor brothers and their circle of naval friends. American privateers were a growing threat to British merchantmen. In the Autumn of 1812, Francis, commanding the *Elephant* (74), was taken from his blockading duties at the mouth of the Scheldt and dispatched to cruise off the Azores. His most notable success, small as it was, was the capture (on 28 December) of a schooner-privateer out of Boston, the *Swordfish* (12), following a chase of eleven hours, upwards of a hundred miles. As successes in the American war were then few and far between, his official letter, reporting this engagement to the Admiralty, was made much of, appearing first in the *London Gazette* and then in the *Naval Chronicle.*[28]

Charles, too, was qualified to talk knowledgeably of the war. He had served for six-and-a-half years on the North American station, for part of that time as Flag Captain to the Commander-in-Chief, Rear-Admiral Warren, and had long experience of intercepting American vessels suspected of trading with Napoleonic Europe. He was familiar with the expanse of sea between the naval stations at Bermuda and Nova Scotia and knew the British Captains and their ships. Of these, the most admired was the *Shannon* (38) commanded by Philip Broke, a friend of Charles since their days together at the Naval Academy in the early 1790s. Broke's name passed into history on 1 June 1813 when he halted the succession of British frigate defeats with the capture of the USS *Chesapeake* (36, but mounting up to 54 guns), a victory gained within the space of fifteen minutes, thanks to Broke's gunnery expertise and his highly-trained crew using effective gun-sights purchased out of his own pocket. The *Naval Chronicle,* grasping at this first opportunity to salvage professional and national pride, went overboard in calling it 'the most brilliant act of heroism ever performed', putting an end to the Americans' 'short career of maritime glory'.[29] The mood of optimism was widespread. A Yankee song marking the famous victory of the USS *Constitution* over the

Guerrière was hijacked and parodied in '*Shannon* and *Chesapeake*', a ballad so popular that it entered the song book of Harrow School and was a favourite at Rugby during the time of Thomas Hughes in the mid-1830's.*

In the last months of the war, however, we hear from Jane of gloomy predictions from Henry's circle (he mixed with naval and military men as well as city merchants and bankers) on the likelihood of the war's continuation and the possibility of a disastrous outcome:

> *His* veiw, & the veiw of those he mixes with, of Politics, is not chearful – with regard to an American war I mean; – they consider it as certain, & as what is to ruin us. The [?Americans] cannot be conquered, & we shall only be teaching them the skill in War which they may now want. We are to make them good Sailors & Soldiers, & [?gain] nothing ourselves. – If we *are* to be ruined, it cannot be helped – but I place my hope of better things on a claim to the protection of Heaven, as a Religious Nation, a Nation inspite of much Evil improving in Religion, which I cannot beleive the Americans to possess.[30]

The 'teaching them the skill in War' and making 'them good Sailors & Soldiers' refers to a long-standing contention on the British side that the American Navy contained a large number of British deserters, trained seamen and marines who had been attracted by better pay and conditions and now provided the skilled core of the American forces. While the Americans admitted to having British-trained crewmen, they argued that these were American nationals who had been illegally impressed into the Royal Navy.[31]

Victory or defeat and 'the protection of Heaven' were heartfelt matters on which Jane was prepared to reveal her deepest hopes and fears. Her correspondent, Martha Lloyd – in 1828, the second wife of Francis Austen – was then staying at a naval household in Bath, the home of a mutual acquaintance, Captain Whitely-Deans-Dundas. The future direction of the war was of wide concern. If it did take a turn for the worse, further naval reinforcements would be needed to face an American Navy now quadrupled in size and Francis might well have been recalled to active service. As it was, the Austens had a further reason for watching the progress of the peace negotiations at Ghent, which began in August 1814. Heading the three British Plenipotentiaries was Francis' old patron, Vice-Admiral Lord Gambier, chosen to reassure the country that its maritime interests were in good hands – although, in reality, Gambier acted wholly on instructions received from London.

---

* Hughes brings it into *Tom Brown's Schooldays* (1857) as a patriotic chorus enthusiastically sung by the boys (p. 120). The words and music are given in *The Oxford Book of Sea Songs* (1986), ed. Roy Palmer, p. 182.

The Peace Treaty, signed on Christmas Eve, was more an occasion for relief than celebration, a mood caught in the *Naval Chronicle*. The Editor observed that the 'strictures on the state of our navy, and the American war' planned for the Preface to the July-December 1814 volume would now be dropped.[32] But quite apart from this ignominious war, other things contributed to the decline in naval morale and its effect upon the public. One was the simple fact of war-weariness, 'the irksome eighteen years' confinement between wooden walls', as Admiral Pellew put it.[33] Desertion was a growing problem, 'running from King's ships' a spreading 'disease', one correspondent wrote in the *Naval Chronicle*.[34] 'Zeal and energy' were found 'wanting', and this among the officers as well as the men.[35] The years of inactivity set the Navy's old fighting spirit in decline. Captain Charles Napier reported that many officers believed 'the falling off of discipline' was to be attributed 'to the length of the war, and the entire disappearance of the enemy, leaving the Navy little or nothing to do'. Whether it was this, or 'the age of the officers', Napier came to a chastening view:

> but it is beyond a doubt, that at the conclusion of the war, more than one half of our ships of the line were in such bad order, and so infamously manned, as to render them unequal to contend with a disciplined enemy; they would have beat a French or a Spanish ship, who were worse than themselves; but I will stake my existence, had an American line of battle ship fallen in with one half of them, they would have been taken . . .[36]

Although the first American ships-of-the-line – 74's, carrying up to 96 guns – were launched only after the war, Napier based his conclusion, in the Summer of 1815, on what he already knew of the size and strength of American frigates. Originally designed as 74's and modified to a rating of 44 guns, the *United States* and the *Constitution* were by far the fastest and most powerful of their class in the world, with up to 62 gun-ports and approaching the length and sail-spread of a British 74. According to Captain Dillon, when the captured USS *President* (44) arrived at Spithead in March 1815, such was its size and fire-power that the vessel 'caused a sensation'.[37]

With the cessation of arms in mid-March 1815, the American War came to an end. On the 29th of the month, Jane Austen completed *Emma*. In mid-June, Napoleon was finally defeated at Waterloo. The following month he surrendered to Captain Frederick Maitland of the *Bellerophon* (74) off Rochefort. At Tor Bay, on 7 August, Napoleon was moved to the *Northumberland* (74), for the voyage to St Helena. On 8 August, the very day that the London newspapers announced 'Bonaparte has sailed', Jane Austen began *Persuasion*.[38]

Against this background of naval defeat and humiliation and, over a longer period, the decline in naval spirit, Jane Austen set out to write a determinedly morale-boosting novel, a story designed (with an eye on the sailor brothers) to show the Navy in its best light, recalling the great days of Trafalgar and St Domingo, high points in the careers of Admiral Croft and Wentworth. Opening as it does in the summer of 1814 – with Napoleon despatched to Elba and the Navy scaling down – *Persuasion* was also designed to show the profession in peacetime. The return of naval men to civilian life in large numbers, after virtually twenty years of war, was a social phenomenon of some magnitude. Unlike the ordinary seamen, these returning officers were not leaving the Navy. No longer required on active service, they remained at home on half-pay. To use Jane Austen's terminology, what was their personal and professional 'character'?[39] What would be their impact on society? How would they be received and how would they fit in? How do their naval 'manners' differ from the manners of polite society?[40] And how are these naval 'manners' to be interpreted? What kind of husbands do they make? What do they look for in their wives? And what marks out a naval wife – the examples are Mrs Harville and Mrs Croft – and how are they shaped by the experience of a naval marriage? These, or something like them, are the questions Jane Austen aimed to answer in *Persuasion*, arranging these aspects of the naval theme around the imaginative and emotional heart of the novel, the story of Anne Elliot, destined, after much suffering, to glory 'in being a sailor's wife'.[41]

These issues of personal and professional 'character' are decisive in the story's pre-history, the events of that momentous 'summer of 1806'[42] when Anne Elliot was 'persuaded'[43] to break off her original engagement to Wentworth, newly-promoted Commander for his part in the British victory at St Domingo. The compelling 'persuasion' was not her father's silent disapproval, his thinking the connection 'a very degrading alliance' (an unpropertied Wentworth ranking far below the offspring of an established Baronetcy), for this was an objection Anne was ready to resist.[44] What drove her to break with Wentworth was Lady Russell's anxiety, amounting to near panic, at the thought of her god-child taking a sailor for her husband. A sailor, moreover, of no fortune or family, a young officer wholly dependent for his success upon 'the chances of a most uncertain profession' and without interest, having 'no connexions to secure even his farther rise in that profession'.* In Lady Russell's eyes, this was a man who would sink his wife 'into a state of

---

* These fictional circumstances, on the money side, are a replication of life not unusual in war-time England. An exactly similar situation can be followed in the Journal of Betsey Wynne. Aged sixteen and in love with a penniless Captain, she sets down her predicament: 'Alas, how will this matter end. If he does not make prize money, it will never do, I should not mind it but my parents would never consent to it without he gets a pretty good fortune.' 'The Spanish War is a great disappointment for us. But it will bring in prize money, a necessary thing for the accomplishment of my happiness.' Entries for 4 and 26 August 1796 (Fremantle, 1937, ii. 119-20, 124). Betsey's story is worth following in full and is referred to later in this chapter.

most wearing, youth-killing dependance!'.[45] Wentworth's confidence, his 'intelligence, spirit and brilliancy',[46] the energy and liveliness which appeal so strongly to Anne, only serve to excite Lady Russell's fears:

> he was confident that he should soon be rich; – full of life and ardour, he knew that he should soon have a ship, and soon be on a station that would lead to every thing he wanted. He had always been lucky; he knew he should be so still. – Such confidence, powerful in its own warmth, and bewitching in the wit which often expressed it, must have been enough for Anne; but Lady Russell saw it very differently. – His sanguine temper, and fearlessness of mind, operated very differently on her. She saw in it but an aggravation of the evil. It only added a dangerous character to himself. He was brilliant, he was headstrong. – Lady Russell had little taste for wit; and of any thing approaching to imprudence a horror.[47]

The irony that Jane Austen leaves unspoken here is that the traits which make Wentworth appear so 'dangerous' to Lady Russell are the very qualities of character which won British Captains mastery of the seas. As for Wentworth himself, 'genius and ardour' set him on a 'prosperous path' to prize-money; and in combat he 'distinguished himself, and early gained the other step in rank' (to Captain). Having watched the 'navy lists and newspapers', with their report of 'successive captures', Anne 'could not doubt his being rich'.[48] The elaborating detail, the precise measure of Wentworth's success, comes later in the novel: his promotion to Captain in 1808 on his posting into a frigate, the *Laconia*, at the age of twenty-five; and his prize-money, when he returns to England in 1813, amounting to £25,000. Riches and naval rank are social advantages and Jane Austen invokes them in closing the story. Now a gentleman of 'independent fortune', Wentworth's standing is 'as high in his profession as merit and activity could place him' (since promotion above Captain was by seniority alone). Nonetheless, what finally carries the day with Sir Walter is Wentworth's 'superiority of appearance', an attribute to match Anne's 'superiority of rank'. This, and a 'well-sounding name' with its aristocratic associations,[49]* brings him up to the mark as a son-in-law to be entered into Sir Walter's 'volume of honour'.[50]**

However, the focus of the novel is not on the process by which Wentworth gains social and financial acceptability in the eyes of Sir Walter, but on the way in which Anne and Wentworth gradually come together again with a new

---

* 'Wentworth' was also the family name of the Earl of Strafford, a connection which is made by Sir Walter (p. 23), informed by his 'favourite volume', 'Dugdale' (pp. 3, 4). This was William Dugdale's *The Ancient Usage in Bearing of Such Ensigns of Honour as are Commonly Called Arms* (1682). The edition of 1811 contains *A Catalogue of the Baronets of this Kingdom of England*, one of whom was William Wentworth, the current Earl, listed on page 70.

** 'honour' carries a punning reference to *Honour* in the title of Dugdale.

understanding of each other's qualities and a rediscovery of their love. We are warned of an uphill path. At twenty-seven, Anne has lost her looks. Meeting her again for the first time Wentworth finds her 'wretchedly altered'. After eight years, he still burns with the resentment of her refusal, regards it as 'a feebleness of character . . . which his own decided, confident temper could not endure', and blames it on Anne's having listened to Lady Russell and given way to 'over-persuasion. It had been weakness and timidity.' Now 'being turned to shore', his object is to marry and settle down, his heart open to 'any pleasing young woman who came his way, excepting Anne Elliot. This was his only secret exception . . .'[51] But, in time, Wentworth's resentment fades, Anne is 'blessed with a second spring of youth and beauty'[52] and we witness the transforming power of love. Yet the sadness of the story (Jane Austen calls it 'this little history of sorrowful interest') – Anne's awareness of lost years and loneliness – is scarcely lifted by the happy ending, and there is a sombreness to the novel as a whole.[53]

The first picture we have of the Navy's homecoming, its peacetime reception in England, close on the formal ending of the war (the Peace of Paris was signed on 30 May 1814), comes in chapter 3. The scene is heavy with irony, the satire caustic. Having preserved the country throughout the war, the Navy, in the person of some 'rich Admiral', as yet unknown, is now to save the bankrupt Baronet in time of peace. Opportunism, not gratitude is in the air. There is no hint of patriotism, not even the slightest show of *amor patriae*. In a minor comedy of 'persuasion', the naval virtues are recited, not those of ardour, zeal and gallantry, but those of 'responsible tenants', men with 'very liberal notions',[54] 'so neat and careful in their ways'.[55] Sir Walter's creatures, the aptly named Mr Shepherd and Mrs Clay, reassure him. Even so, the Baronet remains reluctant and grudging, unwilling to allow even a naval tenant free use (technically, the 'privileges') of the Kellynch house and grounds. All this is too much for Anne and her first words in the novel are spoken on the Navy's behalf:

> 'The navy, I think, who have done so much for us, have at least an equal claim with any other set of men, for all the comforts and all the privileges which any home can give. Sailors work hard enough for their comforts, we must all allow'.[56]

Mild and unemphatic, nonetheless the rebuke is sufficient to introduce Anne as the conscience of Kellynch, the only one to value the Navy for its service to the nation rather than for profit, in Mr Shepherd's naval image as a 'prize' to be exploited: 'If a rich Admiral were to come in our way, Sir Walter . . .'.[57] In retrospect, we are also to understand Anne's intervention as one of the clues to the survival of her love for Wentworth. A second clue soon follows when she promptly identifies the prospective tenant, Admiral Croft, as a 'rear admiral of the white' who took part 'in the Trafalgar action' and has been 'stationed several years' 'in the East Indies',[58]* precisely the service history to catch her eye in the listing of promotions and postings given in the newspapers and Navy List, details which would hold an importance for her and stay in her mind, for Admiral Croft is married to Wentworth's sister, Sophia.

Anne's remonstration is to no effect. Mr Shepherd and Mrs Clay give it a 'Very true' and an 'Oh! certainly'. Her father concedes that 'The Profession has its utility' but, without a pause, goes on to list the ways in which he finds the Navy 'offensive':

> First, as being the means of bringing persons of obscure birth into undue distinction, and raising men to honours which their fathers and grandfathers never dreamt of; and secondly, as it cuts up a man's youth and vigour most horribly; a sailor grows old sooner than any other man; I have observed it all my life.[59]

This speech, running in full to over thirty lines, is a passage of high comedy, continuing the portrait which Jane Austen sets up in the opening pages, the Baronet as a man possessed – 'Vanity was the beginning and end of Sir Walter Elliot's character; vanity of person and of situation' – the very embodiment of a Jonsonian humour, a characterisation which is thin, glittering and unforgettable.[60]

'Vanity' is at the heart of his 'objection' to the naval route of upward mobility, the 'raising' of men 'of obscure birth' 'to honours which their fathers and grandfathers never dreamt of'.[61] The 'Lord St Ives' of his story is readily identified as a composite of Lord St Vincent (the former Sir John Jervis), First Lord of the Admiralty 1801–04, and Nelson, created Baron Nelson of the Nile in November 1798. (At the time, Nelson was a Rear-Admiral. As in the Army, a peerage was so highly regarded that an officer would usually be referred to by his title rather than by his rank.) Just as Lord St Ives' father was 'a country curate', so Nelson was famously the son of a Norfolk clergyman, his humble origin being a feature of the Nelson story, his success owing nothing to the privilege of birth. This is the kind of recent ennoblement to which Sir Walter, as a Baronet, finds himself obliged 'to give place'.[62]

---

* That Admiral Croft is a Rear-Admiral of the White would also indicate to Jane Austen's readers how old he was. In a time-based system of promotion, Flag officers of similar rank could be assumed to be of roughly similar age and an average would place Admiral Croft in his early to mid-forties. As we learn from the first page of the novel, Sir Walter is exactly fifty-four and there is a minor comedy in his view of Admiral Croft as a 'Poor old gentleman' suffering from 'Gout and decrepitude!' (*Persuasion*, p. 166). We know from his own lips that Sir Walter has made the same mistake before, guessing the forty-year-old Admiral Baldwin ('that old fellow') to be not less than sixty (ibid., p. 20).

Not that there has been any breach of precedence, for a Baronet is a commoner, first in rank among the gentry and lowest in the scale of hereditary titles. Sir Walter's objection is on the grounds of upstart creation, a point which Jane Austen establishes in the opening pages. 'Baronetage' in hand, Sir Walter looks with 'pity and contempt' at 'the almost endless creations of the last century' and comforts himself with 'the limited remnant of the earliest patents',[63] those few Baronet families which, like his own, still survive, the Elliots from 'the first year of Charles II'.[64*] In short, Sir Walter's 'vanity' of 'situation' stems from a title conferred in the seventeenth-century on a family, 'ancient and respectable', founded long before that, whereas the tide of naval honours offends him as a freak of the present day.

The language of his 'objection' is familiar. It echoes the charges levelled against Pitt for 'debasing the character of the Upper House with a flood of social inferiors',[65] and 'outnumbering . . . the ancient and hereditary nobles of the land', 'inundating' the Lords 'with a crowd of low born persons'.[66] These accusations relate to the peerages conferred by Pitt (most of them for political advantage) during his first Ministry (1784–1801), with a high point of scandal in the years 1796 and 1797, when thirty-five peerages were conferred. Similar protests arose during Addington's Ministry (1801–04), Pitt's second Ministry (1804–06), Greville's 'Ministry of all the Talents' (1806–07) and in 1814 and 1815, the very moment of *Persuasion,* with the 'victory' distribution over those last two years of thirty new peerages. Eleven of these, given for distinguished naval or military service, were beyond criticism – other than from such snobbish and unpatriotic backwoodsmen as Sir Walter, condemned out of his own mouth.

The second naval episode – Wentworth amongst the Musgroves at Uppercross – could not be more different. Ignorant of naval matters, the household forms an appreciative audience. Jane Austen toys with a classic scene of romantic comedy, the hero returned from the wars to a roomful of young ladies (the Musgrove daughters, Henrietta and Louisa, plus their cousins, the Hayter daughters, unnamed and unnumbered) ready to fall at his feet. Wentworth, flattered and amused, is eager to oblige. He claims the hero's privilege: 'His profession qualified him, his disposition led him, to talk'.[67] He plays to the gallery with tales of success and hair-raising adventures, moving the Miss Musgroves to 'exclamations of pity and horror'.[68] To all this, Anne is a silent and sorrowing observer. Her pain is less at the sight of Wentworth basking in the glow of attention than at the reminders of the past

---

* This dates the Elliot baronetcy to 1660 when Charles II was restored. Charles used the rank to reward those who had stayed loyal to the Stuart cause during the years of his exile, 1649-60. Of the 864 Baronets listed in Dugdale (1682), 159 had been created in 1660.

which arise from his talk of naval life. This is not confined to heroics. The Musgrove sisters enquire about domesticities and Wentworth is amused to answer them in their own terms (as any Captain could, having responsibility for every detail of his ship's fitting out, from its ammunition, masts, cordage etc. to its water and provisions):

> as to the manner of living on board, daily regulations, food, hours, &c.; and their surprise at his accounts, at learning the degree of accommodation and arrange-ment which was practicable, drew from him some pleasant ridicule, which reminded Anne of the early days when she too had been ignorant, and she too had been accused of supposing sailors to be living on board without any thing to eat, or any cook to dress it if there were, or any servant to wait, or any knife and fork to use.[69]

This raising of the past continues when the sisters produce their own copy of the Navy List ('the first that had ever been at Uppercross'[70] – procured, we are to assume, in anticipation of Wentworth's visit) and hunt through it for details of his ships, his first command being the *Asp*, a sloop which he joined in 1806 following the break with Anne, and then the *Laconia*, a frigate.

This chapter is dense in naval detail. Admiral Croft praises the durability of 'old built sloops' – the unspoken comparison being with the more recent war-time vessels, which were less seaworthy because the shortage of good timber meant that fir and other inferior wood was used.[71] Wentworth reads aloud from the Navy List about the *Laconia*, 'the little statement of her name and rate, and present non-commissioned class' (meaning that it is now out of commission, no longer in service, and looked after by a skeleton crew).[72] We hear of Wentworth's service in the West Indies, his success in 'taking priva-teers'[73] and in capturing a French frigate (a notable capture for a sloop) and bringing it into the naval base at Plymouth, his 'pleasant days' in the *Laconia* ('How fast I made money in her'), 'off the Western Islands' (not the Hebrides but the Azores, known at this time as the Western Isles or Islands) a cruising-ground for Francis in the *Elephant*, in 1812 – in search of American prey – and 'in the Mediterranean'.[74]

Anne is not the only person affected by Wentworth's reminiscences. They remind Mrs Musgrove of her son Dick, who died two years before, aged nine-teen. The elements of his story are given in chapter 6: 'sent to sea, because he was stupid and unmanageable on shore', he was such a midshipman 'as every Captain wishes to get rid of' and had, after several moves, arrived at the *Laconia*. During the six months he was under Wentworth's 'influence' he had 'written the only two letters which his father and mother had ever received from him during the whole of his absence; that is to say, the only two disinterested letters; all the rest had been mere applications for money'.[75] Having heard that Wentworth is coming to visit the Crofts at Kellynch, Mrs Musgrove re-reads Dick's letters, including his 'strong, though not perfectly well spelt praise' of Wentworth 'as "a fine dashing felow, only two perticular about the school-master"'.[76] At Uppercross, the sight of Wentworth brings it all back and Wentworth sits down alongside Mrs Musgrove ('of a comfortable substantial size, infinitely more fitted by nature to express good cheer and good humour, than tenderness'),[77] to attend 'to her large fat sighings over the destiny of a son, whom alive nobody had cared for'.[78]

The guying of Mrs Musgrove continues in the next paragraph with a disquisition on the 'unbecoming conjunctions, which reason will patronize in vain – which taste cannot tolerate, – which ridicule will seize'.[79] Does Mrs Musgrove really deserve such a flaying? A trace of Swift or Pope has entered the scene. Was this because Jane Austen still carried a residue of irritation, the memory of an annoying incident, also naval in its connections, from ten years before? This was the occasion in 1805 when Jane Austen and her mother paid a courtesy call in Bath on the Earl and Countess of Leven, whose son, Lord David Balgonie, had served as a Midshipman under Charles. On the morning of their call, the Austen ladies were kept waiting in 'an empty Drawing-room' until 'in came his Lordship, not knowing who we were, to apologise for the servant's mistake, & to tell a Lie himself, that Lady Leven was not within'. But on their way out, they bumped into her Ladyship (like Mrs Musgrove 'a stout woman') coming out of the dining-parlour and 'were obliged to attend her back to it, & pay our visit over again ... By this means we had the pleasure of hearing Charles's praise twice over; they think themselves excessively obliged to him, & estimate him so highly as to wish Ld Balgonie when he is quite recovered, to go out to him' (Charles then having been posted to Bermuda).[80]*

The 'naval' importance of Dick's story is to remind us that yes, there could be duffers, dunderheads and ne'er-do-wells amongst the youngsters at sea, that they were not all as bright, zealous and successful as William Price; and that, fortunately, there were Captains as responsible and good-hearted as Wentworth to care for the youngsters in their charge. Readers of Southey's *Nelson* would remember this too about a great naval hero. In the second chapter, Southey describes Nelson's care for the seamanship of the young Midshipmen and his concern of their 'nautical studies' in 'the schoolroom'.[81]

Apart from Charles' care for Midshipman Balgonie, Jane Austen had another model, nearer to hand. In October 1813, during Charles' time in the

---

* Although Balgonie was dogged by ill-health, he had a successful career, Lieutenant in 1806, Captain in 1812, Vice-Admiral in 1855. He lived to the age of seventy-five and remained a good friend to Cassandra until her death in 1845.

Namur, the vessel was joined by 'Young Kendall', so named in a letter from Jane to Cassandra reporting on his progress. To begin with, 'my Br did not find him forward enough to be what they call put in the Office, & therefore placed him under the Schoolmaster, but he is very much improved, & goes into the Office now every afternoon – still attending School in the morn^g', where he was 'going on very well'.[82] As both Jane and Charles were staying at Godmersham at this time, we can suppose that the news of 'Young Kendall' was a matter of common interest and conversation in the family.

For a youngster's point of view, we have the recollections of Douglas Jerrold, the journalist and *Punch* contributor, who became known as 'the father of nautical melodrama'. The son of a Sheerness actor-manager, he joined the *Namur* as a Volunteer First Class in December 1813, at the age of ten. According to his son, Jerrold remembered the ship – a towering three-decker of 90 guns – looming over him, a 'great floating mass' with all 'the pomp and power of a kingdom about it'. Under Charles's care, the boy was well treated. 'The good Captain Austen received him kindly'; he was allowed to keep pigeons; and found himself 'petted'. Hours were spent in the Captain's cabin reading Buffon's *Natural History* 'through and through'. This was an encyclopaedic work – running from the theory and history of the Earth to molluscs and insects – thorough preparation for an Austen-trained youngster equipped to travel the world with his eyes open.* Much time was also devoted to Jerrold's favourite occupation of getting up 'theatricals'. This was an enthusiasm that Charles was ready to encourage. Like any experienced Captain, he understood the value of entertainment in keeping up a crew's morale. Shipboard theatricals could be ambitious, with primitive scenery and costumes. 'an innocent amusement, much better than being idle and drinking', Captain George Duff wrote home to his wife from the *Mars* (74) at sea, just before 'the gentlemen of the cockpit' (the Midshipmen) put on 'the tragedy of Douglas and the pantomime of Harlequin and the Miller' with painted backcloths and ladies' dresses made out of old sheets and silk handkerchiefs.[83]

The ship's boys ended each day with the singing of a hymn.[84] But there was another side to life on the *Namur*. As the port guardship for Sheerness, one of its functions was as a receiving-ship for men collected by the press-gangs, something Jerrold recounted in 'Jack Runnymede: The Man of Many "Thanks"' (1838). A resentful and mutinous body, these sailors were forcefully disciplined and punishment was a routine feature of shipboard life. Such scenes left their mark on the youngster. Jerrold was to draw on this experience in the graphic description of flogging in *The Mutiny at the Nore: A*

---

* Not, of course, the forty-four volumes of the complete French edition (1749—67) but almost certainly one of the English condensations, reduced in length to a volume or two. Many such editions were in circulation by 1812.

Nautical Drama (1830), which also brings out the horrors of surgery at sea, a sight he witnessed on the *Ernest* (12), transporting the wounded back from Waterloo.

Another 'theatrical' sailor taken in by Charles was the nineteen-year-old William Clarkson Stanfield, later to become famous as a marine and land-scape artist. When Charles was looking for someone to paint a toy coach for one of his children, Stanfield volunteered his services. Apparently, Charles was so pleased with his work 'that he strongly advised him to quit the sea and keep to painting. The captain I believe did something in the way of intro-ducing him to some influential friends; at all events, they became great friends in later life'.[85] Stanfield also painted scenery for the *Namur* theatricals and a few years later, when he had left the sea for good, he was highly successful in taking up scenery-painting as a full-time job.

By this point in the novel, the professional portrait of Wentworth is virtu-ally complete. While his romantic role in the story still has far to go, Jane Austen has little more to tell us about his life as a sailor, the main lines having been established in the scene at Uppercross and his naval 'character' largely accounted for. There remains a single but much-discussed scene, the melo-drama of Louisa Musgrove's fall at Lyme. During his years of service, Wentworth must have witnessed untold scenes of bloodshed, death and mutilation – horrific injuries were suffered on the 'slaughter-house' of a ship's deck raked by enemy fire.[86] The *Naval Chronicle* ran a series of 'Observations on the Character of Sailors' (excerpted from *Ancient and Modern Anecdotes* (1789), by J. P. Andrews) and there was a large degree of truth to the identification of 'intrepidity' and 'presence of mind' as 'Two of the brightest points in the character of a seaman'.[87] Yet, at the mere sight of a girl concussed, Wentworth is made to act like a hysterical civilian, leaving Anne to take command of the situation. Jane Austen's purpose here is two-fold. In part, we are watching a comedy of role-reversal. The competent woman saves the day while the Captain, gallant at sea, is rendered helpless, 'staggering against the wall for his support'.[88] It is a demonstration, for Wentworth's benefit, of Anne's 'fortitude' – a much-prized quality, for Wentworth regards the combination of her 'fortitude and gentleness' 'as perfection itself'[89] – her capacity to face 'The horror of that moment',[90] to fire off first-aid instructions for those frozen or fainting around her, and provide the 'strength', 'zeal' and 'thought' needed to deal with the accident.[91] In this comic tableau, greatly enjoyed by the 'workmen and boatmen about the Cobb',[92] Anne is thrust into the limelight and Wentworth's character as a battle-hardened veteran is momentarily suspended.

No such melodrama attends the relationship of Admiral and Mrs Croft. The comedy of competence, when an emergency arises, is milder and more diffused, and harmony prevails – all this beautifully drawn in Anne's observation of their narrow escapes in the gig with Mrs Croft on the look-out:

> But by coolly giving the reins a better direction herself, they happily passed the danger; and by once afterwards judiciously putting out her hand, they neither fell into a rut, nor ran foul of a dung-cart; and Anne, with some amusement at their style of driving, which she imagined no bad representation of the general guidance of their affairs, found herself safely deposited by them at the cottage.[93]*

The guiding hand of Mrs Croft is seen elsewhere. In the leasing of Kellynch, the questions about 'the house, the terms and taxes' come from Mrs Croft, not from the Admiral; and, of the couple, Mr Shepherd reports, she is the one who 'seemed more conversant with the business'.[94] The Crofts having taken possession of Kellynch 'with true naval alertness',[95] Jane Austen gives us the portrait of a naval wife, a woman whose life at sea is marked in her features and whose solidity, in physique and character, is wholly new to the novels:

> Mrs Croft, though neither tall nor fat, had a squareness, uprightness, and vigour of form, which gave importance to her person. She had bright dark eyes, good teeth, and altogether an agreeable face; though her reddened and weather-beaten complexion, the consequence of her having been almost as much at sea as her husband, made her seem to have lived some years longer in the world than her real eight and thirty. Her manners were open, easy, and decided, like one who had no distrust of herself, and no doubts of what to do; without any approach to coarseness, however, or any want of good humour.[96]

(It is worth noting that in her certainty, decisiveness and self-confidence, Mrs Croft is established as a counter-figure to Anne, whose own future would have been very different if she had possessed these same qualities in the summer of 1806, when she was 'persuaded' to turn Wentworth down.)[97]

For the first time in Jane Austen we meet a woman whose life is shaped by the tides of war. Determined to be with her husband, whether at sea or on his stations abroad, during the fifteen years of their marriage Mrs Croft has been 'a great traveller',[98] and the naval destinations are reeled off in the vivid dialogue of chapter eight: the East Indies, Cork, Lisbon and Gibraltar, and four times across the Atlantic, voyages undertaken whatever the discomforts

---

* This portrait may owe something to the character of Charles's Commander-in-Chief on the North American Station, Vice-Admiral Sir John Borlase Warren, 'one of the most accomplished officers in the service and a perfect gentleman of the old school'. While he was undoubtedly the Admiral, his lady, it is said, was clearly the Commander-in-Chief (quotation in Wilkinson, 1979, i. 293).

and dangers, whether in the confines of a frigate or the 'accommodations of a man-of-war',[99]* and always with a sense of security in companionship:

> I can safely say, that the happiest part of my life has been spent on board a ship. While we were together, you know, there was nothing to be feared. . . . The only time that I ever really suffered in body or mind, the only time that I ever fancied myself unwell, or had any ideas of danger, was the winter that I passed by myself at Deal, when the Admiral (*Captain* Croft then) was in the North Seas. I lived in perpetual fright at that time, and had all manner of imaginary complaints from not knowing what to do with myself, or when I should hear from him next; but as long as we could be together, nothing ever ailed me, and I never met with the smallest inconvenience.[100]

And elsewhere we hear of the 'lodgings' at North Yarmouth and Deal where they made themselves 'snug' together.[101]

This was a litany to warm naval hearts: Cork, the home station of the Irish Squadron; Lisbon, with its fine natural harbour, a base for the Mediterranean Fleet; Gibraltar, the impregnable Rock, guardian of the Mediterranean, where Francis' first command, the *Peterel*, was stationed; not the West Indies, says Mrs Croft, so 'across the Atlantic' would be to the naval bases Charles knew at Halifax and Bermuda on the North American station; Yarmouth, a minor base, servicing the North Sea and Baltic fleets assembling on the Yarmouth Roads, off the Norfolk coast; and likewise Deal, with its dockyard, a base for vessels gathered offshore at the Downs anchorage. Like Mrs Croft, Mary Austen had taken lodgings at Yarmouth and experienced a winter at Deal, where she waited for Francis returning in the *Elephant* from duty with the North Sea Fleet. A few miles along the coast from the resort of Ramsgate, Deal, a working port, was far less fashionable, with lodgings cheap enough to attract naval families. However, unlike Mrs Croft's, their lodgings over Christmas 1812 were far from 'snug' and when Francis returned, they 'established' themselves (as Jane joked to Martha Lloyd) 'once more in fresh Lodgings. I think they must soon have lodged in every house in the Town.'[102]

---

* Presumably the Admiral's Flagship, in which she enjoyed far more spacious quarters, usually twice the size of a Captain's. Betsey Wynne, allowed to travel in the Admiral's quarters of the *Britannia*, a three-decker of 100 guns, found there 'as good accommodation as we would have in any house on shore' Fremantle (1937), ii. 107. In a 32-, 36- or 38-gun frigate, the Captain's accommodation occupied an area of approximately 33 x 26 ft, tapering to about 20 ft at the stern, divided by removable bulkheads. A standard arrangement allowed for three or four compartments: a great cabin, at the stern end, for entertaining, an anteroom or day cabin, a bedroom and a small pantry. A 'water closet' or 'seat of ease' was to be found behind a sliding door on each side of the great cabin. When the ship came into action, the outer bulkheads were dismantled, allowing access to the stern guns within the Captain's area.

What arouses Mrs Croft to such an energetic account of her naval life is her rejection of Wentworth's argument that as the 'personal comfort' of women cannot be provided for at sea, there is no place for them on board ship. This, it seems to Mrs Croft, is an instance of her brother's 'idle refinement!',[103] his having been tainted by the values of polite society, and she and her husband turn on Wentworth with some amusement, in the brisk and emphatic naval style they have in common:

> 'But I hate to hear you talking so, like a fine gentleman, and as if women were all fine ladies, instead of rational creatures. We none of us expect to be in smooth water all our days.'
>
> 'Ah! my dear,' said the admiral, 'when he has got a wife, he will sing a different tune. When he is married, if we have the good luck to live to another war, we shall see him do as you and I, and a great many others have done. We shall have him very thankful to any body that will bring him his wife.'
>
> 'Ay, that we shall.'[104]

As Admiral Croft remarks, it was not uncommon for a friendly Captain to bring a brother-officer's wife out to an overseas station; and, once there, a wife might travel with her husband between bases, just as Fanny Austen accompanied Charles on Admiral Warren's flagship from Bermuda to Halifax, a journey on which she was able to act as a companion to the Admiral's wife. But Mrs Croft has been more than an occasional traveller. She has accompanied her husband on voyages over a long period and is able to speak in terms of the ships she has 'lived in',[105] five in all, and of having 'spent' 'the happiest part' of her 'life . . . on board a ship'[106] – far different from Mrs Admiral Crawford and her niece Mary in *Mansfield Park*: 'Those vile sea-breezes are the ruin of beauty and health. My poor aunt always felt affected, if within ten miles of the sea, which the Admiral, of course, never believed . . .'.[107]

Strictly speaking, it was against regulations to carry women on board ship unless on Admiralty orders, or, after 1806, on orders either from the Admiralty or a Captain's 'Superior Officer'.* Orders would be given, for example, for carrying the families of diplomats, such as the 'Lady Mary Grierson and her daughters' returning from Portugal,[108] whom we can assume to be an Ambassador's family. In practice, however, as Brian Lavery

---

* In the *Regulations and Instructions Relating to His Majesty's Service at Sea* (1790), Article 38 of the instructions to the Captain or Commander reads as follows: 'He is not to carry any Woman to Sea, nor to entertain any Foreigners to serve in the Ship, who are Officers or Gentlemen, without Orders from the Admiralty.' This follows the wording, virtually unchanged, of the *King's Regulations* of 1731. The *Regulations and Instructions* were slightly relaxed in the edition of 1806 insomuch that 'orders' could come from the Captain's 'Superior Officer' as well as from the Admiralty.

tells us, the wives of officers and petty officers were 'often carried to sea' and usually did a specific job, such as 'looking after the sick and wounded',[109] as the wife of the Surgeon's Mate might do. Observance of the regulations varied from ship to ship, depending on the Captain's compliance and the complaisance or otherwise of the Flag officers involved. And while the Captains' wives might be tolerated, the carrying of mistresses was going too far, although aristocratic Captains were prepared to buck the system, as Nelson complained to Sir John Jervis in 1797, pointing out that in the previous war with France (which ended in 1783), 'not an Honourable but had plenty of them; and they will always do as they please. Orders are not for them – at least, I never knew one who obeyed.' Jervis agreed, seeing it as a spreading canker: 'the overflow of Honourables and the Disciples they have made among the Plebeians has been the ruin of the Service. I never permitted a woman to go to sea in the Ship'.[110] Alongside Jervis and Nelson, another veteran was Cuthbert Collingwood. He believed that women on board ship brought bad luck and were makers of 'mischief'.[111] A stickler for discipline, he enforced his views on the Squadrons and Fleets under his command. He heard with contempt of an Admiral coming out to the Mediterranean (where he was Commander-in-Chief) 'with his wife and family on board'. Although, as he wrote to his sister, Collingwood found the prospect appalling, he also managed to see some humour in the situation, envisaging himself a latter-day Othello: 'I do not know what is to become of me at last . . . As I never aspired to command a petticoat, I think, *my* occupation will be lost. It will be time for me to hide my diminished head when admirals cannot be found with hearts hard enough to leave their loves.'[112]*

The official objection to Captains' wives was realistic and commonsensical. Unlike the wives of the lower ranks, they could not be expected to do a job. On overseas stations there was the risk that their husbands would be tempted to loiter on shore, diverted from their duty at sea; and in fighting ships they were a distraction and could only be in the way. Some officers kept to the letter of the regulations. Writing home to his wife from blockade duty off Cherbourg in 1813, Captain James Gordon reported that his Commodore, Captain David Milne, had with him in the *Venerable* (74) his wife, two children and a maid. 'What do you think of that? How officers can act so contrary to their orders I know not.'[113] Occasionally, we get an insight into the circumstances, as in Captain Dillon's decision to take his wife and grown-up

---

* Collingwood's allusion is to 'Farewell! Othello's occupation's gone!' (*Othello*, III, iii. 358), the concluding line to a speech in which Othello blames Desdemona's supposed unfaithfulness for putting an end to his peace of mind and his career as a soldier. Collingwood's strong views are understandable. Commander-in-Chief in the Mediterranean, he served the last six years of his life, until his death in 1810, seeing neither England nor his wife and family.

daughter with him in the *Leopard* (74), then engaged in ferrying troops from England to Portugal:

> After mature deliberation upon my state of affairs, I thought it would be advisable to take my wife to sea, and, by uniting the two incomes together, we might live within our means. . . . I wrote to propose to her to accompany me, judging that, in the command of a troopship, I should not have much cruising against the enemy. Consequently my wife would not be much in the way. She accordingly made her appearance, accompanied by her daughter and maid. I remarked that the officers were pleased at the arrival of the ladies, anticipating an amusing change in the monotony of a sailor's life.[114]

Dillon's daughter stayed in the *Leopard* for no less than ten months, leaving on her marriage to one of the Lieutenants, and his wife remained even longer.

Women such as these could not, in the words of Mrs Croft, afford to behave like 'fine ladies'.[115] Like her, they needed to be 'blessed with excellent health', capable of standing any climate and free from sea-sickness 'after the first twenty-four hours'.[116] It has to be said, however, that Jane Austen skates over a good deal. The gap here between fiction and fact is wide. Even for the wives of Admirals and Captains, there was far more to be endured. A sound witness to this is Betsey Wynne. Before their marriage in January 1797, Thomas Fremantle warned Betsey that she had not seriously considered what life at sea with a frigate Captain would entail, details she recorded in her diary: 'to what I engage myself, to how much misery I shall be espoused, how could I live on board? What shall I do if the ship comes to action? etc.' But she felt that she had properly thought of 'all this' and was confident of enduring 'the inconveniences which must of course occur from being at sea'.[117] Over a period of seven-and-a-half months, travelling from Naples to Portsmouth on the *Inconstant* (36) and the *Seahorse* (38), with stays of several weeks at Elba and Gibraltar, and an attack on Tenerife, Betsey was to face 'misery' and 'inconveniences' she had not anticipated. Despite being a good sailor, her own appetite sharpened by weather that laid other passengers low, there were storms of a violence to confine her to her cabin and give her sleepless nights, as did 'the noise of the guns'.[118] Following the unsuccessful attack on Tenerife, the *Seahorse* took on board the 'sick and wounded'. Betsey found the ship 'worse than a hospital . . . from morning to night and from night to morning you hear nothing but those unfortunate people groan'.[119] Fremantle, too, was injured, suffering a wound in his arm which remained unhealed for many months; and Nelson, more seriously injured, had his right arm amputated before joining Fremantle in the *Seahorse* on its way to England.

Even more distressing were the ship's punishments. Fremantle was a strict disciplinarian and drunkenness, a habitual offence, resulted in 'Much flogging' of the crew. In her cabin, Betsey 'could distinctly hear the poor wretches cry out for mercy', something which 'broke my heart'.[120] To convey the brutality involved, I quote a sailor's description of the cat-o'-nine tails:

> This instrument of torture was composed of nine cords, a quarter of an inch round and about two feet long, the ends whipt with fine twine. To these cords was affixed a stock, two feet in length, covered with red baize.[121]

Three days later came the 'diabolical' punishment (as Admiral Smyth calls it),[122] most feared of all, flogging round the Fleet: 'the three Mariners were punished and flogged along side of every ship'.* On this same day, other sailors were also flogged on board the *Inconstant*. Once again, 'in the cabin' Betsey heard 'all that is going on quite distinctly', leaving her 'miserable all the morning'.[123] For all that she enjoyed her honeymoon at sea, in the privacy of her own 'comfortable cabin',[124] the sail-maker's wife in attendance, and that she could pass her days with her harpsichord, her books and her water-colours, and make music with other passengers, the grim realities of naval life, its cruelty, bloodshed and horror, could not be blocked out.

How much Jane Austen knew of this and how much she assumed her readers to know is uncertain. But she must have been aware that for the ordinary sailor life in these ships was often 'a hell upon earth' – the words of the naval historian William Laird Clowes, writing in 1900.[125] To quote an account from 1812, it was no better than 'dwelling in a prison, within whose narrow limits were to be found Constraint, Disease, Ignorance, Insensibility, Tyranny, Sameness, Dirt and Foul Air: and in addition, the dangers of Ocean, Fire, Mutiny, Pestilence, Battle and Exile'.[126] Besides the injuries and mutilations of war, these were the 'common afflictions' of shipboard life: 'hideous ulcers (a general complaint) arising from bruises received in the course of their hard work, and exasperated by the damp in which they lie, and by the foul water they are obliged to drink'; 'ruptures, an ordinary

---

* Courts martial used this punishment as a substitute for execution for serious crimes such as treason, mutiny or assaulting a superior. To achieve the maximum deterrent effect, it was conducted as a solemn and formalised ritual. The prisoner, lashed to a frame or grating, was paraded in a launch (the largest of a ship's boats) from vessel to vessel, the crews lining the sides to witness his ordeal. With a sentence of 300 lashes, for example, seventy-five might be given alongside the prisoner's own ship and forty-five at each of the five other ships in a Squadron, as determined by the Commander-in-Chief. Full details of this punishment are given in Byrn (1989), pp. 68–71, and a graphic description, bringing out its full horror, is quoted in Clowes (1900). v. 28–29 from *Nautical Economy* (1836) by William Robinson, an account of his experiences on the lower deck of the *Revenge* (74) from 1805 to 1811. The flogging reported in Jerrold's *The Mutiny at the Nore* is a flogging round the Fleet (see above, pp. 272–73).

consequence to young men, from pulling ropes'; 'some with ulcerated lungs'; 'others suffering from lacerations, dislocations and fractures from falls . . .'.[127]

Amongst these rigours and afflictions, punishment came high. For those at home, it was not a taboo subject: 'if those lads do not behave, I must try what the cat will do', and of some deserters, 'Of course, my duty obliged me to flog them', Captain James Gordon wrote to his wife in 1812–13.[120] No passenger could remain long on a ship unaware that naval discipline was a discipline of violence. What else could it be, given the conditions of shipboard life, the quantities of alcohol dispensed, twice daily, in the allowance of grog, and the nature of the crew, some of them criminals released for naval service, some of them unwilling victims of the press-gangs, some of them more or less experienced seamen from all over the world, a mingling of races and nationalities?

As to the guiding principles of good captaincy in ruling his ship, the prevailing orthodoxy is spelt out in a letter – he called it a 'Sermon' giving 'a few hints' – from St Vincent (then First Lord of the Admiralty) to a recently and very rapidly promoted Commander, Francis William Fane. Fane stood in need of advice. A Midshipman in the Spring of 1801 – his father an MP, his second cousin the Earl of Westmoreland, Lord Privy Seal and, on his mother's side, related to St Vincent – he reached the Captains' List in just over two years.

> To the inferior officers and men, your humanity and good sense will naturally incline you to shew all manner of kindness consistently with the preservation of good order and due execution of the Service. Upon complaint being made of any irregularity, investigate it with temper and never delegate these examinations to a Lieutenant, much less the infliction of punishment, which never ought to take place but when absolutely necessary, and the strictest decorum observed in the conduct of it, and whatever your feelings are nothing like passion ought to appear.[129]

But there could be some distance between St Vincent's 'Sermon' and the experience of the crew. At the mercy of the Boatswain and his mates, the seamen were driven by straps, ropes' ends and sticks, an unauthorised and arbitrary punishment known as Starting. Officially abolished in 1809, like Running the Gauntlet,* abolished in 1806, it continued on vessels where a strong lead was not given by the Captain.[130]

---

* A standard punishment for a seaman who stole from his shipmates. Stripped to the waist, the prisoner was tied to a chair or frame and pulled round the deck between lines of his shipmates armed with knotted cords. This ordeal might be repeated two or even three times before the thief's punishment was complete. Sometimes he was marched at sword-point, to his chest and back, to prevent him passing down the lines too quickly.

Grievances were usually not against the system of punishment in itself but at its excesses, a point made by ship's company to Lord Howe when he was investigating the naval minutes of 1797:

> My Lord, we do not wish you to understand that we have the least intention of encroaching on the punishments necessary for the preservation of good order and discipline necessary to be preserved in H. M. navy, but to crush the spirit of tyranny and oppression so much practised and delighted in, contrary to the spirit or intent of any laws of our country.[131]

Certain ships were notorious for brutality, their Captains feared as 'flogging captains', 'tyrants' or 'tartars. According to the recollections of 'Jack Nasty-Face', Charles Paget, Charles Austen's Captain in the *Endymion*, carried such a reputation. He was an officer 'whose name was a terror to every ship's company he commanded' and 'cursed from stem to stern in the British navy'.[132] Francis served under two other men of similar stamp: Captain John Gore and Captain Alexander Frazer. Gore, described by St Vincent (himself a strict disciplinarian) as having 'a most impatient spirit',[133] was known to his crew as a Captain of 'tyrannical disposition'.[134] Frazer too. During his command of the *Shannon* (32), in which Francis served for fifteen weeks, between March and June 1795, as we have heard in chapter 5, Frazer's reign of violence was so unbearable that by mid-1796 the crew was driven to bypass the usual channels and complain to the Admiralty direct, pleading for another Captain or another ship:

> for the Captin is one of the most barbarous and one of the most unhuman officers that ever a sect of unfortunate men eaver had the disagreeable misfortune of being with, which treatment and bad usages is anufe to make the sparites of Englishmen to rise and steer the ship into and enimies port.[135]

This, of course, is an extreme case. We can gauge from the entries in Francis' log-books what could be regarded as a routine level of punishment: twelve lashes for insolence; twelve 'for attempting to strike' an officer; twelve 'for mutinous Expressions'; twelve 'for drunkenness & neglect of Duty'; fifteen 'for Drunkenness & Fighting'; forty-nine for theft; for theft again, probably from his shipmates, 'run the Gantlope' (the Dutch spelling, with the pronunciation 'gantlet', remained fossilized in naval language).[136] Fleet punishments were more ceremonial. In the *London* anchored off Cadiz, the log for 20 October 1798 reads: 'at 1/2 past 6 made the Sig^n. with a Gun for Punishment – at 7 the Boats of the Fleet assembled round us, arrived; at 8 proceeded to put the Sentence paper on Jno Carrol (s) in Execution, by giving him 25 lashes – at 1/2past 9 hand'd down the Sig^n. for Punishment, the

Prisoner having rec^d. the whole of the Punishment awarded him by the Sentence of the Court Martial'. The small procession then continued on its way, the prisoner to receive his quota of lashes alongside each ship of the Fleet. In the *London*, according to the regulations, the Articles of War were read to the crew and they returned to their routine of daily tasks, washing down 'the middle and lower Decks'.[137] Under heavy punishment, prisoners frequently collapsed and for this reason a surgeon was to hand. Such an occasion arose when the *Elephant* was anchored at the Downs in 1812. It was reported to Rear-Admiral Thomas Foley, the Commander-in-Chief, that Thomas Jones 'has received Two Hundred Lashes, being all which in the judgement of the Surgeon he was able to bear at present, alongside the undermentioned [4] Ships'.[138]

In the *Memoir*, we are told of Francis' 'great firmness of character' and his 'strong sense of duty, whether due from himself to others, or from others to himself. He was consequently a strict disciplinarian'.[139] Although Austen-Leigh provides no instances of this side to his uncle's character, from the context it seems that it was Francis' naval reputation he had in mind, probably an aspect of his Evangelical strictness regarding the morals of his crews; and we do know of one instance in 1813 when Francis ran foul of the Admiralty for the number of punishments administered on board the *Elephant*.

Until 1811, the record of a ship's punishments could only be derived from the Captain's or the Master's log; and as these were inspected when a voyage or tour of duty was completed, any excesses would come to light long after the event, far too late to restrain a tyrannical Captain. However, as the war progressed, humanitarian views began to gain ground. A marked change of attitude towards Service discipline became evident. In March 1811, the system of oversight was tightened, the Return of Offences and Punishment now to be made on a quarterly basis. The record was submitted by ships' Captains to their immediate superiors and passed on, if appropriate, with Flag-Officers' comments, for scrutiny at the Admiralty. This was the procedure followed with the Return Francis submitted in July 1813 to Rear-Admiral George Hope, his immediate superior in the Baltic Fleet.

Although the document itself has not survived, we are able to reconstruct from the ship's logs what it was that caught the Admiral's attention. Ninety-eight floggings were recorded, the majority for drunkenness and offences related to it, including disobedience of orders, neglect of duty, insolence and fighting. Writing from his flagship, the *Defiance* (74), on 26 July, Hope sent in the quarterly Return for the twenty vessels under his command, noting in particular 'the very long list of Punishments inflicted on board the *Elephant*', reporting that he had declared his 'sentiments' 'on the subject' 'very strongly' to Captain Austen, whose letter in response he now enclosed, leaving 'their Lordships . . . to determine whether on this statement, it would not be advisable . . . to seperate Men who have been so long together, and who appear notwithstanding every exertion to prevent it, addicted to constant drunkenness'.[140] For this was the substance of the explanation, really a defence, that Francis had submitted to Hope in a letter written from the *Elephant* 'off Rostock' earlier that same day, 26 July, stung by Hope's letter of the previous day:

> whilst I feel most acutely the censure implied in it on my conduct as Captain of the Elephant, I must beg permission in the most respectful manner, to declare that my conscience acquits me of having deserved it.[141]

'The infliction of Punishment', he had 'always felt to be a most ungrateful part of a Captain's duty', although 'experience' had 'convinced' him that it was a 'necessary one'. He went on to account for the level of drunkenness among his crew by the fact that 180 seamen (about half the crew)* had come from a single ship, the *Formidable* (98), where, Francis wrote, they were 'most notoriously addicted to habits of the grossest inebriety' and that the *Formidable*'s previous Captain had told him 'that in the whole course of his Servitude, he had never met with so drunken a Ship's Company'. Ninety more of his crew were drafted from the *Tigre* (80) which 'bore a character not very dissimilar to that of the Formidable's'. The 'germ' of drunkenness, Francis claimed, was 'introduced' into the *Elephant* from the very beginning, before she was fitted out and 'before a regular System of discipline could be established'. And so, he argued, 'the noxious plant' had struck 'deep root, and bid defiance to every attempt to eradicate it'. In this manner, the 'landsmen & new-raised Men' had been led astray. This was the gist of Francis' vehement defence. He protested that there was not a single instance of his having ordered a punishment out of 'whim, Caprice, momentary anger, a disposition to Cruelty' nor of any punishment having been 'improperly severe, or not fully deserved'. His letter ended on a challenging note: that he would 'rather seek than avoid the most urgent enquiry into my conduct on this subject'.[142]

The Admiralty view on this matter is set out in two letters to Hope from John Barrow, the Assistant Secretary. The first, dated 11 August, acknowledges Hope's letter of 26 July and notes having received Francis' letter 'in reply to your animadversions on the frequency of Punishments on board the Elephant'. Barrow also told Hope that the Board approved of the 'strong

---

* Excluding the officers, young gentlemen and boys, there were 370 seamen on the *Elephant*, plus 120 marines with their three officers and two drummers (NMM, MS AUS/17).

notice' he had 'taken of this Subject' and that they would 'take the state of the Crew into account'.[143] The second letter to Hope, of 16 August, communicates 'Their Lordships . . . extreme regret' at 'the continuance of punishments on board the "Elephant"', a comment which suggests that this was not the first time that the matter of punishments in this ship had come to their attention.[144]

Hope's 'strong notice' had some effect. In succeeding quarters the levels of punishment fell sharply. Nonetheless, across a period of eleven months (from 5 April 1813 to 7 March 1814) approximately one in four members of the crew were flogged, about three times the average for the service.* From these figures, and this entire incident, it seems that the problem lay partly with Francis himself, and is not entirely explained by the presence of so many hardened drunkards, the situation eloquently described in his letter to Hope.** On his appointment to the *Aurora* (36) in 1826, Charles Austen faced a very similar problem. According to the *Sailor Brothers*, this was a ship in which 'There had been much insubordination and drunkenness amongst the crew, but under Captain Austen matters were soon altered; he was strict in discipline but kind, much as Douglas Jerrold had found him in those earlier days in the *Namur*.'[145] As we read in Charles' Private Journal, he preferred lecturing offenders to beating them and on 25 December 1826 was happy to forgive 'at least a Dozen offenders . . . in honour of the day'.[146] This positive view of Charles is confirmed in the *Aurora*'s log. From the date she put to sea, on 6 June 1826, for the twelve months until 23 June 1827, there were only twenty-four floggings, received by twenty-three men (under 9 per cent of the crew), figures which cast a cold light on his brother's Captaincy of the *Elephant*.

With this picture of naval punishment before us, we can see a rational basis to the string of evasions and excuses that Wentworth produces when the idea of carrying women in his ships is aired. The reader knows that these passengers might have to face something far more disturbing than physical discomfort. Similarly, looked at afresh, Mrs Croft's determination to accompany her husband, sharing his war-time life at sea whenever she could, reveals a singularly unladylike toughness. Anne, too, has 'fortitude'.[147] But there is no suggestion that her married life will ever take her to sea. The possibility of 'a future war', raised several times in the course of the

---

* There has been no detailed tabulation of ships' punishments for the Navy overall. Byrn (1989) provides a figure of 9 per cent (p. 108), an average arrived at from a survey of ships' logs at the Leeward Islands Station from 1784 to 1812.

** Hope was appointed to the Admiralty Board on 23 October 1813 (serving until 24 May 1816) and this may explain why Francis so speedily withdrew his application for a new command in early May 1814 (see above, p. 51). It may have been intimated to him that such an application would not be favourably considered.

novel, rather implies separation, and this is the prospect which fills Anne with 'dread'.

The naval scheme of *Persuasion* becomes more explicit when the story brings us to Lyme. Having given us two officers flush with prize-money, Jane Austen now shows us the plight of Harville, a Captain who has missed out. His choice of home is not for its picturesque setting not for the 'charms' of the countryside around, the beauties of Charmouth, a few miles along the coast, or the wonders of Pinny nearby, 'with its green chasms between romantic rocks',[148] but because lodgings were cheap in a seaside resort out-of-season and cheapest of all in such nondescript 'small' houses as those found unfashionably 'near the foot of an old pier of unknown date'.[149] When it came to taking prizes, it was, in Wentworth's words, 'Poor Harville'.[150] He had also been out of active service for two years, having suffered a 'severe' leg wound.[151] As a consequence, Harville was supporting his wife and three children as best he could on his half-pay and a pension for his injury.

The predicament of fortuneless officers such as Harville was a problem which increased towards the end of the war and was widely discussed.[152] In part response, during 1814 the Admiralty laid down a new, 'peacetime' pay-scale. This raised the Captain's daily pay (seven shillings to twelve shillings, depending on the rating of his last vessel), to a scale according to seniority: the first hundred on the Captains' List to receive 14s. 9d. per day; the next 150, 12s. 6d.; the remainder, over six hundred of them, 10s. 6d.; the payment to be made quarterly instead of half-yearly as before. This new scale was announced by the Admiralty on 8 June 1814 and was given in the current issue of the *Naval Chronicle*.[153] The Editor commented that 'The dismantling of our victorious fleets must, necessarily, throw a great number of officers out of active service', a serious blow, given the 'increased price of all kinds of the necessaries of life'.[154] In this same volume is announced the birth on 8 January 1814 'of a daughter' to 'The lady of Captain Austin, of HMS Elephant'.[155] So when Francis returned to England in May 1814, he came home to greet his fifth child, Cassandra Eliza, born at Portsmouth. Standing 139th on the Captains' list, Francis received £230 per annum (equivalent to approximately £9200 today), while Charles, 369th, at the bottom of the scale, would receive £192 (£7680) on leaving active service in the Summer of 1816. So without the support of prize-money or some other source of income, half-pay would provide only a bare minimum to live on.

It is very likely that Jane Austen's description of Harville's 'small house' at Lyme – 'rather like a ship on shore', Tony Tanner has described it[156] – owes something to the sight of Charles' economical existence with his wife and children in the cramped quarters of the *Namur* and the scenes of

Francis' family life at Rose Cottage, near Alton;* that Harville's carpentry, carving, toy-making and handicraft reflect Francis' hobbies and skills – the *Sailor Brothers* is sure on this point: 'Certainly in tastes and feelings there is much similarity'; and that the 'domestic happiness'[157] which Anne discovers with the Harvilles was Jane's own experience too on visiting the sailor brothers in their 'small' homes. But the possibility of these biographical origins is of far less importance to us than the value of this episode in illuminating 'the character of the navy'. One aspect of this lies in the warmth and welcoming hospitality with which the Harvilles greet the party from Uppercross. Nelson spoke of his fellow-officers as men joined by ties of friendship, profession and the fire of battle. They were his 'band of friends',[158] his 'brave Brethren',[159] and, quoting Henry V at Agincourt, his 'Band of Brothers',[160]** an affectionate camaraderie that Anne finds in the comradeship joining Wentworth, Benwick and the Harvilles. The pressing invitation to dinner – the Harvilles' 'hospitable . . . entreaties'[161] – is a painful revelation to Anne of the distance between the cold Elliot world of polite society and the naval world of feeling:

> There was so much attachment to Captain Wentworth in all this, and such a bewitching charm in a degree of hospitality so uncommon, so unlike the usual style of give-and-take invitations, and dinners of formality and display, that Anne felt her spirits not likely to be benefited by an increasing acquaintance among his brother-officers. 'These would have been all my friends,' was her thought; and she had to struggle against a great tendency to lowness.[162]

There follows a remarkable passage, central to *Persuasion*'s naval purpose, the description of Harville's 'fitting-up' of the rooms, his practical skills and ingenuity in transforming these indifferent lodgings into a place of comfort, convenience and beauty, a treasure-trove mingling the homely and the exotic. The scene carries a sense of calm and fulfillment. It points to a life

---

* We can touch the spirit of these visits in Jane's letters to Cassandra: 'The Alton 4 [Francis, his wife, a Miss Gibson and Lt. Mark Sweny RN] drank tea with us last night, & we were very pleasant: – Jeu de violon &c – all new to Mr Sweny – & he entered into it very well. – It was a renewal of former agreable evenings. – We all (except my Mother) dine at Alton tomorrow – & perhaps may have some of the same sports again – . . .' Lieutenant Mark Halpen Sweny (1783–1865) served under Francis in 1802, as a Midshipman in the *Neptune* (98) and in the *St Albans*, sailing with him to China in 1809, and later in the *Elephant*. Like Harville, he was wounded in a leg, subsequently amputated. The Austens found their visit to Rose Cottage the next day 'very pleasant' but were disappointed at Sweny's absence, as he had been ordered back to London (4 and 8 September 1816, *Letters*, pp. 318–19, 320). A brief biography is to be found in Gilson (1999).

** *Henry V*, IV. iii. 60–62.

> We few, we happy few, we band of brothers;
> For he today that sheds his blood with me
> Shall be my brother.

which (as Barbara Hardy remarks) 'has nothing to do with great estates or rich possessions'[163] and everything to do with Harville's 'profession, the fruit of its labours, the effect of its influence on his habits,' an observation, and analysis that Jane Austen places with Anne Elliot.

> On quitting the Cobb, they all went indoors with their new friends, and found rooms so small as none but those who invite from the heart could think capable of accommodating so many. Anne had a moment's astonishment on the subject herself; but it was soon lost in the pleasanter feelings which sprang from the sight of all the ingenious contrivances and nice arrangements of Captain Harville, to turn the actual space to the best possible account, to supply the deficiencies of lodging-house furniture, and defend the windows and doors against the winter storms to be expected. The varieties in the fitting-up of the rooms, where the common necessaries provided by the owner, in the common indifferent plight, were contrasted with some few articles of a rare species of wood, excellently worked up, and with something curious and valuable from all the distant countries Captain Harville had visited, were more than amusing to Anne: connected as it all was with his profession, the fruit of its labours, the effect of its influence on his habits, the picture of repose and domestic happiness it presented, made it to her a something more, or less, than gratification.
>
> Captain Harville was no reader; but he had contrived excellent accommodations, and fashioned very pretty shelves, for a tolerable collection of well-bound volumes, the property of Captain Benwick. His lameness prevented him from taking much exercise; but a mind of usefulness and ingenuity seemed to furnish him with constant employment within. He drew, he varnished, he carpentered, he glued; he made toys for the children, he fashioned new netting-needles and pins with improvements; and if every thing else was done, sat down to his large fishing-net at one corner of the room.[164]

These 'rooms so small' command a view of Britain's expanding empire, its trophies modestly assembled in those 'few articles of rare species of wood' of Harville's workmanship, the ebony, padouk, mahogany and teak brought from the West Indies and Far East to add to the indigenous oak, ash, elm, walnut and cherry. Who better than a sailor to fashion a home out of cramped quarters, to make it ship-shape, and turn such a dwelling into a place of comfort and delight, both a cabinet of wonders and a workshop – his bone needles, his ingenious pins – in which to exercise his seaman's dexterity and skills.

At the end of their visit, Anne has much to feel but nothing to say; and Jane Austen gives it to Louisa Musgrove (her heart set on Wentworth) to sing the Navy's praises:

> Anne thought she left great happiness behind her when they quitted the house; and Louisa, by whom she found herself walking, burst forth into raptures of admi-

ration and delight on the character of the navy – their friendliness, their brotherliness, their openness, their uprightness; protesting that she was convinced of sailors having more worth and warmth than any other set of men in England; that they only knew how to live, and they only deserved to be respected and loved.[165]

Within Jane Austen's parade of naval officers, Harville and Benwick provide a contrast in tastes and aptitudes, Harville, 'no reader' but gifted with his hands,[166] a man of invention and contrivance, the other 'a young man of considerable taste in reading' and keen to share his enthusiasms.[167] Benwick belongs to a very recognisable type. It was no embarrassment for a fighting-man to admit to a love of poetry. The *Naval Chronicle* is full of sailors' compositions and verse of the sea. The issue for November 1799 carried an appreciative review of *Lyrical Ballads* by Wordsworth and Coleridge, quoting sections from 'The Ancyent Marinere'. On this account, it was reported by the publishers, Longmans, 'that the greater part' of the edition 'had been sold to seafaring men, who having heard of the Ancient Mariner, concluded that it was a naval song-book, or, at all events, that it had some relation to nautical matters'.[168]

Sea-going versifiers, however young, could find an audience among their shipmates. In 'Pleasures of Naval Life' (1813), a poem of two thousand lines written from his own experience at sea, Thomas Downey describes a Midshipman reciting 'his lays' in the gun-room, 'Sometimes applauded loud, as often vext/By critics near who slyly mar the text'.[169] There were poetic Admirals too. Sir Sidney Smith, under whom Francis served in the Eastern Mediterranean in 1800, was given to reciting poetry by the yard, in English, Latin and French, and celebrated both his victories and his defeats with lengthy poems of his own composition.

Educated sailors, in the mould of the Austen brothers, would have been on the look-out for brother-officers with whom they could share their interests. The absence of such companions, on a lengthy voyage, could be a real deprivation. We have the *cri de coeur* of a contemporary, Captain Francis Beaufort, caught in this very situation in June 1805:

> What an acquisition such a man in a long passage to India! To have had some fund of conversation besides the weather, the beauty of the dolphin, the last sail that was seen, etc. would really be worth a great sacrifice of some desirable qualities in an officer, which he certainly wanted.[170]

Many years before, Midshipman Beaufort had written to his father naming 'books' as his 'food'. While 'philosophy' made up his staple diet, 'poetry and travels' provided his 'banqueting stuff'.[171] With such well-stocked minds, conversation amongst officers in the wardroom or around the Captain's table would range widely. Charles, on the *Phoenix*, could report to Jane that 'Books became the subject of conversation' and that her own novels were praised highly.[172] When Maria Callcott's father was appointed Commissioner of the Navy at Bombay, the family went out in a frigate, the *Cornelia* (32), and found themselves travelling with a group of pleasant and cultivated sailors. The First Lieutenant, Thomas Graham (destined to be Maria's husband), was a young Scotsman, 'A man of warm heart and lively wit' not unlike Wentworth. Into the bargain, he was 'well-read in the general literature of his country'.[173] The 'chief subject' of their conversation was poetry, an interest shared with other officers on board. The year being 1809, their talk was of Walter Scott, the poet of the day:

> So many young people, most of whom had probably those attachments at home that particularly dispose the mind to the warm emotions calculated to taste poetry, could hardly be assembled without making it the subject of conversation, and we had Scotchmen enough to talk of Scotch poetry. Of course, the merits of 'The Lay of the Last Minstrel' [1805] and of 'Marmion' [1808] were compared, and most of us gave the preference to the former.[174]

We are no distance from *Persuasion*, from the poetry-lovers Benwick and Anne in conversation, 'trying to ascertain whether *Marmion* or *The Lady of the Lake* [1810] were to be preferred, or how ranked the *Giaour* and *The Bride of Abydos* [both by Byron, 1813], and moreover how the *Giaour* was to be pronounced . . .'.[175]

Of these poems, *Marmion* was the one with naval connections.* A romance of chivalry with the Battle of Flodden Field (1513) as its centrepiece, it was regarded as a highly patriotic poem. Not a full-blooded celebration of war, *Marmion* nonetheless glorifies 'valour . . . boldness of enterprise and success in battle'.[176] Scott was ready to bring in modern 'success' and Gambier's attack on Copenhagen is alluded to in the poem. Naval hearts would also have been stirred by an extended threnody on the deaths of Nelson and Pitt, here united by Scott as the nation's heroes. Altogether, *Marmion* was inspirational, an heroic poem to strengthen a sailor's resolve, to remind him of the anvil of battle upon which his country had been formed and assert the honour of his cause. Moreover, the poem's cast included an ancient attendant bearing the name of 'Austin', a variant of their own name that the family was used to seeing in the *Naval Chronicle*, the *Gazette* and other papers. So it was probably with mixed feelings, serious and light-hearted, that (in January 1809) Jane Austen despatched a copy of *Marmion* to

---

* *Marmion*, published 23 February 1808, was immensely popular. It reached a third edition before the end of May, selling eight thousand copies. By the end of 1811, in its eleventh edition, twenty-eight thousand copies were in circulation.

her brother Charles in Bermuda. It was a practical gift, too, for a sailor at sea: a long, yet popular and accessible poem, providing much food for thought and discussion, with inspiring lines and lyrics for Charles to recite, to remember and to share with his fellow-officers.

Amongst Benwick's other favourites are 'Lord Byron's "dark blue seas"',[177] an apt quotation, as Anne and Benwick gaze out from the Cobb across the wintry seascape of Lyme Bay; 'seas' which are appropriate, too, for their naval associations. For the 'dark blue sea' appears twice in Byron's poetry of this time: once, in the Second Canto of *Childe Harold* (1812), 'He that has sail'd upon the dark blue sea' opens a fine lyrical section describing a guarding frigate and a straggling convoy, 'spread like wild swans in their flight';[178] and in the very first line of *The Corsair* (1814), beginning a tribute to the sea as the 'empire' and 'home' of seafarers. This is a deeply Romantic poem, glorifying both the sailor's life and the sailor himself, and the Editor of the *Naval Chronicle* promptly took these opening lines as a motto to display on the title-page of the volume for July to December 1814:[179]

> O'ER the glad waters of the dark blue sea,
> Our thoughts as boundless, and our souls as free,
> Far as the breeze can bear, the billows foam,
> Survey our empire, and behold our home!
> These are our realms, no limits to their sway —[180]

The Byronic-Romantic mood enters the Lyme chapters elsewhere. Jane Austen writes of the sea as never before, her tone near-reverential – 'who ever deserve to look on it at all' – her language contained but glowing as she describes the early morning stroll Anne and Henrietta Musgrove take along the shore:

> They went to the sands, to watch the flowing of the tide, which a fine south-easterly breeze was bringing in with all the grandeur which so flat a shore admitted. They praised the morning; gloried in the sea; sympathized in the delight of the fresh-feeling breeze – and were silent . . .[181]

Anne's experience of Lyme is enduring. It remains with her during the weeks at Uppercross and in her meetings with Lady Russell and the Crofts, so strongly so that she can hardly attend to the reports Lady Russell brings of her father's life at Bath:

> Anne would have been ashamed to have it known, how much more she was thinking of Lyme, and Louisa Musgrove, and all her acquaintance there; how much more interesting to her was the home and the friendship of the Harvilles and

Captain Benwick, than her own father's house in Camden-place, or her own sister's intimacy with Mrs. Clay. She was actually forced to exert herself, to meet Lady Russell with any thing like the appearance of equal solicitude, on topics which had by nature the first claim on her.[182]

The Crofts, too, have risen in her estimation. Lady Russell regards calling on them as a painful social duty, a 'trial to us both'.[183] For Anne, the prospect is altogether different:

> for she had in fact so high an opinion of the Crofts, and considered her father so very fortunate in his tenants, felt the parish to be so sure of a good example, and the poor of the best attention and relief, that however sorry and ashamed for the necessity of the removal, she could not but in conscience feel that they were gone who deserved not to stay, and that Kellynch-hall had passed into better hands than its owners'.[184]
>
> In such moments Anne had no power of saying to herself, 'These rooms ought to belong only to us. Oh, how fallen in their destination! How unworthily occupied! An ancient family to be so driven away! Strangers filling their place!' No, except when she thought of her mother, and remembered where she had been used to sit and preside, she had no sigh of that description to heave.[185]

There is a difference of opinion, too, about the Admiral's 'manners'. They 'were not quite the tone to suit Lady Russell, but they delighted Anne. His goodness of heart and simplicity of character were irresistible'. His invitation, like Harville's, is direct, welcoming and unceremonious:

> 'Now, this must be very bad for you,' said he, suddenly rousing from a little reverie, 'to be coming and finding us here. – I had not recollected it before, I declare, – but it must be very bad. – But now, do not stand upon ceremony, – Get up and go over all the rooms in the house if you like it.'[186]

The Admiral continues in this style, half thinking aloud, warning Anne of the practical changes they have made (echoes of Captain Harville at Lyme): the repair to the laundry door; the removal of their umbrellas from the butler's room to the door to the shrubbery (so that they can pick them up for themselves, unattended by servants); and the comic scene we are to imagine of the Admiral and his wife themselves evicting Sir Walter's battery of mirrors:

> 'I should think he must be rather a dressy man for his time of life. – Such a number of looking-glasses! oh Lord! there was no getting away from oneself. So I got Sophy to lend me a hand, and we soon shifted their quarters; and now I am quite snug, with my little shaving glass in one corner, and another great thing that I never go near.'[187]

Anne is lost for an answer, 'and the Admiral, fearing he might not have been civil enough, took up the subject again . . .'[188]

By the end of volume one, Admiral Croft is firmly established in Jane Austen's gallery of naval characters. Readers of *Persuasion* in post-war England would readily identify the 'open hearted, good humoured, jolly English tar', a type that Lady Stanley encountered in the person of Captain James Gordon in 1821.[189] A few years earlier, Gordon had represented himself as 'a rough, uncouth mortal',[190] ill-at-ease and apologetic at carrying into polite society the bluffness and bluntness of his life-long profession, his quarter-deck bearing and his tarpaulin talk. This is the very self-consciousness, the sensitivity of true politeness, that Admiral Croft displays in company with Anne. Jane Austen succeeds in conveying the humour of the Crofts – their quirks, oddities and eccentricities – without letting them stray into staginess or farce, and a certain discipline and fine judgment was required to achieve this. We see this most clearly in the ending that Jane Austen originally wrote to the novel, before rewriting the final two chapters.* The cancelled chapter 10 has the Crofts behaving as sly and interfering matchmakers, a conventional comic role, with Anne and Wentworth tricked into meeting one another, much of the humour turning on the Admiral's noisiness and the comedy of misunderstanding which arises from his heavy-handed hints. All this Jane Austen removed, allowing the Crofts to keep their kindliness and dignity and to remain an endearing and loveable couple whose companionship in marriage has qualities which Anne not only admires but feels that she can enter into and enjoy. In the Bath chapters, Jane Austen makes this a distinctively naval comradeship in which Mrs Croft stands on equal terms with the Admiral and his cronies. On carriage drives with Lady Russell, Anne

> never failed to think of them, and never failed to see them. Knowing their feelings as she did, it was a most attractive picture of happiness to her. She always watched them as long as she could; delighted to fancy she understood what they might be talking of, as they walked along in happy independence, or equally delighted to see the Admiral's hearty shake of the hand when he encountered an old friend, and observe their eagerness of conversation when occasionally forming into a little knot of the navy, Mrs Croft looking as intelligent and keen as any of the officers around her.[191]

* The cancelled Chapter 10 on its own was appended to the Second Edition of the *Memoir* (1871) and to the standard Oxford edition of *Persuasion* (1923). *Two Chapters of Persuasion* (1926) presents the manuscript entire with all its changes. This is described in Grey (1986), pp. 322–23 and, more fully, in Southam (1964), ch. 6. The revision includes one item of naval detail. Where the final text tells us that Sir Walter prepared 'his pen with very good grace for the insertion of the marriage in the volume of honour' (p. 249), Jane Austen first wrote 'for the insertion of F. W. Esqre Post-Capt. of H. M.'s Navy in his chosen volume'.

For the Crofts, Bath is a town of service friends (that 'fine race of seamen' 'generally at Bath in the winter' as one correspondent wrote in 1812).[192] The only cloud is the sight of Admiral Brand and his brother coming down the street. 'Shabby fellows, both of them!' the Admiral explodes to Anne, recalling the 'pitiful trick' they once 'played' him when they 'got away some of my best men',[193] a story he promises to tell in full some other time.* When the Crofts retire to the privacy of their own rooms, they find a 'snug' companionship together, recalling their lodgings long ago in naval sea-towns:

> 'How do you like Bath, Miss Elliot? It suits us very well. We are always meeting with some old friend or other; the streets full of them every morning; sure to have plenty of chat; and then we get away from them all, and shut ourselves into our lodgings, and draw in our chairs, and are as snug as if we were at Kellynch, ay, or as we used to be even at North Yarmouth and Deal.'[194]

For the Elliots and their circle, the groupings are not of profession or friendship but rank. Elizabeth Elliot rules that the Admiral and his wife are unfit to be introduced to her cousin, Lady Dalrymple; they are to be left 'to find their own level' amongst the 'several odd-looking men walking about here, who, I am told, are sailors'.[195] Duty obliges Anne to be with her family and where the Elliots move, a freezing formality takes over:

> the door was thrown open for Sir Walter and Miss Elliot, whose entrance seemed to give a general chill. Anne felt an instant oppression, and, wherever she looked, saw symptoms of the same. The comfort, the freedom, the gaiety of the room was over, hushed into cold composure, determined silence, or insipid talk, to meet the heartless elegance of her father and sister. How mortifying to feel that it was so![196]

William Walter Elliot, Anne's suitor and the heir to Kellynch, both the title and the estate – 'a charm which she could not immediately resist'[197] – belongs to the same world of forms and formality. 'Rank is rank',[198] he declares, and 'Good company' calls for 'birth, education and manners'.[199] A man of 'propriety and correctness', of 'general politeness and suavity',[200] he pleases Lady Russell but repels Anne. Her experience, years before, of Wentworth, and now of Admiral and Mrs Croft, of Harville and Benwick, has given her expectations and values from another world and the desire for 'good company' of a different kind:

---

* 'Shabby' was the naval word for 'dirty' (as in a dirty trick) or 'underhand' (see Dillon, 1956, 2.238–39). The 'pitiful trick' played by the Brands was to impress or otherwise seize members of Admiral Croft's crew on their return from sea to a home port in order to make up the numbers for their own ship's crew.

Mr Elliot was rational, discreet, polished, – but he was not open. There was never any burst of feeling, any warmth of indignation or delight, at the evil or good of others. This, to Anne, was a decided imperfection. Her early impressions were incurable. She prized the frank, the open-hearted, the eager character beyond all others. Warmth and enthusiasm did captivate her still. She felt that she could so much more depend upon the sincerity of those who sometimes looked or said a careless or a hasty thing, than of those whose presence of mind never varied, whose tongue never slipped.[201]

Jane Austen's furthest exploration of naval experience comes in chapter 11 of volume two, the scene at the White Hart leading to Wentworth's declaration of love and reunion with Anne, a resolution that the novelist sets in motion along a decidedly 'naval' path. The naval theme is worth following in some detail, both in the scene-setting and in the discussion, a quasi-debate, that Wentworth overhears between Anne and Harville, and which triggers his letter. The issue is this: separated by war or circumstance, which sex loves longest, which most deeply, men or women? This discussion is sparked by the errand on which Harville had been sent by Benwick, to arrange for the framing of the portrait miniature, once a fiancé's gift for Fanny Harville and now destined for Louisa Musgrove.* This is a change that Harville finds upsetting. He feels his dead sister's memory insulted by the speed with which Benwick has transferred his affections. That Wentworth overhears Anne and Harville and that he is already sitting at a writing-table is not purely fortuitous. As Jane Austen is careful to explain, the framing errand has been passed on to him; when the discussion begins, he is writing to Benwick about this new arrangement.

In the exchanges between Anne and Harville, for the first time Jane Austen explores the unheroic areas of war-time suffering and endurance – the experience of families waiting anxiously at home, the agony of parting for sailors leaving their loved ones, and their impatience to see their families once again at the end of a voyage.

The debate is sparked by Harville's scepticism about how long women's love endures, a challenge which Anne answers by describing what it means to women to have to suffer passively:

> 'Yes. We certainly do not forget you, so soon as you forget us. It is, perhaps, our fate rather than our merit. We cannot help ourselves. We live at home, quiet, confined, and our feelings prey upon us. You are forced on exertion. You have always a profession, pursuits, business of some sort or other, to take you back into the world immediately, and continual occupation and change soon weaken impressions.'[202]

---

* Such miniatures were especially valued in war-time as mementoes or keepsakes. One survives of Francis Austen, painted in 1796, in a Lieutenant's uniform (illus. 3, reproduced in colour in Le Faye, 1998, p. 13). Painted long before he met Mary Gibson, it was not a lover's gift but intended for the family.

Harville counters with the example of Benwick. At the time he heard of Fanny's death 'The peace turned him on shore' and there was no 'exertion' to distract him.[203] If not in 'outward circumstances', replies Anne, then the proclivity to change must lie in Benwick's 'nature'. Harville denies this, on the 'analogy' between men's bodies and their feelings: just 'as our bodies are the strongest, so are our feelings; capable of bearing most rough usage, and riding out the heaviest weather'.[204]* Anne returns the analogy. But she loses the thread of her argument in contemplating what sailors have to endure:

> 'Your feelings may be the strongest,' replied Anne, 'but the same spirit of analogy will authorise me to assert that ours are the most tender. Man is more robust than woman, but he is not longer-lived; which exactly explains my view of the nature of their attachments. Nay, it would be too hard upon you, if it were otherwise. You have difficulties, and privations, and dangers enough to struggle with. You are always labouring and toiling, exposed to every risk and hardship. Your home, country, friends, all quitted. Neither time, nor health, nor life, to be called your own. It would be too hard indeed' (with a faltering voice) 'if woman's feelings were to be added to all this.'[205]

Harville is interrupted by the sound of Wentworth's pen falling, his attention caught by their discussion. When Anne and Harville resume, it is to agree to disagree and Harville tells Anne 'in a tone of strong feeling' what it means to be a sailor, to see his wife and children – 'these treasures of his existence!' – return to land for the last time before he sets sail, and the waiting he endures, at the end of his voyage, returning to a different seaport:

> 'if I could but make you comprehend what a man suffers when he takes a last look at his wife and children, and watches the boat that he has sent them off in, as long as it is in sight, and then turns away and says, "God knows whether we ever meet again!" And then, if I could convey to you the glow of his soul when he does see them again; when, coming back after a twelvemonth's absence perhaps, and obliged to put into another port, he calculates how soon it be possible to get them there, pretending to deceive himself, and saying, "They cannot be here till such a day," but all the while hoping for them twelve hours sooner, and seeing them arrive at last, as if Heaven had given them wings, by many hours sooner still! If I could explain to you all this, and all that a man can bear and do, and glories to do for the sake of these treasures of his existence! I speak, you know, only of such men as have hearts!' pressing his own with emotion.'[206]

---

* This is an image naval men would connect with that most arduous and dangerous of duties, close blockade of the French Channel ports, where the constant problem was holding position in heavy seas. This is what Francis encountered in watching Cadiz harbour in Autumn 1805 (see above, p. 92).

That 'last look', of sad parting and fond farewell, is a recurrent theme in the poetry of the sea and it made its way onto the pottery and porcelain of the period and was the subject of many prints. In ships at sea, 'these treasures of his existence' were the traditional toast for Saturday night, 'Sweethearts and wives', and an old song, a shipboard favourite tells how the wardroom would rise and drink to 'The wind that blows, The ship that goes, And the lass that loved a sailor'. Parting marked the lives of the sailor brothers. Francis recalled 'leaving his wife in an advanced state of pregnancy at home' on joining the *St Albans* at Sheerness only weeks before the birth of his first daughter, Mary Jane, on 27 April 1807.[207] For Charles, it was more painful still, leaving his three children for the *Phoenix* in October 1814, their mother, Fanny Palmer, having died only weeks before, following the death of a fourth child, an infant three weeks old. Francis' Memoir is tight-lipped and reveals little of his feelings. But Charles' diaries tell us of his loneliness at sea and the dreams of Fanny and their children crowding night after night to haunt him. Something of this sadness and desolation would have been carried in his letters home, for Jane Austen to reflect in these pages.

The story of *Persuasion* comes to a close at some indeterminate point in the Spring or early Summer of 1815. Among the Allies, it was a moment of anxiety. Following Napoleon's escape from Elba at the end of February, the threat of renewed war was looming. On 21 March, the Admiralty announced a suspension of demobilisation. The Fleet was to be kept in commission. To bolster public confidence, popular and experienced Admirals were placed in the key commands, Lord Keith, now in his seventies, brought out of retirement to lead the Channel Fleet and Sir Edward Pellew, now Lord Exmouth, recalled to the Mediterranean. But Waterloo set Napoleon on the path to exile; and in Hampshire, Francis remained on half-pay, undisturbed, with his family.

These circumstances are caught in the playful irony of the closing lines. This is a Navy held in the embrace of romantic comedy, a service now 'more distinguished in its domestic virtues than in its national importance'. As Monica Cohen puts it, in *Persuasion* we see the Navy's 'prestige – its influence – changing from one being based on martial deed to one predicated on domestic utility: sailors are good to have around the house because they're so good with their hands.'[208] Anne has no home to look forward to. But she enjoys the happiness of marriage, 'glories in being a sailor's wife' and 'in belonging' to the 'profession'. Yet there are shadows to the 'sunshine': 'the dread of a future war' that a sailor's wife must endure and 'the tax of quick alarm that a sailor's wife must pay'.[209] This was a potent image for readers of *Persuasion*. Property or Income tax, widely regarded as oppressive and inquisitorial, was a war-time measure, introduced in 1799; and Napoleon's escape from Elba reawakened the threat. While politicians debated the issue, a woman of Jane Austen's age was enquiring of her daughter, 'And what do you say about the probability of the war, and the income tax being renewed?'[210] This is the social reality adjacent to the novel's text. 'Future war' is a prospect that Jane Austen allows to surface from time to time during the course of the novel. It holds the promise of naval advancement and success – more prize-money and a knighthood, a Baronetcy even, for Wentworth; a commission for Midshipman Drew; promotion for Benwick (a recently made Commander, he needs such a break, since 'these are bad times for getting on', remarks Admiral Croft); and Admiral Croft looks forward to a future war as an event of 'good luck'.[211] Yet, as Jane Austen intended, the sobering reminders, still fresh in our minds from the conversation of Anne and Harville at the White Hart, are of war's partings and absences, its 'difficulties', 'privations' and 'dangers'.[212] And from earlier in the story, we remember Mrs Croft, alone in her lodgings at Deal, living 'in perpetual fright' wondering when she was to hear next from her husband out 'in the North Seas'.[213]

The testimony of Mrs Barrett, quoted in Chapter One, urges us to read *Persuasion* biographically, to regard the novel as an expression of Jane Austen's enthusiasm for the Navy – a compound of patriotism and pride and affection for her sailor brothers – within a story that embodies the novelist's fantasy of fulfilment in love, a salvation from spinsterhood, in short, Jane Austen's own life salvaged and set right by a naval suitor.

On a footing equally speculative is the possibility that Jane Austen also used *Persuasion* to repair the career of her brother Francis. To outward appearances, it was a career that could not be surpassed. In the dignity of old age, having out-lived every one of his contemporaries and now the last surviving of that elite band, 'Nelson's Captains', Francis attained the Navy's highest rank, Admiral of the Fleet, and of the three officers who currently held that rank, he was the senior. But these trappings of success are misleading. The record of his war-time career tells a different story. He left the Naval Academy, as he noted in his biographical entry for O'Byrne, 'marked out for early promotion'.[214] Yet his Captaincy was slow in coming; and the picture in the later years is equally disappointing. His consuming ambition was to command a frigate, for the possibility of prize-money. Yet even with the support he could muster from Warren Hastings, Moira, and from Nelson himself, Francis could do no better than a succession of Flag-Captaincies or the command of men-of-war escorting convoys or transporting troops.

We are reminded of Admiral Pellew's words to an unsuccessful officer in 1807, someone commissioned in 1778 and unpromoted to the time of his death over thirty years later. If Pellew is bald and to the point, his tone is sympathetic:

> you had no impediment but your interest, you had too many friends of power, who fed your expectations without carrying you over the difficulties every Officer meets in early Life.[215]

Why Francis suffered his disappointments, we are left to guess. Was it because he was a product of the Naval Academy? Was it because of Gambier's unpopularity – a patron unable to raise sufficient interest on his behalf? Or were his own Evangelical leanings a handicap? Or was his competence as a Captain in question? Effective as a First Lieutenant, was he equally able when in sole command – an opportunity which came relatively late in the day, given his successive appointments as Flag Captain? Certainly, bad luck played its part. Nelson wrote on his behalf before Trafalgar; and, following the Battle, it was Barham's intention that Francis should have a frigate, the *Acasta* (40). But through the turn of events he remained on the *Canopus*. He missed out again in 1807. The First Lord, Grenville, promised 'the first good frigate that became vacant'.[216] Instead, his commission to the *St Albans* (64) set him on trooping and convoying for the next three-and-a-half years. The family could rejoice at his 'health & safety' and his brother James could wish Francis 'the reward which your Principles & Exertions deserve in the enjoyment of Domestic Comfort & the Society' of Mary Gibson in marriage.[217] Jane, however, knew her brother's material need: 'he wants nothing but a good Prize to be a perfect Character',[218] she wrote to Cassandra. But that 'good Prize' never came. It was a disappointment that Jane could at last set right in the realm of imagination, granting Francis what he wanted in the 'perfect Character' of Frederick Wentworth and his £25,000.

12

The Aftermath of Persuasion

'Her naval officers are really social portraits'

Richard Simpson, 1870

Persuasion was published alongside *Northanger Abbey* in December 1817, five months after Jane Austen's death. The reviewers bemourned the passing of a talented and entertaining writer. But they had nothing to say about the naval characters of *Persuasion* and it was not for another fifty years that anyone recognised that the sailors compose a distinct social group. The critic in question was Richard Simpson, a Shakespearean scholar and commentator on Catholic affairs; and his observations come in an essay (nominally a review of the 1870 *Memoir*) which remains to this day one of the classic accounts of Jane Austen. Although Simpson's recollection of the novels was faulty in one detail – Mr Price, Lieutenant of Marines, becomes 'Captain' Price – his passage on the naval officers has a modern ring:

If her sympathies were somewhat limited, this was only because her society was limited. Perhaps the assertion that she had no powers of portraying or understanding society as such should be modified in favour of one special class, whose outward life singularly influences its general character. She thoroughly understood the naval officer, whom she could study at home, in her brothers. Her naval officers are really social portraits. A clergyman's daughter, she yet regarded the clergyman's position with a half-quizzical eye. She let the church stand in the churchyard, and did not attempt to transplant it into her novels. But the naval officer was a favourite personage in her later novels; Admiral Croft, Captain Wentworth, Captain Harville, Captain Benwick, Captain Price, and William Price are all admirable portraits, perfectly distinct, and yet all saturated with their professional peculiarities. She even, in Captain Price's case, did what Pope pronounced to be impossible, reconciled the 'tarpaulin phrase' with the requirements of art and civility. Out of these bounds her language never strays. She is neat, epigrammatic, and incisive, but always a lady; there is no brandy and cayenne in her farrago – no 'opinions supercélestes et moeurs souterrains' [unworldly opinion and worldly morality], as Montaigne says. There is no overstepping her own faculties; if she did not know, she felt, that every man, ever so little beyond himself, is a fool. She obeyed the adage, 'ne gladium tollas mulier' [let the woman not bear arms]. She spun out the feminine fibre of the sons of Mars and Neptune, but meddled neither with the sword nor with the trident.[1]

Given that these comments were the first ever to be made on the naval figures, it would not be unreasonable to expect later critics to continue the discussion, whether to agree or disagree, for there is plenty to argue with here. But the 1870s were not the moment; sentiment flourished, critical inertia prevailed, and Simpson's shrewd and challenging remarks passed unregarded.[2]

The private realm, however, reveals a more interesting scene and I want to conclude this account of *Persuasion* with two examples which help us to understand how very deeply this novel entered the experience of Jane Austen's ordinary readers (who were neither reviewers nor academics) in the years after her death and how the naval characters of *Persuasion* found a continuing life outside the novel.

As a young man, Charles Darwin was a voracious reader. At Cambridge, while preparing for the Church, together with beetle-hunting, geologising and pursuing his other scientific interests, he made time to perform what he called, with some justice, the 'Herculean task' of reading Richardson's *Clarissa*.[3] He was not exaggerating. This enormous work, at over a million words, is the longest novel in the English language. In Darwin's eyes, it was also, as he enthused to a Cambridge friend, 'the most glorious novel ever written'.[4] Where Jane Austen stood in Darwin's hierarchy of writers, there is no record. But like the rest of his family, he knew the novels intimately. In time, they were only a short step away, and the Shropshire gentry to which the Darwins belonged enjoyed a style of life in which Jane Austen would have felt at home. 'We are going on much in our usual humdrum style', writes Squire Owen, the father of Darwin's closest childhood friends, in 1832; 'a little hunting, a little shooting, and now and then a little argument about the Reform Bill.'[5] As their letters reveal, Darwin's marriageable sisters were much concerned (as Stefan Collini has remarked) with 'the romantic intentions and tactics of the respectable young gentlemen of the neighbourhood. One almost expects Mr Darcy or Mr Knightley to put in an appearance.'[6] They would not be out of place in the company of the Darwins and their close cousins, the Wedgwoods. Emma Wedgwood, Darwin's wife-to-be, trod warily on meeting a party of officers, 'lest she should appear too Lydiaish'[7] – the allusion being to Lydia, the 'well-grown' younger sister of Elizabeth Bennet, the teenager in *Pride and Prejudice* who welcomes 'the attention of the officers',[8] her enthusiasm unconcealed.

In tracing Darwin's path from Cambridge to HMS *Beagle* (10), we move towards the naval world of *Persuasion*. His joining the expedition as its

'Naturalist' in the Autumn of 1831 was not by way of a formal Admiralty appointment, for the *Beagle*'s main task, on its second expedition, was to chart and survey the coast of South America, from the River Plate southwards round Cape Horn and the Straits of Magellan, continuing northwards as far as Ecuador, improving earlier charts and making new ones for inaccurately or uncharted coastline – a showing of the flag as well as a contribution to hydrographic and geographical knowledge. Darwin's presence was a private arrangement, agreed by the Admiralty, and made with Commander Robert FitzRoy, the ship's Captain, who wanted to travel with a gentlemanly 'companion', a scientist able to study the exotic flora and fauna while he worked along the coast.[9]

FitzRoy came from an aristocratic family with powerful connections. He was the youngest son of General Lord Charles FitzRoy and a grandson of the Duke of Grafton; and his uncles included Lord Castlereagh and, within the Navy, a Rear-Admiral. Yet it was on his own merits that FitzRoy achieved an early career of high success. At the Portsmouth Naval College – much professionalized since the Austens' day – he enjoyed a brilliant career and was awarded the Mathematics Prize with full marks, the first time this had ever been done. And at his Lieutenant's examination in 1824, of the twenty-seven candidates, he was first. These factors all played their part in his choice of Darwin. For as much as FitzRoy wanted a naturalist on the expedition, he sought a gentleman with whom he could feel at ease socially, a university man who could be his equal intellectually, and someone compatible whose company he could stand over the length of a three-year voyage (which, in the event, lasted for almost five) in the confined quarters of a brig only ninety feet long, a vessel carrying officers, crew and supernumeraries such as Darwin himself, numbering seventy-six in all.

At their first meeting, early in September 1831, the two men established an immediate rapport. Darwin was then twenty-two, FitzRoy twenty-six. FitzRoy felt sufficiently at ease with Darwin to propose that he should have the run of his cabin and that they should eat their meals together there. Reporting this to one of his sisters, Darwin could not speak of him too highly:

> Cap Fitzroy is [in] town & I have seen him; it is no use attempting to praise him as much as I feel inclined to do, for you would not believe me. – One thing I am certain of nothing could be more open & kind than he was to me . . . There is something most extremely attractive in his manners, & way of coming straight to the point.[10]

That same day Darwin wrote to the Cambridge Professor of Botany, J. S. Henslow, to whom he was indebted for the introduction to FitzRoy. He opened in the same heightened tones:

My dear Sir,
Gloria in excelsis is the most moderate beginning I can think of. – Things are more
prosperous than I should have thought possible. – Cap. Fitzroy is every thing that
is delightful, if I was to praise half so much as I feel inclined, you would say it was
absurd, only once seeing him. – I think he really wishes to have me . . . You cannot
imagine anything more pleasant, kind & open than Cap. Fitzroys manners were to
me.[11]

Darwin closed his letter to Henslow exactly as he had to his sister, using the
very same words from *Julius Caesar* – 'There is indeed a tide in the affairs of
men'[12] – expressing his sense of the momentous decision that lay before him.
In turn, that same evening FitzRoy wrote to Captain Francis Beaufort, the
Hydrographer of the Navy, who had immediate responsibility for the *Beagle*'s
voyage, giving his impression of Darwin, following their two hours' conversation in the morning and a further meeting over dinner: 'I like what I see and
hear of him, much'; and he asked Beaufort to make an official application for
Darwin's place on the expedition.[13]

By the following day, Darwin had made his decision. He sent instructions
home to his sister Susan for the preparation of his clothes and instruments. It
was, he wrote, as good as settled: 'from Cap. FitzRoy wishing me so much to
go, & from his kindness I feel a predestination I shall start.' Already, from this
early moment, FitzRoy was shaping in his mind as a figure of naval perfection
and he attributed his good spirits 'to the sort of involuntary confidence I
place in my beau ideal of a Captain'.[14*]

A week later, now at Plymouth, having seen the *Beagle* and met the officers
over some 'most jolly dinners', Darwin wrote to Susan again, repeating the
notion of a 'beau ideal' Captain, this time to discard the idea as inadequate.
Having witnessed FitzRoy's dealings with 'a little Midshipman' – 'you cannot
imagine anything more kind & good humoured than the Captains manners
were to him. – Perhaps you thought I admired my beau ideal of a Captain in
my former letters: all that is quite a joke to what I now feel.' As Darwin recognised, this was hero-worship, and it was this consciousness that led him
directly to *Persuasion*. He ended his letter with an extended figure of speech,
comparing his fluctuations of feeling about the voyage to a line of 'little
waves' representing 'all the doubts & hopes that are continually changing in
my mind. After such a wonderful high wrought simile I will write no more'[15]
– words which take us straight to Bath, to Anne Elliot immediately after her
're-union' with Wentworth:

---

* According to the *OED*, the earliest literary use of *beau idéal* was in *Belinda* (1801) by Maria
Edgeworth, a friend of Darwin's mother. So it is just possible that it entered the family from this very
source.

An interval of meditation, serious and grateful, was the best corrective of every thing dangerous in such high-wrought felicity; and she went to her room, and grew steadfast and fearless in the thankfulness of her enjoyment.[16]

Darwin's allusion is apt and exact; and effective too in its communication between readers who knew *Persuasion* through and through, as did the Darwins and their cousins, the Wedgwoods in neighbouring Staffordshire. Having received from Darwin a letter similar to those he had recently written to Susan, Charlotte Wedgwood congratulated him, 'your fate being at last decided, & decided as you wished it . . . I am delighted that you have fallen in with a Captain Wentworth – such an extraordinary piece of good luck is a good omen for every [thing] else.'[17]

With his future now settled, Darwin wrote in gratitude to Henslow, who had made the original introduction. '1831' would be an 'important Epoch' 'in my life', a year of 'memorable events' and new friendships. The *Beagle*'s officers he found 'a fine set of fellows, but rather rough, & their conversation is oftentimes so full of slang & sea phrases that it is as unintelligible as Hebrew to me'; while Fitzroy remained on another plane, 'My beau ideal of a Captain'.[18]

On hearing that FitzRoy was not only an Austen-like character but was also a reader of Jane Austen, Susan wondered if Charles would like to take a copy of *Persuasion* for the voyage. But Darwin declined. The poop cabin, his space for work and sleep, was to be shared with two of the officers, and his own corner was 'most wofully small.'[19] Moreover, the cabin shelves were already packed – with accounts of travels and voyages, with works of natural history and studies of surveying and meteorology (FitzRoy's special interests). For his part, FitzRoy said he would have no time to read *Persuasion*, while Darwin felt that for the very best of reasons he had no need of a copy: 'there is no danger of my forgetting it'.[20]

This was the message Caroline Darwin was to pass on to Susan, and very soon Charles proved his point. In his next letter to Caroline, dated 12 November, with the *Beagle* newly painted and expensively fitted out (mahogany was used throughout the cabins), Darwin reported his delight at the vessel in the very language Jane Austen uses for Louisa Musgrove: 'I get into a fine naval fervour whenever I look at her'.[21] Again, the allusion fits precisely. Anne Elliot is reflecting on the happy match that Louisa, with her 'fine naval fervour', will make with Captain Benwick.[22] One is made for the other, just as Darwin feels at this moment about the match of the *Beagle* and its Captain: the brig 'as good a ship as art can make her', FitzRoy 'as perfect as nature can make him'.[23]

After two false starts, the *Beagle* eventually commenced her 'circumnavigation',[24] setting sail from Plymouth on 27 December 1831. Twice before, gales had forced her back. During one of these stormy days and nights, Darwin spent a 'miserable 24 hours' wracked with sea-sickness and unable to set his hammock straight, a necessary seafarer's skill which he was slow to master.[25] On this occasion, FitzRoy came to his rescue. Amusingly forthcoming about his failings as a sailor, Darwin reported this story of mishap to the family. His sisters replied collectively with a letter of comfort:

> Your account of the Captain was quite sublime – it was the Red Rover's own still quiet manner & 'low distinct tones' heard through all the uproar,* & Papa's eyes were full of tears when he thought first of your miserable night & then of your goodnatured Captain in all the confusion paying you a visit & arranging your hammock – he must be quite a Captain Wentworth every thing you tell us of him makes him more & more perfect.[26]

There were other unpleasantnesses to be endured. One of these was 'the flogging of several men for offences brought on' by their Christmas drinking, what Darwin described in his Diary as their 'crime' of 'drunkedness & consequent insolence'.[27] Despite having to put up with his own chronic and agonising seasickness at this time, the punishment of the sailors he found deeply troubling. It was a harrowing introduction to naval discipline: the drunkard received twenty-five lashes, thirty-one to another for neglect of duty, thirty-four to a third for breaking his leave and disobedience, and forty-four to a fourth guilty of breaking his leave, drunkenness and insolence together.

As time passed, FitzRoy's Wentworthian perfection faded. Darwin penetrated beyond the glamour of his Captain's literary persona, the Austenian *beau idéal*. He found himself serving under 'a very extraordinary person', as he wrote to his sister Caroline from Rio de Janeiro, four months into the voyage:

> I never before came across a man whom I could fancy being a Napoleon or a Nelson. – I should not call him clever, yet I feel convinced nothing is too great or too high for him. – His ascendancy over every-body is quite curious: the extent to which every officer & man feels the slightest rebuke or praise would have been, before seeing him incomprehensible: It is very amusing to see all hands hauling at

---

* The 'Red Rover' refers to James Fenimore Cooper's novel of that name, published in November 1827. Clearly, it was as well-known to the Darwins as *Persuasion*, although the two works are fascinatingly different. One is a largely 'domestic' vision, the other truly nautical, its character well brought out in the *London Magazine* review of January 1828: '*The Red Rover* is a tale of the sea, by an author who has taken the ocean for his element. A ship is the heroine of his stories, and men and women are merely accessories in his plot. He invests a vessel with life . . .' (vol. x, p. 101). The Red Rover himself is a mysterious Byronic Corsair, passing under the name of Captain Heidigger, a swashbuckling pirate with streaks of humanity in his make up and a deep abstracted melancholy.

a rope they not supposing him on deck, & then observe the effect, when he utters a syllable: it is like a string of dray horses, when the waggoner gives one of his aweful smacks. – His candor & sincerity are to me unparralleled: & using his own words his 'vanity & petulance' are nearly so. – I have felt the effects of the latter: but the bringing into play the former ones so forcibly makes one hardly regret them. – His greatest fault as a companion is his austere silence: produced from excessive thinking: his many good qualities are great & numerous: altogether he is the strongest marked character I ever fell in with.[28]

Signing off, Darwin smiles at his glimpse of the aristocratic circles in which FitzRoy moved: 'I must tell you for your instruction that the Captain says, Miss Austens novels are on every body table, which solely means the Jerseys Londonderries etc –'.[29] (FitzRoy's maternal grandfather was the Marquis of Londonderry and Lady Jersey – the eldest daughter of the 10th Earl of Westmoreland and married to George Villiers, 5th Earl of Jersey – was a woman of literary taste and beauty and had been a friend of Byron.)

Back in England, the younger Darwins kept the Austen allusions in play. Susan reported to Charles that his last letter, written from Salvador on the coast of Brazil, 'has been read very often over to Papa (like Mrs Bates)'.[32] When Darwin next brought in *Persuasion*, it was not to evoke Wentworth (a character now absent from his letters home), but the figure of Dick Musgrove. Addressing Catherine from Maldonado, at the mouth of the River Plate, on the subject of his expenses and the books he wanted sent out from England, he added a PS: 'When you read this I am afraid you will think that I am like the Midshipman in Persuasion who never wrote home, excepting when he wanted to beg . . .'.[31] The thought recurred. A year later, in April 1834, writing again to Catherine (from East Falkland Island, 'a wretched place' he found it, apart from the 'fine harbors', abundant 'fresh water & good beef').[32] Unusually, on this occasion, he had nothing to ask for: 'not having any apologetical messages about money, is nearly as odd a feature in my letters, as it would have [been] in Dick Musgrove's. – I am afraid it will be, till we cross the Pacific, a solitary exception.'[33]

Although after Spring 1834 Darwin's extant letters make no further reference to *Persuasion*, Jane Austen could not have been far from his thoughts. Writing from Valparaiso, on the coast of Chile, he enquired of a Cambridge friend whether he was now a married man, perhaps 'nursing, as Miss Austen says, little olive branches, little pledges of mutual affection', a reference to Mr Collins' 'expectation of a young olive-branch',[34] a thought that carried Darwin back from the 'glory and luxuriance' 'of the Tropics' to memories of his friends in England and 'dear Cambridge'.[35] There is no trace now of a Wentworthian Captain. Instead, Darwin foresaw a shadowed and uncertain future for FitzRoy, a view he set down in a letter from Sydney written in

January 1836, this opening the fifth year of their voyage, the previous twelve months having been 'on very Cordial terms with him'.

> He is an extra ordinary, but noble character, unfortunately however affected with strong peculiarities of temper. Of this, no man is more aware than himself, as he shows by his attempts to conquer them. I often doubt what will be his end, under many circumstances I am sure, it would be a brilliant one, under others I fear a very unhappy one.[36]

These speculations proved strangely prescient. FitzRoy's later career was a tragic mixture of failure and success. Appointed Governor and Commander-in-Chief of New Zealand, he was unpopular with the colonials for siding with the Maoris and was recalled to London. In 1850, he resigned from active service in the Navy and in 1854, under the Board of Trade, was appointed 'Meteorological Statist', the first Superintendent of the Meteorological Office. His *Weather Book* (1862) provided the foundation for modern meteorological science, just as the FitzRoy barometer was a key instrument of nineteenth-century meteorological measurement. But a combination of poor health, deafness, indebtedness and over-work broke his spirits. As a final blow, the weather reports issued from his Office early in 1865 were wildly misleading. Held personally responsible, he was pilloried and ridiculed. By the end of April, FitzRoy could stand no more and took his own life.

Alongside the Darwins and the Wedgwoods, the FitzRoys were also readers of Jane Austen. Isabella, a cousin of the Captain was not uncritical. She felt that *Sense and Sensibility* could have been improved, regretting

> that the characters had not been touched up a little before publication of this pretty novel – Mrs Jennings made less vulgar – and the fortunes of her daughters shd. be mentioned as their beauty – and tho' Colonel Brandon was grave why was he to be silent – the best is done to make E. Ferrars seem a mean looking man – and Col. B. must have been good looking, or Marianne never cd. have married him.[37]

Isabella's uncle, Lord William FitzRoy, a younger brother of the 3rd Duke of Grafton, was more enthusiastic. In 1841, Lord William approached Francis Austen for a copy of his sister's 'Autograph'. Francis declined to part with any of Jane's letters but sent a specimen of 'her Signature',[38] a scrap reading 'Yours very affec:ly J. Austen' removed from a letter (since lost) written to Francis at Deal from Chawton on 17 February 1813.[39] To a later American enquiry, however, Francis was more forthcoming, and in this second 'Wentworth' episode we see again how firmly Jane Austen's *beau idéal* of the naval commander was lodged in the public mind on both sides of the Atlantic.

In January 1852, a Miss Eliza Susan Quincy, of distinguished Founding Father stock, wrote to Francis from 1 Beacon Hill, in Boston, Massachusetts. She announced her family's love for Jane Austen: 'For many years, her talents have brightened our daily path, & her name and those of her characters, are familiar to us as, "household words"'; and she sought further information on the author's life than was available in Henry's 'Biographical Notice'.[40] Miss Quincy went on to explain that hearing 'that a brother of Jane Austen held a high rank in the British Navy', she had obtained Francis' address from an American Admiral, and trusted that 'this expression of feeling, will be received by her relatives, with the kindness & urbanity, characteristic of Admirals of *her creation*'; and she went on to request 'The autograph of his sister, or a few lines in her handwriting' to place 'among our chief treasures'.[41] Only a few years before, Francis had visited the United States during his term as Commander-in-Chief of the North American and West India station and had carried away some unfavourable impressions. The men at Saratoga Springs, with their 'vile habits especially that of frequent discharges of saliva, and that without much regard to where they may be'; and the women, with their 'flippant air . . . which seemed rather at variance with the retiring modesty so pleasing in the generality of English women', a comparison he was able to make on the spot as he was travelling with his two unmarried daughters.[42]

Francis was gentleman enough to set these unpleasant recollections to one side. He responded to Miss Quincy's appeal with generosity, setting down some observations on his sister's life and character (see *Appendix* p. 313); and, overlooking her gaffe about Admirals kind and urbane (there are none: the only Admiral we know about is Admiral Croft, a simple and unpolished sailor, kindly, but quite un-urbane), he answered her request by enclosing a letter from Jane to Martha Lloyd, his own second wife, written many years before their marriage. Dated 12–13 November 1800, the letter has some slight naval interest, as it mentions Charles Austen and the marriage of his patron, Captain Sir Thomas Williams.[43]

News of this generous gift went round the Quincy family, enthusing everyone, including Josiah, Miss Quincy's father, a former President of Harvard. In a flight of fancy, Miss Quincy's sister Anna supposed 'Dear Admiral Austin' to have been like 'Captain Wentworth when he was young – and just like what the Captain would have been at eighty years of age' (Francis was then seventy-seven). 'He has replied to your letter with true "naval alacrity", & evidently deserves to be Miss Austin's brother'[44] – 'deserves', because it is 'with true naval alertness' that Admiral and Mrs Croft take possession of Kellynch Hall in *Persuasion*.[45] When Miss Quincy enclosed these flattering remarks with her next letter, Francis was touched by this appreciative correspondence and remarked on the resemblance suggested between himself and Wentworth:

> I do not know whether in the character of Capt. Wentworth the authoress meant in any degree to delineate that of her Brother: perhaps she might – but I rather think parts of Capt. Harville's were drawn from myself – at least some of his domestic habits, tastes and occupations bear a strong resemblance to mine.[46]

Francis was thinking of the likeness between Harville's toy-making, netting and carpentry in the little house at Lyme and his own handyman pursuits of fifty years before – making toys for Edward's children and helping with the furnishing of Castle Square at Southampton in 1807 – and into his old age, knotting nets to protect his cherries and currants at Portsdown Lodge.

Precise to the last, Francis also pointed out to Miss Quincy, who had mis-addressed him that 'I am not a *Vice* Admiral, having for the last 3 years attained the higher rank of *Admiral*.' With Mary Crawford's '*Vices*' and '*Rears*' pun in mind, he went on: 'I wish I could believe that in the change of rank I had left every *vice* behind me'.[47]

Francis' continuing correspondence with Miss Quincy runs to several pages and is of some interest to historians for its views on the American War of Independence and as evidence of Anglo-American attitudes at the mid-century, including views on the War of 1812, 'strenuously opposed' by Miss Quincy's father 'when a member of Congress for Boston'.[48] Unfortunately, however, there is no further speculation about possible connections between Francis and the naval characters. Four years later, Anna Quincy, now Mrs Robert Waterston, came over to England. She set out on what she called her Jane Austen 'pilgrimage'[49] – to Bath, Winchester, Box Hill and Netley Abbey, an excursion from Southampton that Jane made on more than one occasion, and the ramparts at Portsmouth. The high point of the Waterstons' tour was their call at Portsdown Lodge. However, their purpose was not to see 'One of Nelson's Captains', a senior and distinguished naval veteran of seventy years service: the thrill in prospect, as Mrs Waterston wrote to Francis, ahead of her visit, was to meet 'the *brother* of Jane Austen!'[50]*

---

* Indirectly, Charles had a similar experience with James Brooke, the Rajah of Sarawak, who claimed to have read the novels 'a dozen times' since he had taken office 'and am likely to read them a dozen times more. They are unique and inimitable' (Gertrude Jacob, *The Rajah of Sarawak . . . Letters and Journal*, 1876, i.221). Brooke encountered Charles in 1850 when he wanted naval support for a mission to the King of Siam. He was impatient to set out for Bangkok but found it difficult to get angry 'with that pleasant old Admiral Austen, who, being the brother of the author of "Pride and Prejudice", won our hearts by such relationship' (Spencer St John, *The Life of Sir James Brooke . . . Personal Papers and Correspondence*, 1879, p. 221).

At some level, this relegation must have stung Francis. In the last surviving letter of this correspondence, dated 19 May 1863, now aged eighty-nine, he wrote to Miss Quincy of the crippling rheumatism which confined him to a wheel-chair and of his promotion 'to the highest grade in the Naval Service, that of Admiral of the Fleet . . . of which there are now three, and I am the second. It is gratifying to have attained this last step; But it would be bad for England if all her Admirals were such poor enfeebled objects as he who is now addressing you'.[51] In signing off, at least Francis could be his own man, could boast decently of his high rank and joke about his old age and infirmity, rather than submit to being regarded as a relic, the last remaining Austen of his sister's generation, and visited purely on her account. To the end, he preserved his selfhood, his innermost pride, the quality Jane had discerned and celebrated in the birthday poem so many years before, naming it there, very precisely, as his 'best blessing . . . conscious worth'.[52] This was the driving force which, over the course of his life, had proved to be a source of thwarted ambition and disappointment as much as a well-spring of confidence and strength.

To the end of his days, Francis remained an alert and combatant sailor, in spirit, at least, keeping abreast of naval news and developments, and the fortunes of his surviving comrades. One book stirred him deeply, the first volume of *The Autobiography of a Seaman* (1859) by Thomas Cochrane, the Tenth Earl of Dundonald, now Admiral of the Fleet. This was Cochrane of the Basque Roads affair of 1809, recounted here in Chapter 5; Cochrane the witness to Admiral Harvey's mutinous insubordination towards Lord Gambier, his Commander-in-Chief; the same Cochrane who turned on Gambier for failing to follow up his fireship attack on the French Squadron sheltering in the Aix Roads. It was this event that fuelled Cochrane's lifelong resentment: the dashing and phenomenally successful frigate Captain, possibly the most successful of the Long War (Nelson's 'le loup de Mer'), pitched against the armchair Admiral, the much-despised Gambier, an over-cautious Fleet commander. A collision was inevitable. Equally inevitable was Admiralty support for the establishment figure, with Cochrane the victim of a swung Court Martial. The passage of fifty years had done nothing to assuage Cochrane's sense of grievance. No less than five of his twenty-three chapters (in extent over one-fifth of the book) were given over to these events. For him, it remained an unbearable and corrosive episode, an injustice unrighted.

Francis would have turned to Cochrane's *Autobiography* with expectation and interest. They had sailed together in the Mediterranean in the early stages of the war, Francis in the *Peterel*, Cochrane in the *Speedy*; and they had met again only twelve years before, on an official occasion in May 1848, when the

Earl, then a Vice-Admiral, succeeded Francis as Commander-in-Chief of the North American and West India Station.

No one could have anticipated Francis' reactions to the Basque Roads chapters. Far from resenting Cochrane's ferocious attack on Gambier, he took Cochrane's part, indeed, was so moved as to write to him in support. This letter handed Cochrane an opportunity to prolong his side of the story. In the second volume of the *Autobiography*, published in 1860, the first five chapters (no less than a quarter of the book) are taken up with further discussion both of evidence given at the Court Martial and of evidence suppressed. Into this second category came the matter of witnesses '*not summoned to give evidence before the court-martial !*' (the italics and exclamation mark are Cochrane's).[53] According to Cochrane, among these witnesses was 'a gallant officer still living, Admiral Sir Francis William Austen, K.C.B., who was present in Basque Roads but, like other eminent officers, *not examined on the court-martial*' (again, the italics are Cochrane's).[54] Then followed 'an extract from the gallant Admiral's letter':

I have lately been reading your book, the 'Autobiography of a Seaman,' and cannot resist the desire I feel of stating how much pleasure I derived from its perusal, especially of that part which has reference to the movements of the fleet in the Mediterranean from 1798 to 1800. Having been serving for the greater part of those years on that station, your narrative excited in my mind a vivid recollection of former times – as it were living that part of my life over again.

With reference to the latter part of the volume which details the proceedings in the attack on the enemy's squadron in the Charente, I wish to say as little as possible which may inculpate the conduct of the Commander-in-chief, to whom, as you probably know, I owe a debt of gratitude for his kindness to me.

But at the same time I cannot but admit that he appears to me to have acted injudiciously. It would have been far better had he moved the squadron to a position just out of reach of the batteries on Isle d'Aix, when he would have been able to see the position of the enemy's ships, and thus have decided for himself whether they could have been attacked without needless risk, and not have been compelled to from his determination entirely on the report of others.*

Had he done so, it seems probable that he would have seen things in a different point of view, and decided to send in a force sufficient to have captured or destroyed the whole.

I must, in conscience, declare that I do not think you were properly supported, and that had you been so the result would have been very different. *Much of what*

---

* [Cochrane's footnote] Who were more interested in the failure of the action than its success, from the fact shown in the first volume of the ill-feeling manifested towards me in consequence of my being a junior officer temporarily appointed, though against my own will, and after all others had declined the enterprise.

*occurred I attribute to Lord Gambier's being influenced by persons about him who would have been ready to sacrifice the honour of their country to the gratification of personal dislike to yourself, and the annoyance they felt at a junior officer being employed in the service.**

I will only add that I consider your services in the *Speedy, Pallas,* and *Impérieuse* will entitle you to the the warmest thanks of your country, as well as to the highest honours which have been awarded for similar services. Instead of which, you have in numerous instances been persecuted in the most cruel and unrelenting manner.

I desire to subscribe myself, with much respect and esteem,

My dear Lord Dundonald,

Yours very faithfully,

FRANCIS W. AUSTEN.

Admiral the Earl of Dundonald.

Cochrane's mistake was to enrol Francis among the witnesses not called in his defence. At that very time, Francis was in command of the *St Alban*, then at sea more than a week out of Spithead and off the Portuguese coast, past Cape Finisterre, convoying *en route* for Penang and China.

It was a mistake that Cochrane could be forgiven.** Fifty years was enough to dull his memory as to who precisely was at the Basque Roads and who was not; and Francis would be lodged in his recollection as a protégé of Gambier's, something to which Francis himself refers in his letter. Moreover, his letter could very well be read as coming from someone who was on the spot when these events took place. But the facinating and overriding question is not Cochrane's misunderstanding of the letter but Francis' motive in sending it. For despite his averred wish not to 'inculpate' Gambier's 'conduct', the letter has precisely this effect. In view of Cochrane's declared hostility to Gambier, Francis might have guessed that his letter would be seized upon in just this way. We can only suppose that what blinded Francis to this likelihood was his conviction that he was helping to see justice done in declaring the truth, as he believed it to be, even if from afar: the truth that Gambier's tactics were wrong and that his failure to follow up the fire-ship attack was the baneful influence of senior officers jealous and resentful of Cochrane's appointment.

The whole situation smacks of the mid-century, belongs to the world of Trollope rather than Jane Austen. A comedy of errors, on the surface, it seems a tale of mixed motives and confused ends: the innocent, well-meaning act of

* [Cochrane's footnote] Though I had suggested the plan, after all other suggestions had failed to satisfy the Board of Admiralty.[55]

** Not so forgivable are those biographers of Cochrane (among them Ian Grimble (1978), Donald Thomas (1978), and Robert Harvey (2000)) who have carried Cochrane's mistake into the present day. Grimble claims of Francis that he was 'not called as a witness although he was present' (p. 121); Thomas says that Francis' 'evidence' was 'excluded', (p. 180); Harvey writes that Francis 'was not called' (p. 200).

conscience by one octogenarian Admiral fuels the consuming bitterness of
another Admiral, equally aged, and Francis' 'debt of gratitude' to Gambier is
ill-paid. But where does innocence end and intention begin? The man who
wrote that letter had his wits about him, must have known what bait he was
presenting to the lion's den. Was this Francis' final act of revenge, his strike at
the patron who failed him, a resentment long dormant and now re-ignited by
reading Cochrane's account of long ago, a 'narrative' that 'excited in my
mind a vivid recollection of former times – as it were living that part of my life
over again'? If this was the case, it provides a sad but fiery end to Francis'
story.

Francis had written to Cochrane from Portsdown Lodge, his home for over
thirty years, chosen for its glorious naval view down to Portsmouth town, its
dockyards and harbour, and seawards out to Spithead, the old anchorage of
the Grand Fleet. This was the very panorama which had so excited the young
William Cobbett almost a century before. Francis died at Portsdown on 10
August 1865. His niece Caroline noted this in her family record. For the
Austens, it was a moment of history, the passing of a generation, and, with
wording fit for a memorial, she awarded Francis his rightful place:

The last survivor of six brothers and two sisters – several of whom had lived to old
age, but none so old as himself.[56]

Appendix

Francis Austen's account of Jane Austen, letter to Eliza Quincy, 31 January 1852 (Howe, 1925–26, pp. 321–22).

If this strikes us as a strangely distanced and unrevealing picture, it is in exactly the same style as Francis' own autobiographical Memoir. On the score of information, and a brother's knowledge of his younger sister, Francis sets a clear limit to what 'strangers' were entitled to know.

> With reference to the wish of obtaining more information relative to the life of Jane Austen, than is given in the brief memorial affixed to her latest work, I can only say, that there is little I could add to it of a nature to be interesting to strangers. Passing the greater part of her life if not in absolute retirement, yet so much out of what is commonly meant by the World, rarely mixing with any but intimate Friends and near Relations, that it would be a matter of much difficulty to recall any circumstance worth relating.
>
> Of the liveliness of her imagination and playfulness of her fancy, as also of the truthfulness of her description of character and deep knowledge of the human mind, there are sufficient evidence in her works; and it has been a matter of surprise to those who knew her best, how she could at a very early age and with apparently limited means of observation, have been capable of nicely discriminating and pourtraying such varieties of the human character as are introduced in her works. – In her temper she was chearful and not easily irritated and tho' rather reserved to strangers so as to have been by some accused of haughtiness of manner, yet in the company of those she loved the native benevolence of her heart and kindliness of her disposition were forcibly displayed. On such occasions she was a most agreable companion and by the lively sallies of her wit and good-humoured drollery seldom failed of exciting the mirth and hilarity of the party. She was fond of children and a favorite with them. Her Nephews and Nieces of whom there were many could not have a greater treat than crouding round and listening to Aunt Jane's stories.

APPENDIX 1

A note on the religious aspect of the 'Memorandums' from George Austen to Francis Austen by Irene Collins, author of *Jane Austen and the Clergy* (1993) and *Jane Austen: The Parson's Daughter* (1998).

The second paragraph of the letter to Francis shows George Austen to be up-to-date in his religious thinking. He assumes that Francis knows the Catechism by heart and that it will constantly remind him of his duty to God, his neighbour and himself. Clergy had been urged by bishops since the end of the seventeenth century to cate-chise their parishioners in order to instruct them in Protestant doctrine and stave off the Jacobite threat of a return to Catholicism; but many had ceased to do so on meeting with resistance from employers who refused to send their servants to classes and from pupils who declared them boring. The practice had recently revived in certain quarters, however, as a result of the success achieved by Evangelicals in using it not to achieve useless repetition but as a vehicle for understanding. George Austen had apparently interpreted the words of the Prayer Book in the light of his own learning, for the Catechism professes to teach candidates for Confirmation their duty to God and their neighbour only. The idea that it would also remind Francis of his duty to himself derives from the Enlightenment view that self-fulfilment can best be achieved through sympathetic understanding of others.

For further instruction in religion George Austen refers his son to *Elegant Extracts*, having presumably provided him with a copy. The passages from 'approved authors' to which Francis is urged to give his 'frequent and attentive perusal' form 'Part I: Moral and Religious' of the volume devoted to prose *Extracts*. This had been published only a few years earlier in 1783. George Austen would have been predis-posed to think highly of it, since the compiler, Vicesimus Knox, was headmaster of his old school at Tonbridge and a scholar of his Oxford College, St John's. The so-called extracts include complete reprints of John Lewis's *Notes* on the Catechism, Archbishop Secker's 'Essay on Confirmation' and Mrs Hester Chapone's guide to the Scriptures, along with parts of the Book of Common Prayer, a few of Hugh Blair's sermons, and selections from moral and philosophical articles in the *Spectator*, the *Idler* and the *Rambler*.

The remaining parts of the letter are in line with orthodox Old Testament teaching, to the effect that good behaviour brings rewards in this world as well as in the next. Even prayer is recommended to Francis not only as a duty but as being in his own interest. In the Book of Proverbs (especially chapters 3, 8 and 11) Wisdom, or the knowledge of how to lead the good life, is specifically equated with the Prudence which George Austen recommends as a guide for his son. The Church of England at that time was more respectful of the Old Testament than it has become in recent years. Even then, the idea that goodness brings earthly rewards must often have seemed to fly in the face of the evidence; but it should perhaps be remembered that

George Austen was educated during the period when Enlightenment Optimism was at its height. Acceptance of the three orders of society which Francis will find on board ship rests on the Old Testament assumption that inequality is inevitable but can be made bearable by proper conduct at all levels.

APPENDIX 2

The Lloyd's Patriotic Fund Awards

The most notable awards were silver vases from designs by John Flaxman, reputed as the great naval sculptor for his marble bust of Nelson, 1801, and the Nelson monument in St Paul's, commissioned in 1807 and installed in 1818. Between 1804 and 1809, sixty-six vases were presented to Army and Navy officers. In value rising from £35 to £350, their size and lavishness of decoration increased with the rank and perceived heroism of the recipient. For St Domingo, Francis received a £100 Vase, Rear-Admiral Louis a Vase at £350. Swords of honour – of which 153 were awarded between 1804 and 1809, when the presentations ceased – were usually to the value of £30, £50 or £100. Like the vases, the swords were works of art: with blades inscribed and lavishly decorated, and scabbards, belts and fittings of equal elaboration, the *ensemble* contained in a mahogany case with an inscribed brass plate and a card explaining the symbolism of the design. The gift of a sword might be combined with a vase or an item of silver plate. For all these awards there was a cash option. Other gifts included tureens, silver goblets and signalling whistles. For Trafalgar, exceptionally, there were three vases at £500 (actual cost £650), one at £300, on at £200, ten at £100 and twenty-three swords at £100.

For the sailors there were cash sums, typically £40 to the wounded, £20 for bravery, and for their widows, annuities of around £30. By the end of 1812, awards and assistance had been made to 13,250 officers, seamen and private soldiers, widows, orphans and dependants. (Full details are given in Dawson (1932) and Gawler (1993)).

APPENDIX 3

Commemorative Gold and Lesser Medals

These medals were coveted because of their restriction to senior officers at great naval victories. 'Chains and medals are what no fortune or connections in England can obtain', Nelson wrote to his brother (quoted in Warner, 1968, p. 75). The gold chains were only awarded on one occasion, with the Flag-officers' medals for Lord Howe's victory, the Glorious 1st of June, 1794. Thereafter, the Flag-officers' large gold medals, 2 inches in diameter, of which only twenty-two were issued, were suspended by a riband (broad white band between two blue stripes) round the neck. The smaller medals, of 1.3 inches, for Captains, were fastened by a similar riband to the third or fourth buttonhole on the left side of the coat.

For junior officers and sailors there were no official medals, a situation part-reme-died at the Battles of the Nile and Trafalgar by the distribution of officially-sanc-tioned private medals. The Trafalgar medal – gold for Flag-officers, silver for Captains and Lieutenants and bronze or white metal for the lower ranks and sailors – was arranged by Alexander Davison, Nelson's prize-agent. This neglect was not remedied until 1847 when Victoria authorized the award of a silver medal, the Naval General Service Medal, with clasps to mark the successful actions served in between 1793 and 1840.

APPENDIX 4

Francis Austen's Financial Problems, 1805–08

Both before and after Trafalgar, Francis had to endure financial complications and disappointments. At the end of March 1805, he had written to the Admiralty from the *Canopus* in the Bay of Palma at Sardinia, claiming full pay as a Captain of a 3rd rate for the few weeks between his discharge from the *Leopard* and his commission dated 31 January 1805 to take command of the *Canopus*, although his actual joining the *Canopus* in the Mediterranean was not until 29 March. Receiving no reply, Francis sent a copy of this letter on 8 November, when the *Canopus* was still off Cadiz. In fact, his original letter had been received and endorsed: '22 May. Refer to the Navy Board' and '6 June N.B^{d,s} Report'. Seemingly, his request was turned down. (PRO, ADM 1/1451, 1805 A45).

A further indignity was to follow. A Captain received his pay only at the completion of a voyage and when the Admiralty had received the ship's Log Book and all the other official documentation he was required to maintain. During the journey home from Jamaica, in April 1806, 'scudding under a reef'd Foresail in a very violent gale of wind' 'the Tiller' of the *Canopus* 'was carried away and the Ship broached to'. In the resulting 'confusion' the ship's 'Books, Papers and Accounts' were thrown from their 'desk . . . in the Gunroom' and 'so defaced and mutilated, by the water (of which there was then a considerable quantity on the Lower Gun-deck) as to be perfectly illegible'. Francis ordered his Clerk to make 'fresh transcripts'. But such was the quantity of material that these copies were not finished by the time Francis was superseded in the command of the *Canopus* on 23 June and the ship sailed under a new Captain before the copying was completed.

Francis set down these circumstances in a Memorial dated 11 March 1807, sent to the Admiralty from Southampton, requesting that 'the Rules of the Service . . . may be dispensed with' and that he receive his pay without 'the Production' of all the required ship's papers. Not only was he 'sensibly feeling the want of the wages' for his time in the *Canopus*, he was also without 'his subsequent and growing Half-pay, which constitutes a large proportion of his Income . . .'

Receiving no immediate answer to his Memorial, Francis wrote again (from the *St Albans* at Sheerness) on 11 April and once again on 15 May 1807 to enquire about the Admiralty decision; and it was not until January 1808 that he received his *Canopus* pay and the arrears of half-pay due to him.
(PRO, MS ADM 1/1451, 1807, A81).

APPENDIX 5

Patronage by the Sailor Brothers

Some limited degree of patronage was available to the sailor brothers even before they reached the rank of Post-Captain. So in 1809 we find Tom Fowle, a youngster whose father had been a pupil of Mr Austen's at Steventon, serving in the sloop *Indian* under Commander Charles Austen at Bermuda. Charles was pleased to write home that the boy, then sixteen, was 'very well' and 'growing quite manly'.[1] Joseph Sherer, son of the Vicar of Godmersham, entered the Navy as a First-Class Volunteer in 1811, under Charles' protection and Brook-George Bridges served under Francis in the *Canopus*, where he died in August 1807 from wounds received in action.

As Flag-officers, the sailor brothers had a much larger say in the appointment of their following. Two of Charles' sons, Charles jnr and Henry, served under their father in the *Bellerophon* (1838-41). Francis' flag-ship the *Vindictive* (1844-48) was very definitely a 'family ship': for two years, until the end of 1846, the Flag Lieutenant was Francis' fourth son, Herbert; his place was taken by his cousin Charles jnr, then serving as a Lieutenant; in addition, Francis' third son, George, was the Chaplain. Moreover, Francis also brought his two unmarried daughters, Cassandra and Fanny, to assist in his duty of entertaining as Commander-in-Chief of the North American and West India station.

An amused and amusing witness in the *Vindictive* was a young Lieutenant, William King-Hall, who kept a sharp-eyed diary. Cassandra, a woman of forty, features as 'Miss Vindictive' and the 'atmosphere' on board was 'dangerous'. If the ship's Captain (Michael Seymour) were to leave – a possibility, it seems – 'Cass would be the Adl. and commanding Officer.' The danger persisted. In a later entry, when the *Vindictive* had reached Bermuda, he observed that 'She is the Mistress of the Ship, influences the Adl. in every way, and in fact, I *imagine* will soon be Commander-in-Chief'. Such, he commented, were the 'evils of a Family Ship' (King-Hall, 1935, pp. 145–48).

Charles' final acts of patronage were in the Burmese War. His Flag Captain in the *Hastings* was his nephew and son-in-law Francis and amongst the officers in his Fleet were two great-nephews, Commanders Edward Bridges Rice and George William Rice, both sons of his niece Elizabeth Rice (née Knight).

As Flag Lieutenant he also carried George Maitland Purvis, married to Francis' eldest daughter Mary. Among the ladies of the family, there was some dismay at Charles' appointment for the risks it carried for a man of his age. But Francis took some comfort, trusting that it would 'in the end be productive of good to some of the family' just as it proved to be (MS Hampshire Record Office, MS 23 M93/84/17 Letter to Anna Lefroy 21 January 1850).

One instance came to grief. This was John Emilius Bridges, a cousin of twenty one.

---

[1] Letter to Cassandra Austen, 24 December 1809, quoted in *Sailor Brothers*, p. 210.

Discharged from a previous ship for debt and drunkenness, through the good offices of Francis, Charles took him into the *Bellerophon* in 1838, as a mate. But Bridges continued drinking and Charles ordered him to apply for his discharge.[2]

An excellent and detailed account of the Austen and Austen/Knight naval network is given in 'The Naval Connection' by Margaret Hammond (1998).

---

[2] For this information, I am indebted to Margaret Wilson's 'Jane's Sailor Brothers and a Real Dick Musgrove'(1999).

APPENDIX 6

The Commemoration of the Dead

A posthumous 'reward' for military heroes, satisfying to their surviving comrades and descendants, was commemoration in statues and memorials. Money was voted by Parliament in 1795 for monuments to be placed in St Paul's and Westminster Abbey celebrating the feats of British heroes; and between 1802 and 1812 over £40,000 was voted by Parliament for national monuments honouring soldiers, sailors and statesmen. But the memorialising was not untroubled. In the enthusiasm to commemorate Waterloo, the Navy's part in achieving victory over Napoleon was in danger of being overlooked (discussed here on pp. 257–59). The best account of this subject is in Yarrington (1988).

APPENDIX 7

Nelson and Obedience to Orders

That this was an important issue in the public mind as well as within the Navy itself can be judged from Southey's *Life of Nelson* (1813). Southey highlights and explains in detail a number of instances in which, with courage, command of the rules and regulations, and some exercise of ingenuity and wit, Nelson successfully carried through his own course of action in the face of orders to the contrary. See, for example, Chapter Two, the business of the broad pendant, the American traders and the Navigation Act, and the financial abuses in the West Indies. In all three cases, Nelson stood his ground doggedly against orders which he judged to be incorrect or illegal, satisfied that he was doing his 'duty' (p. 34) or demonstrating his 'Political courage' (p. 70). This freedom of judgement Nelson allowed himself out of his experience and confidence in his own ground. To youngsters, however, his advice was very different. Before all else, his 'young gentlemen' were to practise blind obedience: 'you must always implicitly obey orders, without attempting to form any opinion of your own respecting their propriety' (p. 43).

As to the risks Nelson took, these culminate in Southey's Chapter Six with several instances, leading up to the famous blind eye of Copenhagen: 'he had won the day by disobeying his orders; and in so far as he had been successful, had convicted the commander-in-chief of an error in judgement. "Well", said he, as he left the *Elephant,* "I have fought contrary to orders, and I shall, perhaps, be hanged. Never mind: let them!" ' (p. 198).

For Popham, the circumstances were entirely different. He could claim no victory; nor was it an action taken in the heat of the moment, in a compelling situation where an immediate decision was called for. His 'duty' was to have kept to his orders and remained at the Cape.

APPENDIX 8

Henry Austen's Banking Style

Following the death of his wife, Eliza de Feuillide, in April 1813, Henry was not long in recovering his 'Spirits'. As Jane wrote to Francis early in July, 'If I may so express myself, his Mind is not a Mind for affliction. He is too Busy, too active, too sanguine' (3 July 1813, *Letters*, p. 215). An immediate evidence of this resilience was his recent promotion from Deputy-Receiver of Taxes for Oxfordshire to Receiver-General, 'a promotion which he thoroughly enjoys; – as well he may; – the work of his own mind' (ibid.). 'His own mind' was set on money-making, an opportunity open to bankers in the handling of tax receipts, public funds which could be held for private profit. His banking had always been close to the wind. This was evident in his dealing with Moira, whose debts, common talk among London bankers, by 1807 exceeded £270,000. This was true, too, of Henry's original Army and Navy Agency and the banking partnership of Austen, Maunde and Austen which became Austen, Maunde and Tilson. Maunde and Tilson, like Henry himself, were ex-militia officers, exploiting their military connections. It was a high-risk clientele: at Regency card-tables, professional gamblers always passed politely as 'Captain'! Henry used his country connections as well to set up four more partnership banks: two at Alton and the others at Petersfield and Hythe. For many years he was able to live in style, as Caroline Austen puts it, 'at considerable expense, but not more than might become the head of a flourishing bank' (1986, p. 48). With premises successively at smart addresses in St James's, Albany and Henrietta Street, Covent Garden, Henry was a London banker of some distinction and sufficiently in society to be invited to the White's Club ball at Burlington House, a celebration of peace in June 1814 attended by the Prince Regent, the Emperor of Russia and the King of Prussia. As Deirdre le Faye puts it, 'Jane was quite speechless at Cassandra's news: "Henry at White's! Oh, what a Henry" ' (quoting letter of 23 June 1814, le Faye, 1989, p. 191).

Looking back to this period, the Victorian economist and essayist Walter Bagehot (himself a banker by profession) remarked on the 'charmed value' of the name 'London banker': 'There has probably very rarely ever been so happy a position . . . and never perhaps a happier' (*Lombard Street*, 1873, pp. 268–69). But Henry's occupational happiness came to an end in 1815. A crisis spread among the country banks and the collapse of his own small financial empire began. Two years later, he explained it as 'the egregious folly of my partners in a country bank who dissipated £10,000' and 'the unexampled treachery' of Moira, 'who has defrauded me of £6000' (Bearman, 1988, p. 22). A contributing factor in the collapse may have been the serious illness Henry suffered in the Autumn 1815, which must have weakened his control of the business.

By early 1816, the London bank came down as well and Henry's bankruptcy followed on 16 March. Caroline's *Reminiscences* tell us how these events hit the

Austens. 'Uncle Henry's bankruptcy' was the 'most serious misfortune of the year', 'an entire surprise at our house [that of her father, James] and as little foreseen I believe by the rest of the family'. Despite the collapse of his entire banking business, Henry's 'sanguine elastic nature' kept him afloat. 'It was ruin . . .' yet in 'a fortnight he came to Steventon, *apparently* . . . in unbroken spirits' (1989, p. 48). Charles, returning to England after the loss of the *Phoenix*, read the news months later. True to his nature, he took the loss of his money with no more than a wry comment: 'the failure of my Brother's house which perhaps may have left me with a penny' (Diary entry for 19 May 1816, NMM, MS AUS/ 106).

Another niece remembered Uncle Henry kindly, especially his 'hopefulness of temper which, in adapting itself to all circumstances, even the most adverse, served to create a perpetual sunshine' (Hill, 1902, pp. 48–49). Later generations examined him through a less rosy glass, discerning an 'almost exasperating buoyancy of sanguiness of temperament and high animal spirits which no misfortunes could depress and no failures damp' (Austen-Leigh & Knight, 1911, pp. 163–64) – a 'sanguiness' which must have been particularly galling to those of the family whose savings went down with him, not least his Uncle James Leigh-Perrot who lost £10,000 and his brother Edward, who lost twice that sum.

Henry was left 'destitute' but not down-hearted. It was, he said, the work of God. With no regrets and his 'Dreams of Affluence' ended (quoted in Watson, 1960, p. 21), he turned his back on banking for good and took to the Church – the 'best of all professions' (quoted in Bearman, 1988, p. 22), as at last it seemed to him in 1817 – the career on which he had originally been set, before joining the Militia in 1793, and which he now embraced with characteristic energy, high hopes and an opportunist eye. Observing the decline in James's health and anticipating his decease, he addressed the patron of the living of Cubbington, offering himself as the next incumbent to succeed his brother. Although Cubbington never came his way, up to the time of his death in 1850 he enjoyed an honourable and varied clerical career.

Fortunately, very little of Jane's money was lost in these disasters. The £600 profit she had already received on the sale of her novels was wisely and patriotically invested in Navy 5 per cent Stock, while all that stood to her account at the Henrietta Street bank was the sum of £25 7.0, part of her profits on *Mansfield Park*.

Moira seems to have paid off at least some of his debt. In the Hampshire Record Office there is a letter from Francis to James, written from Chawton on 14 February 1819, reporting that the Marquess of Hastings has paid £2000 by Bill of Exchange from Calcutta, a payment which should give hope to the other creditors. In another hand, the letter is inscribed 'M. Hastings acknowledgement of the Debt due to the A [?Austen / Alton] Bank' (MS/23 M93/60/2).

APPENDIX 9

The Grenville Copy of the Popham Trial *Report*

The British Library holds an annotated copy of *A Full and Correct Report of the Trial of Sir Hugh Popham* (1807) BL, G. 19449. This copy came from the library of Thomas Grenville, brother of Lord Grenville in whose Ministry he served first as President of the Board of Control (July–September 1806, with oversight of the East India Company), then as First Lord of the Admiralty (September 1806–March 1807). An inscription reads 'with notes by B. T. Esq late Secretary to the Admiralty'. Benjamin Tucker was St Vincent's Secretary and prize agent in the Channel Fleet, following him to the Admiralty as his Private Secretary when St Vincent became First Lord in February 1801. He was a Commissioner of the Navy 1801–04 and Second Secretary to the Admiralty from January–May 1804 and February 1806 to 8 March 1807.

Tucker's manuscript annotations amount to a sniping commentary on the Popham-inspired or Popham-written Preface, including the observation that 'he is, in general, regarded in the Service as a Naval Quack' (p. xxv). The flavour of Tucker's remarks can be illustrated: 'trash . . . not worth notice' (p. xxiii), 'Sir H's defence is indeed v. ingenious & political & by no means correct as to facts' (p. vii); and against the claim that Popham's 'valour is unquestionable', Tucker has written 'It has never been tried in His Majesty's Naval Service. It is a Question whether he ever saw a Ship of War in action' (p. vi). These remarks can be taken as representing an identifiable 'Admiralty' view of Popham promoted by St Vincent and his followers.

St Vincent was in correspondence with Grenville during the period leading up to the trial, giving general advice on naval matters and personalities as well as in respect of his own command of the Channel Fleet. St Vincent had a further interest in the Court Martial as his second cousin, Thomas Jervis, was counsel to the Admiralty, in effect its prosecuting lawyer in the case.

Notes

PREFACE

1   *Minor Works*, p. 446; Selwyn (1996), p. 7.

CHAPTER 1: THE NOVELIST AND THE NAVY

1   Parkinson (1977).
2   *Memoir*, pp. 13–14.
3   *Mansfield Park*, p. 265.
4   *Persuasion*, p. 156.
5   Ibid., p. 252.
6   Simpson (1870); reprinted in Southam (1981), p. 264.
7   *Persuasion*, p. 98.
8   Ibid., p. 19.
9   *Mansfield Park*, p. 60.
10 *Persuasion*, p. 170.
11 Ibid., p. 99.
12 Ibid., p. 167.
13 Ibid., p. 252.
14 Ibid., p. 30.
15 Julia Kavanagh, 1862; reprinted Southam (1968), p. 195.
16 Woolf, 1923; reprinted Southam (1968), p. 282.
17 West (1928), pp. 263–64.
18 Letter to Fanny Knight, 23 March 1817 (*Letters*, p. 335).
19 For my attempt to disentangle the origins of the tale and relate it to other stories of
    broken romance in Jane Austen's life, see Southam (1961).
20 *Family Record*, pp. 209–10; R. W. Chapman (1949).
21 BBC Television press release for the first showing of *Persuasion*, 1995. (9 March 1995), p.
    16.
22 *Memoir*, p. 5.
23 Ibid., p. 12.
24 *Persuasion*, p. 3.
25 *Persuasion*, p. 19.
26 Quoted in Hill (1902), p. 32.
27 Quoted in Southam (1968), pp. 58–69.
28 Ibid., p. 11.
29 Quoted, ibid., p. 17.
30 Churchill (1952), v. 377. For the circumstances, see Gilbert (1986), p. 609.
31 Pritchett (1969), p. 28.
32 Jane to Cassandra, 11 February 1801 (*Letters*, p. 80).
33 Lane (1984), p. 129.
34 Francis Austen's Memoir, quoted in Hopkinson (1983), p. 256.

35   Letter dated 15–16 September 1793 (*Letters*, p. 10).
36   Letter dated 26 July 1809 (*Letters*, pp. 177–78).
37   Francis Austen's Memoir, quoted in *Family Record*, p. 62.
38   NMM, MS AUS/14.
39   Memoir quoted in Hopkinson (1983), p. 253.
40   *Sailor Brothers*, p. 3.
41   Brabourne (1885), i.37.
42   Ibid., p. 38.
43   Letter to Cassandra, 21–23 January 1799 (*Letters*, p. 38).
44   Letter to Cassandra, 14–15 October 1813 (ibid., p. 239).
45   *Sailor Brothers*, p. 46.
46   Ibid., p. 36.
47   Ibid., p. 54.
48   *Memoir*, p. 15.
49   MS Rice Papers (quoted in Hammond, 1998, pp. 329–32).
50   Family papers (quoted in *Family Record*, pp. 238–39).
51   *Annual Report* (1970), p. 8.
52   *Sailor Brothers*, p. 114.

CHAPTER 2: NAVAL EDUCATION AND THE SAILOR BROTHERS

1   Quoted in Hibbert (1994), p. 119.
2   Cobbett (1796), pp. 16–17.
3   Letter to the Earl of Buckinghamshire, 10 May 1802 (Smith, 1922, ii. 251).
4   Thomson (1767), i. 144.
5   Admiral Sir Thomas Byam Martin, quoted in Parkinson (1934), p. 1.
6   Lloyd (1952), p. 472.
7   Laughton (1907), iii. 298.
8   The full character of Portsmouth – its importance, attractiveness and seamy side – are vividly drawn in chapter 10 of 'Fair Portsmouth Town', *Heart of Oak* (1975), by G. J. Marcus.
9   Lloyd (1966), p. 146.
10   Hamilton (1903), i. 23.
11   Ibid., p. 20.
12   Ibid., p. 23.
13   See St Vincent's *Memoirs*, quoted and discussed in Schom (1992), pp. 128–34, with its slanderous vituperation of Pitt and Melville.
14   Letter to Lord De Dunstanville, 14 September 1801 (Smith, 1922, i. 352).
15   Robinson (1767), i. 150.
16   Letter of 22 July 1787 (Nicolas (1844), i. 249).
17   Ibid.
18   Memoir of Francis Austen; quoted in Lane (1984), p. 89.
19   NMM, MS AUS/14.
20   Information supplied by Francis Austen to O'Byrne (1849), i. 29.
21   See especially Schom (1990).
22   W. and R. A. Austen-Leigh (1913), p. 50.
23   *Sailor Brothers*, p. 16.
24   Parkinson (1954), pp. 432–36.

25 *Family Record,* pp. 61–62.
26 Letter of 14 November 1791 (*Austen Papers,* p. 144).
27 Letter of 11 December 1824, qioted in Honan (1987), p. 378.
28 See Vick (1995).
29 Letter of Eliza de Feuillide to Philadelphia Walter, from Steventon, 26 October 1792 (*Austen Papers,* p. 149).

CHAPTER 3: FRANCIS AT SEA

1 Beaglehole (1974), iv. 440.
2 Ibid., iv. 694.
3 ii.282.
4 India Office Library, MSS Eur.B151, pp. 535, 556–57, Letters from Francis Austen, on board the *St Albans* 'in the Downs', 1, 8 August 1810.
5 PRO, ADM 1/3504: Rules and Orders of the Royal Naval Academy, Article XXXIX.
6 *Mansfield Park,* p. 236.
7 Letter from Cornwallis to Rear-Admiral John Leveson-Gower, undated (in Cornwallis-West, 1927, p. 171).
8 *Historical Manuscripts Commission* (1909), vi. 363.
9 Schom (1992), p. 138.
10 Brenton (1842), p. 6.
11 *Mansfield Park,* p. 251.
12 This account of Cornwallis is based upon *The Naval Chronicle* (1804) xi. 100 (extracted from *Public Characters of 1803–1804*), 207; xvi. 114; and Hickey (1923), iii. 361.
13 Letter to Nelson, early 1791 (West, 1927, p. 202).
14 West (1927), pp. 171–72.
15 Ibid.
16 Ibid., pp. 155–58.
17 Ibid., p. 160.
18 Ibid.
19 *Northanger Abbey,* p. 28.
20 *Sense and Sensibility,* p. 51.
21 *Minor Works,* p. 12.
22 Ibid., pp. 12–29; Tomalin (1997), p. 61.
23 *Minor Works,* p. 36.
24 Ibid., p. 40.
25 *Memoir,* p. 14.
26 *Volume the Second,* pp. 142–43.

CHAPTER 4: LIVES IN THE SERVICE

1 Letter from Nelson to Lord Moira, 30 March 1805 (*Historical Manuscripts Commission,* 1934, p. 241).
2 NMM, MS AUS/17.
3 Quoted in Longmate (1991, edn 1993), p. 258.
4 *Poems* (1807).
5 NMM, MS AUS/6: 'Remarks on the Coast of Kent from the North Foreland to Sandown', 'sent to the Admiralty, August 12th 1803'.

6 Ibid.
7 Lloyd (1955), iii. 146.
8 Letter from Napoleon to Consul Cambacérès, written at Boulogne, 16 November 1803; to the Minister for Home Affairs, 29 November 1803 (Thompson, 1954, p. 104).
9 Letter to John Wilson Croker, 17 May 1814 (MS.ADM 1/1455/107).
10 NMM, MS AUS/105.
11 Marshall (1827), Supplement Pt. II.76.
12 Caroline Austen (1986), p. 47.
13 Mrs Austen to Anna Lefroy, letter dated 21 February 1820 (quoted in *Family Record*, p. 237).
14 Addition to *Sailor Brothers* for the unpublished second edition, p. 274.
15 O'Byrne (1849), i. 26.
16 Hammond (1998), p. 51.
17 Quoted in *Memoir*, p. 15.
18 Memoir quoted in Hopkinson (1983), p. 258.
19 *Sailor Brothers*, p. 285.
20 Martin (1901), iii. 209.
21 *DNB* (1885), ii. 258–59.
22 *Memoir*, p. 207.
23 Quoted in *Family Record*, p. 243.
24 Caroline Austen (1952), p. 9.
25 20 November 1800 (*Letters*, pp. 60–61).
26 8 January 1799 (*Letters*, p. 33).
27 21–22 January 1805 (*Letters*, pp. 95–98).
28 30 June–1 July 1808 (*Letters*, p. 136).
29 1 December 1798 (*Letters*, p. 23).
30 Ibid.
31 8 November 1800 (*Letters*, p. 57).
32 Letter to Cassandra at Godmersham, 25 April 1811 (*Letters*, p. 184).
33 Letter to Cassandra at Godmersham (*Letters*, p. 52).
34 *Persuasion*, p. 252.
35 *Letters*, p. 26.
36 Ibid., p. 28.
37 Ibid., p. 29.
38 Ibid.
39 Ibid., p. 31.
40 Ibid., p. 32.
41 Ibid., p. 33.
42 Ibid., p. 35.
43 Ibid., p. 36.
44 Ibid., p. 38.
45 1802 edn, iii. 197.
46 p. 254.
47 Letter from Bath, 26–27 May 1801 (*Letters*, p. 91).
48 *Letters*, p. 63.
49 Ibid., p. 56.
50 Letter of 20 November 1800 (*Letters*, p. 60).
51 Gardner (1906), p. 180.

52 Letter from Chawton to Cassandra at Steventon, 24 January 1813 (*Letters*, p. 200).
53 Pierpont Morgan Library, MS MA 4500: letter dated 4 October 1813 to James Christie Esten, Chief Justice of Bermuda.
54 Letter from Godmersham to Cassandra at Steventon, 14–15 October 1813 (*Letters*, p. 241).
55 Letter of 14–15 October 1813 (*Letters*, p. 238).
56 Ibid., p. 239.
57 Ibid.
58 Ibid., pp. 240–41.
59 26 November 1815 (*Letters*, p. 301).
60 Ibid., p. 302.
61 NMM, MS AUS/102.
62 Letter of 3 July 1813 (*Letters*, p. 214).
63 Ibid., p. 217.
64 Letter of 25 September 1813 (*Letters*, p. 229).
65 Letter of 5–8 March 1814 (*Letters*, p. 259).
66 *Persuasion*, p. 252.
67 Letter of 18–20 November 1814 (*Letters*, p. 281).
68 Letter of 1 September 1796 (*Letters*, pp. 6–7).
69 Letter of 7–8 January 1807 (*Letters*, p. 115).
70 Letter of 11–12 October 1813 (*Letters*, p. 234).
71 p. 240.
72 p. 297.
73 p. 388.
74 Edward Cooper, quoted in Mrs Austen's letter to Mrs James Austen, 10 April 1806 (*Austen Papers*, p. 237).
75 For these percentages – estimates vary – I have followed figures in Lavery (1989), p. 187.
76 Quoted in Bryant (1942), p. 183.
77 Eliza de Feuillide reporting Jane Austen's words to Philadelphia Walter, 3 May 1797 (*Family Record*, p. 94).
78 Letter of 8 April 1798 (*Letters*, p. 13).
79 Letter to Francis Austen, 22 January 1805 (*Letters*, p. 97).
80 Letter to Cassandra, 15–16 October 1808 (*Letters*, p. 147).
81 Letter to Cassandra, 24–25 October 1808 (*Letters*, p. 150).
82 *Letters*, p. 163.
83 Ibid., p. 173.
84 Letter of 31 May 1811 (*Letters*, p. 191).
85 *Persuasion*, p. 68.
86 Letter of 20 November 1800 (*Letters*, pp. 60–61).

CHAPTER 5: PATRONAGE AND INTEREST

1 The detail of this procedure can be followed in Parkinson (1934), pp. 54–79.
2 Quoted in Edgcumbe (1912), pp. 78, 80.
3 Quoted in Warner (1968), p. 106.
4 Letter of 11 January 1804 (Nicolas, 1845, v. 364).
5 Gardner (1906), p. 174.
6 Quoted in Parkinson (1934), p. 363.
7 Entry in Nelson's Mediterranean Notebooks quoted by Marcus (1971), p. 208.

8   14 October 1803, Nicolas (1845), v. 245.

9   Marshall (1827), Supplement pt II, p. 75.

10   Ibid. (1824), ii. 278.

11   Letter of 10 October 1812, quoted in Parkinson (1934), p. 400.

12   Quoted in Warner (1958), p. 173.

13   Collingwood to Alexander Carlyle, letter dated 15 March 1801 (Hughes, 1957, p. 126).

14   *Times* 6 March 1801; *Naval Chronicle* (1801), v. 268.

15   Quoted in Smith (1922), ii. 313.

16   Quoted in Grimble (1978), p. 41.

17   Quoted in Marcus (1971), p. 208.

18   Letter of 5 May 1804 (Smith, 1922, ii. 359).

19   Quoted in Lloyd (1952), p. 482.

20   Letter of 28 March 1801 (Smith, 1922, i. 338–39).

21   Letter of 30 March 1801 (ibid., i. 340).

22   Letter of 25 February 1801 (ibid., i. 334).

23   Quoted in Lloyd (1952), p. 486.

24   Letter to St Vincent 11 January 1804 (Nicolas, 1845, v. 364).

25   Lloyd (1947), p. 22.

26   Letter of 9 April 1804 (Smith, 1922, ii. 358).

27   Letter of 9 September 1801 (ibid., i. 352).

28   Phillips (1978), p. 230.

29   Laughton (1907), iii. 83–84.

30   Clarke and M'Arthur (1809), ii. 422.

31   Letter 9 March 1805 to his nephew Captain William Lukin (*Windham Papers*, 1929, ii. 252).

32   Quoted in Fulford (1967), p. 151.

33   Letter to Sir John Carter, 17 February 1801 (Smith, 1922, i. 331).

34   Letter to Rear-Admiral Duckworth, 29 March 1801 (ibid., i. 339).

35   Glascock, *Naval Maxims* (1826), quoted in Parkinson (1934), p. 273.

36   House of Commons debate 15 March 1804 (*Hansard*, i. cols 891–93).

37   Quoted in Thorne (1986), iv. 756.

38   BL, Add. MS 39883, fol. 20.

39   BL, Add. MS 29173, fol. 281.

40   Letter to his father, 24 April 1795 (Nicolas, 1845, ii. 32).

41   Letter to Sir Edward Blackett, dated 22 July 1793 (Hughes, 1957, p. 36).

42   Corbett (1913), i. 9–10.

43   Letter from the *Shannon* at Sheerness, 16 June 1796 (quoted in Dobree, 1935, p. 19).

44   Letter of 18–19 December 1798 (*Letters*, p. 26).

45   Letter of 24–26 December 1798 (ibid., pp. 28–29).

46   Letter to Cassandra, 1–2 December 1798 (*Letters*, p. 23).

47   *Letters*, p. 31.

48   The only *Arabian Nights* reference in the novels comes towards the end of *Persuasion*, where 'Mr Elliot's character' (its dark side now revealed to Anne by Mrs Smith), 'like the Sultaness Scheherezade's head, must live another day' (p. 229). There is also a reference in 'The Three Sisters' (*Minor Works*, p. 65).

49   *Letters*, p. 32.

50   BL, Add. MS 34931, fol. 224.

51   Quoted in Caplan (1998), p. 73.

52 Quoted ibid. (1998), p. 81.
53 Quoted in Bearman (1998), p. 22.
54 *Historical Manuscripts Commission* (1934), pp. 240–241. Nicolas (1846, vi. 310) follows the garbled version in Clarke and M'Arthur (1809, ii. 398).
55 Letter to Alexander Davison, 12 December 1803 (Nicolas, 1847, v. 305)
56 Quoted in Pocock (1987), p. 311.
57 Quoted in Russell (1969), p. 312.
58 BL, Add. MS 34911, fol. 167.
59 BL, Add. MS 34916, fol. 3.
60 BL, Add. MS 34931, fol. 224.
61 Nicolas (1846), vii. 63.
62 Ibid., vii. 63. Francis provided a slightly different version in Marshall (1824), ii. 279.
63 MS, Alwyn Austen.
64 NMM, MS AUS/2B.
65 *Sailor Brothers*, p. 175.
66 These had considerable value for their precious metal and Francis was sufficiently proud to record this in Marshall's *Royal Naval Biography* (ii. 281) as 'one hundred pounds'.
67 Letter of 30 January 1805 (*Austen Papers*, p. 236).
68 The document is not known to have survived.
69 Laughton (1907), iii. 331.
70 Letter of 20-22 February 1807 (*Letters*, p. 123).
71 Quoted in Lane (1984), p. 150.
72 *Sailor Brothers*, p. 194.
73 Ibid., p. 195.
74 Details in annotated copy of *Sailor Brothers* and in India Office Library, Minutes of Court Directors and Court of Proprietors, MS Eur. B146, entry for 15 January 1808, p. 1117.
75 India Office Library, ibid., MS. Eur. B151, pp. 538, 556-57, 655, 780, 786-87, 809-10, 815. Francis's first letter was written from the *St Albans* 'in the Downs' on 1 August 1810, his last on 17 October.
76 Quoted in Lavery (1989), p.44.
77 Letter of 18-20 April 1811 (*Letters*, p. 181).
78 See Parkinson (1934), pp. 384-89.
79 Collingwood to his sister, letter of 25 June 1808 (Hughes, 1957, pp. 248-49).
80 Richardson (1908), p. 105.
81 Ibid., p. 106.
82 Ibid., p. 110.
83 Rodger (1994), p. 60.
84 Parsons (1843), p. 23.
85 Evans (1817), p. 361.
86 Talbott (1998); More (1834), iv. 226.
87 Quoted in Marcus (1971), p. 224.
88 Letter to James Currie, 11 May 1805 (Gore, 1963, p. 33).
89 *Monthly Repository* (1808), iii. 504.
90 Quotations in Ralfe (1820), ii. 132, 136, 138.
91 Ibid., (1820) ii. 131.
92 *Annual Register . . . 1805*, p. 543.
93 Ralfe (1820), ii. 135.

94   Ibid., p. 132.
95   Quoted in Clowes (1900), v. 256.
96   Dillon (1956), ii. 269.
97   Gray (1963), p. 395.
98   Aspinall (1968), v. 298.
99   Sanders (1908), p. 150.
100 Undated letter (receipt dated 'Jan. 24') sent from Portsdown Lodge (BL, Add. MS 38039, fol. 184).
101 Letter of 21-22 January 1801 (*Letters*, p. 75).
102 *Mansfield Park*, p. 368.

CHAPTER 6: THE REWARDS OF SUCCESS

1   *Persuasion*, p. 247.
2   James (1826), iii. 403.
3   Southey (1813, edn 1906), p. 267.
4   Letter of 10 November 1805 (Aspinall, 1968, v. 274).
5   *Naval Chronicle* (July–December 1805), xiv. 463–66.
6   Letter to Cassandra, 24 August 1805 (*Letters*, p. 108).
7   Letter of 27 January 1805 (*Austen family ms*).
8   Letter of 28 January 1805 (*Austen Papers*, p. 234).
9   Letter of 30 January 1805 (ibid., p. 236).
10 Nicolas (1846), vi. 443–44.
11 6 October 1805 (Nicolas, 1846, vii. 80).
12 9 October 1805 (ibid., p. 95).
13 Quoted in Schom (1992), p. 307.
14 See above, pp. 93–94.
15 1 October 1805 (Nicolas, 1846, vii. 60).
16 See above, p. 90.
17 See below, p. 131.
18 Letter of 19 August 1804 (Nicolas, vi. 162).
19 Letter of 6 September 1804 (ibid., vi. 193).
20 Burney (1815), p. 354.
21 The rubric of the early nineteenth-century *Book of Common Prayer*.
22 Stephen (1805) quoted in Marcus (1971), p. 125.
23 Ibid., p. 126.
24 'A Discourse of the Invention of Ships', Raleigh (1829), viii.325.
25 Quoted in Colley (1992), p. 65.
26 Letter of 31 January 1799 (Nicolas, 1845, iii. 245).
27 Quoted in Nelson's letter, 3 July 1802 (Nicolas, 1845, v. 21).
28 Ibid., pp. 21–22.
29 Letter of 8 September 1802 (Nicolas, 1845, v. 29).
30 Letters of 8 and 24 November 1802 (quoted in Russell, 1969, p. 250).
31 From the Preamble to the Proceedings of the Fund's inaugural meeting, 20 July 1803, quoted in Gawler (1993), pp. 119–20.
32 Friendly (1977), p. 136.
33 Quoted in Flower (1981), p. 77.
34 *Naval Chronicle* (1807), xvii. 45–47.

35 *Cobbett's Annual Register* (July–December 1803), iv. cols 281–85, 353–59, 415, 448, 471–78, 607.

36 See correspondence in *The Times*, 20, 22 August 1803.

37 *Cobbett's Weekly Political Register* (24 January 1807), xi. col. 105.

38 Ibid., col. 102.

39 Ibid., (19 April 1806), ix. cols 602–3.

40 Ibid., (11 January 1806), ix. col. 41.

41 *Parliamentary Debates*, x. col. 38, 21 January 1808, quoted in Harvey (1978), p. 323.

42 Quoted in Harvey (1978), p. 330.

43 *Naval Chronicle* (February–March 1812), xxvii.254.

44 Anson (1913), p. 177. This splendid example of decorative art is shown in colour in Morriss (1995), p. 97.

45 Fremantle (1937), ii. 172.

46 Brenton (1823–25), i. 193–94; ii. 381–82.

47 Quoted in Lloyd (1947), p. 101.

48 Quoted in Hibbert (1995), p. 236.

49 Vol. x, p. 432.

50 Letter to Sir Alexander Ball, 5 December 1804 (Nicolas, 1846, vi. 285).

51 Letter to Hugh Elliott, 13 January 1805 (ibid., p. 319).

52 Letter to Mrs Bolton, 9 May 1805 (ibid., p. 429).

53 Letter of 29 December 1804 (ibid., pp. 306–7).

54 Edgeworth (1808, 1812), pp. 222–23.

55 Lloyd (1952), p. 484.

56 Letter of 7 September 1798 (Nicolas, 1845, iii. 115).

57 Letter to G. L. N. Collingwood, 15 November 1805 (Collingwood, 1828, edn. 1837, i. 215).

58 Letter of 1 January 1806 (Hughes, 1957, p. 169).

59 Letter of 1 March 1806 (ibid., p. 173).

60 Quoted in Honan (1987), p. 331.

61 Letter of 14 March 1797 (Parkinson, 1934, p. 185).

62 Ibid., p. 187.

63 Ibid., pp. 186–87.

64 Collingwood (1829), i. 338–39.

65 Letter of 11 September 1793 (Nicolas, 1844, i. 325).

66 Letter of 11 February 1801 (*Letters*, p. 80).

67 Letter of 24 January 1809 (*Letters*, p. 169).

68 Letter of 24 December 1808 (*Sailor Brothers*, p. 209).

69 Jane to Cassandra Austen, 26–27 May 1801 (*Letters*, p. 91).

70 *Sailor Brothers*, pp. 72–73; *Steel's Prize Pay Lists*, February 1793 to 1 December 1802, 1803, supplement to 2nd edn.

71 Hall (1998), p. 183.

72 Dillon (1956), ii. 119.

73 PRO, ADM 1/1452 (1808), A85.

74 Letter to her cousin, Philadelphia Walter, now Mrs Whitaker, 18 August 1811 (*Austen Papers*, p. 249).

75 Letter to Philadelphia Walter, 20 March 1812 (ibid., pp. 251–52).

76 Quoted in Kaplan (1992a), p. 118.

77 Vol. xiv (July–December 1805), p. 255.

78 Letter from Mrs George Austen to her sister Mrs Jane Leigh-Perrot, 4 January 1820 (*Austen Papers*, p. 264).

CHAPTER 7: POLITICS AND THE NAVY

1 Quoted in Hopkinson typescript, ch. 3, p. 4.
2 Quoted in Selwyn (1999), p. 53.
3 Letter of 1 October 1808 (*Letters*, p. 138).
4 Quoted in Hill (1901), p. 152.
5 MS Journal, Hertfordshire Record Office, document reference 61175, quoted in Vick (1996), p. 35.
6 Simond (1908), p. 150.
7 Letter of 7 January 1807 (*Letters*, p. 114).
8 Ibid., p. 117.
9 Ibid., p. 115.
10 Letter of 8 February 1807 (ibid., p. 121).
11 Ibid., p. 117.
12 Letter of 8 February 1807 (ibid., p. 119).
13 'Beware of the insipid Vanities and idle Dissipations of the Metropolis of England; Beware of the unmeaning Luxuries of Bath & of the Stinking fish of Southampton' (*Minor Works*, pp. 78–79). Jane Austen may be recalling her first stay in Southampton in 1783 when Mrs Ann Cawley moved her Oxford boarding school there.
14 *Memoir*, p. 82.
15 Letter of 8 February 1807 (*Letters*, p. 119).
16 Ibid.
17 Ibid.
18 Ibid., p. 121.
19 Letter of 20 February 1807 (ibid., p. 123).
20 Ibid.
21 Quoted in Hopkinson, typescript, ch. 3, p. 9.
22 Letter of 20 February 1807 (*Letters*, p. 123).
23 The text given here is that of the original manuscript in Selwyn (1996), p. 7, a version more accurate than the other two sources, Brabourne (1884) or *Minor Works* (1954).
24 Tucker (1994), p. 78.
25 Selwyn (1996), pp. 80–81.
26 *Minor Works*, p. 446.
27 For this information I am indebted to a letter Hugh Popham sent to Deirdre Le Faye in 1992 when Miss Le Faye was herself pursuing this very question of a possible connection.
28 *Austen Papers*, p. 129.
29 Quoted in Harvey (1992), p. 174.
30 General H. E. Fox, forwarding the Reports of Inspecting Field Officers of the Yeomanry and Volunteers in the Home District, to Major-General H. Calvert, 14 March 1804 (quoted in Glover (1973) p. 210).
31 Ham (1945), p. 62.
32 Fremantle (1940), iii. 95, entry for 24 October 1803.
33 *Parliamentary Debates* 3 April 1806, vi. col. 678 (1806).
34 Quoted in Glover (1973), p. 143.
35 Ibid., p. 210.
36 Ibid., p. 45.
37 *The Form and Order of the Service . . . in the Coronation of Their Majesties King George III and Queen Charlotte* (1761), p. 32.

38 Quoted in Twiss (1844), ii. 34.
39 See, for example, J. H. Plumb (1956), p. 145.
40 Quoted in Sawtell (1989), p. 25.
41 In Lefroy (1998) and further in unpublished Lefroy family manuscripts.
42 Quoted in Honan (1987), p. 92.
43 Ibid., p. 232.
44 Letter to Cassandra, 7 January 1807 (*Letters*, p. 116).
45 No. 21.
46 Letter of 10 May 1804 from the Prince of Wales' Private Secretary to Moira, *Historical Manuscripts Commission* (1934), p. 232.
47 Anon. (1819), p. 34.
48 Quoted in Fry (1992), p. 281.
49 Thomas Grenville to his elder brother, the Marquis of Buckingham, 23 February 1807 (Grainger, 1996, p. 164).
50 Same to same, 6 March 1807 (ibid., p. 169).
51 Ibid.
52 Fremantle (1940), iii. 310.
53 PRO, ADM 1/1452 (1808) A.63.
54 Given in the *Naval Chronicle* (1799), i. 480-87, with further documentation ii. 52-55.
55 Nicolas (1844-46), vii. 131.
56 Views quoted in Popham (1991).
57 Mrs Nicholson Croft, quoted in Stokes (1986), p. 868.
58 Letter from Marquess of Buckingham to Lord Grenville, September 1804 (quoted in Popham, 1991, p. 116).
59 See Appendix 9.
60 Unnumbered pages.
61 Quoted in Popham (1991), pp. 44-45.
62 Ibid., p. 30.
63 Ibid., p. 54.
64 Ibid., p. 60.
65 Letter of 25 April 1798 (Corbett, 1913, p. 319).
66 Quoted in *Dictionary of National Biography* (1894), xlvi. 145.
67 January-June 1805, xiii. 136.
68 Lloyd (1952), p. 471.
69 A letter from John Turnbull, a City merchant and a strong ally, to Miranda, dated 17 September 1806, quoted in Robertson (1929), i. 323.
70 Farington, entry for 5 October 1806, viii.2879.
71 Letter to Cassandra, 17 October 1815 (*Letters*, p. 291).
72 Perrin (1928), iii. 202-3, quoting Wilkie, 'Recollections of the British Army in the Late Revolutionary Wars' (*United Services Journal*, 1836, vols i-iv).
73 Quoted in Popham (1991), p. 152.
74 Entry for 2 October 1806, *London's Roll of Fame* (1884), p. 100.
75 Quoted in Popham (1991), p. 152.
76 Ibid., p. 152.
77 *Diary* entry for 6 October 1806 (Farington, viii.2881).
78 *Cobbett's Weekly Parliamentary Record*, vol. x (July-December 1806), issue for 20 September 1806, col. 458.
79 Ibid., issue for 27 September, col. 543.

80 Ibid., issue for 27 December, col. 1006.

81 Ibid., vol. xi (January-June 1807), issue for 24 January 1807, col. 165.

82 Quoted in Gawler (1993), p. 109.

83 Issue for 27 December 1806, vol. x, col. 1006.

84 Issue for 24 January 1807, vol. xi. col. 102.

85 *Annual Register* (1807), p. 209.

86 Ibid., p. 212.

87 Ibid.

88 Quoted in Popham (1991), p. 29.

89 Ibid., p. 34.

90 Popham (1799, edn 1805), p. 35.

91 Quoted in Popham (1991), p. 34.

92 Ibid., p. 29.

93 See Hickey, *Memoirs* (1925, iv. 270–71).

94 *Naval Chronicle* (August–October 1804), xii. 309–13.

95 Quoted in Popham (1991), p. 119.

96 Quoted in Lane (1984), p. 134.

97 Quoted in Popham (1991), p. 118.

98 John, Lord Campbell, letter of 17 May 1804 (Hardcastle, 1881, i. 150).

99 Quotations which follow are taken from the text printed in the *American Historical Review* (April 1901), vi. 509–17.

100 Robertson (1919), i. 278.

101 *Historical Manuscripts Commission* (1934), p. 237.

102 'Memorandum by Henry Dundas . . . for the consideration of his Majestys ministers, 31 March 1800' (Hattendorf, 1993, pp. 346–48).

103 Aspinall (1964) ii. 485, 486.

104 Quoted in *Annual Biography* (1822), p. 288.

105 Letter of 7 July 1806 (Aspinall, 1968, iv. 399–400).

106 Quoted in Oman (1947), p. 551.

107 Quoted in Robertson (1929), i. 316.

108 *Historical Manuscripts Commission* (1934), pp. 240–41.

109 *Hampshire Telegraph*, 9 March 1807.

110 *Hampshire Chronicle*, 16 March 1807.

111 Ibid.

112 Hill (1998), p. 40.

113 Quoted ibid.

114 *Hampshire Chronicle*, 16 March 1807.

115 *Othello*, I. iii. 80–90.

116 *Diary* entry for 16 March 1807 (Farington, viii.2990).

117 *Universal Magazine*, (1807), vii. 329.

118 Ibid., p. 265.

119 Admiralty order quoted in Popham (1991), p. 175.

120 Quoted ibid., p. 178.

121 Ibid., p. 190.

122 Ibid., p. 179.

123 Quoted in Harvey (1992), p. 100.

124 *Monthly Repository* (February 1808), iii. 123.

125 Popham (1991), p. 180.

126 *Gentleman's Magazine* (1820), ii. 274.

127 Letter to Colonel John McMahon, Calcutta, 6 March 1814, (Aspinall, *Letters of George IV*, 1938, i. 398).

128 Quoted in Jupp (1985), p. 382.

129 A comment from Lord Holland, a nephew of Fox and widely regarded as his political heir (Holland, 1854, ii. 112).

130 Letter of 18 September 1807 from Moira to his cousin, General Charles Hastings (*Historical Manuscripts Commission*, 1934, p. 330).

131 Information provided by Mr David Willan, a descendant of Charles Austen and owner of the Sword.

132 Dupuoy (1966), pp. 279, 392.

133 Letter of 24 January 1813 (*Letters*, p. 198).

134 Carnall (1960), p. 123.

135 Pasley (1810), p. 448.

136 11 February 1811, quoted in Harvey (1992), p. 134.

137 *Quarterly Review* (May 1811), p. 437.

138 Wordsworth to Pasley, 28 March 1811 (Wordsworth, 1969, ii. 473).

139 *The Courier*, 4 June 1811.

40 Pasley (1810), pp. 1–2.

141 Ibid., p. 3.

142 Ibid., p. 62.

143 Ibid., p. 117.

144 Ibid., p. 533.

145 Ibid., p. 192.

NOTES TO NAVAL FACT AND NAVAL FICTION

1 Hopkinson MS (quoted in Honan, 1987, p. 156).

2 Fanny-Caroline Lefroy, MS Family History, quoted in *Family Record*, pp. 113–14.

3 *Mansfield Park*, pp. 431–32.

4 Letter to Cassandra dated 3–5 January 1801 (*Letters*, pp. 68–69).

5 Published as *Volume the First* (1933), the *Second* (1963) and *Third* (1951), collected in the *Minor Works*.

6 Letter of 1 July 1808 (*Letters*, p. 138).

7 See, for example, *Letters* nos. 84, 85, 87, 88.

8 Letter of 25 September 1813 (*Letters*, p. 229).

9 Letter of 30 June 1808 (*Letters*, p. 139).

10 Letter of 24 August 1805 (*Letters*, p. 108).

11 Letter of 15 June 1808 (*Letters*, p. 127).

12 Letter of 6 November 1813 (*Letters*, p. 253).

13 Letter of 30 June 1808 (*Letters*, p. 137).

14 *Family Record*, p. 419.

15 *Memoir*, p. 28.

16 See Southam (1961), pp. 464–65, and *Family Record*, pp. 126–27.

17 Letter of 26 July 1809 (*Letters*, p. 178).

18 Scott (1815) in Southam (1968), pp. 59, 63, 67.

19 Preface to *The Spoils of Poynton* (1897), New York edition (1907–17), quoted in Allott (1959), p. 75.

20 *A Personal Record* (1912), quoted ibid., p. 76.
21 Letter to Anna Austen, 18 August 1814 (*Letters*, p. 269).

CHAPTER 8: *MANSFIELD PARK*

1   Letter of 3 July 1813 (*Letters*, p. 217).
2   *Mansfield Park*, p. 461.
3   Butler (edn 1988), p. xvi.
4   *Mansfield Park*, p. 245.
5   Ibid., p. 246.
6   Ibid., p. 234.
7   Ibid., p. 21.
8   Ibid., p. 60.
9   Ibid., p. 21.
10 Ibid., p. 60.
11 Ibid.
12 Letter of 12–13 May 1801 (*Letters*, p. 86).
13 Brophy in Southam (1968a), p. 25.
14 Honan (1988), p. 160.
15 *Mansfield Park* (1996), p. 396.
16 *Minor Works*, p. 148.
17 1811 edn, p. 66; see note, p. 384.
18 *Minor Works*, p. 433.
19 Byron (1980), ii. 15, 63. Cantos One and Two were written and corrected between October 1809 and up to the time of their printing in February 1812. The volume was published on 10 March 1812.
20 *Mansfield Park*, p. 60.
21 Ibid., p. 41.
22 Ibid., p. 63.
23 Ibid., p. 109.
24 Ibid.
25 Ibid., p. 111.
26 Ibid., p. 110.
27 Ibid., pp. 110–11.
28 Ibid., p. 111.
29 Quoted in Oman (1947), p. 628.
30 Thursfield (1951), p. 8.
31 *Regulations* (1806, edn 1808), pp. 247. 248.
32 Lavery (1989), p. 209. There is a high degree of partiality to Mangin's account. He went to sea in 1812 aged 40, serving in the Navy only 14 weeks in all. Appended to his manuscript is this note: 'My object – to show how out of place a clergyman is in a ship-of-war, especially in war-time' (Thursfield, 1951, p. 1).
33 Baynham (1969), p. 94.
34 *Mansfield Park*, p. 110.
35 Steel's *Navy List*, March 1812; also see *Hansard*, Commons, 22 February 1812, col. 885.
36 *Mansfield Park*, p. 198.
37 Quoted in Howse (1953, edn 1971), p. 140.
38 Quoted in Eltis (1974), p. 6.

39 MS addition to *Sailor Brothers*, facing p. 193.
40 *Sailor Brothers*, p. 192.
41 Colley (1992), p. 351.
42 Letter of 4 March 1796 (Nicolas, 1845, ii. 131).
43 Letter of 16 April 1796 (ibid., ii. 154).
44 *Monthly Repository* (1807), ii. 202–03, index.
45 Letter of 10 June 1805 (Balleine, 1908, p. 119). The text given in Nicolas (vi. 451) was taken from Clarke and M'Arthur and is corrupt.
46 Pollock (1977), p. 52.
47 Letter of Creevey to James Currie, 11 May 1805 (Gore, 1963, p. 33).
48 Letter of 24 January 1813 (*Letters*, p. 198).
49 *Mansfield Park*, p. 236.
50 Ibid., p. 235.
51 Ibid., p. 236.
52 Ibid., p. 232.
53 Ibid., p. 233.
54 Ibid., p. 236.
55 Ibid.
56 Ibid., pp. 236–37.
57 Ibid., p. 229.
58 Ibid., p. 232.
59 Ibid., p. 235.
60 Ibid., p. 237.
61 Ibid., p. 254.
62 Ibid., p. 259.
63 Ibid., p. 260.
64 Ibid., p. 271.
65 Ibid., p. 250.
66 Ibid., p. 364.
67 Ibid., p. 266.
68 Ibid.
69 Ibid., pp. 298–99.
70 Dillon (1956), ii. 431.
71 *Mansfield Park*, p. 246.
72 Ibid., p. 299.
73 Ibid., p. 300.
74 Ibid., p. 301.
75 Ibid., p. 235.
76 Ibid., p. 302.
77 Ibid., p. 319.
78 Ibid., p. 328.
79 Ibid., p. 265.
80 Ibid., p. 368.
81 Ibid., p. 372.
82 Ibid., p. 375.
83 Ibid., p. 384.
84 Ibid., p. 388.
85 Ibid., p. 235.

86   Ibid., pp. 21–22.
87   Ibid., pp. 234–35.
88   Auerbach (1972), p. 119.
89   Ryle (Southam, 1968a, p. 113).
90   *Mansfield Park*, p. 400.
91   Ibid., p. 473.
92   Ibid., p. 388.
93   Ibid., p. 389.
94   Southey (1833), i. 2.
95   *Mansfield Park*, p. 3.
96   Ibid., p. 239.
97   See Lowe (1990), 'Commissioned Ranks', pp. li–lxii.
98   Quoted in Lavery (1989), p. 146.
99   John Davis, *The Post Captain* (1805), p. 55.
100 Anon, *Symptoms* (1789), p. vi. The concluding words to the Preface.
101 These stages are recounted in Steele, *The Marine Officer* (1840), i. 26–51. His account covers 1803.
102 See the example given by R. W Chapman in *Mansfield Park*, p. 541.
103 *Regulations and Instructions* (1808), p. 421.
104 Parkinson (1948b), p. 27.
105 Glascock (1826), quoted in Parkinson (1948b), p. 28.
106 *Hansard*, Commons Debates, 12 February 1812, cols. 753–61.
107 Letter to Cassandra, 27–28 October 1798 (*Letters*, p. 18).
108 Letter to Cassandra, 19 June 1799 (*Letters*, p. 48).
109 Letter to Cassandra, 8–9 November 1800 (*Letters*, p. 55).
110 *Mansfield Park*, p. 4.
111 Ibid., p. 3.
112 Ibid., p. 4.
113 Ibid., p. 387.
114 Ibid., p. 440.
115 Ibid., p. 389.
116 Ibid., p. 402.
117 Ibid., p. 379.
118 Ibid., p. 380.
119 Ibid., pp. 380–81.
120 Ibid., p. 383.
121 *Memoir*, p. 14.
122 Article 2, Articles of War of 1749 as amended by 19 GEO III, C.17, quoted in Byrd (1989), p. 203.
123 Quoted in Smith (1808), reprinted in Smith (1869), p. 107.
124 *Mansfield Park*, pp. 548–49.
125 For various conflicting views see *Mansfield Park*, p. 549, and challenged in *Letters*, p. 580; also Thomas (1990), p. 62 and Marcus (1971), pp. 143–44.
126 *Letters*, pp. 102, 164.
127 NMM, MS AUS. 62/103.
128 Quoted in Storey (1997), p. 219.
129 Letter from Chawton, 3–6 July 1813 (*Letters*, p. 217).
130 Letter from Godmersham, 25 September 1813 (*Letters*, p. 231).

131 Clowes, vols 4 and 5.
132 Diary entry for 25 June 1794 (Wilberforce, 1872, p. 123).
133 Quoted in Marcus (1971), p. 142.
134 Jane Austen to Cassandra, 6 June 1811 (*Letters*, p. 194).
135 *Mansfield Park*, p. 432.
136 Ibid., pp. 376–77.
137 Quoted in Vick (1996b), p. 35.
138 *Mansfield Park*, p. 380.
139 Ibid., p. 384.
140 Ibid., p. 400.
141 Ibid., p. 402.
142 Ibid., p. 403.
143 See, for example, J. B. Scott (1930), p. 64; Vick (1996b), pp. 35–36; Climenson (1899), pp. 266–68.
144 *The Portsmouth Guide* (1775), quoted in Sutherland (1996), p. 412.
145 *Mansfield Park*, p. 372.
146 Adeane (1907), p. 98.
147 *Mansfield Park*, p. 404.
148 Ibid., p. 406.
149 Ibid., p. 408.
150 Quoted in Sutherland (1996), pp. 412–13.
151 *Mansfield Park*, p. 409.
152 Ibid., p. 409.
153 Ibid., p. 473.
154 Ibid., p. 387.
155 Ibid., p. 413.
156 Ibid., p. 409.
157 Ibid., p. 384.
158 Ibid., p. 473.
159 *Minor Works*, pp. 431–35. The thirty-eight comments were collected in the autumn of 1814.
160 *Minor Works*, p. 486.
161 Letter of 1 April 1816 (*Letters*, p. 313).

CHAPTER 9: NELSON – HEROISM, HONOUR AND DISHONOUR

1 Letter of 25 September 1813 (*Letters*, p. 231).
2 Ibid.
3 Aspinall (1949), p. 26.
4 *My Aunt*, p. 12.
5 Ibid., pp. 11, 13.
6 *Memoir*, p. 115, the opening page to chapter 7.
7 *Letters*, p. 312.
8 Nokes (1997), p. 484.
9 Letter of April 1816 (*Letters*, p. 312).
10 Ibid.
11 Ibid.
12 *Letters*, p. 307.
13 Quoted in Hibbert (1975), p. 341.

14　Farington, diary entry for 15 July 1807, viii.3088.
15　Letter of 21 December 1815 (*Letters*, p. 307).
16　Ibid.
17　*Naval Chronicle* (1800), iii. 1–38.
18　*Naval Chronicle* (1803), x. 438–40.
19　Brooke (1972), p. 327.
20　*DNB* (1895), xliv. 112.
21　*Naval Chronicle* (1800), iii. 29.
22　*L'Allegro*, lines 26, 151.
23　*Naval Chronicle* (1800), iii. 410.
24　Clarke (1811), p. xx.
25　Clarke (1816), i. v.
26　See Southam (1998), pp. 11–16.
27　Clarke (1816), i. xxix.
28　Ibid.
29　Ibid., p. xxvi.
30　July 1813, 4th series, iv. 11.
31　*Gentleman's Magazine* (December 1810), lxxx. 556. The review, too, was appropriately large in scale, running across three issues (January and April 1811 followed).
32　Steele (1840), ii. 140–41.
33　Oman (1947), p. vii.
34　Nicholas (1844), i. ix.
35　Clarke (1809), i. iv.
36　Clarke (1809), i. 1.
37　Letter of 28 May 1806, BL, Add. MS 34992, fol. 146.
38　'whose ... laying unhallowed hands upon such a subject, I am desired not to spare' (Southey to Charles Danvers, 14 December 1809, quoted in Shine, 1949, p. 14).
39　Southey to John May, 24 November 1805 (Ramos, 1976, p. 105). But Southey was mistaken. The review in the *Monthly Review* (October 1805, xlviii. 113–22) was not by Clarke but by John Ferriar, a regular reviewer.
40　Southey (1810), p. 221. Southey had already reviewed volume one of *Progress* in *The Annual Review 1803* (1804, ii. 12–20), calling Clarke's 230 quarto pages of Introduction 'altogether a work of supererogation' (p. 12), where 'the blind lead the blind' (p. 13). Southey concluded his review expressing his indignation that the *Progress* appeared under the patronage, and with the approval, of the First Lord of the Admiralty, St Vincent.
41　Southey (1810), p. 222.
42　Letter of 19 February 1810 (Southey, 1965, i. 529).
43　Murray to Southey, 28 October 1811 (Smiles, 1891, i. 178).
44　*Edinburgh Review* (January 1814), xxii. 454.
45　The opening four stanzas were first published in the *Courier*, 8 January 1814 and the poem in full later that year.
46　Letter of 11 October 1813 (*Letters*, p. 235).
47　Russell (1969), p. 39. Although this book is unreferenced, as an end-note reveals, it is based on a very wide range of manuscript sources.
48　Letter of 8 January 1799 (*Letters*, p. 33).
49　Southey (1813), p. 131.
50　Ibid., p. 244.

51 Ibid., p. 253.
52 Ibid., p. 149.
53 Ibid.
54 Ibid., p. 154.
55 *Quarterly Review* (April 1814), xi. 73.
56 Edgcumbe (1912), p. 79.
57 *Edinburgh Review* (September 1814), xxii. 399.
58 Ibid., p. 400.
59 Ibid., p. 405.
60 Letter of 12 May 1801 (*Letters*, p. 85).
61 *Letters*, p. 208.
62 Fraser (1996), p. 217.
63 Quoted in Russell (1969), p. 108.
64 Ibid.
65 Nicolas (1846), vii. 140–41.
66 Southey (1906), p. 262.
67 Letter of January 1806 (Sharpe, 1885, i. 251).
68 Aspinall (1938), i. 227–28.
69 Dillon (1956), ii. 122.
70 Letter of 15 November 1799 (Nicolas, 1845, iv. 205).
71 26 June 1800, quoted in Oman (1947), p. 387.
72 Hughes (1957) i. 110.
73 *Mansfield Park*, p. 41.
74 Ibid., p. 456.
75 Ibid., p. 295.
76 Ibid., p. 46.
77 Ibid., p. 467.
78 Ibid., p. 225.
79 Ibid., p. 456.
80 Letter of Fanny Knight, 13 March 1817 (*Letters* p. 333). The Paget story is elucidated by Deirdre Le Faye in the notes (ibid., pp. 463–64, 557 and 560).
81 Letter to Cassandra, 18–19 December 1798 (*Letters*, p. 26).
82 Letter to Cassandra, 24 October 1798 (ibid., p. 15).
83 Letter to Cassandra, 24 October 1808 (ibid., p. 152).
84 Quoted in Harris (1906), p. 433.
85 Brabourne (1885), i. 26.
86 *Minor Works*, p. 431.
87 Selwyn (1996), p. 56.

CHAPTER 10: *EMMA*

1 Quoted in Simmons (1945), p. 140.
2 Ibid., p. 143.
3 Southey (1813), p. 108.
4 Southey (1849–50), iv. 52.
5 Ibid., iv. 53.
6 Ibid., iv. 54.
7 Southey (1965), ii. 92.

8 Diary entry 8 April 1814 (quoted in Tomalin, 1997, p. 242).
9 Letter to Cassandra, 23 June 1814 (*Letters*, p. 264).
10 Letter to Anna Austen, 9 September 1814 (*Letters*, p. 275).
11 *Emma* p. 101.
12 Ibid., p. 106.
13 Ibid., p. 73.
14 Ibid., p. 200.
15 See Cottrell (1989), Hellstrom (1965), Surel (1989) and Wright (1867).
16 *Mansfield Park*, p. 42.
17 Edgeworth (1986), p. 159.
18 *Mansfield Park*, pp. 437, 440.
19 Alfred Percy's unflattering description to his sister Caroline (pp. 301–02).
20 *Emma*, p. 398.
21 Ibid., p. 399.
22 Ibid., p. 146.
23 Ibid., p. 46.
24 Letter of 22 April 1801 (Nicolas, 1845, iv. 345).
25 *Emma*, p. 446.
26 Ibid., p. 149.
27 Ibid., p. 348.
28 Ibid., p. 368.
29 Ibid., p. 57.
30 Ibid., pp. 99–100.
31 Ibid., p. 448.
32 Ibid., p. 223.
33 Ibid., p. 386.
34 Ibid., p. 146.
35 Well discussed in Fiona Stafford's Introduction to the Penguin Classics *Emma* (1996).
36 *Emma*, p. 199.
37 Ibid., p. 178.
38 Ibid., pp. 199–200.
39 Entry for 7 April 1775 (Boswell, 1934, ii. 348).
40 *The Task* (1785), v, lines 495–96.
41 Friendly (1977), p. 139.
42 *Epistulae ex Ponto*, i. 3. 29.
43 *The Task*, i, line 654–58.
44 Edgeworth (1812), p. 141.
45 Edgeworth, *Patronage* (1814), p. 376.
46 *Aeneid*, vi, line 823.
47 Lord Coleridge (1906), p. 106.
48 *Emma*, p. 200.
49 The first edition of *Rural Rides* (1830) collected Cobbett's contributions to the *Political Register*, 1822–26; the second edition, 1853, added further tours.
50 Entry for 21 November 1821 (*Rural Rides*, 1853, p. 38).
51 8 August 1823, *Rural Rides* (1853) p. 209.
52 Butler (1975), p. 272.
53 *Emma*, p. 225.
54 Ibid., p. 100.

55 Ibid., p. 361.
56 Ibid., p. 473.
57 Ibid., p. 100.
58 Stevenson (1813), p. 78.
59 *Emma*, p. 29; See Southam (1971).
60 Stevenson (1813), pp. 73–74.
61 Repton (1816), p. 192.
62 *Emma*, p. 106.
63 Repton (1816), p. 191.
64 Cobbett (1967), pp. 122, 139 etc.
65 *Pride and Prejudice*, p. 249.
66 Ibid., p. 358.
67 Ibid., p. 55.
68 Ibid., p. 56; *The Task*, i. lines 338–39.
69 *Emma*, p. 358.
70 Gilpin (1782), p. 31.
71 *Emma*, p. 358.
72 Bate (1999), p. 545. Bate (2000) provides a valuable discussion of landscape and culture in Jane Austen (see especially pp. 5–13, 130–31).
73 *Emma*, p. 360.
74 Ibid.
75 Ibid., p. 361.
76 Repton (1806), p. 83.
77 *Emma*, p. 360.
78 Gilpin (1798), p. 27.
79 Gilpin (1808), p. 37.
80 Dayes (1805), pp. 2, 268.
81 *Emma*, pp. 364–65.
82 Mitford (1818), i. viii.
83 Bridges (1814), p. v.
84 *Minor Works*, p. 439.
85 Ibid., 436.
86 NMM, MS AUS/106: diary entries for 28 April, 8 May 1816.
87 *Minor Works*, p. 439.
88 Ibid., p. 439.
89 Letter to Cassandra, 26 November 1815 (*Letters*, p. 302).
90 Melville's words for the island of Kokovoko, Queequeg's home, at the opening to ch. 12 of *Moby-Dick*.

CHAPTER 11: *PERSUASION*

1 *Minor Works*, p. 380
2 *Naval Chronicle* (January–June 1814), xxxi, Preface, p. v.
3 *Parliamentary Debates* (29 June 1815), xxxi, col. 1050.
4 Ibid. (February 1816), xxxii. col. 311.
5 Ibid. col. 313.
6 Ibid. cols. 314, 315.
7 Ibid., col. 319.

8 Ibid., col. 320.
9 Ibid.
10 McCahill (1986), pp. 420–21.
11 Baines (1817), ii. 366.
12 Ibid., ii. 370.
13 Diary entry for 9 July 1813 (Haydon, 1960, i. 311).
14 Diary entry for 29 August 1843 (Haydon, 1963, v. 305).
15 The words of Henry Gouldburn, Under Secretary for War and the Colonies, quoted in Jones (1958–59), p. 484.
16 Quoted in Marcus (1971), p. 460.
17 *Edinburgh Review* (November 1814), xxiv. 249.
18 *Naval Chronicle* (July–December 1812), xxviii. 343–44.
19 Ibid., p. 344.
20 *Naval Chronicle* (January–July 1813), xxix. 12.
21 Ibid. preface, p. vi.
22 *Hansard* (vol. xxiv), col. 643.
23 Letter to his wife, 22 December 1812 (Jackson, 1873, i. 448).
24 *Hansard* (vol. xxvi), col. 182, 14 May 1813.
25 Fortescue (1920), *History of the British Army, 1813–1814*, ix. 106.
26 Rear-Admiral Cockburn to Vice-Admiral Warren, quoted in Morris (1997), p. 92.
27 Quoted in Perrett (1998), p. 106.
28 *Naval Chronicle* (January–June 1813), xxix. 80.
29 *Naval Chronicle* (July–December 1813), xxx. 41–42.
30 Letter to Martha Lloyd, 2 September 1814 (*Letters*, pp. 273–74). The editorial interpolations are as printed in the *Letters*.
31 The whole question is discussed in Lewis (1960), pp. 378–79, 434–39.
32 *Naval Chronicle* (1814), xxxii. v.
33 Quoted in Parkinson (1934), p. 412.
34 October 1813, xxx. 409–10.
35 Rear-Admiral Laughton, letter of 20 February 1812, quoted in Parkinson (1934), p. 413.
36 Ibid., pp. 413–14.
37 Dillon (1956), ii. 325.
38 The *Northumberland* actually set sail on 11 August. Historians vary in their dates. I have followed Oman (1942), p. 349 and Bowerbank [1815]. Together, they seem to provide the most convincing timetable for these events.
39 *Persuasion*, p. 99.
40 Ibid., p. 249 etc.
41 Ibid., p. 252.
42 Ibid., p. 26.
43 Ibid., p. 27.
44 Ibid., p. 26.
45 Ibid., p. 27.
46 Ibid., p. 26.
47 Ibid., p. 27.
48 Ibid., pp. 29–30.
49 Ibid., p. 248.
50 Ibid., p. 249.
51 Ibid., p. 61.

52 Ibid., p. 124.
53 Ibid., p. 28.
54 Ibid., p. 17.
55 Ibid., p. 18.
56 Ibid., p. 19.
57 Ibid., p. 17.
58 Ibid., pp. 21–22.
59 Ibid., p. 19.
60 Ibid., p. 4.
61 Ibid., p. 19.
62 Ibid., pp. 19–20.
63 Ibid., p. 3.
64 Ibid., p. 4.
65 Ehrman (1996), p. 490.
66 Henry Clifford, nephew of Lord Clifford, quoted in Harvey (1978), pp. 228–29.
67 *Persuasion*, p. 63.
68 Ibid., p. 66.
69 Ibid.
70 Ibid.
71 Ibid., p. 65.
72 Ibid., pp. 66–67.
73 Ibid., p. 66.
74 Ibid., p. 67.
75 Ibid., pp. 50–51.
76 Ibid., p. 52.
77 Ibid., p. 68.
78 Ibid.
79 Ibid.
80 Letter to Cassandra, 21 April 1805 (*Letters*, p. 105).
81 Southey (1813), p. 26.
82 14 October 1813 (*Letters*, p. 241).
83 Letters of 9 and 10 November 1804, quoted in *Naval Chronicle* (January–June 1806), xv. 281
84 Jerrold (1859), p. 23.
85 Document quoted by van de Merwe (1979).
86 Parsons (1843), p. 21.
87 *Naval Chronicle* (January–June 1807), xvii. 408.
88 *Persuasion*, p. 110.
89 Ibid., p. 241.
90 Ibid., p. 109.
91 Ibid., p. 111.
92 Ibid.
93 Ibid., p. 92.
94 Ibid., p. 22.
95 Ibid., p. 48.
96 Ibid.
97 Ibid., p. 27.
98 Ibid., p. 70.

99   Ibid.

100   Ibid., pp. 70–71.

101   Ibid., p. 170.

102   Letter to Martha Lloyd, 16 February 1813 (*Letters*, p. 207).

103   *Persuasion*, p. 69.

104   Ibid., p. 70.

105   Ibid., p. 69.

106   Ibid., p. 70.

107   *Mansfield Park*, p. 416.

108   Ibid., p. 68.

109   Lavery (1989), p. 141.

110   Nelson to Jervis, 21 June 1797 and Jervis to Nelson of the same date (Nicolas, 1844–46, ii. 398).

111   Quoted in Hughes (1957), p. 251.

112   Letter dated 26 June 1809 (Hughes, 1957, p. 284).

113   Quoted in Perrett (1998), p. 100.

114   Dillon (1956), ii. 172.

115   *Persuasion*, p. 70.

116   Ibid., p. 71.

117   Fremantle (1937), ii. 160.

118   Ibid., p. 187.

119   Ibid., p. 189.

120   Ibid., p. 164.

121   Leech (1857, edn 1999), p. 28.

122   Smyth (1867, edn 1991), p. 582.

123   Fremantle (1937), ii. pp. 164–65.

124   Ibid., p. 163.

125   Clowes (1900), v. 20.

126   Mangin (1951), p. 37.

127   Ibid., p. 29.

128   Perrett (1998), p. 99.

129   Letter dated 21 May 1802 (Smith, 1927, ii. 249–50). Only a few weeks earlier St Vincent had been obliged to explain to the Earl of Westmoreland why it was 'morally impossible' for him to give Lieutenant Fane 'the two steps of Commander and Post-Captain at once' (letter dated 19 April 1802, ibid., pp. 247–48).

130   Lloyd (1955), p. 157.

131   Quoted in Gill (1913), p. 278.

132   Quoted in Baynham (edn 1972), pp. 77–78.

133   Letter to Admiral Markham, 16 May 1806 (Markham, 1904, p. 49).

134   Robinson (1836), p. 27.

135   Letter dated 16 June 1796 (Dobrée, 1935, p. 19).

136   Logs of the *Glory* and *Shannon*, NMM, MS AUS/13.

137   NMM, MS AUS/15.

138   NMM, MS AUS/9. Letter No. 67, dated 1 February 1812.

139   *Memoir*, p. 14.

140   Letter to J. W. Croker, Admiralty, 26 July 1813 (PRO, MS ADM 1/18).

141   PRO, MS ADM 1/18.

142   Ibid.

143 PRO, MS ADM 2/967.
144 Ibid.
145 Addition facing p. 274.
146 Private Journal for 26 September–31 December 1826, NMM, MS AUS/120.
147 *Persuasion*, p. 252.
148 Ibid., p. 95.
149 Ibid., p. 96.
150 Ibid., p. 67.
151 Ibid., p. 94.
152 See, for example, letters addressed to Lord Melville, First Lord of the Admiralty, in the *Naval Chronicle* (July–December 1812), xxviii. 212–13, 375–76; *Naval Chronicle* (July–December 1814), xxxii. 131–32, 202–04; Duke of Norfolk, House of Lords, 11 March 1814.
153 *Naval Chronicle*, (1814), xxxi. 498.
154 Ibid., p. vi.
155 Ibid., p. 87.
156 Tanner (1986), p. 224.
157 *Sailor Brothers*, p. 263. *Persuasion*, p. 98.
158 Nicolas (1845), iii. 109.
159 Ibid., p. 243.
160 Ibid., p. 230.
161 *Persuasion*, p. 98.
162 Ibid.
163 Hardy (1975), p. 163.
164 *Persuasion*, pp. 98–99.
165 Ibid., p. 99.
166 Ibid.
167 Ibid., p. 100.
168 *Naval Chronicle*, ii. 328–30; Allsop (1858), p. 128.
169 From *Naval Poems* (1813), Canto II, p. 57. The long list of Subscribers is largely of naval men and the volume is dedicated to John Wilson Croker, Secretary to the Admiralty.
170 Quoted from Beaufort's Journal in Friendly (1997), p. 132.
171 Ibid., p. 84.
172 Letter of 6 May 1815 (quoted in *Sailor Brothers*, p. 270).
173 Quoted in Gotch (1937), p. 93.
174 Ibid., p. 113.
175 *Persuasion*, p. 100.
176 Scott's 'Chivalry' entry in the *Encyclopaedia Britannica* (1814).
177 *Persuasion*, p. 109.
178 Byron, *Childe Harold*, ii. verses xvii–xxi.
179 *Naval Chronicle*, vol. xxxiii.
180 Ibid., p. 96.
181 *Persuasion*, p. 102.
182 Ibid., p. 124.
183 Ibid., p. 125.
184 Ibid.
185 Ibid., pp. 125–26.
186 Ibid., pp. 127.

187   Ibid., p. 128.
188   Ibid.
189   Adeane (1907), p. 424.
190   Perrett (1998), p. 91.
191   *Persuasion*, p. 168.
192   F. J. Jackson to Mrs George Jackson, 8 May 1812 (Jackson, 1873, i. 371).
193   *Persuasion*, p. 170
194   Ibid.
195   Ibid., p. 166.
196   Ibid., p. 226.
197   Ibid., p. 160.
198   Ibid., p. 150.
199   Ibid.
200   Ibid., p. 249.
201   Ibid., p. 161.
202   Ibid., p. 232
203   Ibid., p. 233.
204   Ibid.
205   Ibid.
206   Ibid., p. 235.
207   Memoir quoted in Lane (1984), p. 184.
208   Cohen (1998), p. 21.
209   *Persuasion*, p. 252.
210   Letter from Maria Joseph Stanley to her daughter Louisa, 13 March 1815 (Adeane, 1899, p. 353).
211   *Persuasion*, see pp. 70, 75, 92, 170 and 171.
212   Ibid., p. 233.
213   Ibid., p. 71.
214   i. 27.
215   Pellew to Alexander Broughton, letter of 22 June 1807 (Parkinson, 1934, p. 376).
216   Letter of Jane Austen to Cassandra (*Letters*, p. 123).
217   Letter of 30 January 1805 (*Austen Papers*, p. 236).
218   Letter of 26 June 1808 (*Letters*, p. 133).

CHAPTER 12: THE AFTERMATH OF *PERSUASION*

1   Simpson (1870), reprinted in Southam (1968b), p. 264.
2   David Spring challenges Simpson's view that Jane Austen's understanding of society was limited to her grasp of naval society, see *Jane Austen: New Pespectives* (1983), ed. Janet Todd, pp. 55-56.
3   Letter to W. D. Fox, 3 January 1830 (Darwin, 1985, i. 96).
4   Ibid.
5   Letter from William Mostyn Owen to Charles Darwin, 1 March 1832 (ibid., p. 212).
6   Collini (1985), p. 511.
7   Letter from Charlotte Wedgwood to Darwin, 22 September 1831 (Darwin, 1985, i. 166).
8   *Pride and Prejudice*, p. 45.
9   Darwin (1985), i. 130 n. 4.
10   Letter to Susan Darwin, 5 September 1831 (Darwin, 1985, i. 140-41).

11 Letter to J. S. Henslow, 5 September 1831 (ibid., p. 142).
12 Ibid.
13 Letter of 5 September 1831 (Darwin, 1985, i. 143).
14 Letter of 6 September 1831 (ibid., p. 144).
15 Letter to Susan Darwin, 14 September 1831 (Darwin, 1985, i. 154-55).
16 *Persuasion*, p. 245.
17 Letter to Darwin, 22 September 1831 (Darwin, 1985, i. 164-65).
18 Letter to J. S. Henslow, 30 October 1831 (ibid., i. 176-77).
19 Letter to J. S. Henslow, 30 October 1831 (ibid., i. 176).
20 Letter to Caroline Darwin, c. 31 October 1831 (ibid., i. 178).
21 Letter to Caroline Darwin, 12 November 1831 (ibid.).
22 *Persuasion*, p. 167.
23 Letter to Caroline Darwin, 12 November 1831 (Darwin, 1985, i. 178).
24 Darwin (1985), i. 540.
25 Letter of 20-31 December 1831 (Ibid., i. 187).
26 Ibid.
27 Diary entry for 28 December 1831 (Darwin, 1988, p. 17).
28 Letter of 25-26 April 1832 (Darwin, 1985, i. 226-27).
29 Ibid.,i. p. 227.
30 Letter of 12 May-2 June 1832 (ibid., i. 234).
31 Letter of 22 May-14 July 1833 (ibid., i. 314).
32 Letter of 6 April 1834 (ibid., i. 380).
33 Ibid., p. 381.
34 Letter to Charles Whitley, 23 July 1834 (ibid., i. 396); *Pride and Prejudice*, p. 364.
35 Ibid., i. 397.
36 Letter to Susan Darwin, 28 January 1836 (ibid., i. 483).
37 See *Letters*, p. 415.
38 Ibid.
39 Letter no. 83 (*Letters*, p. 209).
40 Hampshire Record Office, MS 23 M93/63, letter of 6 January 1852. Unless otherwise indicated, subsequent references are to the manuscripts of the letters held at the Record Office.
41 Ibid.
42 Quoted in Hopkinson (1998), p. 54.
43 *Letters*, pp. 58–60.
44 Undated letter to Susan Quincy.
45 *Persuasion*, p. 48.
46 Draft letter dated 29 March 1852.
47 Letter of 29 March 1852, in Howe (1925–26), p. 328.
48 Letter of 16 August 1852, in *Austen Papers*, p. 311.
49 Letter of 22 April 1856, in Howe (1925–26), p. 328.
50 Letter of 9 June 1856, in *Austen Papers*, p. 313.
51 Typescript transcription at Hampshire Record Office.
52 Letter of 26 July 1809 (*Letters*, p. 176).
53 Cochrane (1861), ii. 40.
54 Ibid., p. 41.
55 Ibid., pp. 41–42.
56 Caroline Austen (1986), p. 67.

Bibliography

Principal Sources

Austen Papers	*Austen Papers, 1784–1856* (1942), ed. R.A. Austen-Leigh.
Family Record	*Jane Austen: Her Life and Letters: A Family Record* (1913), William and Richard Arthur Austen-Leigh, revised and enlarged by Deirdre Le Faye (1989).
Letters	*Jane Austen's Letters* (third edn, 1995, 1997), edited by Deirdre Le Faye.
Memoir	*Memoir of Jane Austen* (1870, 1871, edn. 1926), James Edward Austen-Leigh, edited by R.W. Chapman.
'Memoir' of Francis Austen	Unpublished manuscript. Published quotations from Hopkinson (1976, 1983), Lane (1984), and *Family Record* (1989).
Minor Works	Vol. VI of the Oxford Jane Austen (see below), ed. R.W. Chapman (1954), rev. edn by B.C. Southam(1969).
Novels of Jane Austen	Oxford edition (1923), edited by R.W. Chapman, 6 vols.
Sailor Brothers	*Jane Austen's Sailor Brothers* (1906), John H. and Edith C. Hubback. John Hubback (1844–1939) was a grandson of Francis Austen and Edith his daughter. Reference is made to a copy held at Jane Austen's house, Chawton. This was prepared for an unpublished second edition and carries annotations and other additional material used in this book.

Unpublished Sources

Admiralty papers	Public Record Office.
Austen, Charles	Letters, British Library.
	Diaries and Private Journals, National Maritime Museum, Greenwich.
	Official letters, Public Record Office.
Austen, Francis	Letters, British Library.
	Log books, order books, letter books, naval papers and service records, National Maritime Museum, Greenwich.
	Captain's letters, Public Record Office.
	Papers, including 'Memoir', in possession of the Austen family.
	Charts and Reports, Hydrographic Office of Great Britain.
Austen, George	Section of 'Memorandums' for Francis Austen, in possession of the Austen family.
Barrow, John	Official letters, as Admiralty Second Secretary, Public Record Office.
Clarke, James Stanier	Letters, British Library.
Crimmin, Patricia Kathleen	'Admiralty Administration, 1783–1806', unpublished M.A. thesis, University of London (1969).

Hastings, Warren	Diaries, British Library.
Hopkinson, David	'Niece of Miss Austen'.
Hope (Rear-Admiral), George	Official letters, Public Record Office.
Lefroy family	Family papers.
Louis (Rear-Admiral), Thomas	Official letters, British Library.
Tucker, Benjamin	Second Secretary of Admiralty, annotations to the text of *A Full and Correct Report of the Trial of Sir Home Popham* (1807), British Library.
van de Merwe, Pietre	'The Literary and Theatrical Career of Clarkson Stanfield (1793–1867)', unpublished Ph.D. thesis, Bristol University (1979).

Published Sources

Adeane, Jane H. *The Girlhood of Maria Josepha Holroyd. Recorded in Letters of a Hundred Years Ago* (1897).

——, *Before and After Waterloo: Letters from Edward Stanley* (1907).

Allen, Robert C. *Enclosure and the Yeoman* (1992).

Allott, Miriam, *Novelists on the Novel* (1959).

Annual Register, Selected volumes.

Annual Report, Jane Austen Society Report for the Year (1949 onwards).

Anon., *Memoir of the Marquis of Hastings* (1819).

Anon., *By a Quondam Sub, Symptoms of Advice to the O*****RS of an Amphibious Corps* (1789).

Anson, W.V., *Life of John Jervis, Admiral St Vincent* (1913).

Arnell, J. C., 'Bermuda as Naval Base', *Bermuda Historical Quarterly*, vol. 35, no. 3, pp. 58–63.

Aspinall, A. *Cornwallis in Bengal* (1931).

——, ed. *The Letters of King George IV, 1812–30* (3 vols, 1938).

——, ed. *The Letters of the Princess Charlotte, 1811–1817* (1949).

——, ed. *The Correspondence of George, Prince of Wales* (8 vols 1963–71).

Auerbach, Nina Joan, 'O Brave New World: Evolution and Revolution in *Persuasion*', *English Literary History*, 39 (1972), pp. 112–28.

Austen, Caroline, *My Aunt Jane Austen: A Memoir* (1952).

——. ed. Deirdre Le Faye, *Reminiscences* (1986).

Austen-Leigh, Mary Augusta, *Personal Aspects of Jane Austen* (1920).

Austen-Leigh, William and Knight, Montague George, *Chawton Manor and its Owners* (1911).

Bainbridge, Simon, *Napoleon and English Romanticism* (1995).

Baines, Edward, *History of the Wars of the French Revolution, From the Breaking out of the War in 1792, to the Restoration of a General Peace in 1815; Comprehending the Civil History of Great Britain and France During That Period* (2 vols, 1817).

Bamford, Francis, *Dear Miss Heber: An Eighteenth-Century Correspondence* (1936).

Barr, John, *Britain Portrayed: A Regency Album, 1780–1830* (1980).

Barrow, John, *The Life and Correspondence of Admiral Sir William Sidney Smith* (2 vols, 1848).

Bate, Jonathan, 'Culture and Environment: From Austen to Hardy', *New Literary History* vol. 30, no. 3 (1999).

——, *The Song of the Earth* (2000).

Batey, Mavis, *Jane Austen and the English Landscape* (1996).

Baugh, Daniel A., *British Naval Administration in the Age of Walpole* (1965).

Baynham, H., *From the Lower Deck: The Old Navy 1780-1840* (1969; edn 1972).

Beaglehole, J.C., ed. *Journals of Cook* (4 vols 1968–74).

Bearman, Robert, 'Henry Austen and the Cubbington Living', *Persuasions*, 10 (1988).

Bennett, Geoffrey, *Nelson the Commander* (1972).

Birley, Derek, *A Social History of English Cricket* (1999).

Blake, Richard Charles, 'Aspects of Religion in the Royal Navy, *c.* 1770–*c.* 1870', unpublished M.Phil., University of Southampton (1980).

Bloom, Harold, *The Western Canon: The Books and School of the Ages* (1994; edn 1995).

Bloomfield, Peter, *Kent and the Napoleonic Wars* (1987).

Book of Common Prayer (edn of 1818).

Bowerbank, John, *An Extract From a Journal, Kept on Board HMS Bellerophon, July 15– August 7, 1815* [1815].

Brabourne (Lord), Edward, ed. *Letters of Jane Austen* (2 vols, 1884).

Brenton, Edward Pelham, *The Naval History of Britain 1783 to 1822* (5 vols, 1823–25).

Brenton, Jahleel, *Memoir of Captain Edward Pelham Brenton* (1842).

[Bridges, George Wilson] *A Member of the University of Oxford, Alpine Sketches, Comprised in a Short Tour . . . Switzerland in 1814* (1814).

Brooke, John, *King George III* (1972).

Brophy, Bridget, 'Jane Austen and the Stuarts', in Southam (1968).

Brown, Ford K., *Fathers of the Victorians: The Age of Wilberforce* (1961).

Brown, Julia Prewitt, *Jane Austen's Novels: Social Change and Literary Form* (1979).

Bryant, Arthur, *The Years of Endurance, 1793–1802* (1942).

Burke, Edmund, *Reflections on the French Revolution* (1790; Everyman edn, 1910).

Burrey, W., *Universal Dictionary of the Marine* (1815).

Butler, Marilyn, *Jane Austen and the War of Ideas* (1975; new edn 1988).

——, 'Introduction', *Jane Austen Selected Letters 1796-1817* ed. R. W. Chapman (1955; edn 1985).

——, 'History, Politics and Religion' in Grey (1986).

——, ed. *Mansfield Park* (World Classics edn, 1990).

Byrn, J.D., *Crime and Punishment in the Royal Navy: Discipline on the Leeward Islands, 1784-1812* (1989).

Byron, George Gordon, *Complete Poetical Works*, ed. Jerome J. McGann (6 vols, 1980–91).

Campos, Christopher, *The View of France: From Arnold to Bloomsbury* (1965).

Caplan, Clive, 'Jane Austen's Soldier Brother: The Military Career of Captain Henry Thomas Austen of the Oxfordshire Regiment of Militia, 1793–1801', *Persuasions*, 18 (1996), pp. 122–43.

——, 'Jane Austen's Banker Brother: Henry Thomas Austen of Austen & Co., 1801–1816', *Persuasions*, 20 (1998), pp. 69–90.

Carnall, Geoffrey, *Robert Southey and his Age: The Development of a Conservative Mind* (1960).

Castle, Terry, Introduction, *Emma* (World Classics edn, 1995).

Chapman, R.W., 'Jane Austen's Friend, Mrs Barrett', *Nineteenth Century Fiction*, 4 (December 1949), pp 171–74.

——, 'A Reply to Mr Duffy on *Persuasion*', *Nineteenth Century Fiction*, 9 (1954–55), p. 154.

Chesterfield, Lord, *The Letters of Lord Chesterfield to his Son* (1774), ed. Charles Strachey (1901).

Churchill, Winston, *The Second World War* (1952).

Clarke, James Stanier, *Naval Sermons, Preached on Board His Majesty's Ship, the Impetueux* (1798; new edn, 1801).

——, *The Progress of Maritime Discovery* (1803).

——, *Naufragia; or, Historical Memoirs of Shipwrecks and of the Providential Deliverance of Vessels* (2 vols, 1805, 1806).

——, *The Life of James the Second Collected out of Memoirs Writ of his Own Hand* (1816).

——, with M'Arthur, John

——, *The Life and Services of Horatio, Viscount Nelson, from his Lordship's Manuscripts* (2 vols, 1809).

Climenson, Emily J., *Passages from the Diaries of Mrs Philip Lybbe Powys* (1899).

Clowes, William Laird, *The Royal Navy: A History* (vol. iv, 1899; v, 1900; vi, 1901).

Coad, Jonathan, 'The Historic Architecture of HM Naval Base Portsmouth, 1700–1850', *Mariner's Mirror*, 67 (1981), pp. 21–27.

Historic Architecture of the Royal Navy: An Introduction (1983).

Cobbett, William, *The Life and Adventures of Peter Porcupine* (Philadelphia, 1796).

——, *Rural Rides* ed. J.P. Cobbett, 1853 (Dent edn 1912).

——, ed. George Woodcock (Penguin, edn, 1967).

——, *Cobbett's Annual Register*

——, *Cobbett's Weekly Parliamentary Record.*

——, *Cobbett's Weekly Political Register.*

Cochrane, Thomas, *The Autobiography of a Seaman* (2 vols, 1859, 1860).

Cohen, Monica F., 'Persuading the Navy Home: Austen and Married Women's Professional Property', *Novel*, vol. 29, no. 3 (Spring 1996), pp 346–66.

——, *Professional Domesticity in the Victorian Novel: Women, Work and Home* (1998).

Colby, Robert A., *Fiction with a Purpose: Major and Minor Nineteenth-Century Novels* (1967).

Coleridge (Lord), Bernard John Seymour, *The Story of Devonshire House* (1906).

Colley, Linda, *Britons: Forging the Nation, 1707–1837* (1992; Vintage edn, 1996).

Collingwood, G.L.N., *A Selection from the Public and Private Correspondence of Viscount Collingwood* (4th edn, 1829).

——, ed. *Correspondence and Memoirs of Collingwood* (1828; 5th edn, 1837).

Collins, Irene, *Jane Austen and the Clergy* (1993).

Cookson, J.E., *The British Armed Nation, 1793–1815* (1997).

Corbett, J.S. and Richmond, H.W., *The Private Papers of George, 2nd Earl Spencer, 1794–1801* (4 vols, 1913–24).

Corley, T.A.B., 'Jane Austen and Her Brother Henry's Bank Failure 1815–16', *Jane Austen Society Report* (1998), pp. 12–23.

Cottrell, Stella, 'The Devil on Two Sticks: Franco-Phobia in 1803', *Patriotism: The Making and Unmaking of British National Identity*, i , *History and Politics*, ed. Raphael Samuel (1989).

Cunningham, A.E., *Patrick O'Brian: Critical Appreciations and a Bibliography* (1994).

Darwin, Charles, ed. Frederick Burkhardt and Sydney Smith, *The Correspondence of Charles Darwin* (9 vols, 1985–91).

——, ed. Richard Darwin Keynes, *Charles Darwin's Beagle Diary* (1988)

[Davis, John,] *The Post Captain* (1805; ed. R.H. Case, 1928, from 3rd edn, 1808).

Dawson, Warren R., *The Nelson Collection at Lloyd's* (1932).

Dayes, Edward, *A Pictorial Tour Through the Principal Parts of Yorkshire and Derbyshire* (1805).

Dictionary of National Biography, (DNB).

Dillon, William Henry, *A Narrative of my Professional Adventures* (vol i, 1953; ii,1956), ed. Michael A. Lewis.

Dobrée, Bonamy and Manwaring, G.E., *The Floating Republic: An Account of the Mutinies at Spithead and the Nore in 1797* (1935; Penguin edn, 1937).

Downey, Thomas, *Naval Poems: Pleasures of Naval Life, and the Battle of Trafalgar* (1813).

Doyle, Francis Hastings, *Reminiscences and Opinions* (1886).

Duffy, Joseph Michael, 'Structure and Idea in Jane Austen's *Persuasion*', *Nineteenth Century Fiction*, 8 (1953–54) pp. 272–89.

Dundonald, Earl of (see Cochrane, Thomas), *The Autobiography of a Seaman.*

Dupouy, Walter, ed., *Sir Robert Ker Porter's Caracas Diary 1825–1842: A British Diplomat in a Newborn Nation* (Caracas, 1966).

Eastwood, David, 'Patriotism Personified: Robert Southey's *Life of Nelson* Reconsidered', *Mariner's Mirror*, 77 (1991), pp. 143–49.

Edgcombe, Richard, *The Diary of Frances Lady Shelley, 1787–1817* (1912).

Edgeworth, F.A., *Memoir of Maria Edgeworth* (1862).

Edgeworth, Maria, *Patronage* (1814).

Edgeworth, Richard Lovell, *Essays on Professional Education* (1808; 2nd edn, 1812).

Ehrman, John, *The Younger Pitt: The Consuming Struggle* (1996).

Eltis, David, 'The British Trans-Atlantic Slave Trade after 1807', *Maritime History*, 4, no. 1 (1974), pp. 1–11.

Evans, Maurice, *The Aegis of England; or The Triumphs of the Late War as they Appear in the Thanks of Parliament* (1817).

Everett, Barbara, 'Hard Romance', *London Review of Books* (8 February 1996).

Everett, Nigel, *The Tory View of Landscape* (1994).

Farington, Joseph, ed. Kenneth Galbraith and Angus MacIntyre, *The Diary of Joseph Farington* (16 vols, 1978–84).

Farrer, Reginald, 'Jane Austen', *Quarterly Review* (July 1917), in Southam (1987).

FitzRoy, Robert, *The Weather Book: A Manual of Practical Meteorology* (1862).

Flower, Raymond and Jones, Michael Wynn, *Lloyd's of London* (1974; rev. edn, 1981).

Fortescue, J.W., *A History of the British Army* (13 vols, 1899–1930).

Fraser, Flora, *Beloved Emma: The Life of Emma, Lady Hamilton* (1986; edn 1994).

——, *The Unruly Queen: The Life of Queen Caroline* (1996).

Fremantle, Anne, ed., *The Wynne Diaries*, vol ii, 1937; vol iii, 1940.

Friend, William, *Patriotism: or The Love of our Country: An Essay . . . Dedicated to the Volunteers of the United Kingdom* (1804).

Friendly, Alfred, *Beaufort of the Admiralty: The Life of Sir Francis Beaufort* (1977).

Fry, Michael, *The Dundas Despotism* (1992).

Fulford, Roger, *Samuel Whitbread, 1764–1815* (1967).

Fulford, Tim, *Landscape, Liberty and Authority: Poetry, Criticism and Politics from Thomson to Wordsworth* (1996).

——, 'Wordsworth, Cowper and the Language of Eighteenth-Century Politics', in Thomas Woodman ed. *Early Romantics: Perspectives in English Poetry from Pope to Wordsworth* (1998), pp. 117–33.

——, 'Romanticizing the Empire: The Naval Heroes of Southey, Coleridge, Austen, and Marryat', *Modern Language Quarterly*, 60:2 (June 1999), pp. 161–96.

Furneaux, Robin, *William Wilberforce* (1974).

Gardiner, Robert, ed. *The Naval War of 1812* (1998).

Gardner, James Anthony, ed. R. V. Hamilton and J. K. Laughton, *Above and Under the Hatches: The Recollection of James Anthony Gardner* (1906).

Gawler, Jim, *Britons Strike Home: A History of the Lloyd's Patriotic Fund 1803–1988* (1993).

George, Mary Dorothy, *Catalogue of Political and Personal Satires Possessed in the Department of Prints and Drawings in the British Museum* (vols vii–ix, 1942–49).

Gilbert, Martin, *Road to Victory: Winston S. Churchill, 1941–1945* (1986).

Gill, Conrad, *The Naval Mutinies of 1797* (1913).

Gilpin, William, *Observations on the River Wye* (1782).

——, *Observations on the Western Parts of England* (1798; 2nd edn, 1808).

Gilson, David, *A Bibliography of Jane Austen* (1982; rev. edn, 1997).

——, 'Books and their Owners: Some Early American Editions of Jane Austen', *Book Collector*, 48, no. 2 (Summer 1999).

[Glascock, W.N.] *Naval Sketch-Book: or The Service Afloat and Ashore* (1826; 2nd edn, 1834).

Glover, Richard, *Britain at Bay: Defended against Bonaparte 1803–1814* (1973).

Gore, John, ed., *The Creevey Papers* (1963).

Gotch, Rosamund Brunel, *Maria, Lady Callcott* (1937).

Grainger, John D., ed., *The Royal Navy in the River Plate, 1806–1807* (1996).

Gray, Denis, *Spencer Perceval: The Evangelical Prime Minister, 1762–1812* (1963).

Gretton, Peter, *Former Naval Person: Winston Churchill, and the Royal Navy* (1968).

Grey, Jack, ed., *The Jane Austen Handbook* (US edn, *Companion*) (1986).

Grimble, Ian, *The Sea Wolf: The Life of Admiral Cochrane* (1978).

Grocott, Terence, *Shipwrecks of the Revolutionary and Napoleonic Eras* (1997).

Grose, Frances, *Dictionary of the Vulgar Tongue* (1785; edn 1811).

Halévy, Elie, *England in 1815* (1913; edn 1949).

Ham, Elizabeth, ed. Eric Gillett, *Elizabeth Ham by Herself, 1783–1820* (1945).

Hamilton, R.V., ed., *Journals and Letters of Sir Thomas Byam Martin* (1903).

Hamilton, R. Vesey and Laughton, John Knox, *Recollections of James Anthony Gardner, 1775–1814* (1906).

Hammond, M.C., *Relating to Jane: Studies on the Life and Novels of Jane Austen with A Life of her Niece Elizabeth Austen Rice* (1998).

——, 'The Naval Connection', *Jane Austen Society Report* (1998), pp. 47–54.

Hansard (Parliamentary Debates) Selected volumes.

Hardcastle, M.S., *Life of John, Lord Campbell* (1881).

Hardwick, Mollie, *Emma, Lady Hamilton* (1969).

Harris (Lord), George, *The History of Kent County Cricket* (1906).

Harvey, A.D., *Britain in the Early Nineteenth Century* (1978).

——, *English Literature and the Great War with France* (1981).

——, *Collision of Empires: Britain in Three World Wars* (1992; edn, 1994).

——, *A Muse of Fire: Literature, Art and War* (1998).

Harvey, Robert, *Liberators: Latin America's Struggle for Independence, 1810–1830* (2000)

——, *Cochrane: The Life and Exploits of a Fighting Captain* (2000).

Hattendorf, John B., ed. (with R.J.B. Knight, A.W.H. Pearsall, N.A.M. Rodger, Geoffrey Till), *British Naval Documents, 1204–1960* (1993).

Hay, Denys, 'The Historiographers Royal in England and Scotland', *Scottish Historical Review*, 13 (1951) pp. 15–29.

Haydon, Benjamin, ed. William Bissell Pope, *The Diary of Benjamin Robert Haydon* (5 vols, 1960–63).

Hayward, Karla M., *Cruise of HMS Vindictive on the North America and West Indies Station 1845–1848* (exhibition catalogue) [2000].

Hazlitt, William, 'William Wordsworth and Robert Southey from 1807 to 1830', *Taits Magazine* (July 1839) in *Reminiscences of the English Lake Poets*, Everyman Edition (n.d.), p. 184.

Hellstrom, Ward, 'Francophobia in *Emma*', *Studies in English Literature*, 5 (1965) pp. 606–17.

Helmsinger, Elizabeth K., *Rural Scenes and National Representation: Britain, 1815–1850* (1997).

Henderson, James, *The Frigates: An Account of the Lesser Warships of the Great French Wars, 1793–1815* (1970).

Hibbert, Christopher, *George IV: Prince of Wales* (1972); *Regent and King* (1974) (Penguin edn, one vol., 1976).

——, *Nelson: A Personal History* (1994; Penguin edn, 1995).

Hickey, William, ed. Alfred Spencer, *Memoirs* (vol. iii, 1923; vol. iv, 1925).

Hill, Constance, *Jane Austen, her Homes and her Friends* (1902).

Hill, J.R., *The Oxford Illustrated History of the Navy* (1995).

——, *The Prizes of War: The Naval Prize System in the Napoleonic Wars, 1793–1815* (1998).

Historical Manuscripts Commission, Various Collections (1909), vi, p 363.

——, *Manuscripts of Cornwallis Wykeham-Martin* (1909).

——, *Manuscripts of Reginald Rawdon Hastings* (1934), lxxviii, vol. 3.

Hodges, H.W and Hughes, E.A., ed., *Select Naval Documents* (1922).

Holland (Lord), H.R., *Memoirs of the Whig Party during My Time* (2 vols, 1852–54).

Honan, Park, *Jane Austen: Her Life* (1987; rev. edn, 1997).

Hopkinson, David, 'The Naval Career of Jane Austen's Brother', *History Today* (September 1976), pp. 576–84.

——, 'The Later Life of Sir Francis Austen', *Jane Austen Society Report* (1983).

——, 'The Austens and North America', *Persuasions* (1998).

Hoste, William, *Memoirs and Letters of Captain Sir William Hoste* (2 vols, 1833).

Howarth, David and Stephen, *Nelson: The Immortal Memory* (1988).

Howe, M.A.D., 'A Jane Austen Letter', *Yale Review*, new series 15 (1925–26), pp. 319–35.

Howells, William Dean, *Heroines of Fiction* (2 vols, 1901).

Howse, E.M., *Saints in Politics: The 'Clapham Sect' and the Growth of Freedom* (1953; edn, 1971).

Hughes, Edward, ed., *The Private Correspondence of Admiral Lord Collingwood* (1957).

Hughes, Thomas, *Tom Brown's Schooldays* (1857; World Classics edn, 1989).

Humphries, R.A., *Liberation in South America, 1806–1827: The Career of James Paroissien* (1952).

Hunt, John Dixon, *Gardens and the Picturesque: Studies in the History of Landscape Architecture* (1992).

Jackson, George, ed. Lady Jackson, *The Bath Archives: A Further Selection from the Diaries and Letters of Sir George Jackson* (2 vols, 1873).

Jaffe, Patricia, *Lady Hamilton in Relation to the Art of her Time* (1972).

——, *Drawings by George Romney, Fitzwilliam Museum* (1977).

James, William, *The Naval History of Great Britain (1826; edn 1886)*.

Jerrold, Douglas, *The Mutiny at the Nore: A Nautical Drama* (1830).

——, 'Jack Runnymede: The Man of Many "Thanks"', in *Men of Character* (3 vols, 1838).

Jerrold, W. Blanchard, *Life and Remains of Douglas Jerrold* (1859).

Johnson, Claudia L., *Jane Austen: Women, Politics and the Novel* (1988).

Jones, M.G., *Hannah More* (1952).

Jones, W.D., 'A British View of the War of 1812 and the Peace Negotiations', *Mississippi Valley Historical Review*, 45 (1958–59), pp. 481–87.

Jupp, Peter, *Lord Grenville, 1759–1834* (1985).

Kaplan, Deborah, 'Domesticity at Sea: The Example of Charles and Fanny Austen', *Persuasions*, 14 (1992a), pp. 113–21

——, *Jane Austen Among Women* (1992b).

King-Hall, L., ed., *Sea Sagas: Being the Naval Diaries of Four Generations of the King-Hall Family* (1935).

Kirkham, Margaret, *Jane Austen: Feminism and Fiction* (1983; rev. edn, 1996).

Knutsford (Lady), Margaret Jean, *Life and Letters of Zachary Macaulay* (1900).

Lane, Maggie, *Jane Austen's Family: Through Five Generations* (1984).

——, *Jane Austen's England* (1986).

——, *Jane Austen and Food* (1995).

——, 'The French Bread at Northanger', *Persuasions* (1998).

Laughton, John Knox, ed., *Letters and Despatches of Nelson* (1886).

——, ed., *Letters and Papers of Charles, Lord Barham, 1758–1813* (3 vols, 1907).

Lavery, Brian, *The Ship of the Line* (2 vols, 1983, 1984).

——, *Nelson's Navy: The Ships, Men and Organisation, 1793–1815* (1989; rev. edn, 1990).

——, *Shipboard Life and Organisation, 1731–1815* (1998).

Le Faye, Deirdre, 'Fanny Knight's Diaries: Jane Austen through her Niece's Eyes', *Persuasions: Occasional Papers*, 2 (1986).

——, 'Anna Lefroy's Original Memoirs of Jane Austen', *Review of English Studies*, new series, 39 (1988) pp. 417–21.

——, *Jane Austen* (1998).

Leavis, Q.D., 'A Critical Theory of Jane Austen's Writing', *Scrutiny*, 10 (1941), pp. 61–90, 114–42; (1942), pp. 272–94; 12 (1944), pp. 104–19; reprinted in *A Selection from Scrutiny*, ii (1968), ed. F.R. Leavis, pp. 1–80. (See Southam, 1962, 1964).

Leech, Samuel, *A Voice from the Deck: Being a Record of the Thirty Years Adventures of Samuel Leech* (1857; edn 1999).

Lefroy, Helen, 'Everyone Here Tells of War', *Jane Austen Society Report* (1988), pp. 23–29.

Leslie, John Randolph Shane, *Mrs Fitzherbert: A Life Chiefly from Unpublished Sources* (1939).

——, ed., *The Letters of Mrs Fitzherbert and Connected Papers* (1940).

Lewis, Michael, *A Social History of the Navy, 1793–1815* (1960).

——, *The Navy in Transition, 1814–1864: A Social History* (1965).

Lloyd, Christopher, *Lord Cochrane: Seaman - Radical - Liberator* (1947).

——, ed., *The Kirk Papers: Selection from the Papers of Admiral Viscount Kirk* (3 vols, 1950–55).

——, ed., *The Naval Miscellany*, iv (1952).

——, *The Nation and the Navy: A History of Naval Life and Policy* (1961).

——, 'The Royal Naval College at Portsmouth and Greenwich', *Mariner's Mirror*, 52 (1966) p. 146.

London's Roll of Fame, 1757–1884: Notes and Addresses on the Presentation of Honorary Freedom (1884).

Longmate, Norman, *Island Fortress: The Defence of Great Britain, 1603–1945* (1991; edn 1993).

Lowe, J.A., *Records of the Portsmouth Division of Marines* (1990).

Lucas, John, *Mansfield Park* (1970), Oxford English Novels edn.

Lynch, John, 'British Policy and Spanish America, 1783–1808', *Journal of Latin American Studies*, 1, no. 1 (1969).

MacLean, Alistair, *Captain Cook* (1972).

Mangin, Edward, ed. H.G. Thursfield, 'Edward Mangin's Journal', in *Five Naval Journals, 1789–1817* (1951).

Marchand, Leslie A., *Byron: A Biography* (3 vols, 1957).

Marcus, G.J., *A Naval History of England*, i, *The Age of Nelson* (1971).

——, *Heart of Oak* (1975).

Markham, Clements ed., *Selections from the Correspondence of Admiral John Markham* (1904).

Marryat, Frederick, *Peter Simple* (1834; ed. Oliver Warner, 1969).

Marshall, John, *Royal Naval Biography* (6 vols, 1823–35).

Marshall, P.J., *The Impeachment of Warren Hastings* (1965).

M'Arthur, John, *A Treatise of the Principles and Practice of Naval and Military Courts Martial* (1792; 4th edn, 2 vols, 1813).

——, *System of Universal Signals by Day and Night* (1800).

Martin, Thomas Byam, ed. R.V. Hamilton, *Letters and Papers* (1901).

McAleer, Michael J., 'The Gift of Freedom', *Connoisseur*, 208 (December 1981), pp. 263–67.

McCahill, Michael W., 'Peerage Creations and the Changing Nature of the Political Nobility, 1750–1850' in Clive and D.L. Jones ed., *Peers, Politics and Power: The House of Lords, 1603–1911* (1986).

Milford, John Jnr, *Observations, Moral, Literary, and Antiquarian made during a Tour through the Pyranees, South of France, Switzerland etc. in the Years 1814 and 1815* (1818).

Millar, Oliver, *The Queen's Pictures* (1977; edn, 1984).

Mineka, F.E., *The Dissidence of Dissent: The Monthly Repository, 1806–38* (1944).

Mitford, Mary Russell, *Our Village* (2 vols, 1st and 2nd series, edn 1848).

Monthly Repository of Theology and General Literature, Selected volumes.

More, Hannah, ed. William Roberts, *Memoirs of the Life and Correspondence of Mrs Hannah More* (4 vols, 2nd edn, 1834).

Moron, Guillermo, *A History of Venezuela* (1956; edited and translated by John Street, 1964).

Morriss, Roger, *The Royal Dockyards during the Revolutionary and Napoleonic Wars* (1983).

——, et al., *Nelson: An Illustrated History* (1995).

——, *Nelson: The Life and Letters of a Hero* (1996).

——, *Cockburn and the British Navy in Transition: Admiral Sir George Cockburn, 1772–1853* (1997).

Namier, Lewis and Brooke, John, *The House of Commons, 1754–1790*, i (1964).

Naval Chronicle, Selected volumes.

Neale, Jonathan, *The Cutlass and the Lash: Mutiny and Discipline in Nelson's Navy* (1985).

Nelson, Horatio, ed. Geoffrey Rawson, *Nelson's Letters* (1960).

Nicolas, Nicholas Harris, *Dispatches and Letters of Vice-Admiral Lord Viscount Nelson* (7 vols, 1844–46).

Nokes, David, *Jane Austen: A Life* (1997).

Notman, Susanne, 'The Austen File', *The Bermudian*, August 1999.

——, 'Fanny's Letters', *The Bermudian*, March 2000.

O'Byrne, W.R., *A Naval Biographical Dictionary* (2 vols, 1849; new edn, 1861).

[Oliver, Francis], *Memoirs of Lady Hamilton: With Illustrated Anecdotes of Many of her Most Particular Friends and Distinguished Contemporaries* (1815; 2nd edn 1815).

Oman, Carola, *Britain Against Napoleon* (1942).

——, *Nelson* (1947).

Parkinson, C. Northcote, *Edward Pellew, Viscount Exmouth* (1934).

——, *Trade in the Eastern Seas, 1793–1813* (1937)

——, ed., *The Trade Winds: A Study of British Overseas Trade, 1793–1815* (1948a).

——, *Portsmouth Point: The Navy in Fiction, 1793–1815* (1948b).

——, *War in the Eastern Seas, 1793–1815* (1954).

——, *Britannia Rules: The Classic Age of Naval History, 1793–1815* (1977; edn 1994).

Parsons, G.S., *Nelson's Reminiscences: Leaves from Memory's Log: A Dramatic Eye-Witness Account of the War at Sea, 1795–1810* (1843; edn 1998).

Pasley, C.W., *Essay on the Military Policy and Institutions of the British Empire* (1810).

Paulson, Ronald, *Literary Landscapes, Turner and Constable* (1982).

Perkin, Harold, *The Origins of Modern British Society, 1780–1880* (1969).

Perrett, Bryan, *The Real Hornblower: The Life and Times of Admiral Sir James Gordon, GCB* (1998).

Perrin, W.G., ed., *The Naval Miscellany III* (1928).

Pettigrew, Thomas Joseph, *Memoirs of the Life of Vice-Admiral Lord Viscount Nelson*, (2 vols, 1849).

Pevsner, Nikolaus, *London*, i, *The Cities of London and Westminster (The Buildings of England)*, 3rd edn, revised by Bridget Cherry (1973).

Philips, C.H., *The East India Company, 1784–1834* (1940, 1961).

Phillips, I.L., 'Lord Barham at the Admiralty, 1805–6' *Mariner's Mirror*, 64 (1978).

Plumb, J.H., *The First Four Georges* (1956; edn 1966).

Pocock, Tom, *Horatio Nelson* (1987).

——, *A Thirst for Glory: The Life of Admiral Sir Sidney Smith* (1996; edn 1998).

Pollock, John, *Wilberforce* (1977; edn 1986).

Popham, Home Riggs, *A Description of Prince of Wales Island* (1790; edn 1805).

Popham, Hugh, *A Damned Cunning Fellow: The Life of Sir Home Popham* (1991).

Prentice, Rina, *A Celebration of the Sea: The Decorative Art Collections of the National Maritime Museum* (1994).

Priestley, J.B., *The Prince of Pleasure and his Regency, 1811–20* (1969; edn 1971).

Pritchett, V.S., *George Meredith and Comedy* (1969).

Quarterly Review, unsigned review of Repton's *Fragments on the Theory and Practice of Landscape Gardening, 1816*, 16 (January 1817) pp. 417–30.

Raleigh, Walter, 'A Discourse of the Invention of Ships', 1597–98, rev. *c.* 1608, in *The Works of Sir Walter Raleigh*, ed. William Oldys and Thomas Birch (8 vols, 1829), viii, pp. 299–316.

——, 'Excellent Observations and Notes, Concerning the Royal Navy and Sea-Service' (published 1650), in *Sir Walter Raleigh: Selections from his Writings in Peace and War*, ed. W. Roy Macklin (n.d.), p. 151.

Ralfe, James, *The Naval Chronology of Great Britain, 1803–1816* (3 vols, 1820).

Rasor, Eugene L., *Reform in the Royal Navy: A Social History of the Lower Deck 1850 to 1880* (1976).

Rawson, Claude, 'Introduction', *Persuasion* (World Classics edn, 1990).

Rawson, Geoffrey, ed., *Nelson's Letters* (1960).

Regulations and Instructions Relating to His Majesty's Service at Sea (1806; edn 1808).

Report of the Trial of Sir Home Popham (1807).

Repton, Humphrey, *An Enquiry into Changes of Taste in Landscape Gardening* (1806).

——, *Fragments on the Theory and Practice of Landscape Gardening* (1816).

Richardson, Joanna, *George IV: A Portrait* (1966).

Richardson, William, ed. Spencer Childens, *A Mariner of England* (1908).

Roberts, Michael, *The Whig Party, 1807–1812* (1939).

Roberts, Warren, *Jane Austen and the French Revolution* (1979, 1995).

Roberts, William, *Memoirs of the Life and Correspondence of Mrs Hannah More* (4 vols, 2nd edn, 1834).

Robertson, William Spencer, *The Life of Miranda* (2 vols, 1929).

Robinson, William (Jack Nasty Face), *Nautical Economy: or Forecastle Recollections of Events during the Last War* [1836].

Rodger, N.A.M., *The Admiralty* (1979).

——, 'The Naval World of Jack Aubrey', in A.E. Cunningham (1994).

——, *The Wooden World: An Anatomy of the Georgian Navy* (1986; edn 1988).

Ryle, Gilbert, 'Jane Austen and the Moralists' (see Southam, 1968a).

Sanders, Lionel, *The Holland House Circle* (1908).

Sawtell, George, 'Four Manly Boys', *Jane Austen Society Report* (1982).

Schom, Alan, *Trafalgar: Countdown to Battle, 1803–1805* (1990; edn 1992).

Scott, J.B., *An Englishman at Home and Abroad* (1930).

Scott, Walter, Review of *Emma*, *Quarterly Review*, 14 (October 1815) pp. 188–201 (in Southam, 1968b).

Selwyn, David, ed., *The Poetry of Jane Austen and the Austen Family* (1996).

——, *Jane Austen and Leisure* (1999).

Sharpe, Charles Kirkpatrick, ed. Alexander Allardyce, *Letters from and to Charles Kirkpatrick Sharpe, Esq.* (1888).

Shine, H. and H. C. *The Quarterly Review under Gifford* (1949)

Simmons, Jack, *Southey* (1945).

Simond, Louis, ed. Christopher Hibbert, *An American in Regency England: Journal of a Tour in 1810–11* (1968).

Simpson, Richard, Review of *Memoir*, *North Britain Review*, 3 (April 1870), pp. 129–52; (in Southam, 1968b).

Smith, David Bonner, ed., *Letters to Admiral of the Fleet The Earl St. Vincent* (2 vols, 1922, 1927).

Smith, Sydney, 'Methodism', *Edinburgh Review*, 11 (1808), pp. 341–62.

——, *The Worlds of the Rev. Sydney Smith* (1869).

Southam, B.C., 'Jane Austen: A Broken Romance?', *Notes and Queries*, 206 (1961), pp. 464–65.

——,'Mrs Leavis and Miss Austen: The "Critical Theory" Reconsidered', *Nineteenth-Century Fiction*, 17 (1962), pp. 21–32.

——, *Jane Austen's Literary Manuscripts* (1964).

——, *Critical Essays on Jane Austen* (1968a).

——, *Jane Austen: The Critical Heritage, 1812–70* (1968b).

——, 'Robert Martin and the Agricultural Reports', *Jane Austen Society Report* (1971), pp. 9–11.

——, *Jane Austen: The Critical Heritage, 1870–1940* (1987).

——, 'The Silence of the Bertrams: Slavery and the Chronology of *Mansfield Park*', *Times Literary Supplement* (17 February 1995), pp. 13–14.

——, 'Jane Austen and the Political Context', *Women's Writing*, 5, no. 1 (1998), pp. 7–26.

Southey, Robert, ed. Jack Simmons, *Letters from England: By Dom Manuel Alvarez Espriella* (1807, 1984).

——, Review of Nelson biographies, *Quarterly Review*, 3 (February 1810) pp. 218–62.

——, Review of Pasley (1810), *Quarterly Review*, 5 (May 1811), pp. 403–37.

——, *Life of Nelson* (1813; Everyman edn, 1906).

——, *Lives of the British Admirals* (1833–40)

——, ed. Charles Cuthbert Southey, *The Life and Correspondence of Robert Southey* (6 vols, 1849–50).

——, ed. Maurice H. Fitzgerald, *Poems of Robert Southey* (1909).

——, ed. Kenneth Curry, *New Letters of Robert Southey* (2 vols, 1965).

——, ed. Charles Ramos, *The Letters of Robert Southey to John May 1797 to 1838* (1976).

Southwick, Leslie, 'The City of London Presentation Awards', *Antique Dealer and Collectors Guide* (1983).

Steele, Robert, *The Marine Officer: or Sketches of Service* (2 vols, 1840).

Steel's Prize Pay Lists, Selected volumes.

Stephen, James, *War in Disguise: or The Frauds of Neutral Flags* (1805).

Stevenson, William, *General View of the Agriculture of the County of Surrey* (1809; rev. edns 1813, 1815).

Stokes, Winifred, 'Popham' entry in *History of Parliament, 1770–1820*, iv (1986).

Stone, Laurence, *Road to Divorce: England, 1530–1987* (1990)

——, ed., *An Imperial State at War: Britain from 1689 to 1815* (1994).

Storey, Mark, *Robert Southey: A Life* (1997).

Surel, Jeannine, 'John Bull', *Patriotism: The Making and Unmaking of British National Identity*, iii, *National Fictions*, ed. Raphael Samuel (1989).

Sutherland, Kathryn, ed., *Mansfield Park* (Penguin Classics edn, 1996).

Talbott, John E., *The Pen and Ink Sailor: Charles Middleton and the King's Navy, 1778–1813* (1998).

Tanner, Tony, ed., *Mansfield Park* (Penguin edn, 1966)

——, *Jane Austen* (1986).

Tave, Stuart M., *Some Words of Jane Austen* (1973).

Taylor, Gordon, *The Sea Chaplains: A History of the Chaplains of the Royal Navy* (1978).

Thomas, B.C., 'Portsmouth in Jane Austen's Time', *Persuasions* (1990).

Thomas, Donald, *Cochrane: Britannia's Last Sea-King* (1978).

Thomas, F.M.G., *Portsmouth and Gosport: A Study in the Historical Geography of a Naval Port*, unpublished University of London M.Sc. thesis (1961).

Thompson, Edward, *Sailor's Letters Written to his Select Friends in England, 1754–1759* (2 vols, 1766; 2nd edn, 1767).

Thompson, J.M., ed., *Napoleon's Letters* (1934; edn 1954).

Thorne, R.G., ed., *The House of Commons 1790–1820*, i (1986).

Thursfield, H.G., ed., *Five Naval Journals, 1789–1817* (1951).

Tours, Hugh, *The Life and Letters of Emma Hamilton* (1963).

Trilling, Lionel, Introduction to *Emma*, Riverside Edition (1957a).

——, 'Jane Austen and *Mansfield Park*', in *From Blake to Byron: The Pelican Guide to English Literature*, 5 (1957b), ed. Boris Ford.

Trumpener, Katie, *Bardic Nationalism: The Romantic Novel and the British Empire* (1997).

Tucker, George Holbert, *A Goodly Heritage: A History of Jane Austen's Family* (1983).

——, *Jane Austen the Woman: Some Biographical Insights* (1994).

Turberville, A.S., *The House of Lords in the Age of Reform, 1784–1837* (1958).

Twiss, Horace, *The Public and Private Life of Lord Chancellor Eldon* (3 vols, 1844).

Vane, Charles, ed., *Memoirs and Correspondence of Viscount Castlereagh* (12 vols, 1848–53).

Vick, Robin, 'Cousins in Bath', *Jane Austen Society Report* (1995), pp. 24–29.

——, 'The Royal Naval Academy at Portsmouth', *Jane Austen Society Report* (1996a), pp. 24–28.

——, 'A Tourist's View of Southampton and Portsmouth in 1811', *Jane Jane Austen Society Report* (1996b), pp. 34–36.

Viveash, Chris, 'Jane Austen: The Divine and the Donkey', *Persuasions* (1994).

Voorhis, Harold, *Freemasonry in Bermuda*, (n.d.) [?c. 1961].

Warner, Oliver, *A Portrait of Lord Nelson* (1958).

——, *Life and Letters of Vice-Admiral Lord Collingwood* (1968).

Watkin, David, *The Royal Interiors of Regency England from the Watercolours First Published by W.H. Pyne in 1817–1820* (1984).

Watson, Vera, *Mary Russell Mitford* (1948).

Watson, Winifred, *Jane Austen in London* (1960).

Webb, William, *Coastguard! An Official History of H.M. Coastguard* (1976).

West, G. Cornwallis, *Life and Letters of Admiral Cornwallis* (1927).

West, Rebecca, *The Strange Necessity* (1928).

Whateley, Richard, Review of *Northanger Abbey* and *Persuasion*, *Quarterly Review*, 24 (January 1821), pp. 352–76 (in Southam, 1968b).

Wilberforce, Samuel, *Life of William Wordsworth* (1872).

Wilkinson, Henry C., *Bermuda from Sail to Steam: The History of the Island from 1784 to 1901* (2 vols, 1973).

Williams, Raymond, *The Country and the City* (1973).

Williamson, Tom and Bellamy, Liz, *A Social History of Land Ownership and the English Countryside* (1987).

Wilson, Margaret, 'Jane's Sailor Brothers and a Real Dick Musgrove', *Jane Austen Society Report* (1999), pp. 35–37.

Windham, William, *The Windham Papers* (2 vols, 1913).

Wollstonecraft, Mary, *A Vindication of the Rights of Men* (1790).

Woolf, Virginia, 'Jane Austen at Sixty', *Athenaeum*, 15 December 1923 and *New Republic* (New York), 30 January 1924 (in Southam, 1968b).

Wordsworth, William, ed. Hugh de Selincourt, *The Letters of William and Dorothy Wordsworth*, rev. Mary Moorman (2nd edn, 1969), vol. 2.

Wright, Thomas, *Caricature History of the Georges* (1848; rev. edn, 1867).

Yarrington, Alison, *The Commemoration of the Hero, 1800–1804: Monuments to the British Victors of the Napoleonic Wars* (1988).

Zuill, William Sears, 'The Gibraltar of the West: A History of Admiralty and War Department Lands', *Bermuda Historical Quarterly*, 10, no. 3 (1953), pp. 84–106.

Index

Notes

1. The titles of the novels are reduced to initials.
2. Similarly, these names: Jane Austen JA, Francis Austen FA, Charles Austen CA, Henry Austen HA.
3. *MP*, *E*, and *P* are treated, respectively, in Chapters 8, 10, and 11. References to the characters occur throughout and are only indexed when they relate particularly to the naval or thematic material under discussion.